The Joseph Paradox

ALSO BY HILLEL I. MILLGRAM

Four Biblical Heroines and the Case for Female Authorship: An Analysis of the Women of Ruth, Esther and Genesis 38 (McFarland, 2008)

The Joseph Paradox
A Radical Reading of Genesis 37–50

HILLEL I. MILLGRAM

McFarland & Company, Inc., Publishers
Jefferson, North Carolina, and London

Unless otherwise noted, all chapter and verse references in this book are to the text of the Hebrew Bible, Masoretic Text (MT), with an English translation by the author.

LIBRARY OF CONGRESS CATALOGUING-IN-PUBLICATION DATA

Millgram, Hillel I., 1931–
The Joseph paradox : a radical reading of Genesis 37–50 / Hillel I. Millgram.
    p.   cm.
Includes bibliographical references and index.

ISBN 978-0-7864-6850-8
softcover : acid free paper ∞

1. Joseph (Son of Jacob)
2. Bible. O.T. Genesis XXXVII–L— Criticism, interpretation, etc.
I. Title.
BS580.J6M55 2012   222'.1106 — dc23   2012014727

BRITISH LIBRARY CATALOGUING DATA ARE AVAILABLE

©2012 Hillel I. Millgram. All rights reserved

No part of this book may be reproduced or transmitted in any form or by any means, electronic or mechanical, including photocopying or recording, or by any information storage and retrieval system, without permission in writing from the publisher.

On the cover: *Joseph Interpreting the Dreams of the Baker and the Butler* (Benjamin Cuyp, circa 1630); background © 2012 Shutterstock

Manufactured in the United States of America

*McFarland & Company, Inc., Publishers
Box 611, Jefferson, North Carolina 28640
www.mcfarlandpub.com*

For my father and mother,
Abraham Ezra and Ita Haya
Proverbs 6:20–23

*We are such stuff
As dreams are made on, and our little life
Is rounded with a sleep.*
— William Shakespeare, "The Tempest," IV

*Two roads diverged in a wood, and I–
I took the one less traveled by,
And that has made all the difference.*
— Robert Frost, "The Road Not Taken"

*Many are the intentions in the human heart,
But it is the will of God that will come to pass.*
— Proverbs 19:21

Table of Contents

Preface	1
Introduction	5
Prologue: The Way of the Fathers	31
1. A Family Tragedy	41
2. Rehabilitation	54
3. The Slave	68
4. The Interpreter of Dreams	76
5. The Egyptian	88
6. Cat and Mouse	96
7. The Entrapment	108
8. The Unmasking	123
9. The Long Farewell	135
10. The Egyptian Trajectory	150
11. The Write-Off	158
12. Legacy	169
13. The Closing of Accounts	182
14. Conclusion 1: Between God and Man	197
15. Conclusion 2: Joseph's Place in History	207
Appendix 1.: Who Sold Joseph into Egypt?	221
Appendix 2.: Can Judah and Tamar Be Fitted into the Joseph Narrative?	225
Appendix 3.: What Is a Poem Doing in the Joseph Story?	228
Glossary of Terms and Place Names	233
Who's Who in the Joseph Story	239
Bibliography	243
Scriptural Index	247
General Index	249

Preface

This book is an outgrowth of my earlier work, *Four Biblical Heroines and the Case for Female Authorship* (McFarland, 2008). One aspect of that study explored what I consider to be the birth of the approach to the human condition that we nowadays call "the theology of Providence." This work is, in part, meant to round out the story of the origin of this, for its time, radical doctrine.

More specifically, this book is an attempt to come to a new understanding of one of the most famous and well-loved tales in the annals of mankind: the Joseph Story. For more than a century scholars have approached the tale as simply a part of the larger work of Genesis (which, of course, it is), employing the tools of source criticism they used to study the Pentateuch to identify the various components of the Joseph Story's composition, while giving insufficient attention to the literary aspects of the tale that are the primary sources of its long-lasting appeal. This essentially reductionist approach has yielded results that leave much to be desired.

Our reevaluation, while bearing in mind the larger context in which the story is embedded, will focus almost exclusively on the tale itself as a self-contained literary unit, and will attempt to understand it as such. It will involve revising and nuancing our view of its hero from the generally laudatory and simplistic evaluation of almost two thousand years of readers. It moreover will demand of us a more profound appreciation of the artistry and sophistication of the way the tale is told, and insist that we question exactly what were the intentions of the ancient author who penned it.

Nothing has been more common (and nothing, I would add, more misleading) than to see the Joseph Story as a simple rags-to-riches Horatio Alger tale; a stirring triumph of faith, courage, perseverance and — yes, let us say it — clean living. And nothing, we will contend, is further from the truth. Our reevaluation will force upon us the need to closely reread this ancient text, paying careful attention to the vocabulary used to tell this tale, the implications of the structure and its emphases, both in terms of the narrative itself and in terms of the broader agendas of the Book of Genesis in which it is embedded. What will emerge, we will suggest, is a cautionary tale, darker by far than usually perceived. The astounding "success story" of Joseph's Egyptian career emerges as the precursor to the enslavement of his descendants; the hero himself is ultimately seen to be rejected by his family, by his people, and by Scripture. It becomes a startling example of how success can breed failure, and how the struggle for a place in the sun can end in deep shadow.

The tale that emerges is far more complex than a study of the self-defeating nature of the pursuit of worldly success. It also highlights a deep clash of values; a struggle between two disparate ways of life, and passes judgment upon them. Moreover, in what appears on the surface as a humanistic tale of family conflict and resolution, we will discover a thinly masked theological inquiry into the relationship between humanity and God. Through the tale, the author is proposing a radical theological approach to human life on this planet, one far removed from what we normally think of as the way the Bible pictures God's ways with man.

The methodology of our study consists of a once popular but nowadays largely overlooked format: that of commentary. Proceeding systematically verse by verse, sometimes word by word, the three-thousand-year-old text is analyzed and explicated, the implications and conclusions emerging in the form and order the author originally intended. The analysis of the narrative is preceded by a general introduction to the specific textual issues addressed, and a prologue which places the Joseph Story in its larger context. It is followed by two final chapters which sum up the conclusions reached. From explosive beginnings to dark dénouement, the tale is exposed in all its stark power, clarified rather than smothered in analysis. This work is not intended as an academic monograph but rather as a vehicle designed to return the Joseph Story to the general public that has provided its enthusiastic readers over the centuries and, when all is said and done, for whom it was originally written.

As I have remarked in one of my previous books, no one writes without having read. My debt to those who have preceded me in this study of the Joseph Story — from the rabbis of the Talmudic Age and the medieval commentators, to the scholars of the modern era — is beyond measure. Their numbers far exceed the room available for citation. Those whose works have proved most immediately helpful are listed in the bibliography, while those of the medieval commentators relied upon are to be found in the glossary. I have tried to give credit to those Bible scholars and commentators who are the sources of the premier ideas and insights that have directed my steps, either by lighting the way or by providing theories against which I have reacted (a not less vital service). To all those specifically acknowledged, as well as those whose indirect influence cannot be thanked by name due to space constraints, my deepest gratitude. Without them this book could never have been attempted, much less written.

Two names deserve, I feel, special mention. The first is that of an institution: The Gramcord Institute. This nonprofit organization produces a most amazing computer software package that has revolutionized the study of the Bible, making tasks that previously took weeks accomplishable in minutes, and opening to the serious student of the Bible vistas that were previously attainable solely by scholars of genius, and then only after the better part of a lifetime of study. My especial thanks go to Dr. Paul A. Miller, who guided me in my first halting steps in acquiring the skills necessary to utilize these powerful tools, and helped me over the pitfalls of computer glitches and compatibility problems. His help, and that of Dr. Dale Wheeler, made my entry into this new world possible.

The second name deserving special mention is that of Leon R. Kass, who first made his name in the disciplines of medical ethics and philosophy. His magisterial work, *The Beginning of Wisdom*, a philosophical close reading of the Book of Genesis, is eye-opening in both its breath and its depth of insight. My copious quotes and references to this book do not do justice to the extent of my indebtedness to his approach. His shadow looms large over this work.

Two people have read the complete draft manuscript of this book: my son, Professor Elijah Millgram, whose suggestions, based upon his expertise in philosophy, and his editorial skills have, as with past books, improved this work beyond measure. Debby Millgram, my wife and intellectual goad of more than half a century, has interacted with me constantly during the period of writing, both on the text and the issues underlying it. She has read, edited and commented on multiple drafts of every chapter, and her comments and corrections have proved invaluable in making this book what it is. To both of these, as to my other readers, I owe a massive debt of gratitude.

Victor Hamilton quotes Dr. Paul Rees who, when once asked, "Do you like to write?" answered, "Yes, I like to write, but I like it better to have written." He expresses to perfection my feelings as I contemplate the completed manuscript, and ready it for dispatch to my publisher. It was long in gestation, laborious in the writing and rewriting, and invigorating in realization. Moreover, as it concludes the project on the biblical origins of a theology of Providence begun with my book *Four Biblical Heroines*, its completion brings a sense of closure.

Introduction

> *To travel hopefully is a better thing than to arrive, and the true success is to labour.*
> — Robert Louis Stevenson,
> *Virginibus Puerique*

The Amazing Technicolor Dreamcoat

In 1967 Alan Doggett, head of the Colet Court School[1] music department, commissioned two young unknowns to write a work for the school's first musical production. The young men were Andrew Lloyd Webber and Tim Rice, aged 19 and 23, respectively. The theme chosen was the biblical story of Joseph. In March 1968, *Joseph and the Amazing Technicolor Dreamcoat* debuted at the school, put on by the school choir, a rock group named The Mixed Bag, and the school orchestra. Within the following eight months it had been performed, in an expanded version, in St. Paul's Cathedral and reviewed in *The Times*. In the following year it was released by Decca Records and *Joseph*, Andrew Lloyd Webber and Tim Rice were on their way to fame and fortune.

Obviously the captivating music of Webber and the charming lyrics of Rice, which retold the Joseph Story in modern idiom, were critical ingredients to what was to become one of the most dependably profitable titles in musical theater, but it was the magic of this old biblical tale that was central to its success. By the time of the 1991 restaging at the London Palladium, *Joseph and the Amazing Technicolor Dreamcoat* had been produced for TV, been successfully put on by more than 20,000 schools and amateur theater groups and as well it had numerous professional stagings in London, New York and even South America. What had begun as a 15 minute pop cantata had metamorphosed into a two hour musical phenomenon that shows no signs of abating.

What is it about the story of Joseph that so captivates audiences? This phenomenon is not new. In its written form the Joseph Story has been casting its spell upon readers for almost three thousand years, seizing their imaginations and never palling. To penetrate behind this seductive magic, to attempt to understand how it works and what are the secrets that power one of the most fascinating tales ever told are the rationale and the motivation behind this book.

The Mystery of the Joseph Story

The tale of Joseph is arguably the best-known of all the stories in the Bible. It is both a complex, exhilarating account brilliantly told, and the longest connected narrative in Genesis, comprising almost 450 verses.[2] Of all the human beings portrayed in the vast panorama that is the Hebrew Bible, only Moses and David are given more space. Yet, strangely, the tale is superfluous to the main plot line of Genesis.

This statement requires explanation. Genesis begins with the creation of the world and with mankind. It then traces the development of mankind from its humble beginnings: its spread over the face of the earth, its differentiation into tribes, nations and language groups, and especially the growth of violence from individual incidents into a systematized and continuous phenomenon. All this is background.

The focus then shifts to the true subject of the biblical narrative: the development of a family that will become God's special people, a people whose purpose will be to lead mankind, by precept and by example, out of the self-destructive downward spiral of ever escalating violence into which it has entered by providing an alternative: a new and better way in which to live. As with mankind, this new family begins with a single couple. By the time we have concluded with the 35th chapter of Genesis we have followed this family through three generations of struggle and vicissitude. From a rocky start beset with uncertainty, the family has stabilized and grown. It is now on the verge of becoming a clan.

In Genesis 35, Benjamin, the last member of the fourth generation, is born. The family is now complete. God has reaffirmed, definitively, that this new generation will be the fulfillment of His promise to Abraham and Isaac, the founders of the family, and that out of them the new people will emerge. The chapter concludes with a summary of the completed composition of the new generation, and an account of the death of Isaac. All that now remains to tell is the descent into Egypt. One chapter would suffice to cover this transition, and then we could move on to Exodus, Chapter 1, where the mega-drama of enslavement, redemption and covenant proceeds and gains the momentum that carries it to the very end of the Bible.[3]

Seen in this light the entire story of Joseph is superfluous, an apparent digression from the main plot line of the Bible. So the question arises: fascinating though it may be, why was the tale intruded into the narrative, and moreover given such prominence? This book is an attempt to answer this question.

My central contention is that, far from being a digression, the Joseph Story is a necessary segment of the structure of Genesis, and of the larger plot of the Bible. Beyond filling in the details of how the family gets to Egypt in the first place, the function of the narrative is to raise a number of issues that will prove to be central to the larger biblical agenda. Among them are the following: The fourth generation of the family, the one immediately following that of the founders — the Fathers of the people to be — will prove decisive in determining the path that God's people will take; for good or for ill, the sociological patterns of this people are determined here. The Joseph narrative also raises theological issues that will determine the future direction of the Israelite religion, such as the role of God in a world that seems to us to be secular, and the issue that has become known as the problem of free will. The narrative explores prototypes that will continue to appear in the Jewish people over the millennia. And not least, the Joseph Story explores, for the first time, how this new people, mandated to exert a redeeming influence on the peoples of a world steeped in self-destructive patterns of tyranny and violence, are to function in this unredeemed world. Seen in this light, the tale of Joseph and his brothers sets the stage for everything to come. Without it the subsequent biblical narrative would lose much of its meaning and, in part, become incomprehensible. Demonstrating these points is a part of the agenda of this book.

How Are We to Proceed?

As this is a book about the Bible, or to be more exact, a part of one of the books of the Hebrew Bible,[4] it is only proper that before analyzing the Joseph Story we be clear in our minds what exactly we mean when we speak of the Bible, and precisely how we intend to approach it.

The Hebrew Bible is the creation of a people known as the Children of Israel,[5] or in shorthand the Israelites, who were the ancestors of the present-day Jews. The thirty-nine books that became the Hebrew Bible we currently possess were composed over a period of close to a thousand years. They are the end result of the sustained efforts of this unusual people to reach an understanding of itself, of its place in the world and of its tortuous, and often tortured, relationship with its God. The insights reached during this millennial undertaking (known subsequently as the Biblical Age) and embedded in the books of the Hebrew Bible, have not only shaped Judaism and its daughter religions, Christianity and Islam, but have determined the form and direction of civilization in the modern world.

The Bible contains literary works composed in different periods and in vastly divergent conditions, and these encompass radically different literary forms. There are surges of exhortation alternating with vehement denunciation; dry legal codes side by side with philosophical speculation; odes of joy and sadness, comedy and tragedy, phrased sometimes in poetry, sometimes in prose and sometimes both intermingled, side-by-side with long stretches of narrative. This last includes stories, biographies, reportage and, most of all, history. It is within this last category, narrative prose, that we find the book of Genesis, whose last third comprises the Joseph narrative.

How did the story of Joseph and his brothers come into being? For close to two centuries it has become pretty much a scholarly consensus that the book of Genesis is a composite creation, pieced together from various "documents," "sources" and "traditions" by a team of editors and redactors. As a result, the regnant approach to the Joseph narrative, as indeed to the Pentateuch as a whole, has been to attempt to identify the putative documents or sources that form the separate components of the narrative. In more recent years this approach has been increasingly recognized as sterile. A painstaking and indeed definitive chemical analysis of all the pigments used by Leonardo da Vinci in painting his Mona Lisa tells us very little about either the subject of the painting or its composition, much less why it is universally considered a masterpiece. In like manner, assigning one verse to a supposed source "E," while determining that the following verse (minus two words which belong to a third source) belongs to source "J," really tells us very little about the Joseph Story, even if the analysis is correct.[6] This has led in recent years to an increasing abandonment of so-called "source criticism" in favor of literary approaches: the attempt to see the narrative as a connected and unified whole, and to understand its overall meaning as well as how it works as a literary masterpiece. This is the approach that I have adopted.[7]

A Literary Approach

Every work is, of necessity, undergirded by preconceptions and assumptions. As should by now be clear, one of the fundamental assumptions underlying this book is that the Joseph narrative is a unitary work, the product of one author.[8] A second assumption is that it is a great work of literature. This is in no way meant to diminish its religious status or character.

The notion that religious works and works of great literary merit are incompatible categories is not only refuted by counterexample, but highly denigrating to religion as a whole. Excluding the Bible from discussion for the moment, some of the most important, indeed formative religious works of the West, from Augustine's *The City of God* or his *Confessions*, through Dante's *Divine Comedy*, to Kierkegaard's *Fear and Trembling* and *Purity of Heart* are universally considered magnificent works of literature. Far from their literary excellence diminishing their religious worth, it has enhanced both the quality of their religious message and its appeal.

This truism was foundational to the Age of the Bible. It would have been considered disrespectful to God, indeed outright insulting, to treat of Him and His concerns with anything but the highest of which man is capable. Nothing but superlative and sophisticated literary technique would receive a hearing when treating of what we today would term religious subjects. And of those written, only the very best would eventually make it into the Bible as it was finally canonized.[9] Thus only through an appreciation of biblical books as works of high literature can we begin to make sense of them at all. Robert Alter, who pioneered the contemporary literary approach to the Bible, states, "I would ... insist on a complete interfusion of literary art with theological, moral, or historiosophical vision, the fullest perception of the latter dependent on the fullest grasp of the former."[10] It is this revised understanding of both what religious works and literary works are, an understanding now increasingly respectable in biblical studies, that underlies this book.

The central literary technique employed to understand the Joseph narrative is one called a close reading of the text. This literary method, I would contend, is especially suited to explicating the extraordinarily dense and rich biblical narrative texts that have come down to us. Indeed, close reading as we know it today[11] is an outgrowth of, among other sources, the exegesis of religious texts. The scriptural commentaries of the ancient rabbis embedded in the Talmud[12] and those of the rabbinic medieval commentators are commonly cited as early predecessors to close reading.

Because this is so central to this entire work, a brief excursus here becomes necessary. When one writes, one translates one's ideas, experiences and purposes into words. The result, if effectively written, contains the author's aims and ideas encoded in the sentences, paragraphs and overall structure of the resultant text. Our task as readers thus becomes to decode the text to reclaim the original ideas, experiences and intentions of the author. This is the aim of close reading.

This task is not simple. In the first place we have to contend with our own often unconscious prejudices and preconceptions which act as filters, coloring and distorting our understanding of what the author intended to convey. We project our meanings into the text, unintentionally distorting or violating the original meaning of the author. This is especially the case when the selection in question — as in the case of a text from the Bible — was written thousands of years ago, and thus reflects a world remote from our experience. To make matters worse, the Bible employs unfamiliar literary conventions. It therefore requires discipline and sophistication to retrieve both the meanings and the intentions of the ancient author.

Part of the method must be historical. All authors write within the context of their times, and unless we can reconstruct, at least minimally, the material, social and ideational environment in which the author worked, we have little chance of recovering his or her meaning. When one peruses the way biblical texts were interpreted only one hundred years ago, when our knowledge of the Ancient Near East was minuscule, one is easily shocked by what are now obviously misunderstandings and distortions typical of the period.[13] Thankfully, in the course of the past century historical and archaeological progress has opened up the expanse of the Ancient Near East before our eyes. The outlines, and often even details, of the world in which Joseph and his brothers lived out their lives, as well as the world of the author of our tale (the two were not the same by any means)[14] are now available to us. Part of the analysis of this book, therefore, will be historical: an attempt to make comprehensible to the reader what, in the light of contemporary knowledge, these worlds were like and how they functioned.

With the context in place the focus will return to close reading, that is, careful, sustained interpretation of the text. We will accordingly place great emphasis on the particular as opposed to the general, and will pay close attention to individual words, to how they are used, to the syntax, and to the order in which sentences and ideas unfold. Through them we attempt to arrive at the author's purpose in writing.

Close reading is more than a discipline. It presumes the active engagement of the reader, and an active dialogue with the long-dead author, in which one actively questions the use of every metaphor, every turn of phrase, every juxtaposition to tease out what the author is getting at. Once the various parts fall into place and a coherent system of meaning emerges, the technique we call close reading approaches its goal. This goal is the appreciation of the text as an integrated whole expounding the central ideas of the author, his or her message and purpose.

Let me pause to identify the intended audience of this work. As with my previous books, this work is not intended for a scholarly or academic readership. While I hope that some biblical scholars may find positions that I have taken to be of interest, they are not my target audience. I am addressing the type of person for whom the Joseph Story was originally written, that is, the intelligent layman. Over the years these have been the people who provided the captivated audience for the Joseph Story, and it is to the twenty-first century successors of this longstanding appreciative audience that this book is directed.

Because the aim is to make the often complex issues posed by the text available, and to dissolve the barriers that prevent appreciation of, and identification with, this more than three thousand-year-old saga, I presuppose no prior knowledge of ancient history, biblical studies or related matters. Where background knowledge or explanation is needed, it will be supplied on a need-to-know basis. All that is required of the reader is an open mind.

With these assumptions understood, we can now proceed to more immediate concerns.

Fact or Fiction?

If we intend to approach the Joseph narrative as literature, it behooves us to begin by addressing the question: what kind of literature is it? In recent years there has been a tendency to define the Joseph Story as a novella.[15] What is a novella? As Humphreys defines it: the term "novella is currently used in literary criticism to denote a type of prose narrative that stands between the novel and the short story, sharing characteristics of each."[16] As such, novellas "are fiction. They do not report events or describe persons as they actually took place or lived in the past.... they are not historical.... What is reported in them is not designed ... to meet any tests of historical accuracy." Novellas are "the conscious creative work of generally a single author.... They reveal from beginning to end the artful stamp of a single controlling craftsman.... They intend to entertain."[17] Humphreys considers the Joseph Story a prime example of the novella form in the Bible.[18]

I consider this characterization problematic and misleading. In the first place, the novella is a relatively recent Western literary form, unknown in the ancient world.[19] To read it back twenty-five hundred years, and into a different culture, is anachronistic. Furthermore, to see the Joseph Story as merely fictional entertainment is to fail to take seriously both the narrative itself and the entire culture of the Biblical Age out of which it emerged. The Bible we hold in our hands today was intended as Scripture, that is, a compendium of works designed to direct and instruct humankind in the meaning and purpose of life on this earth and of what God expects of His creatures. At the very least, it was conceived to be a compendium of works composed under the influence of divine inspiration; to some it amounted to the very Word of God. As such, any work not meeting these high standards was not admitted to the canon.[20] Works designed simply for entertainment, and with no transcendental purpose, were rigorously excluded.[21]

This impinges on a central question pertaining to the Joseph narrative: is it fact or fiction? To define it as a novella brands the tale from the start as fiction. This is not a categorization that should be accepted without a supporting argument. It is far more appropriate, on the face of it, to classify the Joseph Story as an instance of a frequent and distinctive biblical literary form: that of historical prose narrative. Historical narrative was one of the great inventions of the ancient Israelites; a form of writing previously unknown, created to enable them to express their revolutionary theology. The monotheistic revolution ruthlessly suppressed the pagan gods; this entailed abolishing mythology, the stories of the gods. This in turn had the effect of shifting the focus of attention from the heavens to the earth. In a universe with but one omnipotent deity, there was nothing to tell about Him: no birth, no mating, no quarrels with other deities, no love affairs, no scandals. All that there was to tell was of His creative acts and of His relations with humanity. By default, attention turned to human beings, their relations with God and with each other: that is, with their history, and so historiography—the writing of history—was born,[22] which is why Baruch Halpern calls the Israelites of the Biblical Age, "The First Historians."[23] Thus I agree with Kenneth Mathews' evaluation of the Joseph Story: "It is better to conclude that it appears historical because it *is* historical. The historical nature of the story is recognizable because it authentically reflects historical events."[24]

But even accepting the Joseph Story as historical narrative, to what degree can we rely upon it for historical *accuracy*? When one considers the complexity of the story, the detailed conversations and subtle interactions, short of first person reporterage—an impossibility as the author was not a contemporary of the events related—how can we see the tale as anything but fiction?

Where he got his information we will discuss below. At this stage of the discussion it is important to point out that the question is itself anachronistic. The biblical historians were not writing history the way we do. They were asking different questions than the ones we ask. The discipline of history as it has developed and assumed its present form over the past several centuries is concerned with *what* happened and *how* it happened. The biblical view of history is concerned with a different issue: *what does it mean*? This led to the development of a different technique of writing history than that currently practiced in the Western world.

We have said that one of the few things that can be told about God is an account of His relations with human beings. The reason why so much of the Bible is structured as history and as biography (which is merely personal history) is a conviction that, to come to an understanding of God's purposes, the study of the development and the vicissitudes of humanity, and especially of the People of Israel, is one of the surest routes.

As the Bible sees it, the purpose of the study of history is to draw lessons of universal import, applicable to human beings whenever and wherever they might be. But such conclusions are only as reliable as the sources from which they are drawn. If one is to get the conclusions right, one must first get the facts right. This implies that we should take seriously what we would think of as the basic historical data that the narrative contains.

As a general rule, the biblical authors choose their episodes with an eye to the lessons that they wish to draw. But once the subject is chosen, the author takes scrupulous care to get his facts right. The biblical authors saw matters in terms of factual foundations shaped by realistic art. It was accepted literary practice in the biblical period, and later in the Greek world, that when the author knew, in greater or lesser detail, the gist of what had been said or what had taken place, he would frame speeches for his protagonists, giving form and dramatic impact to the known contents. The noted historian J. B. Bury explains this style of historical writing in his analysis of the speeches in the works of the Greek historians. Of Thucydides, the greatest of the Greek historians, he states:

> The persons who play leading parts in the public affairs which he relates reveal their characters and personalities, so far as required, by their actions and speeches. The author, like a dramatist, remains in the background, only sometimes coming forward to introduce them with a description as brief as in a playbill.... His general rule was to take the general drift and intention of the speaker, and from this text compose what he might probably have said.... His speeches in general served two purposes. In the first place they were used by the author to explain the facts and elements of a situation, as well as underlying motives and ideas.... [Thus] he uses the actual expositions of politicians — genuine political documents so far as the main tenor went — as the most useful means of explaining a situation.... His speeches had the second function ... of serving the objective dramatic method of indicating character.... The general plan was that the men, as well as the events, should speak or be made to speak for themselves, with little or no direct comment from the writer.[25]

Bury's account sums up one of the main techniques of the biblical historians as well.

So how can we answer our original question? It would seem that with the Joseph Story we are dealing with a narrative based on historic fact. This has been sculpted into a work of art through conscious choice of what to present and how to present it, for the purpose of creating a vehicle capable of conveying messages of universal import. It is partly this sculpting, but mostly the embedded messages, that gives the narrative its enduring value, and which led it ultimately to become part of the heritage of the world.

This will be our working hypothesis. As we proceed in our investigation of the Joseph narrative, we will see how well our hypothesis holds up to the realities of both the text and the results of modern historical and archaeological research.[26]

When Did the Events Related in the Joseph Narrative Take Place?

Given our working hypothesis, that the Joseph narrative is based on historic fact, we are now able to pose the question: when did the events portrayed take place? Inasmuch as our aim is to understand the narrative, our method will be to start with the text itself rather than some arbitrary starting point, and use the text to set the parameters in the search for the proper period of investigation. Having defined the Joseph Story as literature, and having concluded that in its own context it appears to be historical narrative, we can now begin by questioning how this answer accords with the reality of the Ancient Near East.[27]

The most common current view of the narratives to be found in Genesis, of which the Joseph Story is a part — or at the very least, an appendix — considers them to be pure fiction, myths and legends committed to writing sometime during the first millennium.[28] As such, they should have little in common with the literature of the second millennium BCE. Yet K. A. Kitchen, after an exhaustive comparison of these narratives (including the Joseph Story) with analogous literatures of the second millennium Ancient Near East finds clear analogies. He concludes his survey as follows:

> Purely on literary type and content — as measured against the self-existent criteria of the biblical world — the patriarchal narratives stand closest to historically-founded narratives.... This by itself does *not*, of course, prove that the patriarchs are, or were, historical people. But these facts (based on external, tangible comparison) do favor understanding the patriarchs as having been historical persons within historically-based traditions, and equally clearly go against any arbitrary assumption that they "must" have been simply a myth or legend.... If the patriarchal narratives are not historical or quasi-historical, then they must be specimens of a type of imaginative, "realistic-fiction" novel not otherwise known to have been invented until several millennia later, in fact approaching modern times. That, in itself, would be more than passing strange.[29]

Further evidence that these narratives come from an earlier period than the first millennium can be found in the fact of the narrator's acceptance of practices that were taboo in Mosaic Law, such as marrying one's half-sister, as in the case of Abraham and Sarah.[30]

Kitchen brings several additional lines of reasoning to bear in order to fix the time of the Age of Abraham, Isaac and Jacob, and thus to determine the date of Joseph. Among them are:

1. The head of the Syrian-Canaanite pantheon during the first half of the second millennium was the high god El, "but after circa 1500 in round terms, he was overtaken throughout the Levant by Hadad the weather/storm/fertility god, increasingly under his title Baal ('Master').... The total absence of Baal from the patriarchal tradition indicates its antiquity, in effect before 1500."[31]

2. And most decisively, only twice in all its long history was Egypt ruled from a capital in the Delta. The better known of these was during the Nineteenth Dynasty under Ramses II (1279–1213) when Egypt was ruled from Pi-Ramesses (in use until circa 1130). But earlier, from 1970–1540 BCE (the Twelfth-Fifteenth Dynasties) the Egyptian kings had an East Delta residence at Ro-waty. Somewhat prior to 1944 BCE, the Pharaoh Amenemhat I established a royal estate and temple here. This was expanded into a major settlement by Sesostris III (c. 1860 BCE), which in turn the Hyksos rulers of the Fifteenth Dynasty used as their East Delta capital which they called Hat-waret. This was the Avaris of Manetho, which remained the capital of Egypt until 1540 BCE.[32] "Thus the visits by an Abraham or a Jacob to a pharaoh at an East Delta Palace are only feasible in Egyptian terms within circa 1970–1540 BCE, if they are not to be turned into contemporaries of Moses!... for Abraham to visit a pharaoh's palace, or Joseph to serve in one, or Jacob and family to visit and reside within reach of one, their successive presences ought to be located chronologically within circa 1970–1540, and preferably circa 1860–1540 ... the Ramesside period is too late."[33]

To my mind the above (in conjunction with additional evidence Kitchen brings[34]) is decisive.[35] I therefore accept his placing the events of our tale in the late Middle Kingdom-Second Intermediate Period of Egyptian history, with Joseph's arrival in Egypt tentatively dated to 1720/1700 BCE, and Jacob's entry into Egypt circa 1690/1680 BCE.

When Was the Joseph Story Written?

We have defined the Joseph Story to be historical narrative as opposed to narrative fiction. We now need to refine our understanding a bit further. Historical narrative, as we are employing the term, also excludes reportage, the firsthand witnessing of events. By utilizing the term *history*, we are implying composition of the work subsequent to the events discussed in it, often long after they occurred, with the resultant advantage of hindsight and perspective. Our contention is that the Joseph Story, as an historical narrative, was composed long after the events it relates took place.

This leads to two questions: having more or less fixed the date of the events, how long after them was our narrative written? And secondly, how did the author know? What were the sources of his information?

To begin with the first question: my view is that the Joseph Story, as we know it today, was composed in the tenth century BCE, that is some seven hundred years after the events it portrays. Before exploring the implications of this large gap in time between occurrence and composition, let us first review some of the reasons for fixing on the tenth century as the date of our narrative. The first major factor is style. The dynamic and extremely sophisticated style of the Joseph Story, including the language employed, closely resembles that of the Books of Samuel and of Ruth, works that couldn't have been written before the latter part of the reign of David,[36] that is, the beginning of the tenth century. That the Joseph Story, Samuel and Ruth all possess a similar style argues that all of these works were written in the same period. This era, the age of the United Monarchy and the Davidic Empire, has been called by Gerhard von Rad the "Solomonic Enlightenment,"[37] a time crowned by a magnificent cultural and literary flowering. This, I would contend, was the environment in which the Joseph Story was composed.

A further, internal indicator of compositional dating is Genesis 38:29, the climax and denouement of the dramatic tale of Judah and Tamar; the raising of the curtain on the major sub-plot and counter-thesis of the Joseph Story.[38] The announcement of the birth to Tamar of a son by the name of Perez implies knowledge of David as king of Israel on the part of the reader. Without this knowledge, the story has no punch-line and the tale of Judah and Tamar loses its point.[39] This not only sets the reign of David as the earliest possible date for the composition of the Joseph Story, but also probably precludes a date of composition much after the death of Solomon (c. 930 BCE). The collapse of the Empire and the breakup of the United Kingdom would have robbed David's name of much of its luster, especially in the Northern Kingdom of Israel, which specifically revolted *against* the "House of David." The punch line would also not have worked following the collapse of the "House" that David built.

Having indicated why I have joined the large group of scholars who date the composition of the Joseph narrative to the tenth century,[40] we are now free to address the second question: what were the sources that can explain our author's knowledge of events that transpired some seven hundred years before his birth?[41] This is a real problem for, beyond the specifics of the story itself, the author provides us with a wealth of detailed description of the tale's Egyptian background. This setting, when examined in the light of our current knowledge, demonstrates intimate acquaintance with the Egyptian conditions and practices current in the seventeenth century BCE. Furthermore, many of these changed considerably over time, and did not resemble at all the Egypt of the tenth century. Even had the author been familiar with the Egypt of his day, this would not, by itself, have enabled him to reflect the Egypt of a bygone era.

To answer this question we return to our starting point: our characterization of the Joseph Story as literature. And not simply literature, but a beautifully crafted and highly sophisticated historical narrative with complex plot lines and deep psychological penetration. Such high literature is not born fully formed from nowhere; "sprung fully armed from the head of Jove," as Athena's birth is described in Greek mythology. Literature develops by stages. As von Rad opines: "It should be assumed that such a complex literary structure had, from the point of view of the history of the narrative, its preliminary stages. This assumption finds support in a number of tensions and roughnesses in the shaping of the material."[42]

I likewise propose the existence of a literary history, a chain of works, oral and written, on the subject of Joseph, his family and his career, with our narrative the grand culmination of a long process. Specifically, there is the magnificent poem encased in Genesis 49, which we have entitled "The Testament of Israel." This is universally accepted as one of the oldest compositions in the Bible, and it long predates the Joseph narrative of which it is a part.[43] In addition I believe we should assume the existence of a prior written narrative containing, in a simpler form, the basic story of Joseph and his brothers. Let us, for ease of reference, call this hypothetical document the "Ur-Joseph Tale."[44] These two provided the major, if not the exclusive, sources for the composition of our narrative. So when our author sat down to put pen to paper,[45] he was in a very similar situation to the one in which Shakespeare found himself when he sat down to write *Hamlet*.

When Shakespeare decided to compose a play on the subject of Hamlet, Prince of Denmark, he could not simply commence de novo. He was confronted with a well-known tale hundreds of years old. It was part of the traditional history of Denmark, first incorporated into written literature in the second half of the twelfth century.[46] In 1514 this version was printed in Paris, reprinted elsewhere, and came to the attention of Francois de Belleforest who, in 1576, wrote his version of the Hamlet story. The next version was an English play of the 1580's based on Belleforest. Most modern authorities agree with the noted poet and literary critic, T. S. Eliot, who attributed this play to the Elizabethan playwright Thomas Kyd (1557–1595?), the author of *The Spanish Tragedy*.[47] This play, though often performed, was never printed and its manuscript has been lost. We know of it only from contemporary references and from its influence. It is called by scholars the "Ur-Hamlet" and it served as the immediate source of Shakespeare's play. Of this play Eliot remarks:

> *Hamlet* is a stratification.... It represents the efforts of a series of men, each making what he could out of the work of his predecessors. The *Hamlet* of Shakespeare will appear to us very differently if, instead of treating the whole action of the play as due to Shakespeare's design, we perceive his *Hamlet* to be superimposed upon much cruder material which persists even in the final form.[48]

This sketch of Shakespeare's *Hamlet* and its relation to its antecedents can serve as a model for the Joseph narrative we possess today. The basic story of Joseph and his family, incorporating much descriptive background, was very likely to have been transmitted first in oral and then in one or more written versions from pre–Mosaic times down to the tenth century.[49] The penultimate stage of this process produced the "Ur-Joseph Tale" which contained the data utilized in the Joseph narrative we possess today.

If we accept this hypothesis (and as I shall attempt to show in our subsequent analysis of the Joseph text there are strong indications which argue for its acceptance), what are the implications for the composition of the Joseph Story as we have it? In the first place it explains how our author was in possession of detailed and accurate information about the conditions in a foreign land, Egypt, and events that transpired there seven centuries before his time. But at the same time this "Ur-Joseph Tale" constrained the author. He was not free to design his story as he saw fit. Just as Shakespeare could not, for instance, omit Rosencrantz and Guildenstern[50] or the episode in which the king sends Hamlet to England bearing sealed instructions to the English king to kill Hamlet on arrival — everyone who was anyone had seen the "Ur-Hamlet" play and was expecting them[51] — so our author was not free to alter any significant element of the traditional tale he had inherited. Everyone knew the basic outline of the story — it was a pivotal part of the cultural heritage of Ancient Israel — and would expect tradition to be upheld. Then what remained for the author to do? If the characters and the plot could not be changed, then what remained was language and interpretation: to turn a pedestrian script into high literature and artistry, and to present the old plot in a new manner so as to impart new meaning and new significance to the well-known tale. In just this manner, in addition to replacing the bombast of Kyd with incomparable poetry, and turning the two-dimensional cardboard figures of the "Ur-Hamlet" into three-dimensional characters of great psychological depth, Shakespeare reinterpreted the story of Hamlet, turning a simple revenge melodrama into a universal meditation on the tragedy of the human struggle against destiny. In much the same way our author, by rewriting the tale in an elevated literary style, raised what he had inherited to the level of high art, and by adding new meaning and significance to well-known events, transformed a simple Horatio Alger success-story into the complex psychological and theological drama which has captivated a hundred generations. By imposing on the basic story larger philosophical, political and theological themes, a religious work of great depth was born, bringing the Book of Genesis to its climax and becoming one of the high points of the Bible.

If such is the case, then the issue of the historical accuracy of the literary tradition that culminated in the Joseph Story we now possess becomes of secondary importance. What becomes primary is the literary-religious significance of the tale, and the implications that flow from it. Most literary discussions of the Joseph Story have focused on the tensions within the plot and their resolution. But the truth of the matter is that there are no tensions and no suspense. Everyone knew how the story would "all come out." The narrative as we have it concentrates not so much on plot resolution as on issues of character, human motivation, and the larger theological implications of free will and God's governance of human affairs; it takes up the destiny of the seed of Abraham and the unavoidable conflict between the New Way of Abraham — God's way — and the old way, the "way of the world." The focus thus becomes not so much what happens as what it all means.

And so I suggest that the original, traditional story — the "Ur-Joseph Tale" — was no more than a rather simple success story with Joseph cast as the hero — or anyway, something on a par with such a story.[52] With the benefit of hindsight, our author has rethought the events, reinterpreted them, and produced a tale with a burden of his own choosing. Very much aware that the Joseph "success story" proved to be the precursor of the enslavement and oppression of the Israelites, the assessment of Joseph is reevaluated. A subplot featuring

Judah as a counterpoise to Joseph is introduced.⁵³ The matter of assimilation to Egyptian values becomes of central concern, and ethical issues move to the center stage. In the process of this rewriting, the Joseph Story became more than a retelling of a pivotal turning point in the development of the Israelite people; it turned into an archetype of the alternatives that lie before humanity at all times and in all places, and a theological thesis proposing to explicate the ways of God to man.⁵⁴

*The Question of Literacy in Ancient Israel*⁵⁵

Let us summarize our argument to this point: we are contending that the Joseph Story, in the form we have it today, is a sophisticated literary composition. It takes the form of a historical narrative (as the Ancient Israelites and Greeks understood this term), and as such reflects with a high degree of accuracy the events and conditions that it portrays. We further contend that, like all mature literary compositions, the Joseph Story is the end product of a long process of development which only took its final form in the tenth century BCE. There remains but one further step to complete our argument: to demonstrate that this thesis is indeed feasible within the conditions that prevailed in the eleventh and tenth centuries, the putative period for the gestation and composition of the literary *tour de force* that is the Joseph narrative.

The primary objection that can, and in all probability will, be raised against our thesis flows directly from an observation made by Humphreys, and whose truth is incontrovertible: that the Joseph narrative is a composition "rooted in a life setting characterized by a high level of literacy ... [it] presupposes a literate audience."⁵⁶ The question thus becomes: did the level of literacy that was the necessary prerequisite to the emergence of high literature exist in the tenth century?

It therefore becomes necessary to address the question of literacy in the Ancient World in general and Ancient Israel in particular. I will attempt to demonstrate that the appropriate level of literacy did exist in the tenth century. I will also contend that we have consistently underestimated the size of the reading public in Ancient Israel.⁵⁷

Until recently it had been universally assumed that during the Biblical Age virtually all Israelites were illiterate. Such literacy as did exist (and that largely only from the eighth century) was believed to have been confined to a very small class of professional scribes who performed such reading and writing activities as were necessary for rulers and the elite. As was the case in other illiterate societies, it was taken as a given that most "compositions" and "traditions" were oral, and were transmitted by bards and "storytellers" who wandered from village to village and from tribe to tribe.⁵⁸

Over a century ago, the German scholar Julius Wellhausen advanced the thesis that Israel had its origins in a conglomeration of primitive desert tribes who were, of course, illiterate.⁵⁹ As with so many nineteenth century theories constructed in a time when virtually nothing was known of the Ancient Near East, the explosion of knowledge produced by twentieth century discoveries — especially the vast libraries and archives of ancient Ugarit, Mari and Ebla — have rendered most of the views of Wellhausen and his school obsolete.⁶⁰ Ancient Israel did not exist in a vacuum. We now have a picture of the wider environment in which Ancient Israel existed, and as more and more of that larger context is filled in, we gain a correspondingly better understanding of what really went on in that small part of the whole that was Israel. The presumption of near total illiteracy in Ancient Israel is a holdover from discredited nineteenth-century theories, and can be classed as more a blind faith than historical knowledge.[61] Or as K. A. Kitchen puts it:

> [It is] the persistence of long-outdated philosophical and literary theories (especially of the 19th century stamp), and ... wholly inadequate use of first-hand sources in appreciating the earlier periods of the Old Testament story.[62]

The earliest form of writing, invented in Sumer in a long series of stages and reaching maturity about five thousand years ago, was a very complicated mixture of hundreds of signs representing whole words (logograms), signs for syllables or parts of words (syllabaries) and unpronounced signs used to indicate to which category of things a phonetic sign belonged (determinatives).[63] As such knowledge of writing was very hard to master, it was mainly confined to professional scribes in the employ of the king or of a temple. Writing was mostly used for clerical purposes: keeping records of goods collected as taxes, rations paid to workers as wages and so on. Only slowly did writing, by becoming even more complicated, become sufficiently flexible to be able to be used for such purposes as state propaganda and the recording of myths. From the beginning writing was designed to facilitate the functioning of the centralized state (which included the state religion), therefore its effective restriction to state-employed professionals was seen as advantageous.

The invention of the alphabet, sometime around 1700 BCE by Canaanites somewhere in Southern Syria-Palestine, changed everything.[64] Using a mere 22 signs to represent the consonants, any word could be constructed. It was so simple that virtually anyone could easily master it. Writing ceased to be the monopoly of professionals. We can get some idea of the revolutionary impact of alphabetic writing from the history of its introduction into Greece. The Greeks got their alphabet from the Phoenicians,[65] and from the moment of its appearance it was a private vehicle used for private purposes. Thus the first example of Greek alphabetic writing we possess appears scratched onto an Athenian jug from about 740 BCE, and is an announcement of a dancing contest: "Whoever of all the dancers performs most nimbly will win this vase as a prize." The very next example is three lines of poetry scratched onto a drinking cup: "I am Nestor's delicious drinking cup. Whoever drinks from this cup, swiftly will the desire of the fair-crowned Aphrodite seize him."

> The earliest preserved examples of the Etruscan and Roman alphabets are also inscriptions on drinking cups and wine containers. Only later did the alphabet's easily learned vehicle of private communication become co-opted for public and bureaucratic purposes. Thus, the developmental sequence of uses for alphabetic writing was the reverse of that for the earlier systems of logograms and syllabaries.[66]

With this background in mind, we now return to that area of the Ancient Near East where the alphabet had been invented more than half a millennium before it was introduced into a Greece just beginning to emerge from its dark age. Even as in Greece, the invention of the alphabet, by simplifying to an amazing extent the art of reading and writing, had the effect of dramatically democratizing literacy in Canaan. The beginning of national existence for Israel coincided with the streamlining of an alphabetic script. Mounting evidence indicates that by the beginning of the eleventh century BCE "writing was clearly part of everyday life and not restricted solely to a special scribal elite."[67]

K. A. Kitchen has provided numerous examples taken from archeological discoveries in both pre–Israelite Canaan and from Israel's immediate neighbors of a literacy not confined to elite and scribal circles. We have evidence from late thirteenth century Canaanite Lachish,[68] from a ninth century BCE private home in Tell Deir Alla in the Transjordan,[69] and from a late ninth-early eighth century BCE caravanserai, a fortified stopping-off place for caravans and merchants, located at Kuntillet Ajrud near a junction of two international trade routes in the northeast Sinai,[70] to name but a few. It is especially significant to our subject that the three earliest Israelite inscriptions yet discovered are abecedaries (schoolboy pads for practicing the writing of the alphabet); the earliest, from the little farming village of Izet Sartah,[71] dates from the twelfth century BCE. If tiny farm towns, some, like Izbet Sarta, numbering less that two dozen houses, had schoolchildren occupied with practicing their a-b-c's, we have evidence for a much wider distribution of literacy at this early period than had previously been suspected.[72]

I hope by this point to have established a strong presumption that literacy was sufficiently widespread by the tenth century BCE to allow us to posit a reading public for whom authors could write.[73]

A Word on Translation

This volume is designed as a companion to and commentary on the Joseph Story. As such, it contains the full text of Genesis 37–50. You may be used to reading the Bible in the King James translation, or in one of the more modern versions. While the King James translation is by far the greatest rendition of the Bible into English, the archaic language of this version no longer facilitates understanding, but instead acts as a barrier to most people.[74] On the other hand I feel that many of the modern translations, in striving to be relevant, are too free in their renderings, often imposing contemporary agendas on the text that distort the original meaning. Some modern translations I simply find wooden. And most modern versions, unfortunately, commit "the unacknowledged heresy" of using the translation "as a vehicle for *explaining* the Bible instead of representing it in another language, and in the most egregious instances this amounts to explaining away the Bible."[75] All this has led me to translate the text anew.

I have tried to make the translation simple and to keep it in contemporary English. The translation is a literal one in which I have stayed as close to the Hebrew original as possible, avoiding euphemism and paraphrases, while conforming to proper English usage. In a word, I have tried to render just what the text says while avoiding stilted and convoluted English. This not only facilitates ease of reading but also, to my way of thinking, conveys best the feel of the simple and lucid style of the original text.[76]

The Egyptian Setting

We now turn to the historical background of the land which provides the setting for our tale. Most of the story takes place in ancient Egypt, a civilization so alien to the modern denizen of the West as to be virtually incomprehensible. Without some guidance the reader will almost inevitably misinterpret much of what takes place. What follows is not intended to be a comprehensive introduction to this totally foreign society — multiple volumes would not suffice for this task — but it is simply a brief survey covering a few points that are relevant to the understanding of our topic. Hopefully they will serve as an aid to penetrating an unfamiliar world as we follow our story in a society completely at odds with everything we know and take for granted. Ancient Egypt was a "different planet" from the one we currently inhabit.

Egypt has the distinction of having become the first nation-state in human history. This state was a totalitarian theocracy, and served as the framework of a culture of extraordinary strength and durability which lasted for three thousand years.[77] Before discussing this state and the culture it embodied, it would be wise to establish an overall chronological outline of Egypt's historical development.

The determinative moment in Egyptian history was its unification into a nation-state around 3100 BCE. Before this seminal event, in the era referred to as predynastic, Egypt consisted of villages strung out along the Nile which gradually coalesced into mini-states,[78] then into two kingdoms, one in the South (the Nile Valley proper, referred to as Upper Egypt[79]) and the North (the Delta, referred to as Lower Egypt). Unification occurred when the southern kingdom conquered the North, and a united capital was established at Memphis.[80]

Formally Egyptian history begins with the first dynasty, founded by one Narmer, the conqueror of Lower Egypt.[81] But its true beginning was with the Third Dynasty, around 2686 BCE. This opened the first major historical age, the Old Kingdom, a period covering the Third through the Sixth Dynasties and lasting about five hundred years. This was the first great peak of Egyptian civilization. In all the critical elements it provided the template for everything that was to come. Its forms and ideas were, over the succeeding two thousand years, to be modified but never substantially changed. This was the creative period of Egyptian history, the glorified ideal for all the ages yet to be.

The Sixth Dynasty ended in collapse and chaos[82] with the breakdown of The Two Lands.[83] This chaotic period, known as the First Intermediate Period, was a time of anarchy, foreign incursion and social revolution. It took approximately one hundred years before Egypt pulled itself together into a new era of stability that has become known as the Middle Kingdom. But despite the reassertion of unity and order, the kings could never regain their former stature or power. From a totalitarian tyranny the land had become a feudal society. Whatever the theory — and the theoretical model of a totalitarian society ruled by an absolute despot, the Pharaoh, was unalterable — in practice power had to be shared with the Nomarchs, the great barons who ruled the districts. During the Old Kingdom all land belonged to the Pharaoh. Any gift of land was not inheritable, and the land normally reverted to the crown. But now land, and with it power, became dispersed among the nobles and the priests.[84] In time the feudal system extended to the peasantry as well, and they became holders of homesteads in fief.

As the nobles of Thebes[85] had been in the forefront of the reestablishment of Egypt as a unified state, it was Thebes in the South that now served as the capital for most of the Middle Kingdom. But towards its end the pharaohs established an East Delta residence at Ro-wati ("Door of the Two Ways") and ruled from there.[86] The Twelfth Dynasty, and with it the Middle Kingdom, collapsed in 1790 BCE, bringing on the Second Intermediate Period which was to involve two hundred years of debility, Semitic influx, subjugation and foreign rule. It was during this period that Joseph made his appearance in Egypt. With this rough sketch we have an overall background to the history leading up to the time of our tale.[87]

We now return to our definition of Egypt as a totalitarian theocracy. Egypt was ruled by the Pharaoh, and the Pharaoh was a god. More, he was not simply *a* god, he was all the gods, becoming each as the occasion demanded. But pre-eminently, the Pharaoh was Re, the god of the sun, among the most ancient of the gods of Egypt.[88] Moreover, the Pharaoh was the only official priest to all the gods; all priests were, strictly speaking, his vicars.[89] At his coronation the Pharaoh acquired *niswt* and entered into the realm of the divine; after his death he was wholly divine. The theory and practice of Pharaonic kingship conferred stability on Egyptian society. One of the gods occupied the throne. Pharaoh being divine, his rule insured a harmonious integration of nature and society at all times, one of the primary goals of all pagan religion.

Pharaonic power was not static. It grew during the Old Kingdom, reaching its peak in the Pyramid Age (the Fourth Dynasty). Afterward it slowly declined.[90] But the doctrine of Pharaonic divinity was believed absolutely by everyone, including the Pharaoh himself, irrespective of his actual power.

No monarch before the age of television was more visible to his people than the Pharaoh. Constant appearances at public ceremonies — laying cornerstones of new temples, canal openings, liturgical events — as well as frequent travel up and down the Nile in his royal barge — the great majority of Egyptians lived within a few miles of the river — kept him constantly in the public eye. Yet even those of highest rank had to keep their distance from the royal presence. Too close an approach meant death.

Central to Egyptian thought was a belief that there was a proper order for everything. The word for right order was *maat*, which also stood for justice and morality. It was the Pharaoh, as a god, who determined what was *maat* and what wasn't. Unlike the Israelites whose religion would center on a written code of law, the Egyptians had none.[91] They lived by unwritten custom based on the Pharaonic judgments, and altered by the Pharaoh whenever he saw fit. The Pharaoh embodied *maat* and he dispensed it.

As to the Egyptians — they considered themselves as a people to be unique. Egypt was conceived as being the center of the earth and its people the only legitimate inhabitants of the earth. All lands belonged to Egypt by divine right. Unlike the later Israelites,

> the Egyptians did not regard themselves as a chosen people; they were, quite simply, people. Other humans fell into another category. The Egyptian word for "man" as distinct from gods and animals ... applied only to Egyptians. A text ... which dates from the breakdown of the Old Kingdom, complains: "Strangers from outside have come into Egypt ... foreigners have become people everywhere."[92]

While the origins of Egyptian religion are hypothesized as springing from a consciousness of power embedded in creatures and natural phenomena,[93] requiring appeasement through priestly intermediaries and pious sacrifice, in its more developed phase religion was built on the twin poles of death and eternity. To this must be added the notion that hard stone could be identified with eternity. Therefore, stone was reserved mainly for religious use. Houses, even palaces, were built of mud brick that eventually would crumble. Temples, and especially tombs, were expected to be eternal and so were built of stone. As Paul Johnson comments with regard to royal tombs:

> The Egyptian theory of death and eternity ... presupposes that the exact reproduction, on the funerary plane, of life on earth, was the guarantee that it would be perpetuated into eternity. So tomb patterns are mirror images of what went on in real life.... The whole purpose of the [royal tomb] was that it should be built for eternity.... The logic of the association between stone and immortality ... reproduced in stone every material element of Egyptian daily life.... Wooden doors, copper hinges, metal bolts, mat hangings are all faithfully and exactly imitated in stone. In effect he [the architect] took a working Egyptian palace and petrified it into a tomb, so that it would last forever, and so insure the immortality of the king and his dependents.[94]

As with much else, what was once the prerogative of the Pharaoh alone — eternal life — progressively became democratized over time. In the same way that land ownership became available to ever wider circles of Egyptians, so immortality, once a monopoly of the pharaohs, increasingly became an option for, at first, the nobility, then the middle classes, and finally even the humble peasant. But while the average Egyptian might grasp at "privileges" once inconceivable, and guard his gains jealously, the feeling persisted that this was not progress but quite the reverse. Egypt was deteriorating. The days of the Old Kingdom, when the Pharaoh had been everything and everyone else nothing, remained in the popular imagination the Golden Age, looked back on with deep nostalgia. Those were the days when *maat* prevailed, when everyone knew his place and was in his proper place. Those were the days when the gods beamed down on Egypt and all was right with the world.

As dreams and their interpretation assume a pivotal role in the Joseph Story, it is in place to comment briefly on the role dreams played in Egyptian culture. It is necessary, however, to differentiate between the dreams of Egyptians as described in the Bible, and the dreams of Israelites (including Joseph). Dreams of Israelites are always clear and self-explanatory. The dreams of Egyptians are clothed in symbolism and are opaque to the dreamer; their enigmatic imagery requiring interpretation, normally at the hands of a professional dream interpreter.[95]

In the context of Ancient Egyptian society dreams served a decisive function. No Egyptian would for a moment contemplate making any important decision on the basis of personal inclination or the relevant objective facts alone. The realm of the divine must be consulted by means of omens and prophecies. Whether to go out after dark, cross a river, use a boat, swim or even engage in sexual intercourse or refrain from doing so were all dependent upon oracular advice. Among the sources of divine direction, dreams played a pivotal role.

The Egyptians carefully studied their dreams for direction at all moments of their lives. Dream interpretation was treated as a science, and a highly trained order of dream interpreters, working from hoary and detailed manuals of types of dreams and their meanings,[96] was routinely consulted by all classes of society. It was normative to take dreams and their interpretations with the utmost seriousness. Even in matters of State—issues such as the dispatch of expeditions, the date on which to fight a battle or where to locate a temple—dreams would play a major, even a decisive role. And while Egyptians did not normally ask the opinion of Asiatics on topics which had a religious bearing, in the matter of interpreting dreams it seems that they often acknowledged Asiatics as their superiors.

With this short introduction we will make do for the present.[97] Much further information about various aspects of Egyptian life, death and belief will appear at appropriate points throughout the book.

And Finally, a Note on Notes

We have already mentioned that this book, being designed for the general reader, is not written in the format typical of academic literature. So what is all that small print doing at the end of each chapter?

It is true that endnotes are a scholar's tool, their primary purpose being to facilitate peer review. Meticulously documenting every fact and opinion with its scholarly source allows specialists to check up on each other to see how well they have done their homework, whether they are accurately reflecting the views of those upon whom they rely, and therefore how seriously one can take their results. None of this is appropriate for a work that is not destined for the world of biblical scholarship, but rather for the intelligent and interested layman. In this book the endnotes serve different purposes entirely.

The purposes are three. The first is to play fair by letting the reader know whenever the translation departs from the Masoretic Text (MT), the standard Hebrew version of the Bible.[98] As most readers will have little or no command of Hebrew, they will have no way of knowing when their guide has departed from the accepted Masoretic Text. These notes are just a way of keeping the translation transparent, and of not relying on different versions without the reader's knowledge.

The second purpose is plain common courtesy. Whenever there is a direct quotation from some work it is the polite thing to give the author credit. So whenever an author is mentioned or quoted directly that author is given his or her due.

But by far the greatest number of endnotes serve the purpose of optional enrichment. Some readers work on the principle that the shortest distance between two points is a straight line. Anything extraneous to the matter at hand is an annoyance, to be avoided at all costs. Others, myself included, far from finding digressions distracting, discover in them half the reward of reading: detours open new vistas, expand horizons and deepen understanding. Many of the endnotes, those with more than one or two lines, fall into this category of short side excursions.

Assuming that at least some of my readers will have the same kind of temperament that I have, while others will prefer to get on with the task at hand, I have arranged to remove most side issues from the main body of the text and put them into the endnotes (and into a selected series of Appendices at the end of the book). Some of these will give a deeper understanding of the subject under discussion; sometimes they will give a view of some related field or issue. The endnotes at the end of this introduction are a taste of what you can expect. Those who prefer to stay with the main text will find that it is fully self-contained. But for those inclined to explore side issues, the doors have been left open.

In Conclusion

An extraordinary writer has the power to be immanent in the written page; his personality triumphs over time and death. The author of the Joseph Story is a presence directly confronting us with his unique understanding of life. Through the medium of a tale of bygone years, his subtle and revolutionary treatment reveals a vision of unsuspected potentialities and opens up new areas for human self-understanding. It is our task as readers to open ourselves to him so that, under his guidance, we can achieve insight into a fuller meaning of such basics as responsibility and brotherhood as they impact human life. Through the retelling of a series of events, already ancient in his day, and now almost thirty-eight hundred years in our past, he created a human drama that has gripped the imagination of millions over the intervening millennia. He has opened the eyes of his readers to the possibility that we need not remain trapped in our constricted pettiness, but have the capacity to grow into persons that transcend the limits of our current imaginations. It is the power of this vision, as well as the direction of the possibilities that can open to us, that led our narrative to be included in the Bible; it is this vision that challenges us today.

It is with this challenge that we commence our journey, turning back the clock nearly forty centuries to begin by probing the sources of our saga, an epic tale that retains the power of its implications undimmed by the passage of the years.

Notes

1. Colet Court is the preparatory school for St. Peter's School, one of the leading (as well as one of the oldest) public schools in England.

2. To be exact, 448 verses. This count includes Genesis 38 (30 verses) and Genesis 49 (26 verses), which, while forming independent units that can stand on their own, are nonetheless integral parts of the Joseph narrative. See Chapters 2 and 12 for an analysis of the relationship of these chapters to the whole.

3. The grand climax of this drama is the decree of Cyrus the Great freeing the Israelite captives in Babylon and permitting them to return to their ancient homeland to rebuild Jerusalem and the Temple of God. The structure of the mega-plot of the Hebrew Bible, which ends with Chronicles, has been obscured in the Christian rearrangement of the components of what they rename the Old Testament, mainly by moving the Books of the Prophets to the end of the OT. See also note 4 below.

4. So called because it is mostly written in the Hebrew language (a few parts are written in Aramaic, a sister language to Hebrew). To Christians the Hebrew Bible is known as the Old Testament (OT), to differentiate it from the New Testament (NT), which is written in Greek. The Hebrew Bible is the Holy Scriptures of the Jews. It, together with the New Testament, forms the Holy Scriptures of Christianity. All chapter and verse references in this book are to the text of the Hebrew Bible. These may, in rare instances, differ, though never more than by a few verse numbers, from those given in most English translations.

5. That is, the descendants of Israel, the third of the Fathers (see Glossary), who is also known by the name of Jacob (see Genesis 32:23–33).

6. "The division into the sources 'J' and 'E' of the Pentateuch, as it was maintained not without a polemical undertone by Wellhausen almost one century ago [is in error]. His statement is interesting because he seems to have realized that the story was fundamentally unitary; but he nevertheless chose to argue that 'the main source is, also for this last section of Genesis, "JE"...; our previous results require this assumption and would be shattered, if it were not provable.' But the problem is that this assumption is not required, nor can it be proved; not only so, it seems also extremely improbable, as has been rightly seen already by Gunkel in 1922 and Gressmann in 1923. Both authors came to the conclusion that the Joseph Story has a unitary and coherent plot, an element that would be lost by dividing it along source lines. But having realized this, they did not draw the obvious consequence: that the Documentary Hypothesis is not applicable to the Story" (J. A. Soggin, "Notes on the Joseph Story," in *Understanding Poets and Prophets: Essays in Honour of George Wishart Anderson,* ed. A. Graeme Auld [London: Sheffield Academic Press, 1993], 336).

7. As can be seen from the remarks of J. A. Soggin (note 6 above), I am not unique in holding to the view of a unified work as opposed to an assemblage of disparate sources. A growing number of serious scholars, especially those approaching the books of the Bible with the tools of literary analysis, are coming to this conclusion. To quote one more, David W. Gooding has little patience with "a great deal of the (until recently) standard literary criticism of the OT ... [whose proponents] claim to prove irreconcilable discrepancy, and therefore multiple authorship, by selecting a detailed feature from one context, contrasting it with a detailed feature from another context, without carefully examining the place each feature holds and the function it performs in the thought-flow of its own particular movement.... To understand a narrative from a literary point of view, we must first listen to the narrative as it stands, trying to see where and how each part fits into the thought-flow of the whole. In other words we must first give the narrative the benefit of the doubt; for if we start out with the assumption that the narrative is likely to be composite and discrepant, we shall too easily find imaginary discrepancies that confirm our original assumption.... [M]y presupposition would rather be that a biblical (or classical) narrative should be presumed to be a unity unless indisputable evidence is adduced for considering it composite" (David W. Gooding, *The Story of David and Goliath: Textual and Literary Criticism,* eds. D. Barthelemy, D. W. Gooding, J. Lust, and E. Tov [Gottingen: Vandenhoeck und Ruprecht, 1986], 58, 117).

8. "Suffice it to say here that most scholars are agreed that the Joseph narrative is a (redactional) unity composed by a single author" (Kenneth A. Mathews, *Genesis 11:27–50:26* [Nashville: Broadman & Holman, 2005], 50).

9. Canonization simply means the formal recognition and acceptance of a given book as holy or "inspired" by an authorized body. Works so recognized became as consequence Sacred Scripture, writings that were authoritative and binding. Genesis was canonized c. 445 BCE See Glossary.

10. Robert Alter, *The Art of Biblical Narrative* (New York: Basic, 1981), 19. He then quotes Rosenberg's statement, "The Bible's value as a religious document is intimately and inseparably related to its value as literature. This proposition requires that we develop a different understanding of what literature is, one that might — and should — give us some trouble." To which Alter adds, "The proposition also requires,

conversely, that we develop a somewhat more troublesome understanding of what a religious document might be." Alter takes the quote from Joel Rosenberg, "Meanings, Morals and Mysteries: Literary Approaches to the Torah," *Response* 9:2 (Summer 1975): 67–94.

11. The technique as currently practiced was pioneered in the English-speaking world by I. A. Richards (1893–1979) and his student William Empson (1906–1984), and later developed by the "New Critics" of the mid-twentieth century.

12. See Glossary.

13. It is well to remember that while archeological excavation in Syria-Palestine and Mesopotamia had its beginnings in the latter part of the nineteenth century, publication of the results, especially the ancient archives and libraries unearthed, only began in earnest after World War I. Before this virtually nothing was known of pre–Hellenistic times in the Ancient Near East, and biblical scholars were free to theorize (some would say fantasize) with no fear of contradiction by inconvenient facts. It was during this period that what became the regnant theories of biblical scholarship took form. It is only with W. F. Albright and his followers, from the early 1920s and onward, that a coherent picture of the Ancient Near East began to emerge to influence and to challenge the misconceptions underlying the theories developed in the nineteenth century. Unfortunately, old misconceptions die hard.

14. They were separated by about seven hundred years. See below.

15. For example, Gunkel, Humphreys, Redford, Soggin, etc.

16. W. Lee Humphreys, "Novella," in *Saga, Legend, Tale, Novella, Fable: Narrative Forms in Old Testament Literature*, ed. G. W. Coats (London: Sheffield Academic Press, 1985), 82.

17. Ibid., 83.

18. Ibid., 85. In his view, other examples of novella in the Bible are the Samson story (Judges 13–16) and The Book of Esther.

19. The term itself is Italian. The novella first took shape in fourteenth century Italy, Giovanni Boccaccio's *The Decameron* (c. 1348 CE) being one of its earliest examples.

20. See "canon" and "canonization" in Glossary.

21. This is not to say that the style of the work could not be entertaining. Pedantry was hardly a prerequisite. But the *contents* of a work had to be spiritually serious to qualify it for consideration as Scripture.

22. For a more comprehensive treatment of the monotheistic revolution and its consequences, see Hillel Millgram, *The Invention of Monotheist Ethics* (Lanham, MD: University Press of America, 2010), 18–20.

23. Baruch Halpern, *The First Historians: The Hebrew Bible and History* (San Francisco: Harper & Row, 1988).

24. Mathews, *Genesis 11:27–50:26*, 53.

25. J. B. Bury, *The Ancient Greek Historians* (New York: Dover, 1958), 108–117.

26. Some Bible scholars make much of the fact that no direct evidence has been unearthed to confirm the biblical account of Joseph's career in Egypt. Egyptologists, on the other hand, do not find this surprising. In the first place, the Bible depicts Joseph's career as having taken place in the Delta. Unlike Upper Egypt where the extremely dry climate preserves written documents, the wet soil of the Delta is destructive of written matter. Everything that can rot rots. If the vast archives of the great Ramses II have completely vanished, why should anyone expect any different fate for the records of the lesser pharaohs of the Thirteenth Dynasty under which Joseph would have served? A second point should also be considered: unlike Upper Egypt which has been extensively explored and excavated over the past two centuries, only in the past few years have archeologists seriously begun to turn their attention to the Delta, which remains largely unexplored territory. Under these circumstances, that Egyptologists find a lack of direct evidence for Joseph is exactly what one would expect. When it comes to *indirect* evidence, however, the picture is very different. There is an abundance of indirect evidence that tends to corroborate the biblical account. The Egyptologist James Hoffmeier (*Israel in Egypt: The Evidence for the Authenticity of the Exodus Tradition* [New York: Oxford University Press, 1996], 77–106) minutely surveys the data currently available and comes to the conclusion that "the narratives ought to be considered historical until there is evidence to the contrary ... the indirect evidence ... tends to demonstrate the authenticity of the story" (97). I share this conclusion, which forms one of the starting points of this study.

27. Inasmuch as historical narrative was an Israelite convention, we should not expect to find this genre part of the literary spectrum of the Ancient Near East. But some aspects of this new literary departure were at least partially analogous to extant Near Eastern forms, such as autobiography. Historical narrative was not a case of *creatio ex nihilo*. All new forms of literature grow out of, and are adapted from, previously existent forms. Israelite literature, while unique in many ways, was part of an international literature of the period.

28. This attitude has its roots in the position taken by Julius Wellhausen (1844–1918) who dominated the field of biblical scholarship a century ago, and whose views continue to influence many Bible scholars to this day. See the section "The Question of Literacy in Ancient Israel" below.

29. K. A. Kitchen, *The Bible in Its World: The Bible and Archaeology Today* (Eugene, OR: Wipf & Stock, 1977), 65.

30. "It is difficult to conceive of tradents creating out of whole cloth such [stories of taboo] practices while at the same time venerating the Fathers. If the narratives are first millennium, reflecting a later political and social setting, one wonders why the religious life and customs of the exilic period are not also refracted upon the Fathers" (Mathews, *Genesis 11:27–50:26*, 36f). Among other patriarchal practices that became taboo in post-settlement Israel were: Abraham could set up altars next to trees, but such "high places" were proscribed under the laws of Moses (Deut. 12:2; cf. Hosea 4:13); sacred stones (like Jacob's) were also barred (Deut. 16:22) and to be smashed (Deut. 7:9; 12:3). Examples of smashed-up images, etc., were found in late Bronze Hazor — which would correspond to the commands to Israel (and most likely done by them), but *not* to other people's customs in Canaan (K. A. Kitchen, *On the Reliability of the Old Testament* (Grand Rapids: Eerdmans, 2003], 332).

31. Ibid.

32. After the expulsion of the Hyksos the site was abandoned as a center of government. Through the Eighteenth Dynasty (1540–1295) there was no royal residence at this location, only a fort compound. It once again became a royal residence only in the Nineteenth Dynasty under Ramses II.

33. Kitchen, *Reliability*, 319, 348.

34. See ibid., 313–372.

35. Donald Redford, in his comprehensive *A Study of the Biblical Story of Joseph (Genesis 37–50)* (Leiden, E. J. Brill, 1970) disagrees with this early dating and attempts to demonstrate a mid-seventh to mid-fifth century BCE province for the tale (Saite or Persian period). In his "Review of Redford, *A Study of the Biblical Story of Joseph* (1970)," *Oriens Antiquus* 12 (1973), Kitchen answers Redford's argument and effectively demolishes it.

36. See my *Invention of Monotheist Ethics*, 4, 7–12, for the dating of the Book of Samuel, and my *Four Biblical Heroines and the Case for Female Authorship: An Analysis of the Women of Ruth, Esther and Genesis 38* (Jefferson, NC: McFarland, 2008), 24–26, dating the composition of the Book of Ruth.

37. Much of von Rad's perhaps overly enthusiastic assessment of an Enlightenment, suspiciously similar to the European awakening of that name (Gerhard von Rad, "Joseph Narrative and Ancient Wisdom," in *Studies in Ancient Israelite Wisdom*, ed. J. Crenshaw [New York: Ktav, 1976], 440–441; Gerhard von Rad, *Old Testament Theology*, trans. D. M. G. Stalker [New York: Harper, 1962, 1965], 1:48–56), has been justly called into question in recent years. But his main contention, that the unification of the tribal constellations into a unified kingdom and the creation of an empire by David gave rise to urban centers and a dramatic rise in living standards among the new elite — creating a leisure class which formed the basis of a reading public, and which in turn led to a literary flowering — seems to me correct, nonetheless.

38. As I will demonstrate, Genesis 38 is integral to the Joseph story, and indeed necessary to the ultimate resolution of the main plot line of the tale. See page 64, notes 4 and 13.

39. See Chapter 2. The mention of the birth of Perez, in and of itself, would be sufficient to trigger the necessary associations at the height of David's reign. David's ancestry was well known; indeed his genealogy, beginning with Perez, is featured in the epilogue to the Book of Ruth, a work that I hope to be able to establish was in the public domain and circulating at the time "Joseph" was being written.

40. Among them are to be found A. Mazer, G. von Rad, G. Rendsberg, G. Wenham, and C. Westermann. Their reasons often differ from mine; what I find to be significant is this convergence from different starting points to a common dating.

41. Those scholars who hold the Joseph story to be a "novella," and hence pure fiction, do not have to contend with this problem. They simply claim that the author invented the tale out of whole cloth.

42. von Rad, *Old Testament Theology*, 1:172, note 12.

43. See Chapter 12.

44. The name is patterned upon the "Ur-Hamlet." See below.

45. He would be writing on papyrus, a kind of paper made in Egypt from the stems of the papyrus plant. The sheets would be glued together to make a scroll (which was called a *sefer* or book). Pens in ancient Israel seem to have been made from reeds, split at one end and used as brushes. Ink was charcoal-based, dissolved in oil or gum (Menachem Haran, "Scribal Workmanship in Biblical Times," *Tarbiz* 50 [1980–1981]: 65–87; and Menachem Haran, "Book-Scrolls in Israel in Pre-Exilic Times," *Journal of Jewish Studies* 33 [1982]: 161–173).

46. It was one Saxo Grammaticus who incorporated the tale in his *Historia Danica*. Despite the barbaric

nature of this early version (for example, the body of the prototype of Polonius is thrown into an open latrine to be devoured by scavenging hogs), all the basic elements of Shakespeare's plot are to be found there, as well as all the chief characters of the play.

47. T. S. Eliot, "Hamlet and His Problems," in *The Sacred Wood: Essays on Poetry and Criticism*, 4th ed. (London: Methuen, 1934), 96–99.

48. Ibid., 96–97.

49. Kitchen insists that we not overlook the possibility that there was no oral stage to the tale. He reminds us that Joseph was literate (see below, Chapter 3, page 69) and possibly other members of his family as well. Thus the possibility exists that either Joseph himself, or a family member, penned a memoir of the events for the future edification of the family. If such a memoir was indeed penned, it would have perforce been written in Egyptian, and would have to have been translated at some time into Hebrew to avoid becoming a closed book to subsequent generations. But Kitchen reminds us that "the recently invented West Semitic alphabet, a vehicle designed by and for Semitic speakers (and writers)" has been demonstrated to have been in use in seventeenth century Egypt. "These oldest examples occur in homely, informal contexts, showing that it could be, and was, readily utilized by anyone who cared to do so, and not solely by government elites.... This system of not more than thirty simple, semipictographic letters would have been very easy to use in writing up (on papyrus) a 'first written edition' of the patriarchal traditions from Abraham to Jacob, to which a Joseph account could be added" (Kitchen, *Reliability*, 371). That such a "first written edition" was the precursor of the "Ur-Joseph Tale," which in turn was the source used by the author of our Joseph narrative, is a possibility that should not be dismissed lightly.

50. As Laurence Olivier, in his 1948 film *Hamlet* saw fit to do.

51. Indeed, these characters and these elements of the plot were already part of the earliest version of the tale.

52. If Joseph himself was the author of the original tale, a not unlikely possibility, casting himself as hero only would be natural.

53. I am of the strong opinion that Judah had little if any role in the original tale.

54. I will not go into the questions involved in the transmission of the text, i.e., how a work written almost three thousand years ago reached our hands, as even without this discussion the Introduction will be overlong, and because I have already dealt with the issue in my previous books. For those interested, see *The Invention of Monotheist Ethics*, 14–16.

55. Versions of the following section appeared in my previous works, *Four Biblical Heroines* and *The Invention of Monotheist Ethics*. Because of its importance in establishing the viability of my thesis, I am including a modified version here.

56. Humphreys, 83, 96. Humphreys, as we have previously noted, supposes the Joseph Story to be fiction. But he would agree that the definition of the Joseph Story as either fiction or history is irrelevant to the issue that the appearance of a work of high literature cannot emerge without a literate audience as a prerequisite. Humphreys accepts the tenth century as the period of the Joseph Story's composition and posits "middle to upper class circles in the royal establishment of King Solomon, especially those broadly within the effective reach of court schools in Jerusalem" to have been the intended audience for which it was composed (96).

57. As we have consistently maintained, a body of highly sophisticated literature with a well-developed style (the Bible) evidences the existence of a well-established reading public with the taste that appreciates and demands that sophisticated style.

58. With regard to the classical prophets, "schools" of "disciples" were postulated who memorized the words of their masters, and then passed them down from generation to generation until they were committed to writing sometime in the post-exilic age.

59. Wellhausen categorically dismissed everything the Bible has to say about Israelite origins — specifically almost everything reported from Genesis through Joshua — as fictions invented by post-exilic Jews. "We attain [in Genesis] to no historical knowledge of the patriarchs, but only of the time when the stories about them arose in the Israelite people; this later age is here unconsciously projected, in its inner and its outward features into hoar antiquity, and is reflected there like a glorified mirage" (Julius Wellhausen, *Prolegomena to the History of Ancient Israel*, trans. Black and Menzies [New York: Meridian, 1957], 318–319).

60. Wellhausen used primitive pre–Islamic Arab tribes as his models for what the earliest Israelites were like. We now recognize this model as pure anachronism.

61. Wellhausen took it for granted that the invasion of "primitive" Israelite tribes into "civilized" Canaan produced results similar to those of the Doric invasions of Mycenaean Greece at roughly the same time: a dark age of barbarian illiteracy that lasted for centuries. The Dorian conquest of Greece took place at approximately the midpoint of the Age of the Judges in Israel (about 1100 BCE). The oldest Greek inscriptions

date only from the eighth and seventh centuries. Homer flourished in the ninth century; the masterpiece attributed to him, *The Iliad*, was transmitted orally by wandering bards and by guilds of "rhapsodes" (from *raptein*, to stitch together, and *oide*, a song) until finally being reduced to written form in Athens under the dictatorship of Pisistratus (died 527 BCE, and thus a contemporary of the Babylonian Exile). The illiteracy of Greece during almost the entire First Commonwealth period was naively taken as a model for Israelite society just across the Mediterranean.

62. Kitchen, *Bible in Its World*, 7.

63. Egyptian Hieroglyphic writing, equally complicated, emerged also about 5,000 years ago, but apparently without the long period of experimental development that preceded Sumerian cuneiform. This leads some scholars to conclude that the Egyptians did not invent hieroglyphic writing from scratch, but got the original idea of writing from the Sumerians and then proceeded to develop their own system of writing based on the same principles.

64. The alphabet was the invention of those Semitic-speaking peoples who used what we currently call Western Semitic languages. Hebrew, Phoenician and Aramaic, which are part of this language group and are closely related, were all soon using the alphabet. (By the thirteenth century BCE, the original 27 letters representing consonants had been reduced to 22.) To the best of our knowledge, this discovery was unique in human history. All alphabets, past and present, derive from this original alphabet.

65. A Semitic people located in what is now western Lebanon, who specialized in sea-born commerce. They were the Semites with whom the Greeks were in contact, and it is from them that the Greeks borrowed the Phoenician-Hebrew alphabet, even retaining the Semitic names of the letters.

66. Jared Diamond, *Guns, Germs and Steel: The Fates of Human Societies* (New York: W. W. Norton, 1999), 236. The Greek examples are also taken from this book.

67. The full quotation reads: "With this limited set of simple signs [letters] to spell any word by its consonantal framework, literacy steadily became possible for a far greater number of people.... We have ... private letters (ostraca, Hebrew and Aramaic), some papyri (mostly Aramaic), and innumerable personal stamp-seals bearing the name of their owners (practically all dialects), use of which presupposes that many people could read enough to distinguish between them. There are inscribed arrow heads, notations of person, place, or capacity on jar handles — the list of everyday uses is quite varied. Thus certainly from 1100 BC (and probably rather earlier), writing in Canaan, then in Israel, Phoenicia, and round about was clearly part of everyday life and not restricted solely to a special scribal elite" (Kitchen, *Bible in its World*, 18). (This was written before 1977; since then further data has strengthened this evaluation.)

68. "The locals could write. A splendid two-foot-high ewer was decorated in deep red paint with a series of animals, over which the artist had jotted, very informally, a dedication: Gift (of) an oblation, O my [lad]y Goddess [? and Reshe]ph! This is only one of several fragmentary inscriptions from thirteenth-century Lachish, all informal such that any reasonably intelligent Canaanite might have inked them onto bowls and basins — and did" (Kitchen, *Reliability*, 407).

69. "...a remarkable text written out on the white-plastered surface of a wall.... There is nothing 'religious' about this room in a ninth-century dwelling; benches against the other walls may have served readers of the text as seats. The text is titled 'The Book of the Afflictions of Balaam Son of Beor,' and has a visionary content.... The language is West Semitic with Aramaic affinities.... What is it doing here? A question unanswered, and not answerable with certainty" (ibid., 412–413). Kitchen's assumption is that the seats were for a stream of people who came to read the inscription which was on public display.

70. "The doorway passage from the guardhouse into the fort's inner court was flanked by two narrow side rooms with benches and storage jars (*pithoi*). The latter bore remarkable sketches ... and some even more remarkable jottings in Hebrew and Phoenician." To summarize Kitchen's lengthy analysis, the jottings were dedications, blessings and graffiti and were undoubtedly scribbled by Phoenician and Israelite travelers, merchants and common soldiers, not by scribes or educated professionals (ibid., 413–415).

71. Izbet Sartah is the name of an archaeological site in the foothills of Samaria named after the adjacent Arab village. We currently are unsure as to what its original biblical (Hebrew) name was.

72. I append here from personal observation an example of my own: a recently discovered tomb from the early monarchic period, cut into bedrock in the Kidron Valley opposite the Temple Mount of Jerusalem, bears an inscription advising potential grave robbers that it will be unprofitable for them to break into the tomb as there is nothing there to take. But should you disregard this advisory, the inscription continues, and do break in, may a curse fall upon you and all your descendants. Just as today we post Beware of the Dog signs with the expectation that potential trespassers will be able to read the sign and be warned off, so does the ancient inscription presuppose the ability of the grave robbers of those days to read and so be deterred.

73. This does not in any way imply that one could make a living by writing literature. Writing was an

avocation, not a paying proposition. But for one who had something to say, one could write knowing that there were people able and willing to read what one had written. More: the extraordinary levels of sophistication and artistry of biblical books (we will repeatedly comment on it even though this will not always be germane to our line of inquiry) implies that there were readers who could appreciate this high level of literature, even demand it. We have no way of estimating the size of the reading public at any given period; we can only suggest that it was sufficiently rooted to have developed good taste.

74. Actually, the language used was already archaic in 1611, when the Authorized Version (which is the official title of the King James translation) was published. "Thee"s and "thou"s had long since ceased to be used in everyday speech. The Bishops' Committee that was responsible for the translation made the conscious choice to use "old-fashioned" language in order to give its Bible a tone of solemn antiquity. The Committee felt that everyday language would cheapen the text. And strangely enough, though they themselves were unaware of the phenomenon, this is exactly what the original authors of the Bible did. We are currently alert to the fact that the prose of the Bible was not in use by the people in their daily lives. Biblical prose was written in a "high literary style" employing only the most respectable and "elevated" terminology. As we have previously noted, only the best was good enough when dealing with God and His works. This explains why biblical prose vocabulary is so limited in the number of its words; common everyday words were excluded as a matter of principle. The solemn and stately English of the King James translation thus actually mirrors the kind of language employed in the Bible.

75. Robert Alter, *Genesis: Translation and Commentary* (New York: W. W. Norton, 1996), xii. Emphasis in the original.

76. A word about the way we refer to God in our translation of the biblical text. The Bible routinely uses two separate ways of referring to the deity: the general term *elohim*, which simply means "deity" and is virtually universally rendered as "God," and what is termed as "the Tetragrammaton," the four-letter personal name of God. This is often rendered by modern scholars as "Yahweh," or "Yahveh," or sometimes without vowels as "YHVH." These are current attempts to reconstruct God's personal name (a previous attempted reconstruction was "Jehovah"). But since biblical Hebrew was written with a consonantal alphabet (there were no vowels), and because we really have no idea how the consonants were pronounced in those days, all reconstructions are highly speculative. Jews ceased pronouncing God's name more than two thousand years ago, out of a sense that it was improper to address God by name. Instead they substituted the title *Lord*, a convention adopted by the Bishop's Committee that issued the English Authorized Version of the Bible (known as the King James Bible). This convention has been used in most subsequent translations down to the present day. We have continued this tradition in our translation. There is a further point to be considered, one succinctly expressed by Norman Podhoretz: "I prefer LORD because YHVH ['Yahweh'] in English willy-nilly makes God seem a tribal deity (which is in fact what some scholars—wrongly, I believe—think He was to the earliest of His Israelite devotees)" (*The Prophets: Who They Were, What They Are* [New York: Free Press, 2002], 12). Like him, I only allow this putative reconstruction into my books when I am quoting someone else.

77. It is impossible to imagine the civilization of ancient Egypt outside its unique geographic setting: a river winding its way through a narrow productive valley surrounded on all sides by desert. In effect Egypt is one continuous oasis 750 miles long, from the first cataract to the Mediterranean Sea (see map number 2). This geography imposes the three central conditions that, from its formative period, determined the path Egypt would take: isolation from the rest of the world, the Nile River as a regulator of life (and the great highway that bound Egypt together), and the immediate proximity of the surrounding desert. Isolation fostered an extraordinary conservatism. Egyptian society was deeply resistant to the adaptation of technological and cultural innovations of other cultures; for example, the wheel only came into general use a thousand years after it had become common in Mesopotamia, while the manufacture and use of bronze was delayed for 500 years after it became the common technology of the rest of the Ancient Near East (but see note 63 above for a significant exception to this generalization). The annual rise and fall of the Nile determined the agricultural rhythm of the land, while the three-month period of enforced leisure during the annual flood made available a vast labor force for a series of public works culminating in the pyramids. The close proximity of life-supporting waters with sterile desert encouraged a neurotic focus on the conflict between life and ever-encroaching death that was to dominate the culture to its very end.

78. These mini-states remained intact as districts (Nomes) of the unified state, their hereditary rulers now functioning as their governors.

79. Because it was upstream.

80. Memphis, near the site of present day Cairo, was at the junction of Upper and Lower Egypt.

81. A dynasty is a line of kings, beginning with the founder or first king of the line, and ending when a king either fails to produce a male heir or is murdered and a stranger usurps the throne. The conceit of

organizing Egyptian history by dynasties was established by Manetho, an Egyptian priest living in the first part of the third century BCE, who compiled the first systematic history of dynastic Egypt.

82. Pepi II, the last king of the Old Kingdom, died in 2181 BCE

83. This is what the Egyptians themselves called Egypt. The Hebrew name for Egypt, *mitzraim*, (grammatically a plural form designating a pair) preserves the reality that Egypt was the unification of two kingdoms. This was also proclaimed by the crown worn by the Pharaoh (the official title of the king), a combination of the white crown of Upper Egypt and the red crown of Lower Egypt.

84. This last was a direct result of the frenzy of pyramid building in the Old Kingdom. The pyramids were gigantic tombs of the Pharaohs. But every tomb had a temple and chapels attached, where perpetual priestly intercession was to take place for the *ka* (the spirit, the personality and vitality) of the deceased. These priests had to be supported in perpetuity, so land was ceded to them by the king to pay for eternal priestly service. As time went on and tombs multiplied, more and more land came into the hands of the priests until they came to be among the greatest landholders in Egypt, rivaling the king in this regard.

85. The ancient capital of Upper Egypt, on the site of present-day Luxor.

86. See page 12 above. This move was possibly necessitated by ever increasing Asiatic incursions from Canaan and Syria. Indeed, a growing Canaanite presence became a major element of its population during the Twelfth–Thirteenth Dynasties. When the Hyksos invaded and conquered Egypt, they renamed the site Hat-waret and made it their capital. (This was the Avaris of Manetho.)

87. The eventual expulsion of the Hyksos invaders by Amosis, founder of the glorious Eighteenth Dynasty, and the birth of the New Empire, the last great age of Egypt, lies beyond the horizon of Joseph and his world.

88. Osiris and Seth were more ancient but neither was appropriate for a Pharaoh. Osiris was the god of the dead (his brother Seth had murdered and dismembered him), while Seth was the god of the desert.

89. To us these statements seem one mass of contradictions, but the ancient Egyptians did not see it that way. They were perfectly content to live with these, and even more blatant, contradictions.

90. Originally the Pharaoh was divine from birth; he was Re! This belief was slowly supplanted by the doctrine that the Pharaoh was not Re but an "incarnation" of Re. Then from an "incarnation" of the god he became (in the age of our story) "the son of Re." From full divinity to merely an incarnation of the god, then to divine sonship charts a tale of progressive deterioration in religious status that mirrors a slow erosion of power. In much the same way, Pharaoh's status as Sole Priest to the gods deteriorated over time to that of Chief Priest, the first among many.

91. At least, as far as we currently know.

92. Paul Johnson, *The Civilization of Ancient Egypt* (London: Seven Dials, 2000), 42.

93. Hence the multitude of gods, the majority in animal or semi-animal form, who embodied the various forces of nature.

94. Ibid., 35–37.

95. The distinction also holds with regard to the dreams of Babylonians as dreamed in Babylon (cf. Daniel 2, 4).

96. For example, dreaming of a deep well meant prison, a face in a mirror meant a second wife in the offing, and a shining moon meant forgiveness.

97. I wish to express my deep appreciation to Paul Johnson, and his wonderful book, *The Civilization of Ancient Egypt*, for much of the information and insight in the foregoing analysis.

98. See "Masorite" in the Glossary. There are times when I rely on some of the ancient versions. Whenever I depart from the Masoretic Text (MT) I always will indicate in an endnote that I have done so, on what basis, and will include the MT reading for comparison. In this way it is possible for the reader to come to an independent conclusion, deciding whether to go along with me or to stick with the MT. For a discussion of the origins of the ancient versions and why sometimes I see fit to rely on them, see my *Four Biblical Heroines*, 4–6.

Prologue:
The Way of the Fathers

As for Me, this is My covenant with them, says the Lord:
My spirit that is upon you, and My words which I have placed
in your mouth shall not depart out of your mouth, and from the
mouth of your seed, nor out of the mouth of your seed's seed,
says the Lord, from now and forevermore.
— Isaiah 59:21

Meir Sternberg opens his groundbreaking study of biblical narrative prose with several seminal questions: "What goals does the biblical narrator set for himself? What is it that he wants to communicate in this or that story, cycle, book?" He then reaches the conclusion: "Like all social discourse, biblical narrative is oriented to an addressee and regulated by a purpose or set of purposes involving the addressee. Hence our primary business is to make purposive sense of it."[1] Or to put it another way, our principal task as readers is to discover how the author wished his narrative to be read. The author no longer being present, we must look to his work for hints.

Our first hint is that we have received the Joseph Story, not as an independent book such as the Book of Amos or the Book of Job, but as an integral part of a larger work known to us as the Book of Genesis. Thus it would be reasonable to assume that we were meant to read the Joseph narrative in the context of Genesis as a whole.[2] Acting on this assumption, we will begin our quest for understanding with an analysis of the structure of Genesis and of the Joseph Story's place within it.

The Book of Genesis, like Caesar's Gaul, is divided into three parts. These may be termed, for convenience of reference, The Primeval History (chapters 1–11), The Travails of the Fathers (chapters 12–36) and The Joseph Story (chapters 37–50). Each of these sections, while containing elements that predate the composition of the division into its present form, has been integrated by the author of the segment into a unified and coherent composition which exhibits a sophisticated theological point of view.[3] Each division of the book, moreover, acts as the prelude to the succeeding section, while Genesis as a whole serves as the prologue to its successor, the Book of Exodus. Thus, despite the very different rhetorical styles exhibited by the three parts of Genesis, the book does not import a sense of three disparate units being tacked together, but gives the reader a feeling of organic development of subject matter, plot and ideology which extends beyond the borders of Genesis to encompass its sequel.

The Primeval History (Genesis 1–11)

The Primeval History recounts the beginnings of the universe and of humanity, the pinnacle of creation. It then recounts the story of the development of civilization and the spread of human beings over the face of the earth, a narrative that is simultaneously an account of recalcitrance — a rebelling against divine will — and of progressive degeneration. This account is presented in five distinct narrative installments:

A. Creation
B. Adam and Eve
C. Cain and Abel
D. Noah and the flood
E. Babel and dispersal

These narratives are separated by chronologies which, despite their seeming lack of interest for the modern reader, actually embody a distinct ideology and serve to advance some of the main arguments of the Primeval History.

Two central issues dominate this segment of Genesis: the preciousness and the sanctity of life, especially human life, and its obverse, the threat to life posed by escalating violence. The first, the supreme value of life, is encapsulated in the primary divine command: be fruitful and multiply and fill the earth.[4] God is presented as seeing every new creature, and especially every new human being, as an unqualified blessing. The second, the threat to life, is seen as stemming from human intransigence. Endowed with free will, man thwarts the divine will with violence. Cain murders Abel. Matters escalate until "the earth was filled with violence" (Gen. 6:11).[5] Killing becomes the norm and the world is awash with blood.

Running parallel to these two major concerns, a subsidiary issue is treated in the Primeval History: the growth of civilization. The narrative enumerates the stages: the founding of cities, the growth of technology, and the cultivation of the arts. Isaac Kikawada insists that the entire Primeval History, and especially Genesis 4:17–26, is one sustained "indictment of civilization, an indictment that associates civilization with a murderous disregard for human life."[6] It is the murderer, Cain, who is credited with being the founder of the first city (v. 17), and it is his descendants who are named as the fathers of technology and of the arts (vv. 21–22). Despite its many benefits, the dark underside that civilization inherits from its beginnings contains an ineradicable streak of violence. Civilization inevitably acts as a lens, serving to give focus to human aggressiveness and acting as well as a multiplier, engendering the phenomenon of mass warfare. It is this that emerges as the central problem of humanity.[7]

The Primeval History concludes with the human attempt to build a world city that would concentrate all mortals into one homogeneous humanity, focused on one monumental public project.[8] But God concludes that a pluralistic world is a better setting for human beings, so He changes the one universal language into many; the people cease building the city[9] and scatter over the face of the earth, forming nations in the process.

The History ends with Abraham's family leaving "Ur of the Chaldees,"[10] mirroring the earlier dispersal of humanity from Babel, the world city.

The Travails of the Fathers[11] (Genesis 12–36)

Dispersal is no solution to patterns of behavior that are inimical to life. It is, at best, no more than temporary damage control. The behavioral patterns remain, embedded in a way of life so pervasive as to seem the natural order of things. This has become the "way of the world." It is this "way" that must be changed for humanity to have the possibility of rejecting violence and affirming life. But to change one must have the option of an alternative to set off against the accepted pattern. This is to become the task of Abraham, the first of the Fathers, and of his descendants: to become the embodiment of an alternative way, a life-affirming way, designed to become a blessing to mankind. To mark just how Abraham must have seemed to a perceptive contemporary, I will call this alternative the "New Way."

This becomes the larger theme of the second division of Genesis. God has come to a strategic decision: in a world that is now the abode of many diverse nations, He will create a special people, one animated by an alternative way of life that, by force of example, will open new options and thus bring blessing to all humanity. It is to be the mission of one Abraham, son of Terah — in his day an obscure inhabitant of Ur of the Chaldees — to become the founder of this uniquely tasked people.[12]

Let us spend a few moments examining Ur, Abraham's birthplace and the environment which nurtured his early years. Located some 140 miles south of present-day Baghdad, Ur was one of the greatest cities of the Ancient World. Now long past its prime (at its height it had been the capital of the Sumerian Empire, dominating all of Mesopotamia), in the days of Abraham it was still one of the great commercial, religious and cultural centers in the world, holding a monopoly of the trade with India.[13] This swarming metropolis was overshadowed by its great multicolored ziggurat[14]; it and its surrounding temple and the palace complex served as the focus of the religious and civil life of the inhabitants. Living for the well-to-do was comfortable, cosmopolitan, cultured and urbane.[15] It was from these surroundings that Abraham's family uprooted itself to relocate about 550 miles to the northwest, in Haran in present-day Turkey. If Ur to the south, port and center of foreign trade, was the New York of ancient Mesopotamia, then Haran was its Chicago, the great transportation and trade hub at its northern extreme. What led to the move we have no idea. All that we are told is that it is in Haran that Abraham emerges from obscurity by a great act of renunciation: he turns his back on civilization and all the certainties of his past.

We must be clear as to the significance of this act. Abraham was no primitive. He was the product of the highest and most sophisticated civilization of his time. His decision to leave Haran, to reconfigure his life into that of a pastoral semi-nomad, cutting himself off from family and friends, must be seen as a rejection of civilization itself and all that it stands for.[16] This was more than the act of a Henry Thoreau, simplifying his life by leaving urban Boston for the tranquility of Walden Pond, although this element of simplification was present. Abraham's resolve amounted to a complete rejection of the values by which mankind had lived since time immemorial, and an attempt to forge an alternative way of life.

We can better understand the boldness of the break with the past initiated by Abraham if we grasp the essentials of the pagan world view, both as manifested in the Mesopotamian civilization on which Abraham has turned his back and in the form it took in the Egyptian civilization which his great-grandchildren were destined to confront.

> The differences between the Egyptian and Mesopotamian manners of viewing the world are very far reaching. Yet the two peoples agreed in the fundamental assumptions that the individual is part of society, that society is embedded in nature, and that nature is but the manifestation of the divine. This doctrine was, in fact, universally accepted by the peoples of the ancient world with the single exception of the Hebrews....
>
> The dominant tenet of Hebrew thought is the absolute transcendence of God. Yahweh[17] is not

in nature. Neither earth nor sun nor heaven is divine; even the most potent natural phenomena are but reflections of God's greatness.... [This] means that all values are ultimately attributes of God alone. Hence all concrete phenomena are devaluated....Nowhere else do we meet this fanatical devaluation of the phenomena of nature and the achievements of man; art, virtue, social order — in view of the unique significance of the divine.

It has been rightly pointed out that the monotheism of the Hebrews is a correlate of their insistence on the unconditioned nature of God. Only a God who transcends every phenomenon, who is not conditioned by any mode or manifestation — only an unqualified God can be the one and only ground for *all* existence.[18]

All this is embodied, in essence, in Abraham's rejection of the world into which he had been born. But where did this revolutionary rejection come from?

What we are told is that Abraham acted in response to a command from the one and transcendent God:

Now the Lord said to Abram,[19] *"Go forth from your land, and from your place of birth, and from your father's house to the land I will show you. And I will make you a great nation, and I will bless you, and I will make your name great;* [therefore] *be a blessing. And I will bless those who bless you, and he that curses you shall I curse; and in you shall all the families of the earth be blessed* [Gen. 12:1–3].

Embedded in this command is the first statement of the Promise which will motivate Abraham and his descendants: the prospect of becoming the father of a great nation, the assurance of world renown and the guarantee of being a blessing to all humanity. And bundled within the Promise is the command to be a blessing, i.e., to live and act in such a way as to bring blessing to all.

It is significant that, while being ordered to leave his past, both physically and spiritually, Abraham is neither told what his destination is to be geographically nor with exactly what he is to replace the heritage of his fathers that he is directed to abandon. The remainder of his life is to be consumed with a search to fill these lacunae. The first discovery is physical; setting out westward with his immediate family[20] he reaches Canaan, there to be informed by God that he has arrived at his destination. More, the Promise is enlarged: *Now the Lord appeared*[21] *to Abram and said, "To your seed will I give this land"*[22] (Gen. 12:7). With this pledge the land of Canaan has been transmuted into "The Promised Land." This was the easy part. Delineating the parameters of a new way of life, a spiritual goal, was to prove the real challenge.

The first challenge this new way of life was to pose was to dominate much of Abraham's life. It was predicated upon an ongoing life of faith in a God who was invisible, unlike all the gods men had known heretofore; indeed, He was to forbid any attempt to represent Him. He was moreover not limited to any territory nor was He bound to any natural phenomena. Faith in this transcendent God and His Promise was made doubly difficult by Abraham's circumstances — circumstances that seemed designed to nullify any possibility of the Promise ever being fulfilled.[23] The "old way," the pagan way of the world to which human beings had become inured — calculating, down-to-earth, pragmatic — would not have room for an ideal that flew in the face of reality as it was then seen.[24] Yet the New Way demanded a faith that would transcend the expediency that the old way, the pagan way, imposed upon mortals thus constricting their horizons. The challenge was to break the mental bonds of the civilization in which he had been reared and to open himself to previously unimaginable opportunities. *He had faith in the Lord, and He* [God] *recorded it to his merit* (Gen. 15: 6).

Map 1

Canaan During the Age of the Fathers
(c. 1900–1600 BCE)

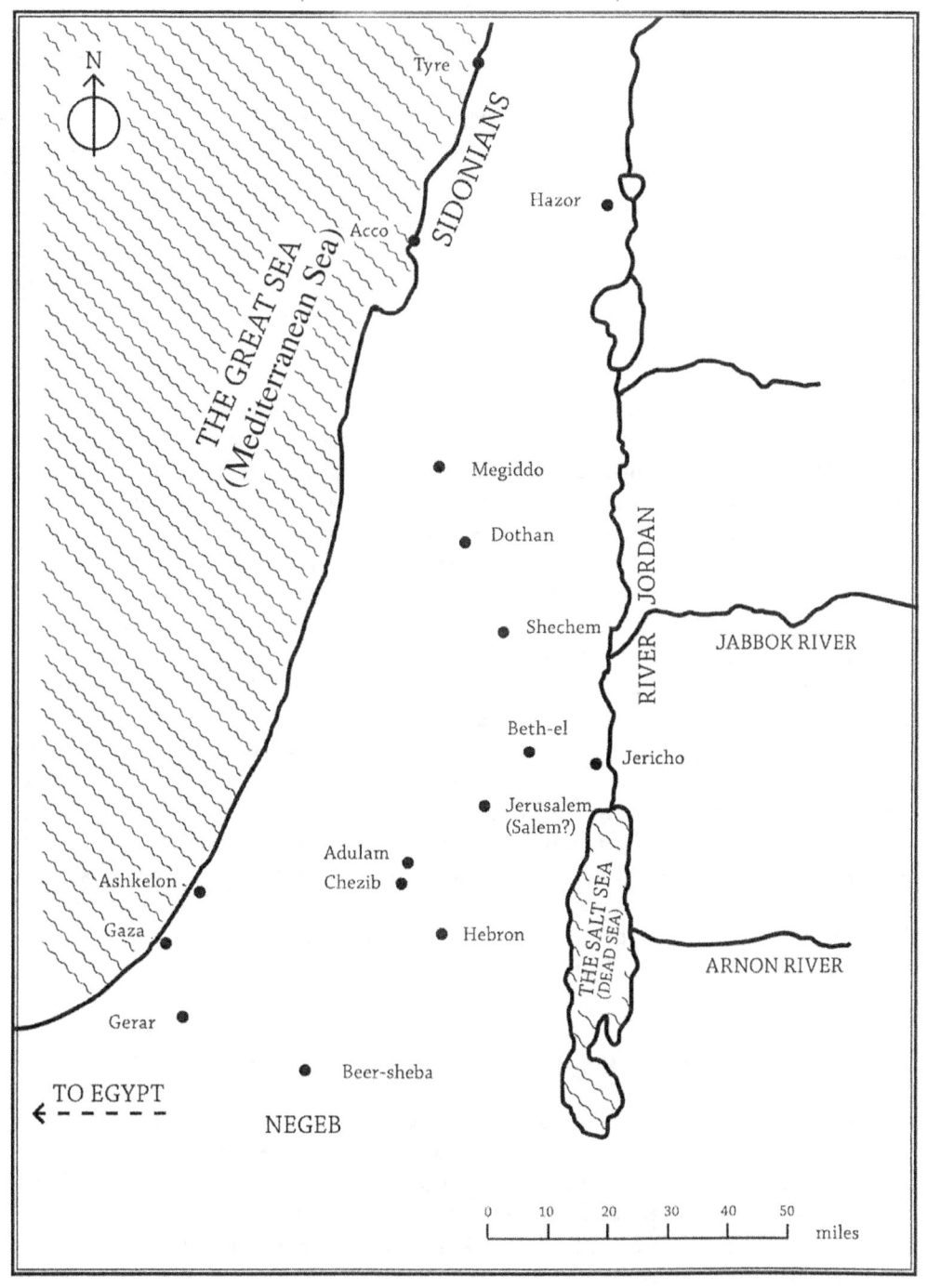

The second challenge, revealed in the context of a reaffirmation of the Promise and only after many years of sojourning in the land, is embedded in the command:

"Walk before me and be whole-hearted"[25] [Gen. 17:1].

There is a double emphasis here. Whatever Abraham does, he must be *tamim*, that is, he must behave with wholehearted sincerity and uncompromised commitment. But the "walking before God" is an equally vital part of the injunction. One "walks" through life in tiny, incremental steps as he tries to concretize his dedication to the covenant. For God "cares" about the fulfillment of the covenant — every detail of its fulfillment.[26]

And the final challenge is to be found in God's mandate to Abraham and his descendants:

"For I have known him, that he may command his children, and his house after him, that they keep the way of the Lord to do righteousness and justice, in order that the Lord may bring upon Abraham that which He has spoken of him" [Gen. 18:19].

Here, for the first time, it is made explicit to Abraham that the fulfillment of the Promise is contingent on *moral performance*, and not merely one's faith or beliefs. One must *do righteousness and justice*, not simply hold them as ideals.[27] The basic ground rules for walking before God are being laid down.

In sum, what Abraham learns in the course of his struggle to reject the old and lay hold on the new, the Way of the Lord, amounts to no more than a sketch, an outline: to have faith that because God created the universe and rules it, that the seemingly impossible is indeed possible; that because God is just and righteous, it is the task of human beings, created in His image, to do what is just and right; and to walk before God, that is, to walk in the Way of the Lord, sincerely and unreservedly. From this embryonic beginning much is to grow. The commitment by Abraham to hold fast to this New Way and to walk in it, and the concomitant Promise on the part of God, was formally contracted in a solemn agreement, to become known as the covenant.[28] This covenant or agreement was later ratified and made permanent (Gen. 22:15–18).

Absent is any prescribed form of worship, ceremonial or religious ritual.[29] Absent also is any decreed code of social behavior or preferred form of social organization; the autonomous individual and his offspring are the sole and essential current units of this new constellation. But life is not built from generalizations. It must be lived in the concrete from hour to hour. To spell out the specific meanings of these generalizations and to establish the parameters of living God's Way was to be deferred to the future. For the present a direction has been chartered, a path radically different from that of the old way of the world. The great totalitarian civilizations with their institutionalized violence and their ruthless use of human beings as the means to aggrandize the power lusts of the elite, often the aggrandizement of a single individual, self-proclaimed as a god, have been decisively repudiated.

The Trials of Transmission

To originate a new way of life may seem challenging, even romantic. In practice it can prove to be an excruciatingly difficult process. One must remain constantly focused, ever alert, always aware that any lapse of concentration will result in an inevitable backsliding into habitual patterns. Tradition and habit, instead of acting as buttresses to one's conduct of life, become inimical forces. Life becomes an endless series of trials, testing endurance as much as faith and creativity.

To introduce a new way requires the capacity to turn a few vague and, at best, half-understood principles — generalizations whose far-reaching implications cannot even be imagined — into concrete decisions as to how to shape one's responses to the daily dilemmas of living. In the relatively isolated pastoral lifestyle of Abraham and his son Isaac — and to a lesser degree his grandson Jacob — these centered on conduct within a family setting. The family thus became the initial laboratory, through trial and error incrementally giving content to the vague imperatives of integrity and sincerity, of "doing righteousness and justice;" and an incubator within which embryonic forms could take shape. This process could have had no chance while subjected to the pressures of an urban environment. Only in the relative isolation of a life on the edge of the desert, on the very fringes of the civilized world, could new patterns take hold.

The point to be emphasized is how tenuous the process of crystallization was, how uncertain of success and how stressful and all-consuming it was to the Fathers who had the task of shepherding it to a viable consummation. Nor are we to assume that the Fathers were uniformly successful in their endeavors. Old prejudices and patterns were heartbreakingly difficult to abandon. In relations with the outside world, Abraham was to prove inordinately inept. For example, arrogantly assuming himself to be the sole possessor of a high morality, and darkly suspicious of the possessors of cultures alien to him as being irredeemably corrupt (unbridled rapists of beautiful women and murderers of inconvenient husbands), he relapsed into the old patterns of expediency. In order to avert what he perceived as a life-threatening danger to himself, he prevailed upon his wife, Sarah, to pretend to be his unmarried sister, leading to her recruitment into the harems of the rulers of, first Egypt, and then the principality of Gerar (Gen. 12:10–20; 20:1–18). Of course the deceptions were discovered. Abraham stood revealed as a liar and worse, as endangering the moral health of these communities by sowing the seeds of potential adultery.[30] These extremely unprincipled lapses, the result of falling back on the classic immoral expediency that the New Way so starkly rejected, were rendered all the more embarrassing by the fact that it was the practitioners of the old way who were left holding the moral high ground. For Abraham, as for his immediate descendants, embedding the New Way as an integral aspect of their lives was to prove a desperate, even heroic lifelong struggle.[31]

Beyond the personal struggle loomed the larger issue of transmission to the future. This was to prove one of the central challenges facing the Fathers: to whom to bequeath the Promise, the blessing and the burden? Not everyone is capable of such a life of constant trial, unsupported by well-established patterns. Not everyone is suited to be a pioneer. It is possible to surmise that in no case was the successor wholly able to maintain a righteous and just life. One could question whether Isaac had the profound faith and the powers of endurance of Abraham. Jacob's character as a young man was problematic, to say the least: opportunistic, dishonest, scheming, always on the lookout for the main chance. Neither seemed a particularly promising choice; they both were the lesser of the evils, the best of those available. Yet surprisingly, despite the poor prognosis, in each case they rise to the occasion, accepting the burden, adding refinements and handing the trust on to the next generation. This section of Genesis, chapters 12–36, a record of trial, struggle and occasional failure must be deemed on the whole a ringing success. A new way of life at the end emerged, sufficiently formed and resilient to survive character flaws and the vagaries of human variability.

> It is a poignant myth, this Hebrew myth of a chosen people, of a divine promise made, of a terrifying moral burden imposed — a prelude to the later myth of the Kingdom of God, that more

remote and spiritual "promised land." For in the myth of the chosen people the ineffable majesty of God and the worthlessness of man are correlated in a dramatic situation that is to unfold in time and is moving toward a future where the distant yet related parallels of human and divine existence are to meet in infinity.[32]

What yet remains to be determined is how well this embryonic New Way can hold up in direct confrontation with the established way of the world. For the New Way cannot remain in an incubator forever. The world has a way of pressing in upon us. And there is no way that the family, now grown to the size of a small clan, can maintain its isolation. The issue now becomes this: thrust into direct and continuous interaction with the wider world, and especially with the way of the world as enshrined in high civilization, will the New Way be able to withstand direct competition with the old? With these issues as Prologue, we now turn to the third division of Genesis: The Joseph Story.

Notes

1. Meir Sternberg, *Poetics of Biblical Narrative* (Bloomington: Indiana University Press, 1987), 1.
2. As we shall discover, the Joseph Story presupposes much that precedes it in the earlier portions of Genesis, its meaning determined by the frame into which it has been set.
3. This statement is in no way meant to exclude the possibility that the authors of the three divisions of Genesis may turn out to be one and the same person. But this issue will not be pursued as it lies outside the scope of the present study.
4. To aquatic creatures and birds: "And God blessed them and said, 'Be fruitful and multiply and fill the water in the seas, and let the fowl multiply in the earth'" (Gen. 1:22). To land creatures, and specifically to human beings: "And God blessed them, and God said to them, 'Be fruitful and multiply and fill the earth and conquer it'" (v. 28).
5. Leon Kass, focusing on the passages immediately preceding this culminating statement, which refer to the *Nephilim*, the "heroes of yore, the men of renown" (Gen. 6:4), suggests the crystallization of a "Heroic Age," i.e., a warrior culture, which glorified the warrior to the extent that he proves himself an efficient and copious killer of other warriors, with all the inevitable "collateral damage" such unending bloodshed engenders (*The Beginning of Wisdom: Reading Genesis* [New York: Free Press, 2003], 154–162). Kass' lengthy and sophisticated analysis goes beyond the confines of this brief survey, and is heartily recommended for its insights.
6. Isaac M. Kikawada and Arthur Quinn, *Before Abraham Was: The Unity of Genesis 1–11* (Nashville: Abingdon Press, 1985), 57.
7. Kikawada lists a related issue: civilizations, due to enhanced efficiency of food production, have a tendency to rapidly rising populations. Being city cultures, they are prone to the congestion of their urban centers. The problem is exasperated by great cities tending to drain the countryside of their population. Civilizations usually respond to overpopulation by falling birthrates, often promoted by forcible restriction of family size. As every new human being is seen by the biblical narrative as an unlimited blessing, social structures that dam the flow of new human beings are deemed an evil, a violation of the divine mandate to "be fruitful and multiply."
8. The story seems to take for granted that the social structure is totalitarian. The "Tower" probably reflects the construction of the great Ziggurat of Babylon. More on Ziggurats later.
9. The common misapprehension is that the Tower is the problem. But the Tower is only a part of the city which is to contain all human beings. It is the building of *the city* that God frustrates (11:8), diversifying human cultures and opening multiple options for future development.
10. The author added the modifier, "of the Chaldees," to the name of the city, Ur, to differentiate it from other cities of the same name.
11. This is how the Hebrew Bible refers to Abraham, Isaac, and Jacob (cf. Genesis 48:21; Exodus 13:5; Deuteronomy 1:8; 6:18; 9:5; 10:15; 29:12; 30:20; Joshua 24:3, etc.). The term widely used today, "patriarchs," does not appear in the Hebrew Bible. It is a Greek term (from *patri* = family/clan and *archus* = ruler, thus "ruler of the family or clan") which passed to the Roman world, and thus from Latin into English. The application of this term to the fathers of the Israelites is completely inappropriate. Unlike Greek and Roman patriarchs who were rulers in every sense of the term, and who held the power of life and death over their wives and children, Abraham held no such authority nor did his descendants. They were not rulers but

fathers (and often hen-pecked husbands at that). Therefore, we will avoid the use of the term "patriarch" except when we are quoting or referring to its use in a citation, and revert to the term used in the Bible and by Jews ever since: *Ha-Avot*, The Fathers.

12. Actually, he had originally been named Abram, meaning "Mighty Father," a title of the moon god (Ur was a center of moon worship). Only later was the name Abraham, by which he came to be known, bestowed upon him by God by the enlargement of his original name (Gen. 17:5). We will refer to him throughout by the name by which he is known to history: Abraham.

13. K. A. Kitchen argues that various lines of evidence converge to date Abraham to the early nineteenth century BCE (*Reliability*, 316–343). Some of the reasoning has already been cited in the Introduction with regard to the dating of Joseph (see page 00).

14. The Ziggurat, a monumental stepped pyramid topped by a shrine, was the premier architectural expression of the Sumerian civilization. The "Tower of Babel" tale was undoubtedly based on the Ziggurat of Babylon. All major Sumerian cities had one. The Ziggurat of Ur is the only one to survive sufficiently intact to enable a reliable reconstruction. It rose in three massive stages; the 50 foot high base colored black, the second stage red, while the shrine perched at the summit was covered with blue tiles and (probably) capped with a gold covered dome. The terraces seem to have been planted with trees and other greenery. Ceremonial processions in brilliant garb solemnly proceeded up the huge staircases to the "bedroom of the god" at the pinnacle, in the presence of vast worshipful throngs — a spectacle never to be forgotten.

15. There is no reason, a priori, to deny Terah and his family a place in the middle class of Ur. There are those who assume that since Abraham emerges later as a semi-nomad, that that is what he and his family always were; not residents of Ur but pastoral hangers-on, pitching their tents on the fringes of the vast agricultural zone surrounding Ur. There is no evidence to support this contention, and much that argues against. If they were indeed well off— and they seem to have had ample funds — they may have lived in a comfortable two-story house like those from that period that have been excavated, houses very similar to middle and upper-class Arab houses of about 100 years ago. (This note, and the one preceding, are based on the report of the excavations of Ur by Sir Leonard Woolley, *Ur of the Chaldees: A Record of Seven Years of Excavation* [Harmondsworth, UK: Penguin], 1952.)

16. Despite the fact that God's call to Abraham, and Abraham's decision to heed the call, took place in Haran, God is always remembered as bringing him out of Ur of the Chaldees (Gen. 15:7; Neh. 9:7). It would seem that the emphasis is being placed on Abraham rejecting civilization at its highest rather than that of the second-rate version extant in Haran.

17. See Introduction, note 76 for the term "Yahweh."

18. Henri Frankfort, H. A. Frankfort, J. A. Wilson, and T. Jacobson, *Before Philosophy: The Intellectual Adventure of Ancient Man* (Harmondsworth, UK: Penguin, 1949), 241–243.

19. See note 12 above.

20. This included his wife and orphaned nephew and his retainers, including bondsmen. We are also informed that he took with him the wealth that he had amassed. Abraham, we are clearly being informed, was neither a solitary nor penurious (Gen. 12:5).

21. The term, *vayaira*, "now he appeared," is used in Genesis to introduce a theophany, or divine revelation, to one of the Fathers. It appears six times in this context. For a significant exception, see Chapter 9, page 140.

22. This promise of the land of Canaan is only for the distant future when Abraham's seed (i.e., his descendants) will have multiplied to the extent of becoming a great people. This additional promise is dependent on the fulfillment of the original pledge.

23. Abraham's wife being childless precluded his having any descendants, much less their multiplying and becoming as multitudinous as "the stars of the heavens and the sand on the shores of the sea." (cf. Gen. 15:5–6; 22:17)

24. The way of the world would say: "If she can't have children then she can't have children. Make your peace with the way things are. Find a practical way to deal with your problem: take a second wife or adopt a child. Don't expect miracles."

25. Or, "Walk before me in wholeheartedness." The Hebrew *tamim* is often rendered nowadays as "blameless," largely on the grounds that ritual texts use the term in the sense of "without blemish" (cf. Lev. 1:3). However, the word is an adjective from the verb *tamam*, "to be complete," and in non-ritual texts "it implies only spiritual perfection (Deuteronomy 18:13)" (Jacob Milgrom, *Leviticus 1–16*, The Anchor Bible, C3 [New York: Doubleday, 1991], 147). Therefore, our rendition of "wholehearted;" the understanding being that one of the primary meanings of this term involves loyalty to God. See Joshua 24:14.

26. Avraham H. Feder, *Torah Through a Zionist Vision*, 2 vols. (Jerusalem: Gefen, 2008), 220. The nounal form of the verb "to walk," *halachah*, came to mean Jewish law in the post–Biblical Age, but the

term never lost its meaning of the steps one takes as one walks through life, the requirement of wholehearted sincerity in these steps nor the sense that one is walking in the presence of God.

27. What "righteousness and justice" are, in the concrete and not in the abstract, and how one "does them," are issues that will remain central throughout the Biblical Age. The concepts will be given legal form in a vast corpus of law, beginning with the Ten Commandments. The prophets will push the frontiers of righteousness and justice beyond the limits that law can cover and into the cracks and crevices of human relationships where only the vigilant conscience can reach. The aim, always an ideal ever striven for but never fully attained, will be that every aspect of life, no matter what changes time will bring, will be conducted and lived by their light.

28. The formalization of the covenant between God on the one hand, and Abraham and his descendants on the other, will be discussed in Chapter 9.

29. The one exception being the ritual of circumcision, which was to serve as a permanent reminder of the covenant, the mutual relationship between God and the special people that bound the Promise to the mandate of championing the Way of the Lord and being a blessing to the world (Gen. 17:9–14). Of course the Fathers worshiped God, adapting some of the standard forms of ancient worship to their needs. They built altars and offered sacrifices; they dedicated pillars as sacred monuments, etc. But this was on their own initiative. And worship was always private and individual, without intermediaries or intercessors. Formal "religion" was to wait for the emergence of a full-fledged people.

30. Adultery was considered one of the most horrendous sins in the Ancient Near East, a crime against civil society and a sin against the gods.

31. This same failure was to be repeated by his son, Isaac (Gen. 26:6–11).

32. Frankfort, et al., 244–245.

1

A Family Tragedy

*All happy families resemble each other,
each unhappy family is unhappy in its own way.*
— Leo Tolstoy, *Anna Karenina*

Death solves all problems — no man, no problem.
— Josef V. Stalin, 1918

This chapter, which sets the stage for all that is to come, is an unusually dense and ambiguous narrative. As such it deserves our intense scrutiny.

Our tale opens in the vicinity of Hebron,[1] the current residence of Isaac[2] and site of the burial cave of his parents, Abraham and Sarah. Jacob has at long last come home after about twenty years "abroad" in Paddan-aram.[3] With him are three of his four wives (two of them concubines) and thirteen children — a family that is on its way to becoming a clan. He has done well financially in foreign climes, returning to the land of his birth a well-established, semi-nomadic herdsman, his wealth represented mainly by herds of sheep and goats. After an aborted attempt to settle at Shechem in the north, a venture which consumed several years and ended disastrously,[4] he has now settled down at the side of his aged father. The adventurous part of Jacob's pilgrimage on this earth is now behind him. In his declining years one paramount task yet awaits him: to raise his family to be worthy of the Covenant of his fathers and to determine who, among his many children, is fittest to guide the brethren in the new ways initiated by their great-grandfather, Abraham.

This, as he already realizes, will be no easy task. In the first place the primal curse of families, fraternal enmity, has made its appearance among his children. This is not a united and harmonious generation. It will require strong, even inspired leadership to cement them into a cooperative unit and to direct them forward on the path of their forefathers. But who is to assume this role?

His eldest three sons have already exhibited serious character flaws — sufficiently severe to disqualify them in their father's eyes from any leadership role.[5] His middle sons seem inept and unlikely candidates for leadership. It is among his younger sons that his best hopes seem to lie. In his next to youngest Jacob detects signs of great native ability and real promise. His attention increasingly focuses on Joseph.

A Spoiled Brat

Now Jacob dwelt in the land of his father's sojournings, in the land of Canaan. These are the happenings that befell Jacob[6]: *Joseph, seventeen years of age, was shepherding the flock with his brothers; he was helping[7] the sons of Bilhah and the sons of Zilpah, his father's wives. And Joseph gave a defamatory account of them to their father[8]* [Gen. 37:1–2].

Following a brief note which locates the events that are to unfold in the land of Canaan, we are presented with the central figure of our narrative, Joseph. The introduction is not flattering. A teenage boy apprenticed to his fully mature brothers, he reveals himself as a tattletale, running to his father with reports of their misdeeds, real or invented.[9] There seems to be more here than simply currying favor with his father. Joseph, the son of his father's favorite wife, Rachel, has been apprenticed to brothers who are sons of Bilhah and Zilpah, the maids of Jacob's premier wives. They had been given by their rival mistresses to Jacob for the sole purpose of being surrogate breeders of children at a time when both Rachel and Leah were incapable of bearing.[10] Their offspring, while full legal sons of Jacob, nonetheless inherited from their mothers a lower social status than that of the children of their father's full wives. Can we postulate here a sort of "upstairs-downstairs" situation with the concubines (who remained the maids of their mistresses so long as they were alive) and their children relegated to servant's quarters?[11] If so, their children, who remained with their mothers until puberty, would have been socialized differently from the sons of Jacob's wives, Leah and Rachel. This, in turn, could have led to an actual behavioral divide between "upper class" and "lower class" half-brothers, with all the differences in speech and social behaviors typical of a social system with a highly differentiated class structure, such as prevailed in the Ancient Near East. Thus there is more than a hint of social snobbery inherent in the situation.[12] Joseph, by virtue of being the son of his father's favorite wife, may well have felt his position as an apprentice to these particular brothers demeaning, despite the very real difference in age. In this case affront may have been as much the motive of his talebearing as seeking his father's approbation.[13] Whatever the motives, Joseph's actions can only have led to anger and deep resentment on the part of those brothers whose dirty linen had been laid bare before their father, and contempt on the part of all his older brothers. No one respects a tattletale, or worse, an informer.

This insight into Joseph's character and the deep rifts among the brothers is but the beginning. Once their father is brought actively into the picture, this situation begins to assume explosive proportions.

Now Israel loved Joseph more than any of his sons, for he was the child of his declining years,[14] and he made him a robe of many colors.[15] And his brothers saw that it was he whom their father loved more than all his brothers, and they hated him and could not speak peaceably to him[16] [Gen. 37:3–4].

Jacob seems to have a knack for mismanaging family affairs. He mishandled the two sisters who ended up as his wives, not even making a pretense of evenhandedness ("Now he loved Rachel more than Leah ... and the Lord saw that Leah was hated" 30:30–31). He allowed himself to get involved in the surrogate fecundity contest between his two wives, a conflict driven by envy, thus adding Bilhah and Zilpah to the simmering mix. Thus he sowed the seeds of a disastrously divided brood. He now carries the blatant favoritism forward to the next generation, compounding the damage inherited from the past. We are told that he loved Joseph more than all his brothers because he was born late in life.[17] But then again the fact that he is the son of Rachel, his beloved wife, must have played a large part. Jacob had loved her obsessively; it had been love at first sight and the love had never abated. A good case can be made that with Rachel's death that love had shifted to her oldest son.

And herein lies the paradox inherent in Jacob's treatment of his sons. This section enlarges on Joseph's less than sterling character traits: his squealing on his brothers, his insensitivity to the feelings of others and, as we shall soon learn, his arrogance and ambition to dominate his family. Together they render him most unlovable.[18] A number of his brothers, as we shall learn, exhibit far more endearing characteristics. Yet it is Joseph that his father loves.

It is suggestive that their father, at this point, is called Israel rather than Jacob. He received his new name at Peniel, just before he reentered Canaan on his return from Paddan-aram.[19] Shortly thereafter Rachel died. One possible interpretation of the use of his name Israel would be that the favoritism displayed toward Joseph only began after his renaming and the death of Rachel which shortly followed. Equally significant is one of the ways Israel expresses his love: outfitting his favorite with a special coat (undoubtedly expensive). It is clear that this garment was a symbol of status; more, it is probable that this designated the wearer as a future leader of the clan.

There is another way of looking at this choice of Joseph as heir apparent. It is hardly by accident that after beginning his story by speaking of Jacob and his son, the narrator suddenly switches names on us, using the name Israel which Jacob received so dramatically in his encounter at Peniel. Perhaps the narrator is reminding us that in becoming Israel, God has confirmed him as the recipient of the covenant of Abraham (35:9–12), and thus the bearer of not only the Promise but of the burden of designating who, in the next generation, will be the recipient of the mantle. As things will turn out, the blessing will pass to all of his sons; none will be left out. Does Jacob/Israel, at this early date, know this? If so, he needs to choose who among his sons is best suited to lead the family (in the process of evolving into a clan) on the difficult path of Abraham:

> *That he may command his sons and his house after him, that they keep the way of the Lord to do righteousness and justice* [Gen. 18:19].

Under these circumstances it would be reasonable to assume that he would assess the qualities of his very different sons for those attributes best suited to the role. By this time it must have become clear that Joseph is by far the most naturally talented of his children. That his native brilliance signally fails to include those traits most essential to winning the necessary consent of his peers to his leadership in a community of equals seems to have escaped their father. Perhaps it is here that the displaced love of his beloved Rachel blinded him to the obvious until it was too late to back off.

Passing over all the older brothers to place the mantle of future leadership on the shoulders of the next to the youngest son, a mere teenager, could not but store up a reservoir of resentment. Joseph becomes a pariah in his own family: "they could not speak peaceably to him," or as Robert Alter renders it: "they could not speak a kind word to him" (Gen. 37:4). Joseph does not seem to be in the least perturbed. As long as he basks in his father's love, his brother's feelings to him are irrelevant.

The Dreamer

> *Now Joseph dreamed a dream, and he told it to his brothers, and they hated him all the more. He said to them, "Please, hear this dream which I have dreamed. Behold, we were binding sheaves in the field, and behold, my sheaf arose and stood upright, and behold, your sheaves gathered around and bowed low to my sheaf." And his brothers said to him, "What! Do you mean to reign over us! Do you mean to rule us!" And they hated him all the more because of his dreams and because of his words.*

Now he dreamed another dream and told it to his brothers. And he said, "Behold, I dreamed another dream and behold, the sun, and the moon and eleven stars were bowing low to me." But [when] he told it to his father,[20] his father reprimanded him and said to him, "What is this dream that you have dreamed? Is it possible that I, and your mother and your brothers will come and bow low before you?" So his brothers were violently jealous of him, and his father took the thing to heart[21] [Gen. 37:5–11].

Joseph's complete self-absorption, his total obliviousness to the effect of his words upon the others, comes to its fullest expression in the dreams that he insists upon relating to his family. In both the dreams of which we are informed[22] the symbolism is transparent and does not need a trained psychoanalyst to interpret. His brothers, and later his father, instantly grasp their import. The world didn't have to wait until the advent of Freud to realize that dreams can reveal the desires and ambitions of the dreamer. The immediate response of his brothers, "What! Do you mean to reign over us! Do you mean to rule us!" show us how well they read the intentions of this young narcissist growing up in their midst. Worse even than these intentions are his presumptuousness and insensitivity to his brother's feelings in smugly proclaiming his vaulting ambitions to them. And, as the robe of many colors he is wearing seems to proclaim, as their father's successor he will one day have the means of realizing his ambitions. Small wonder this proclamation brings his brothers' hatred to new heights of fury.

The second dream brings Joseph's arrogance to full flower. The symbolism has become celestial: the sun, the moon and the stars. These heavenly bodies only owe obeisance to their Creator. By dreaming that the heavenly bodies are bowing to him, Joseph, in his own mind, has raised himself to divine status. This is blasphemy, and any pretense of filial piety has been abandoned. Even his parents must now grovel before him to satisfy his inflated ego.

Having examined what the dreams and their telling reveals about Joseph's character, and what effects they are having upon his brothers, it behooves us to direct our attention to several curious aspects of the dreams themselves. The first is the way the dreams are introduced and related: "Now Joseph dreamed a dream" (v. 5). This is an extraordinary phrasing. Not that the coupling of a noun with its verbal cognate is unusual in the Bible,[23] but Israelites do not "dream dreams." In the Bible, the phrase is used exclusively by pagans, and about pagans.[24] Israelites, on the other hand, see or hear things "in a dream."[25] The only exception to this general rule is Joseph. This phrasing is emphasized by being repeated no less than six times in our episode. The implications of this anomaly will only surface later.

The second curious aspect of the dream is its setting. Joseph and his brothers are binding sheaves in a field. But the family is not made up of farmers. They are shepherds. Shepherds don't bind sheaves.[26] When Jacob dreams, he dreams of sheep as one would expect a shepherd to do (Gen. 31:10–13). And unlike serf farmers, semi-nomadic shepherds are not in the habit of bowing. The setting of this dream is not the Highlands of southern Canaan where the family resides; it is far more at home in Egypt, a land of omnipotent rulers and self-abasing masses. This background of his dream is as alien to young Joseph as the implications are to his brothers.

Which brings us to the question: are Joseph's dreams prophetic? In the ancient world it was commonly accepted that dreams can have a supernatural origin and accurately predict the future. This does not by any means imply that every dream is an augury. The ancients recognized that usually a dream is simply a dream born of the concerns and anxieties of the dreamer.[27] The brothers obviously relate to Joseph's dreams in this manner, seeing them as simple projections of the little monster's arrogance and egomania. In their hatred of Joseph, they cannot do otherwise. Moreover, augury is absolute and can only be met by resignation: what will be, will be. But Joseph's dreams provoke not resignation but active opposition. Far from admitting the dreams to be prophetic, the brothers see Joseph's dreams as a warning of what awaits them unless the threat is nipped in the bud. Only their father perhaps suspects that there might be more to the dreams then youthful arrogance.[28]

But leaving the reactions of the family aside, how do we, the readers, understand the nature of these dreams? More than a hundred generations of readers, knowing the end of the story, have tended to take these dreams as prophecies of how things will spin out. But is this assessment valid? They, no less than we, have been subject to the magic of the Joseph "success story." We are thus predisposed to a bias in favor of Joseph, seeing him larger than life and taking what he says at face value. But does the text actually support such an evaluation? Because of our tendency to see Joseph as a hero, it behooves us to be very careful and resist jumping to hasty conclusions. So for the present let us just say that it is too early for judgment. On the one hand we cannot rely on the conviction of the brothers; although they know him best, they are clearly biased against him. Nor at the present can we rely on our own judgment. Because of a superficial acquaintance with the tale, often going back to Sunday school, we tend to take an overly sanguine view of the main protagonist. This question of prophecy will have to be but the first of many questions on which we will need to defer judgment until the tale's end. Things may not be as simple as they seem. And, as all who are familiar with Greek legends know, even auguries often surprise us in the end.

To summarize: we have been introduced to a teenager who is very full of himself. He squeals on his brothers, is arrogant and insensitive, and thus has succeeded in stirring up a storm of hatred and jealousy. It is significant that, while his father rebukes Joseph for the presumptuousness he displays in his second dream, the brothers no longer react but remain ominously silent.[29] We have been introduced to a father who, by loving not wisely but too well, has favored this son over all his brothers and, by investing him with that unique robe, has designated him as his heir apparent, the future leader of the clan. Together, father and son, they have sown the seeds of tragedy. The harvest will not be long delayed.

Fratricide

Now his brothers went to pasture their father's flock at Shechem. And Israel said to Joseph, "Your brothers are pasturing [the flock] *at Shechem. Go* [get ready], *and I will send you to them." And he said to him, "Here am I." And he said to him, "Please go and see if it is well with your brothers and well with the flock,*[30] *and bring me back word." So he sent him forth from the Vale of Hebron,*[31] *and he came to Shechem.* [There] *a man found him wondering about in the field, and the man asked him, saying, "What are you looking for?" And he said, "I am looking for my brothers. Please tell me where they are pasturing." And the man said, "They have journeyed on from here, for I heard them say, 'Let us go on to Dothan'"* [Gen. 37:12–16].

Hard upon the account of Joseph forcing his dreams of dominance upon his now tight-lipped brothers and his public rebuke by their father, comes the terrible denouement. At least several weeks have elapsed. These the narrator passes over in silence. His last words were: "His father took the thing to heart" (v. 11). We can imagine Jacob/Israel brooding over what has taken place and its implications. Then this father, who up to now has allowed himself to remain uninvolved in all the critical happenings in his children's lives, suddenly acts. He sends Joseph to Shechem, thus triggering the tragic cascade that follows.[32] Whatever prompted him to this disastrous act? Is Jacob simply being obtuse? Is he as oblivious to the boiling hatred of the brothers as Joseph is? If so, then he scarcely deserves the title of father except in the very limited biological sense. But this seems hardly credible. Things have gone too far for that.

There are commentators who hold that Jacob is indeed by now fully aware of the explosive tensions that threaten to tear the family apart. The second dream and the grim silence of the brothers are an eye-opener. It is this awareness that causes Jacob to side with the majority of his sons when he publicly slaps Joseph down for his presumptuousness. But this attempt to defuse the issue is insufficient. Matters are building up to a crisis. Jacob now realizes that his attempt to foist Joseph off on his sons as the future leader of the family has backfired. His open favoritism has proved fatal. He has come to appreciate that only if he takes himself out of the picture and lets Joseph and his brothers work things out on their own has the most gifted of his sons any chance of being freely accepted by his brothers as their leader. But at this late stage what chance has he?

There are those who are of the opinion that Jacob alone, among all those before whom Joseph paraded his dreams, accepts the possibility that they are indeed prophetic. If so, then his brilliant younger son may yet be able to prevail upon his brothers; good sense may yet overcome hostility and envy. If heaven is on his side, the impossible can become the possible, even the probable.[33] There is a sense of grasping at straws here. There is also a sense of desperation. The next generation must have a leader, and it is becoming painfully obvious to Israel that none of his older sons are up to the job. So with eyes wide open, Jacob sends his beloved Joseph to cope on his own with his brothers in a setting far removed from the dominating presence of their father.

I seriously doubt that Jacob had any idea of the extent of the danger into which he is sending Joseph. Rejection of Joseph by his brothers would seem to be the limits of Jacob's fears; for if they do reject him what will become of God's Promise in the absence of the right kind of leader? But real physical danger does not appear to be in the forefront of Jacob's mind. Yet the tone of the narrative is ominous. The language hauntingly recalls that of the *Akedah*, the binding of Isaac. Especially suggestive is the use of the terms *Hineni*, "Here am I" (Gen. 22:7; 37:13) and "Please take" and "Please go" (22:2; 37:14). The stories are in no way parallel, but a similar language is, I believe, meant to create a frisson of horrified anticipation in the perceptive reader. Joseph is being sent to the vicinity of blood-drenched Shechem.[34] Has Jacob so quickly put out of his mind the violence and mayhem associated with the site?[35] Most ominous of all, this is one of the very few chapters in the Bible in which there is no mention of God. So while Jacob may not be aware of the extent of the risk, we, alerted by the narrator, are.

Is Joseph in anyway apprehensive? He certainly accepts his commission like a good son; with alacrity and voicing no reservations. Like Abraham on the road to Moriah, he has plenty of time to think things over. It is a full fifty miles from Hebron to Shechem, a journey of several days by foot. Was he using the time to think through his relationship with his brothers, planning a new approach? We are given no indication.

Arriving at Shechem, Joseph cannot find his brothers. Instead, an unnamed stranger finds him wandering about in the fields. Who is this mysterious stranger who so unerringly directs Joseph on the path to calamity? At Shechem the main road forks; without assistance Joseph would have no way of knowing which direction his brothers had taken, and not knowing it is likely he would have returned home, thus aborting the looming confrontation. Yet suddenly there appears a mysterious stranger to take matters in hand and ensure that the impending crisis will not be deterred. There is a sense of an emerging destiny about the entire affair, almost as though all things are conspiring to hasten us to tragedy. Several commentators have suggested the possibility that this mysterious "man" is indeed the very same equally mysterious "man" who wrestled with Jacob that momentous night at Peniel, and from whom Jacob rung the blessing of his renaming as Israel.[36] This would imply the guiding hand of Providence, a tempting thought, though admittedly with no direct warrant from the text. Yet the suspicion that the text is nudging us in this direction cannot simply be dismissed. The narrator must have some purpose in intruding this seemingly extraneous episode into the terse narrative. Whatever our opinions, with this intervention the tale assumes the cast of inevitability.

Suitably directed, Joseph takes the northwest fork to Dothan,[37] an ancient fortress town about thirteen miles from Shechem.

> *So Joseph went after his brothers and he found them at Dothan. Now they saw him from afar, before he came near to them, and they plotted[38] against him to kill him. And they said each man to his brother, "Behold, here comes that Lord of Dreams![39] Come now, let us kill him and throw him into one of the cisterns and say that a wild beast[40] has devoured him; then we shall see what will become of his dreams"* [Gen. 37:17–20].

When asked by the mysterious stranger what he was looking for Joseph replied, "I am looking for my brothers" (v. 16). Equally his siblings relate to each other as brothers. But this sense of brotherhood does not include Joseph. Focusing on the Hebrew word *mirahok* (from afar) as reflecting emotional as well as physical distance between them and Joseph, Feder comments that "they did not look on him as brothers should look at a brother, but rather as a man who was as distant from them as a stranger." Having distanced themselves from Joseph, they no longer see him as a brother but only as "the other," an alien for whom they bear no responsibility. They are no longer their brother's keepers for in their hearts he is no longer their brother. They can now, with relative ease, plot to murder him or otherwise dispose of him. "Essentially they wish to rid themselves of him, to condemn him to oblivion."[41] This distancing of their brother from themselves will be repaid in time with compound interest.

The level of hatred that Joseph has generated is appalling. To the suggestion of murder, followed by a cover-up, no one dissents. Only the eldest brother, Reuben, opposes the general consensus, yet he dare not give voice to his opposition. He temporizes, insisting that to murder Joseph with their own hands would be to incur the heinous stigma of blood-guilt. Throw him into a cistern and let nature take its course, he counsels. Not having "laid hands on him" (v. 22), we can with plausibility deny direct complicity in his death. In either case the result will be the same. But behind his words, the narrator tells us, lies the aim of buying time so as to make rescue possible. His prescription seems to win consent.

> *But Reuben heard, and saved him from their hands. And he said, "We will not take his life."*[42] *And Reuben said to them, "Do not spill blood. Throw him into this cistern here in the wilderness, and lay no hand upon him"—that he might save him from their hands, to return him to his father. So it came to pass that when Joseph came to his brothers they stripped Joseph of his robe, the robe of many colors that was upon him, and they took him and threw him into the cistern—now the cistern was empty, there was no water in it. And they sat down to eat* [Gen. 37:21–25a].

Cisterns were artificial reservoirs, usually cut into bedrock, for collecting and preserving rainwater for use during the dry season. Many were bottle-shaped with a small opening at the top. Where the native bedrock was porous, as is often the case in the hill country of Samaria, the cisterns had to be sealed with lime plaster to prevent leakage. Cisterns have to be kept covered, usually with a stone over the opening.[43] Such cisterns were hewn out in pastureland outside the cultivated areas, i.e., "the wilderness," to enable shepherds to water their flocks. At the end of the dry season, many of these, their water used up, would be dry. Into such a designated tomb is Joseph hurled after having been stripped of his hated robe. The future leader, imposed on them by their father, has been disposed of. And the brothers who are no brothers to Joseph, having accomplished a good day's work, now sit down to eat.[44]

We are not to assume that Joseph accepted his fate with resignation. He must have struggled wildly as he was stripped and hurled into the dark pit. Much later we will be informed that, from the depths of the cistern, he continued to shriek and plead with his brothers; cries and pleas that remained engraved on their minds, even though, with a stony-hearted indifference, they stolidly continued to turn a deaf ear to them as they munched their bread.

> *Raising their eyes they saw, and behold, a caravan of Ishmaelites coming from the Gilead, their camels bearing gum, and balm and labdanum,*[45] *going to take it down to Egypt. Now Judah said to his brothers, "What profit is there in killing our brother and covering up his blood? Come, let us sell him to the Ishmaelites and let not our hand be upon him, for he is* [after all] *our brother, our own flesh." And his brothers agreed*[46] [Gen. 37:25b–27].

The difference between the ploys of Reuben, the oldest of the brothers, and thus the natural candidate to be their leader, and that of Judah, the fourth oldest, gives us pause. Reuben's intentions are good; his means are flawed. His aim is to save Joseph's life and return him to the protection of his father — good as far as it goes — but even if accomplished would merely postpone the crisis, for it does not relate to the burning hatred that would be bound to reignite on some later occasion. His means are counter-productive. He issues preemptive orders; he makes no attempt to win his brothers over. All he gains is a temporary stay. The text pointedly does not say that he gained his brothers' agreement. As things turn out his plan is preempted by the onrush of events.

Judah's true motives, on the other hand, remain unclear. On these the narrator remains silent. The reasons Judah gives his brothers — let's turn a fast buck — may be his true motive, or it could be simply a ploy to save Joseph. His argument amounts to this: our aim is to get rid of Joseph. Selling him into slavery in a foreign land will do the job as well as if we killed him, and we can make a profit on the deal as well. This argument wins over the brothers. "And his brothers agreed." Thus Reuben emerges as a man of good intentions but a poor leader, and thus incapable of implementing his purposes. Judah emerges as a leader of men, capable of obtaining the consent of his peers to his leadership. He has just made his first tentative step toward the leadership of the family. It is Judah's character and purposes that remain unclear. We have a long way to go before we will be in a position to evaluate them.

What takes place next is more than a little confusing. It has posed a problem to commentators for centuries.

> *Now some Midianite merchant men passed by, and they drew Joseph up and lifted him out of the cistern, and they sold Joseph to the Ishmaelites for twenty* [shekels] *of silver,*[47] *and they brought Joseph to Egypt* [Gen. 37:28].

Who sold what to whom? One way to look at the matter is to postulate that the brothers have removed themselves from the immediate vicinity of the cistern. Joseph's screams may have disturbed their lunch and so they move out of earshot.[48] In their absence a group of passing Midianite merchants, attracted by Joseph's cries and pleas, draw him out of the pit and sell him to the Ishmaelites, who in turn sell him into Egypt.[49] It is worth noting that all the participants in this sordid affair are close relatives. The brothers obviously; Midianites are descendants of Abraham by his concubine Keturah, and Ishmaelites (if the name is not here used as a generic term for nomadic traders[50]) were also of the seed of Abraham by his concubine Hagar. In fact all the participants are either brothers or cousins. From start to finish this remains a family affair.

> *Now Reuben returned to the cistern and behold, Joseph was not in the cistern! And he rent his clothes and returned to his brothers and said, "The boy is gone![51] And as for me, where shall I go?"* [Gen. 37:29–30].

Reuben, obviously, has no idea of what has happened to Joseph. In shock he tears his clothing, an ancient symbol of mourning, clearly indicating that he believes Joseph to be dead.[52] He seems to have leapt to the conclusion that some wild beast — a leopard or a lion perhaps, creatures that freely roamed the wilderness areas of Canaan and often intruded into the cultivated regions — had pounced upon Joseph, killed him, and carried off his corpse. This interpretation appears to have been accepted by the brothers. They now reactivate their original cover-up plan.

> *So they took Joseph's robe, and slaughtered a young goat, and dipped the robe in the blood. And they sent*[53] *the robe of many colors and brought it to their father, and said, "This have we found. Please, do you recognize* [this]*? Is this your son's robe or is it not?" And he recognized it, and said, "It is my son's robe! A wild beast*[54] *has devoured him! Torn! Torn to pieces is Joseph!" And Jacob rent his garments and put sackcloth on his loins, and he mourned for his son many days. Now all his sons and all his daughters rose up to comfort him, but he refused to be comforted. And he said, "*[No]*, I will go down to Sheol*[55] *to my son, mourning." And his father wept for him* [Gen. 37:31–35].

The cover-up is brutal, wantonly so. One suspects the brothers of exacting their revenge not only on Joseph but also on their aged father who has preferred him and loved him more than themselves. To present their father with a bloodied robe that had been the mark of Joseph's preferment and to ask him to identify it is cruel. Jacob's response is all that could have been desired. He is totally taken in by the deception, even using the very words used by the brothers when they concocted the plot,[56] but his reaction is excessive. He goes into deep mourning and refuses to snap out of it after a reasonable amount of time has past. His extravagant, almost histrionic behavior[57] begins to alarm his children. But despite their concentrated efforts to console him, he refuses comfort. He will continue to grieve, he insists, until he finally joins his son in the grave. This almost pathological reaction leads us to suspect that more than grief is involved. Does Jacob now blame himself for being the cause of his son's death, having sent Joseph out alone in a dangerous country? In those days a lone individual was strikingly vulnerable to mishap. He had once himself been out alone when he had fled home in his youth. He of all people should have known better. A large burden of guilt seems to be weighing on Jacob and on the brothers as well. All apparently believe Joseph to be dead. All seem convinced that they had a part in his demise. Their father can express his mixed feelings, and does so in extravagant fashion. The brothers, not having this option as they must preserve appearances, can only repress their guilt. If the condition of the family before Joseph's "demise" was explosive, it has now become pathological.

So the family struggles to adjust to the fact that Joseph "is no more."[58] But ironically, the narrator insists, neither Jacob nor his sons have any idea of the true situation. As each in his own way grieves and/or feels guilt for Joseph's decease, we are reminded that he is very much alive.

Now the Midianites had sold him into Egypt, to Potiphar, the Head of Security,[59] a high official[60] of Pharaoh [Gen. 37:36].

But before we can discover what will become of Joseph, our narrator opts to tell us what happens to another of Jacob's sons; the one who came up with the idea of selling his brother into slavery — Judah.

Notes

1. Hebron is an ancient city midway between Jerusalem to the north and Beersheba to the south. According to Numbers 13:22, the city was founded seven years before the Egyptian city of Tanis. This would place its establishment as a fortified center at about 1737 BCE There is evidence of an unfortified settlement on the site as early as the third millennium BCE

2. Though Isaac never appears in our narrative, simple arithmetic determines that he will not die until twelve years after Joseph's sale into Egypt. His death notice in Genesis 35:27–28 has been tacked on to the end of the "Adventures of Jacob" narrative to keep him from being, in his dotage, a distracting factor in the Joseph story.

3. Paddan-aram is in Mesopotamia, and probably refers to the area of Haran, the home of his uncle Laban.

4. See Genesis 34 for the sorry tale of an enterprise that got off on the wrong foot, progressed to the rape and abduction of Jacob's sole daughter, only to reach its nadir in deception, treachery and massacre.

5. These will be explored in Chapter 12, page 172–173.

6. Following Ibn Ezra (see Glossary); literally, "these are the *toldot* of Jacob." The Hebrew term *toldot* comes from a root that means "to give birth." While *toldot* usually refers to the giving birth to successive generations, it also refers to "where no family tree follows but only stories of subsequent events, the formula is used figuratively for 'a record of events'" (Nahum M. Sarna, *Genesis*, JPS Torah Commentary [Philadelphia: Jewish Publication Society, 1989], 16). The phrase "these are the *toldot*" is a formula that appears eleven times in Genesis. It serves as a marker to indicate the beginning of a new section containing fresh and significant developments. Here it also, in its primary meaning of giving birth, refers back to Genesis 35:22b–27 where a list of Jacob's wives and concubines, and the sons they bore, and of the family's arrival at Hebron where his father and grandfather sojourned, concludes the saga of Jacob and his adventures. Thus this phrase serves the dual function of indicating the beginning of the tale of Joseph and his brothers, and is a bridge between this tale and the previous account of the adventurers of Jacob. (Genesis 36, which separates the two sagas, is taken up with an excursus concerning the progeny of Esau, Jacob's brother.)

7. Literally, "and he was a lad." The Hebrew term *naar* has the meaning of a young male, one who has not yet reached the status of an adult, and also the meaning of an apprentice, one who is learning a trade. Having already been told Joseph's age, the intention here would seem to be to indicate that he has been attached to his older brothers as an assistant so as to learn the trade of shepherding.

8. More literally, "and Joseph brought an evil report of them to their father." The Hebrew term *dibah* has the sense of vilification. The only other place this term is used is with regard to the report of the spies who had been sent to reconnoiter the Promised Land (Num. 13:32; 14:36–37). There both the consequences of the calumny and the punishment for it were extreme.

9. Significantly, we are given no clue as to the nature of these "misdeeds," whether they related to their job performance or to their extra-curricular activities. All that we are told is that the defamation was such as to severely compromise the brothers in the eyes of their father.

10. It is important to notice that while Bilhah and Zilpah held the status of concubines, they are here pointedly referred to as Jacob's wives. Have they been raised to the status of full wives after the death of their mistresses, Rachel and Leah, as suggested by Ramban (see Glossary).

11. There is little doubt that servants (and Jacob had them — note the differentiation between Jacob's "house," i.e., his immediate family, and "all who were with him" in Gen. 35:2), were housed in a separate tent compound from that of Jacob's wives and their children.

12. To keep matters straight in this fragmented family, here is the scorecard:
    Wives of Jacob
    Children of **Leah**: Reuben, Simeon, Levi, Judah, Issachar, Zebulun, and Dinah.
    Children of **Rachel**: Joseph and Benjamin.
    Concubines of Jacob
    Children of **Bilhah**, maid of Rachel: Dan and Naphtali.
    Children of **Zilpah**, maid of Leah: Gad and Asher.

13. Some commentators read this situation differently: they see Joseph as having been placed by his father as an overseer over his brothers despite their being full-grown men. It is indeed possible to render the text in this manner: "Joseph, being 17 years old, shepherded his brothers along with the sheep though he was [but] a lad, that is, the sons of Bilhah and the sons of Zilpah, his father's wives" (Sacks, *A Commentary on Genesis*, 307). If we accept this as the meaning of the text, then the resentment would have been all on the side of the humiliated older brothers.

14. Literally, "a child born to someone of advanced years."

15. Rendering as do LXX (Septuagint, see Glossary) and Vulg. (Vulgate, see Glossary). The Hebrew term *ketonet passim* has more recently been rendered variously as "a long robe with sleeves" (RSV, see Glossary), "an ornamented tunic" (NJPS, see Glossary; Alter, *Genesis*) and classically "a coat of many colors" (AV, see Glossary). The only other place in the Bible where this term appears is in 2 Samuel 13:18, where it is described as a garment worn by unmarried daughters of royalty. Thus in both cases it would seem to have been a special status symbol. The term means literally, "a garment of stripes." A fourteenth-century BCE Egyptian fresco, roughly contemporaneous with the period of Joseph, shows Canaanite noblemen dressed in robes made of multicolored wide longitudinal panels sewn together, and may be versions of the garment Joseph's father made for him. At any rate, no certainty having been reached as to the exact meaning of the term, I prefer to use "a robe of many colors," the rendition of LXX and Vulg.; this is the origin of the rendition of the King James Bible "coat of many colors."

16. Or, "they could not speak a kind word to him." In some such manner the phrase is usually rendered. On the other hand, "the Hebrew *dabbro* is unique. Usually the suffix attached to the verb carries a possessive sense, meaning 'his speech.' The passage would then be translated, 'They could not abide his friendly speech.' In other words, they rebuffed every attempt of Joseph to be friendly" (Sarna, *Genesis*, 256).

17. But then his affections should have been centered on Benjamin, his youngest. But Benjamin was a very late surprise. Perhaps his love had already fixed on Joseph long before Benjamin was born. Only after Joseph's seeming death is the possessive love free to settle on his youngest son. Or perhaps, as Benjamin's birth was what killed his beloved Rachel, his youngest son was passed over in his father's affections because of that traumatic event (Kass, 514, note 5).

18. Ibid., 516, note 8.

19. Jacob spent eighteen years in Paddan-aram, at the home of his uncle Laban, acquiring wealth and family, and in the process stirring up such enmity that he had no choice but to leave and return home to his father in Canaan. For the renaming incident see Genesis 32:23–33; for the epiphany when God confirmed the name-change see 35:9–15.

20. Reading with LXX; MT adds "and his brothers."

21. Literally, "kept the thing" [in mind]. I have rendered the phrase this way because of the implication that he took the event seriously. Milgrom, on the other hand, basing himself on Akkadian cognates, which mean "to be angry, to rage," insists that the phrase "implies that when told by Joseph that he was destined to bow down to him, 'he (Jacob) became enraged at the matter'" (Milgrom, *Leviticus 17–22*, 1,651).

22. The fact that the narrator concludes his account of the *first* dream with the words, "and they hated him all the more because of his dreams (plural) and because of his words" (v. 5), we can conjecture that there may have been previous similar dreams of which we have not been told, this being merely the latest of a series. The "words" then could relate either to past explanatory remarks by Joseph or to the "bad reports" he made to his father.

23. In fact it is quite common. Examples are "to offer incense," literally, "to incense incense" (1 Samuel 2:28); "to sacrifice a sacrifice" (2:13); "to petition a petition," (1:17, 27); "the youth was young," literally, "the youth was a youth," (1:24); "to seed seed," (Gen. 1:12, 29); "to pledge a pledge," (Exod. 22:25); etc.

24. Egyptians "dream dreams" (Gen. 40:5, 41:15), Babylonians "dream dreams" (Dan. 2:3, 5), Midianites "dream dreams" (Judg. 7:13); etc.

25. Such as Jacob (Gen. 28:12–15; 31:10f; etc.).

26. Sarna (*Genesis*, 256) is of the opinion that at harvest season farmers would recruit pastoralists to

27. In our saga dreams come in pairs. Joseph will later insist that when dreams come in pairs, the second serves as a confirmation of the first, validating the two as a genuine augury. But for this we only have Joseph's opinion, and perhaps a self-serving opinion at that.

28. However, see note 21 above.

29. The brothers are not deferring to their father. Joseph has forced his brothers to listen to him before going to repeat his dream to their father. Unlike the first dream when the brothers reacted with shock at its presumptuousness, here they greet his grand follow-up in stony-faced silence.

30. Literally, "if it is shalom with..." I.e., "is it peace with...?"

31. Possibly the pasture below the city. Hebron was on a hill, but Jacob and his family did not live in the city. They dwelt in tents close to their flocks.

32. He does not react overtly to Reuben's bedding of his concubine (Gen. 35:22). He is impotence personified in the events that follow the rape of his daughter. The only overt intrusion into the lives of his children that is chronicled up to this point is his designation of Joseph as a future leader of the clan, signaled by presenting him with a robe of many colors. We are told he intervened by calling down Joseph for his grandiose posturing. Now, for the third time, he intervenes.

33. Cf. Kass, 520.

34. Feder, *Torah Through a Zionist Vision*, vol. 1, 104–106.

35. The kidnapping and rape of his daughter, and the slaughter perpetrated by his sons. See Genesis 34.

36. Feder, 1:110; Kass, 521. Kass also calls to mind the mysterious "men" that appeared at Abraham's tent (Gen. 18:2) who are later revealed as angels (Kass, 521, note 14).

37. Dothan is situated in a valley known for its rich pasture land (Sarna, *Genesis*, 258).

38. The Hebrew root *nakal* carries the connotations of craftiness and vileness.

39. The appellation is meant to be sarcastic.

40. Literally, "an evil creature."

41. Feder, 1:104–105.

42. Literally, "strike down on his soul."

43. P. J. King and L. E. Stager, *Life in Biblical Israel* (Louisville: Westminster John Knox Press, 2001), 126–127.

44. One is reminded of Haman and Ahasuerus, some twelve hundred years later, having issued the genocidal decree mandating the death of all the Achaemenian Empire's Jews, sitting down to a pleasant round of drinks to celebrate a task well done. Ironic situations have a way of repeating themselves. See my discussion of the irony in *Four Biblical Heroines*, 140.

45. Plant extracts of extremely high value, prized for their medicinal and/or aromatic properties, and used in compounding medicines, perfumes, and incense.

46. Literally, "heeded" [him].

47. K. A. Kitchen observes that the price Joseph fetched (twenty shekels of silver) allows us to date the events related in our narrative. Our expanding knowledge of the Ancient Near East allows us nowadays to plot the rising market price of young adult male slaves over time (then as now inflation was a serious long-term problem). Twenty shekels was "approximately the right price in the 18th century. This is the average price (expressed as one-third of a mina) in the laws of Hammurabi and in real-life transactions at Mari (exactly) and in other Old Babylonian documents.... Before this period slaves were cheaper, and after it they steadily got dearer, as inflation did its work" (*Reliability*, 344; see also graph, figure 43, 639).

48. Since Reuben intended to sneak Joseph out of the cistern and return him to his father, and thus had an interest in distancing his brothers from the vicinity to give him the chance to do so, it may very well have been he who was the one who suggested the move.

49. The implications of this reading will be significant. For alternative readings and for why we chose this one see Appendix 1: Who Sold Joseph into Egypt?

50. See Judges 8:24 and Appendix 1, note 6.

51. Literally, "the boy is not!"

52. The ceremony of rending one's garments, called *keriah*, is still practiced today, in attenuated form, by Jews at the funeral of a close relative.

53. To take and present the robe would be to accept responsibility — the last thing the brothers wish to do. By "sending" they distance themselves from what has happened or might have happened. Note the verb *send*. We will soon confront it again.

54. Literally, "an evil creature."

55. The underworld, the realm of the dead.

56. Compare Genesis 37:20 and 37:33. As opposed to the conventional reading which accepts that Jacob is completely taken in by the brothers' cover-up, Robert Sacks, *A Commentary on the Book of Genesis* (Lewiston, NY: Edwin Mellen, 1990), 313–314, sees things differently. Relying on Skinner and Davidson without quoting them (see Bibliography), which take the term "wild beast" in Ezekiel 34:25 (and by extension the identical term in Leviticus 26:6 from which Ezekiel probably borrowed the term) as a metaphor for vicious human beings (invaders and marauders), he then transfers this metaphoric usage to Genesis 37. Thus in the Sacks reading, when Jacob cries out, "A wild beast has devoured him," he is seeing through the brothers' deception and realizing that it is they who are the "wild beasts," the murderers of Joseph. This reading and its implications, intriguing as they may be, cannot be sustained. The metaphorical understanding of "wild beasts" here and elsewhere is shown by Moshe Greenberg to be mistaken (*Ezekiel 21–37*, The Anchor Bible, 22A [New York: Doubleday, 1997], 702–703). It would appear that "wild beasts" are simply wild beasts and no more, and that when Jacob cries out that Joseph was eaten by a wild beast, he meant that and only that. So we return to the conventional reading that Jacob's sons intended to deceive their father, and their deception succeeded.

57. "All this language of mourning and grieving suggests a certain extravagance, perhaps something histrionic" (Alter, *Genesis*, 215).

58. The euphemism later used by the brothers to refer to the "decease" of Joseph (Gen. 42:13).

59. Many translations render Potiphar's office as "the Chief Steward." The title comes from a root that means to slaughter, to kill. From the first meaning of slaughtering animals for food, the title here might mean Chief Steward; from the second meaning, Chief Executioner. (The difficulty of this second rendering in modern English is that it recalls to mind the office of the Lord High Executioner in the satiric Gilbert and Sullivan operetta *The Mikado*, with its ridiculous associations with the tailor Ko-Ko and the Town of Titipu.) From Genesis 40:3 we know that the holder of this position was responsible for the royal prisons. In a later period a Babylonian high official with a similar title seems to have been in charge of the royal bodyguard (2 Kings 25:8). With these considerations in mind, I have opted to render the title as "Head of Security," with the understanding that the office included the responsibility for the execution of those convicted of capital crimes. In all events this position was one of great power and prestige. As a member of the ruling class of Egypt, it was in full keeping with Potiphar's rank that he possessed a large estate and was in the market for slaves to work it.

60. The term *saris* is often rendered as "eunuch," which meaning it does have. It is a loan word from the Akkadian *sa resi*, literally, "the one at the head," i.e., a high official. It gained a secondary meaning of eunuch in Mesopotamia as it was a common practice to use eunuchs in high government positions. But here the term probably retains its original meaning inasmuch as "there does not seem to be evidence of eunuchs as an institution in ancient Egypt" (Sarna, *Genesis*, 263). Kitchen agrees ("Joseph," *The New Bible Dictionary*, ed. J. D. Douglas [Grand Rapids: Eerdmans, 1962], 658).

2

Rehabilitation

Sow an act, and you reap a habit. Sow a habit, and you reap a character. Sow a character, and you reap a destiny.
— Charles Reade, *Attrib.*

In what follows I may appear to be repeating myself. An earlier version of this chapter appeared in my previous book, *Four Biblical Heroines*. There the material was treated as a self-contained unit (which indeed it is), with, as its focus, the struggle of Tamar for dignity of place in the world. Our present treatment looks at this chapter as an integral episode within the larger framework of the Joseph saga, and focuses on the character development of Judah that makes him a contender for the leadership of the covenantal family.

Until fairly recently this view of Genesis 38 would have been considered untenable. It was a scholarly consensus that what we now know as chapter 38 is an independent literary unit arbitrarily inserted into the Joseph saga, which breaks the natural continuity between chapters 37 and 39.[1] Indeed, the blatant chronological contradictions between chapters 37 and 39, and chapter 38, made the notion of a harmony between them seem absurd.[2] It was Robert Alter who led the reevaluation of this chapter and brought the scholarly world to the realization that, far from being a foreign body, it was originally written as part and parcel of the structure of the Joseph narrative.[3] He accomplished this by definitively demonstrating that both linguistically and conceptually it forms an integral part of the larger epic. In a sense, Genesis 38 acts in the same way that the chapter entitled "The Grand Inquisitor" functions in *The Brothers Karamazov*: the chapter forms a self-contained unit that can be understood on its own terms, yet also serves as one of the keys that unlock the meaning of the novel.[4] It is as part of an antiphonal structure, the story of Judah and Tamar as a counterpoint to the tale of Joseph's betrayal by his brothers that we have just concluded, that we will now read our current chapter.

The Dropout

The brothers may have been left in a quandary as to exactly what happened to Joseph, but of one thing they are certain: he is gone. And as, in their minds, the assumption of his death solidifies into certainty, the full realization of their complicity in his elimination morphs into a chronic ache that cannot be ignored.[5] The picture becomes even more bleak if we add to this the opinion of some commentators that father Jacob, fully aware of the violent antagonism felt for Joseph by his brothers, sent Joseph to them for the express purpose of provoking a crisis in a spot far removed from any possible intervention on his part. They posit that Jacob's hope was that, in a moment of truth, family feeling would triumph over hatred and jealousy; the outcome being a mending of the increasingly fractured family.[6] On both counts Jacob has been proven wrong: Joseph is no more; and as to the family's dysfunction—far from being mended, the family begins to fall apart. Joseph is gone; now Judah is the next to go.

> *Now it came to pass at that time that Judah went down from his brothers and pitched his tent near a certain Adullamite[7] whose name was Hirah. And Judah saw there the daughter of a certain Canaanite whose name was Shua, and he took her [to wife], and went in to her; she conceived and bore a son, and he called his name Er. She conceived again and bore a son, and she called his name Onan. Yet again she bore a son, and she called his name Shelah; she[8] was in Chezib[9] when she bore him* [Gen. 38:1–5].

These five verses form the prologue, which sets the scene for our mini-drama.[10] We are presented with the names of most of the protagonists involved in the tale (though, strangely, Judah's wife is not named—she will remain merely "Shua's daughter"). We are told when the events take place. And finally, we are informed that it is Judah's relocation from the central highlands to the plains near Adullam that triggers the action in our chapter.

The opening words of our narrative, "now it came to pass around that time that Judah went down from his brothers" (v. 1), is more than a bridging phrase meant to provide a smooth transition from the previous chapter. It raises in our minds the suspicion that the very act of selling their brother has triggered the next step in the disintegration of the family: Judah is distancing himself from the circle of father and siblings.[11] As we know, the family at that time was located in the vicinity of Hebron, one of the highest points of the region.[12] Breaking with the past practice of pasturing the family herds collectively, Judah removes his sheep and makes the seasonal migration to the plains alone (note the words *went down*).[13] Why he makes this move we are not told, but the suspicion arises that, after years of being immersed in an atmosphere of seething jealousy which culminated in the traumatic betrayal and disposal of their brother, Judah feels the need to break clean, start afresh and make a new life for himself. He makes friends among the locals (we will learn that Hirah is not just a neighbor but becomes Judah's bosom companion), finds a girl, marries and settles down to raising a family. By the time his third son is born he has relocated his family to Chezib. Judah has taken up permanent residence in the plains.

The terseness of the account—"he saw," "he took," "he went in" followed by the staccato three time repetition of the phrase "she bore a son"—emphasizes the feverish rapidity with which the events unfold: meeting, marriage, consummation; another year another son. And now, as if in reaction to this frenetic pace, the story dries up. More than a dozen years will flow by until our tale resumes. Judah is now in his late thirties.

> *Now Judah took a wife for Er, his first born, and her name was Tamar* [Gen. 38:6].

Now a middle-aged father of teenage sons, Judah takes responsibility for their future. His oldest is now of marriageable age. So Judah, the responsible parent, finds an appropriate bride for his oldest son, Er. Though we are not specifically told, she, like his wife, is undoubtedly of Canaanite stock.

There is something interesting going on here. Judah's great-grandfather, Abraham, was insistent that his son not marry a Canaanite girl, and took great pains to ensure the proper choice of a bride for his son from among his own people.[14] Isaac, in his turn, was equally insistent that his son, Jacob, not take a Canaanite bride, and sent him abroad specifically to choose a wife for himself from among his own kin.[15] Jacob, on the other hand, does not seem to have been particularly concerned as to whom his children marry, or to have made any efforts to ensure appropriate marriages for them. (Indeed, Jacob seems to have exercised hardly any control over his children.) We have already seen that Judah left home, married whom he willed, and whom he willed was a Canaanite woman. However, with regard to his son, the freedom of choice that he seized for himself will most decidedly not be permitted Er. *He* makes the choice for him; and considering his own marriage to a Canaanite woman he hardly has any scruples in the matter with regard to his son. What will become of God's Promise to Judah's progeny seems to be of little concern. More on this issue later.

> *And Er, Judah's first born, was evil in the sight of the Lord, and the Lord slew him. Then Judah said to Onan: "Go in to your brother's wife, and perform the duty of a brother-in-law to her, and raise up seed to your brother"* [Gen. 38:7–8].

Things don't work out very well. How much time elapses between the marriage and Er's untimely death we are not told, but it does not seem to have been very much.[16] All that is relevant is that he leaves behind a young and childless widow (given the customs of the period, Tamar was probably no more than fourteen years of age).

What comes next may seem strange to us; it is based on the widespread custom of those times (later codified into law) of levirate marriage. This custom was based on the strongly held conviction that it was imperative that no individual family line be allowed to die out. The practice that grew out of this conviction amounted to the following: if a man dies childless, leaving no heirs to carry on the family name, then his brother (or lacking a brother, some other close relative) has the duty to marry the widow for the express purpose of producing an heir to carry on the family name. The first child born of this union will legally be the son and heir not of the biological father, but of the late husband of the widow.[17] This practice is alluded to in three separate instances in the Bible: in the narratives of Genesis 38 and the Book of Ruth where the workings of this practice are depicted, and Deuteronomy which legislates the rules that govern levirate marriage — one of the specific forms this practice takes. The passage reads as follows:

> *If brothers dwell together, and one of them dies childless, the wife of the deceased shall not be married to a stranger; her husband's brother shall go into her, and take her to him to wife, and perform the duty of a husband's brother to her. And it shall be that the first-born [son] that she bears shall succeed to the name of the dead brother, that his name be not blotted out of Israel* [Deut. 25:5–6].[18]

It is vital that Er have heirs; his family line must not be allowed to die out. Onan, a year or so younger than Er, should be around sixteen at this point, possibly only fifteen. He may be a bit young for marriage by the standards of the time, but not overly so; he is certainly capable of "doing his duty by his brother." So Judah gives Onan his marching orders and Tamar moves in with him (or is it the other way around?) Note that Judah does not refer to Tamar by name, only as "your brother's wife." More on this too later.

> *Now Onan knew that the seed would not be his, so whenever he went in to his brother's wife he spilled it* [his semen] *upon the ground, so as not to give seed to his brother. Now what he did was evil in the sight of the Lord, and He slew him also* [Gen. 38:9–10].

Er's childless death has been a windfall for Onan. As one of two surviving sons, he can now look forward to inheriting fully half of Judah's estate. But should he father a son by Tamar, that son would become Er's heir, and Onan's share of the estate will revert to a mere third.[19] This Onan will do his utmost to prevent. We do not know if, at this early period, brothers had the right to refuse their duty to "raise up seed to (dead) brothers."[20] If Onan had no right of refusal, he will prove guilty of betraying his brother and his duty to him. If he had the right to refuse, he will be in addition guilty of hypocrisy — pretending to carry out his duty but secretly sabotaging it.

The means he employs is that whenever he beds Tamar, he withdraws before reaching climax, "wasting" or "spilling" his seed upon the ground.[21] This gives Onan the best of both worlds: he has full and frequent sexual use of Tamar but also prevents her from producing an heir to her late husband. Again we are not told how long this continues, but apparently in short order Onan follows his brother into the grave.

Judah now has a problem. This girl (whom, to his chagrin, he himself had chosen) has now buried two of his sons. Law and custom require him to provide her with his last remaining son, Shelah, to do what Onan had refused to do — provide an heir to Er. But what if this girl is a hex, a husband-burier? She may hasten his youngest son out of this world just as she dispatched his brothers. This Judah determines to prevent. He cannot simply refuse to give Shelah to her; both the law and public opinion will not permit open defiance of clear duty. So Judah takes the road of his late son: hypocritical pretense at compliance and secret sabotage.

> *Then Judah said to Tamar his daughter-in-law: "Remain in widowhood in your father's house until Shelah, my son, grows up;" for he thought*[22]*: "He too might die like his brothers." So Tamar went and lived in her father's house* [Gen. 38:11].

Judah's excuse is that Shelah is too young to marry.[23] Go home and wait, he tells Tamar. Don't call me; I'll call you when he is ready.[24]

Judah's treatment of Tamar is not only unjust but it is brutal. Instead of providing sympathy and support to his young daughter-in-law (who is undoubtedly traumatized by the rapid successive deaths of two husbands), Judah packs her off and washes his hands of her. Given the customs of the time, Tamar has no choice but to comply.

Tamar is now in an unenviable position. She is a widow but not free to remarry. Under the rules of levirate marriage, she is "betrothed" to Shelah and may marry only him.[25] Yet Judah has no intention of ever allowing the union to take place. Judah is leaving her with no options and with no future. He is even refusing to provide support, turning her out of her home and unloading her on her probably less than enthusiastic parents.[26] Judah's behavior can be summed up as self-serving and irresponsible.

The Hooker at the Crossroads

Out of sight, out of mind. How long Tamar remains warehoused in her parents' home we are not told.[27] In the meantime Shelah grows up and nothing happens. A further question: how much time passes before Tamar realizes that she has "been had"? Again we are not told, but as a year or so passes and Shelah reaches the age when Onan had been given to her, and then another year and he has reached the age of Er when he married, the truth of the matter begins to sink in. Judah, of course, appreciates that Tamar will eventually realize that she has been hung out and left to dry, but expects that, after a period of complaining, she will resign herself to her fate. After all, given the status of women in the Canaanite world, what can she do? He has not counted on Tamar.

But then again why should he? It is quite clear that he does not know her. It is significant that not once does he refer to her by name. To him she is always a daughter-in-law, a wife of one of his sons, an appendage tacked on to the family. The arrangements for her marriage to his oldest son, Er, were made with her parents. It is questionable if the immature twelve-to-fourteen-year-old girl was even asked as to her opinion of her prospective bridegroom, or of the family into which she was destined to enter. Girls did what they were told. To Judah, Tamar has always been an object, not a person. And so, never having known her, and having removed her from his presence during the years in which she was metamorphosing from girl into woman, Judah is completely unprepared for what awaits him.

In the meantime Judah has other things to occupy his mind. Even though he has shepherds to manage his flocks the business needs constant oversight. And then once again death strikes in the immediate family circle.

> *In the course of time*[28] *Shua's daughter, the wife of Judah, died; and when Judah was comforted*[29] *he went up to Timnah*[30] *to his sheepshearers, he and his friend Hirah the Adullamite. When Tamar was told: "Behold, your father-in-law is going up to Timnah to shear his sheep," she took off her widow's garments, covered herself with a veil, and perfuming herself*[31] *seated herself invitingly at Enayim, which is by the road to Timnah,*[32] *for she saw that Shelah had grown up but she had not been given to him as wife* [Gen. 38:12–14].

His wife's death and the incumbent period of mourning take Judah out of circulation for a while, but with the end of the mourning period business calls. Judah departs his home in the plains for the highlands where his sheep are being pastured. It is sheep-shearing time, a laborious and labor-intensive undertaking of several days' duration, which demands the involvement and oversight of the owner. The preparations for leaving take a little while, and Tamar learns of her father-in-law's imminent departure. The news stirs her into desperate activity.

Desperate is hardly the word for it. Tamar, as we shall see, is taking her life into her hands. For Tamar proposes to become, if only for a day, a prostitute; and if she is caught in the act, as a married woman, the penalty is death.[33] That this is no momentary impulse is evident. Advance planning and preparation are necessary to carry it off, not least being the ready availability of clothing appropriate to her "profession." It must have taken time to secretly accumulate the necessary garments (and cosmetics?) and to prepare a discreet retreat where she can switch costumes unobserved. Everything about Tamar's actions speaks of long and careful planning.

What impels Tamar to risk her life in so problematic a way? We have just been told: "for she saw that Shelah had grown up but she had not been given to him as wife" (v. 14). She understands fully what is being done to her, and she will not allow herself to be discarded like a worn out sandal if there is anything she can do to prevent it. Her options are terribly limited: there is no one to whom she can appeal; there is no one to whom she can turn for help. Only through her own action can she alter her situation, and then only at appalling risk. She will fulfill her obligation to her late husband, Er, and bear him an heir. She will not permit his family line to die out if she can help it.

As we learn from the Book of Ruth, custom dictated that when the closest relative is for some reason unavailable to marry the widow, then the obligation passes to the next in line. Er's brother, Shelah, being denied her, the next relative in line is none other than her late husband's father, Judah himself. So Tamar single-mindedly sets out to get herself pregnant by Judah.

She has planned carefully. Judah, of course, will never cooperate. In fact he is the very cause of the present impasse. He will have to be tricked and seduced, something impossible to do in his home territory where she would likely be recognized. Only off his home ground, in unfamiliar circumstances, can such a plan have any chance of success. She must get to him when away from his home. His departure to oversee the shearing of his sheep is the chance she has been waiting for.

There is another factor working in Tamar's favor. The death of Judah's wife, (with possibly a preceding illness), and the mourning period that followed have enforced a period of sexual abstinence on him. He is now especially vulnerable to sexual advances.

Tamar acts! Stealing out of her parent's home to her secret retreat, she removes the widow's weeds that have been her garb these last bitter years, and dresses in clothing such as a common prostitute would wear. Then, repairing to the approaches of the town of Enaim, she takes up her position by the crossroads where Judah must pass on his way to Timnah, and assumes the attitude of a roadside prostitute soliciting customers. In due course Judah and his friend Hirah make their appearance.

> *When Judah saw her he thought she was a prostitute, for she had covered her face. So he went over to her at the roadside and said: "Here, please let me come in to you," for he did not know that she was his daughter-in-law* [Gen. 38:15–16a].

No sooner does Judah see her than he gets right down to business (his prolonged abstinence must have made matters very urgent for Judah). No time for preliminary banter: "Look here, I want you!" But despite the urgency Judah remains the gentleman; he does not forget to add "please." The text stresses that he does not recognize her — her face was covered by her veil.[34] But I am not sure that he would have recognized her even without the veil; Tamar is now a grown woman, and with her face appropriately made up for the part (the use of cosmetics was a highly developed art in the Canaanite world), it is doubtful that she looked anything like the nubile girl that is all Judah could have remembered. At any rate, the text insists that he had no idea whom he was addressing. So on to business: the woman being willing, all that remains is to agree on price.

> *She replied*[35]*: "What will you give me that you may come into me?"* [38:16b].

No delicacy here. She feeds his blunt language right back to him, offering to let him propose the price. This creates a problem for Judah. He was not expecting to proposition a prostitute. This is a spur of the moment initiative prompted by what to him seems a chance encounter. He has no cash on him (no one normally carried cash — lumps of silver — it was mainly a barter economy). He has no alternative but to ask for credit. He is on his way to his flocks for the annual spring sheep shearing. He will send someone from there with a baby goat for her.[36]

> *And he said: "I will send you a kid from the flock." And she said:* [Only] *if you give me*[37] *a pledge until you send it." And he said: "What pledge shall I give you?" And she said: "Your signet, your cord and the staff that is in your hand." So he gave them to her and went into her, and she conceived by him. Then she rose and went away; she took off her veil and put on her widow's garments* [Gen. 38:17–19].

The offer of a kid some time in the future leaves her cold; she does not accept promises in return for her services. She is willing, however, to offer secured credit: if he will leave with her an item of value as a deposit, to be held against the delivery of the kid, she will give him credit. Upon his asking what she will accept as a pledge, she demands his signet, his cord and his staff.[38] These were all highly personal items, unique to the individual and of use only to him. But equally to the point, the owner would be seriously inconvenienced without them. Judah would want to get them back, and thus they guaranteed a speedy delivery of the promised kid. Robert Alter has compared them, in modern terms, to a demand that one leave all of one's major credit cards with a prostitute as pledge for cash payment.[39] It is a mark of the urgency felt by Judah that he surrenders them without argument.

The terms mutually agreed, the transaction is consummated. Judah seduced, and with proof of her customer's identity in her hand, Tamar now packs up, removes her disguise, and reappears as the doleful widow dutifully residing with her parents. Though she cannot yet be sure, her encounter has indeed succeeded: she is pregnant.

Payment Deferred

Morning finds Judah at Timnah, fully involved with the shearing of the sheep, yet increasingly uneasy over having surrendered his signet and staff. The sooner he recovers them the better. So despite the pressure of the work on hand, Judah relieves his friend Hirah of his tasks and sends him with a kid to redeem his pledge. Once again no need for delicacy — having been present, Hirah knows exactly what went on and where to find the "woman of easy virtue."

> *Now Judah sent a kid by the hand of his friend the Adullamite to take* [back] *the pledge from the woman, but he could not find her. So he asked the locals*[40]*: "Where is the courtesan,*[41] *she that was by the roadside at Enayim?" And they said: "There has been no courtesan here"* [Gen. 38:20–21].

She isn't there! At first this is not particularly worrisome. She must live somewhere in the vicinity and, as a "professional," will be well known. But inquiries meet a stone wall. The locals insist that there isn't, and never has been, a "courtesan" who frequented the entrance to the town. Perplexed, Hirah returns to Timnah to report.

> *So he returned to Judah and said: "I could not find her; also the locals said: 'There has been no courtesan here.'" Then Judah said: "Let her keep it* [the pledge] *lest we be put to shame. I have sent this kid but you could not find her"* [Gen. 38:22–23].

Judah's reaction is interesting. Valuable as the articles are to him, he is ready to forgo them. Pursuing the matter will only result in publicizing the episode, and branding him as a person who patronizes common street prostitutes. This will hardly do wonders for his reputation. Indeed, he fears that he may become the laughing stock of the region — which is what the Hebrew term we have rendered as *"put to shame"* embodies. "Let it go," Judah counsels, "further inquiries will only result in my becoming the butt of dirty jokes. My conscience is clear. I promised to send payment and I did. It is only her fault if she was not there to receive it." So Judah writes off his signet, cord, and staff, hoping that by maintaining a low profile scandal will be averted. And there, for three months, the matter rests.

But Tamar is pregnant, and it is only a matter of time before the fact becomes evident.

> *About three months later it was told to Judah: "Your daughter-in-law, Tamar has played the harlot; what is more, she is with child by harlotry!" And Judah said: "Bring her out and let her be burned!"* [Gen. 38:24].

It seems that legally, despite living in her parents' home, Tamar is still under the jurisdiction of the father of her late husband. Judah's relations with his daughter-in-law have been cavalier in the extreme. He has refused her Shelah, he has avoided the expense of supporting her; indeed, since he sent her packing he has had (so far as he knows) nothing to do with her. But where *his honor* is concerned (note the phrase *"your daughter-in-law"*), the matter assumes a very different hue. Without even giving her a hearing, he brutally orders her taken out to the city gate and burned.[42] Leaving matters to the very last moment, Tamar sends[43] a message to Judah along with the signet, cord, and staff she has been holding against this very eventuality.

> *When she was brought forth she sent* [word] *to her father-in-law: "I am pregnant by the man to whom these belong. Please, do you recognize*[44] *to whom these belong — the signet, and cord, and the staff?" And Judah recognized* [them] *and he said: "She is more in the right than I, inasmuch*[45] *as I did not give her to Shelah, my son." And he did not lie with her again.*[46] [Gen. 38:25–26].

Judah has finally gotten his pledge back, but the price he now finds he must pay for his fling is far higher, and bitterer, than ever he anticipated. Not only has he to live with the ongoing embarrassment of his patronizing roadside prostitutes becoming common knowledge, but also he is now forced to publicly face his formidable failures of responsibility as a head of family. But deeper and much more traumatic, Judah is being forced to face his role in the "disposal" of Joseph and the fracture of the family. By the careful choice of words in the recounting of the events ("sent" and "Please, do you recognize ... these?") the narrator is tying the threads together, showing us that Judah's behavior in the lowlands is a continuation and direct outgrowth of his previous behavior in the highlands; that his treatment of his brother and his daughter-in-law are all of one piece — when someone becomes inconvenient, you discard him/her like a broken pot. More, the narrator is suggesting that by being forced to face his treatment of Tamar, he is simultaneously being forced to face his treatment of Joseph, and incidentally of his father as well.

Up to now Judah has not been presented to us in a very flattering light. It was he who proposed the sale of his brother into slavery.[47] It is he who then continues the process of breaking up the family by pulling his sheep out of the common herds, moving away and establishing residence in the lowlands among the Canaanites. It is he who first breaks the Abrahamic taboo against marrying Canaanite women, and his treatment of his Canaanite daughter-in-law has been callous in the extreme. What seems to underlie all this reprehensible behavior is an unwillingness to accept responsibility: as a brother, as a family member, as an heir to a sacred tradition and as a father and father-in-law. Here, for the first time, Judah breaks the pattern. Instead of getting defensive, or angry at being publicly put on the spot, he proves big enough to admit that it is he who is in the wrong and it is Tamar who is in the right. In fact, as Leon Kass acutely notes, Judah is the first person in the entire Bible to publicly admit his *own* unrighteousness. He also implies that his callous self-preoccupation is far worse than harlotry.[48]

It was he who had refused Tamar his third son, Shelah; worse, he had selfishly denied to his dead eldest son an heir. Unconventional though her actions were, Tamar had done the right thing. Having been denied the proper surrogate for her dead husband she had simply skipped to the next in the priority list. Denied the brother she had gone on to the father — Judah — and tricked him into "raising up seed" to her late husband. She presented Judah with an example of responsibility taken to an extreme which shames him. His admission does more than vindicate Tamar; it also marks the beginning of the process of maturation and assumption of responsibility that is to end with Judah becoming the moral leader of his brothers. It is Tamar who jump-starts Judah's rehabilitation.

Epilogue: The Fruits of Fortitude

Tamar's courage vindicated, her motives and actions approved by all,[49] the narrative hastens to its consummation.

> *Now when the time came for her to give birth, behold there were twins in her womb. And while she was in labor* [one of them] *thrust forth his hand, and the midwife took it and tied on his hand a scarlet thread, saying: "This came out first." But as he drew back his hand behold his brother came out. And she exclaimed*[50]: *"What a breach you have made for yourself!" Therefore his name was called Perez.*[51] *And afterwards his brother, upon whose hand was the scarlet thread, emerged; his name was called Zerah.* [Gen. 38:27–30].

Perez is a name that should be familiar to readers of the Bible. The Book of Ruth concludes with these words: "Now these are the generations of Perez: Perez was the father of Hezron ... and Salmon was the father of Boaz, and Boaz was the father of Obed; and Obed was the father of Jesse, and Jesse was the father of David." (Ruth 4:18–22). So to put things into the larger picture, just as the Book of Ruth is the prequel to the story of David, what we have been reading in Genesis 38 is really the prequel to the story of Ruth.[52] And now we can understand the blessing in the Book of Ruth that the elders and the people in the gate bestow upon Boaz: "May your house become like the house of Perez, whom Tamar bore to Judah" (Ruth 4:12). For not only was Tamar's legacy to the future her son, founder of the most illustrious clan in the tribe of Judah, it was ultimately King David. Her remarkable story still resonated more than half a millennium later in Ruth's time, and still resonates among us today.

So how can we sum up Tamar? She was a woman of courage and determination. She was a person who had a clear understanding of right and the will to see that right be done, come what may. She would be defeated neither by natural calamities nor the injustice of others. All this yes, and far more — she was an immature Canaanite girl co-opted by marriage into a strange and God-possessed family. She eventually came to take its dark destiny far more seriously than did the members of the family itself. If they proved too preoccupied to take responsibility for the future of the Promise, then she would shoulder the burden that was rightfully theirs, and do what had to be done that the family fulfill its promise. In so doing she not only preserved the future physical existence of the seed of Judah, but by her example she lit an answering fire of responsibility in heart of her wayward father-in-law. Tamar's triumph was as much the making of the character of Judah as it was mothering the line that would bring forth kings.[53]

An Interim Reckoning

The time has come for a review of the road Judah has taken. Up to the debacle of Joseph's betrayal, Judah has not figured significantly in the biblical narrative. Unlike his older brothers, Reuben, Simeon and Levi, and his young sister, Dinah, who have all made their mark with (mostly negative) exploits,[54] Judah has remained a cipher, simply the fourth son of Leah. The first time that Judah pushes himself into the limelight is when he acts to prevent his brothers from committing fratricide. His first recorded attempt at leadership is successful: he persuades his brothers to forgo murder in favor of the lesser crime of selling Joseph into slavery. But his initiative comes to naught. Joseph disappears, leaving the brothers to come to the perhaps understandable conclusion that he has met with death. Judah then has no alternative but to go along with the ghastly charade of presenting Joseph's torn and bloody robe to their father, driving him to distraction. In Judah's eyes he has failed in his attempt to influence his family for the better.

Stained by the guilt of his complicity in the elimination of Joseph, and revolted by the cover-up that followed, Judah turns his back on his fratricidal brothers and his dysfunctional father who is trapped in an endless orgy of mourning for his favorite son. But, as Kass points out, in washing his hands of his family, he himself is symbolically committing fratricide (and patricide as well). He has "eliminated" them from his horizon. His "going down" from the Highlands to the plains of Adullam is not only a physical descent but a moral decline as well.[55]

In the plains, having put his family behind him, he makes friends and starts a family. But one's past is not so easily left behind. His refusal to be his brothers' keeper returns to haunt him in the person of his own children. The sin of Onan — his refusal to be his brother Er's keeper — is ratified by Judah when he refuses to give Shelah to Tamar. The evasion of responsibility has become a family trait spanning the generations. Judah's treatment of his daughter-in-law is just a manifestation of his entire attitude to life.

There is one gleam of promise during the close to twenty years in which Judah has cut himself off from his family,[56] and it would be wrong of us to overlook it. Judah makes friends, or at least one friend: Hirah the Adullamite. This seems a small thing, but in the context of the Bible it is not. We are never told of Joseph making a friend; indeed, in my reading of the text, he was incapable of making them. In any case, friendships are rare in the Bible. In the entire Book of Genesis there is only one other friendship on record.[57] Moreover the use of the term with regard to Hirah is repeated twice for emphasis. The ability to make close friends, especially among persons of different backgrounds than oneself, and to keep them long-term, bespeaks an outgoing and empathetic personality. Perhaps the author is here hinting that there is more to Judah than has so far been made manifest.

During his long stay on the plains, unbeknownst to himself, Judah has been recapitulating in his own life some of the most traumatic experiences in the life of his father, Jacob. As his father lost his wife Rachel, so Judah loses his wife. As his father has "lost" two sons (Joseph and Judah) so does Judah lose two sons. And as Jacob favored his son Joseph over all his brothers (and in the future will favor his youngest, Benjamin, over all the others), so will Judah repeat the pattern: favoring his youngest, Shelah, over the memory and progeny of his eldest, Er. One can argue that these successive traumas prepare Judah, once the breakthrough has taken place, to be able to empathize with his father, and to make reconciliation between them possible.

It is Tamar who forces Judah to confront his "patricide" and "fratricide" — his act of disavowal of father and brothers. With the words *haker na*, "Please, do you recognize," Judah finds himself back at the terrible moment from which he has turned away and tried to shut out of memory. He is once again among his brothers presenting the torn and bloody robe to their father with the cynical words, *haker na*, "Please, do you recognize [this]? Is this your son's robe or is it not?" And in this moment of truth, he is forced to face not only his sin against his brother and his father, but admit to himself his sins against his son Er and against his daughter-in-law Tamar. With his public confession of his wrong, "She is more in the right than I," Judah is commencing the process of reassumption of all the responsibilities discarded over the past twenty years.

When the story returns to Judah, we will find him reconciled with his father and brothers. With him are Tamar and his two grandsons,[58] whom he has adopted as his own, replacements for his lost sons Er and Onan.[59] He has emerged the prime support of his father and his is the most persuasive voice in family councils. He is well on his way to becoming the true keeper of his brothers.

Having recorded the beginning of the rehabilitation of Judah, our author now turns the clock back twenty years to follow up on the fate of that precocious seventeen-year-old, Joseph.

Notes

1. The dominant assumption was that the editor (or possibly the final redactor) of the Joseph narrative had inherited an independent narrative tradition relating to the "patriarch" Judah, and loathe to leave it out but not knowing what to do with it, arbitrarily inserted here for want of a better place (Victor P. Hamilton, *The Book of Genesis: Chapters 18–50* [Grand Rapids: Eerdmans, 1995], 431; Gerhard von Rad, *Genesis*, trans. D. M. G. Stalker [Philadelphia: Westminster, 1972], 356–357; E. A. Speiser, *Genesis* [Garden City, NY: Doubleday, 1985], 299–300; Claus Westermann, *Genesis: A Practical Commentary*, trans. David E. Green [Grand Rapids: Eerdmans, 1987], 268; etc.).

2. For centuries commentators on this chapter have stressed the impossibility of packing all its happenings into the tight time frame of twenty-two years. Some would go so far as to say that even forty years might be too little. But what has been obvious to medieval and modern scholars should have been equally obvious to the author (unless we assume that he never made it past second grade arithmetic). We shall attempt to indirectly address the issue of the timing of the sequence of events in our treatment of the text. For a more detailed analysis of the chronological problems posed by the relationship between this chapter and the larger Joseph saga of which it is a part, see Appendix 2: "Can Judah and Tamar Be Fitted into the Joseph Narrative?"

3. His groundbreaking treatment first saw the light of day in his article, "A Literary Approach to the Bible," *Commentary* 60, no. 6 (1975): 76.

4. This linguistic unity is demonstrated by the use of key terms that connect chapters 37 and 39. For example, various constructions of the root *yrd* (to go down): chapter 37 ends with Jacob wailing, "No, I will *go down* to Sheol to my son, mourning" (v. 35); chapter 38 begins by informing us that Judah *went down* from his brothers; while chapter 39 continues the theme with the words, now Joseph had been *taken down* to Egypt (v. 1). These repeated usages establish all three chapters as part of a larger narrative. See also note 13 below.

5. The fact that their hands were not directly involved in the implementation of their intention to either murder him or sell him into slavery proves of little help to their guilty consciences. They "set him up," and therefore rightly feel morally responsible for whatever occurred to him.

6. Sacks, 309; Kass, 519–520. They both take the phrase, "So his brothers were violently jealous of him, and his father took the thing to heart" (Gen. 37:11), to mean that Jacob had become aware of the true fury the brothers felt toward Joseph, and it was this that motivated his sending his favorite son to cope on his own with his brothers outside the home and immediate vicinity where he could protect him. More, relying on the similarity of language to that connected with the Akedah (the binding of Isaac, Genesis 22), they posit that Jacob was fully aware that he could be "sacrificing" his son, sending him to his death (see chapter 1, page 46).

7. A man native to Adullam, a Canaanite walled city in the lowlands about thirteen miles southwest of Bethlehem and twelve miles northwest of Hebron.

8. Reading with LXX, MT reads "he."

9. Probably identical with the town of Achzib, another lowland town, southwest of Adullam, mentioned in Joshua 15:44 and Micah 1:14.

10. This chapter, Genesis 38, is in many ways very like the Book of Ruth. Like Ruth, it is a self-contained unit not directly dependent on that which precedes it, nor overtly connected to that which follows it. It stands alone; and like Ruth, it has a prologue, a central portion, and a concluding epilogue. It seems likely, due to the large number of similarities in theme and organization, that one of these two served as the inspiration and model for the other.

11. It further implies that the events in our chapter take place during the twenty-two years during which Joseph is working his way up from household slave to Viceroy of Egypt, before the events that will once again unite the family.

12. Genesis 37:14.

13. Hebron is over 3,000 feet above sea level while Adullam is about 1,000 feet. So on the simplest level, the phrase "went down" in the current chapter reflects a descent of about 2,000 feet from the heights of Hebron to the plains of Adullam. But on a deeper level the verb *yarad* (to go down) reminds us of the wild grief of the aged Jacob who refuses to be consoled for the (supposed) death of his son Joseph. The previous chapter concluded with his wail: "No, I will go down (*ayred*) to Sheol to my son, mourning" (Gen. 37:35). But of course Joseph is not dead. The coming chapter will begin with the words: "Now Joseph was taken down (*hurad*) to Egypt..." (39:1). These three versions of the same verb, much more obvious in the Hebrew than in translation, is one expression of the ongoing and deeply ironic way the text treats the discrepancies between the reality of our actions, the way we perceive them and their unsuspected outcomes.

2. Rehabilitation

14. "Swear by the Lord, the God of the heavens and the God of the earth, that you will not take a wife for my son from the daughters of the Canaanites among whom I dwell, but will go to the land of my birth and get a wife for my son Isaac" (24:3–4).

15. "He commanded him [Jacob] saying: 'You shall not take a wife from among the daughters of Canaan. Arise, go to Paddan-aram, to the house of Bethuel, your mother's father, and there take a wife from among the daughters of Laban, your mother's brother'" (28:1–2)

16. Umberto Cassuto feels that "in view of the phrasing of the text ... in the opinion of the author of our chapter Er died immediately after his marriage, in the very same year, and that Onan married his sister-in-law Tamar also in that year" (Umberto Cassuto, "The Story of Tamar and Judah," in *Biblical and Oriental Studies*, vol. 1., trans. Israel Abrahams [Jerusalem: Magnus, 1975], 39–40). We are also not told in what way he was evil (it is irrelevant to the story). There may have been nothing at all. Inasmuch as in those days it was assumed that any sudden or untimely death must be God's doing, since God killed him He must have had good reasons for doing so. In other words, this may be no more than a conventional cliché.

17. The philosophical reasoning behind this complex of custom and law can be described as follows: "The heart of marriage, especially but not only biblically speaking, is not primarily a matter of the heart; rather it is primarily about procreation and, even more, about the transmission of a way of life. Husband and wife, whether they know it or not, are incipiently father and mother, parents of children for whose moral and spiritual education they bear a sacred obligation — to ancestors, to community, to God ... Precisely because of their communal commitment to righteousness, they must not ... cease to be their brother's keepers.... In levirate marriage, all these central principles are defended. A man serves literally as his brother's keeper: he refuses to let his brother die without a trace.... Taking seriously the commandment 'Be fruitful and multiply,' levirate marriage elevates the importance of progeny above personal gratification, and hence, the importance of lineage and community above the individual. In accepting the duty a man simultaneously shows reverence for his ancestors, respect for the meaning and purpose of marriage, and devotion to the future of his family and his people" (Kass, 530–531).

18. It is also important to understand that there are significant differences between the case in which there are surviving brothers and the case where there are none. When a brother survives the deceased, we are dealing with a case of levirate marriage. The term "levirate marriage" comes from the Latin word for a husband's brother, *levir*: thus "husband's brother marriage" in plain English. The legislation in Deuteronomy 25 deals with this case alone. Here the widow is not free to marry whom she wills. She *must* marry her brother-in-law. Relations with any other man are treated as adultery. Only if the brother-in-law refuses to marry her — in which case he is forced to undergo a public humiliation ceremony in which his sister-in-law spits in his face, removes his shoe, and publicly reviles him (25:7–10) — is she released from obligation to the family and freed to remarry. In the case where there are no surviving brothers, the widow is bound by no restrictions. Similarly the social stigma cast upon a more distant relation who declines to marry the widow is correspondingly lessened.

19. When we speak of Judah's estate we refer to his moveable property, and especially the herds.

20. They had this right at a later period, albeit at the price of public humiliation (see note 18 above). There is much that we don't know about law and its development in Israel and the Ancient Near East; "the simple fact [is] that the ancients mainly used law ... without chattering their heads off about it all the time" (Kitchen, *Reliability*, 496).

21. This practice, called *coitus interruptus*, was a primitive form of birth control.

22. Literally, "for he said" [to himself]. This is another of the very few instances in the Bible where we are explicitly informed as to a person's motives, rather than leaving us to guess at them (note the case of Reuben's motives for saving Joseph in Genesis 37:21–22). All ambiguity has been banished. We are not being permitted to give Judah the benefit of the doubt, but are being forced to condemn the hurtful and unjust nature of his actions.

23. Shelah may be only fourteen at this junction; he may even be younger than Tamar. As such Judah's claim is credible.

24. "Understandably, Judah seeks to preserve his own son, his youngest and last. Not without cause, he very likely fears a curse on his sons through Tamar, and he attempts to escape it. But we notice that in doing so he is willing to sacrifice not only the rightful claims of his daughter-in-law, whom he further humiliates by keeping her, a twice-married woman, confined to her father's house. He is also willing to ignore the duties that are owed to another son. To save one son, Shelah, he is willing to allow Er to disappear without a trace.... More generally, he is willing to neglect future generations in favor of the present one: he neglects the claims of lineage and future community needs for the sake of the love he feels for his youngest son" (Kass, 529).

25. Shelah, of course, is under no such restriction. Given that polygamy was accepted practice in the Ancient Near East, despite his legal tie to Tamar, Shelah could marry any other woman of his choice.

26. For some reason or other most commentators seem to be blind to Judah's repudiation of financial responsibility for his bereaved daughter-in-law.

27. See note 28 below.

28. Literally, "Now the days multiplied"; a vague and indeterminate expression that can mean anything from a year or two to as much as twenty years (1 Samuel 7:2).

29. That is, when the period of mourning was over.

30. This is not the Timnah in Philistia made famous by Samson, but the location in the highlands, southeast of Hebron, mentioned in Joshua 15:57.

31. Adopting the rendering of Dahood, who bases himself on Ugaritic and Arabic cognates (M. J. Dahood, "Northwest Semitic Notes on Genesis," *Biblica* 55 (1974): 80).

32. Understanding the phrase *bepetah enayim* to be a *double entendre* (*enayim* meaning both a place name, "Enayim," and "eyes"). Thus the phrase can mean both the spot where she waited for Judah, the "opening" or entrance to Enayim, and also the attitude of open sexual invitation that she adopted, as an "eye-opener" (Ira Robinson, "*Bepetah Enayim* in Genesis 38:14," *Journal of Biblical Literature* 96 (1977): 569)

33. Technically, as "betrothed" to Shelah, Tamar's condition is that of a married woman; sexual relations with any but Shelah would fall into the category of adultery, which was a capital offense.

34. From everything we know, women were normally *un*veiled in those days. Tamar veils herself specifically so as not to be recognized.

35. Literally, "she said."

36. Judah's flocks, as was common then, consisted of goats as well as sheep. A kid was probably an overpayment, but Judah was in no mood to bargain. Besides, he is asking for immediate services on credit.

37. Reading with LXX and Syr. (see Glossary); MT omits *me*.

38. The signet, probably a cylinder seal, was a small tubular object made of metal or semiprecious stone and engraved on its outside surface with a unique design so that when rolled over soft clay it would leave an impression that was recognized as the owner's signature in all matters legal. It was usually worn around the neck by means of a cord passed through its hollow interior. The cord itself might have also been distinctive, woven in an unusual pattern of colored threads. The staff was probably carved with an original identifying design and may have been embossed with the name of the owner as well. Taken together these items not only identified the bearer but also proclaimed his status. Only a person of status would have such objects. Only a person of substance would be willing to temporarily part with them, certain of being able to immediately redeem them. Despite overpaying, a kid was small change for Judah.

39. Alter, "A Literary Approach to the Bible," 76.

40. Literally, "the men of the place" (LXX and Syr.); MT reads "the men of her place."

41. The Hebrew term *k'deshah* (literally, "holy woman") usually referred in biblical times to a woman who, as a devotee of one of the pagan fertility cults that flourished in the Ancient Near East, would offer herself to partakers of these religious rites. This term is often rendered as "cult prostitute." Jeffrey Tigay and Victor Hamilton point out, however, that in all the Ancient Near East there have been found no examples of "outreach" — that is, "cult prostitutes" ever operating outside temples and religious shrines, and certainly not at roadsides. Taken in conjunction with the fact that the term *k'deshah* is only used in conversation between Hirah and the locals, pagans all, and in Hirah's report to Judah in which he quotes the townspeople, whereas the narrator refers to her as a common professional, a "hooker," or as "the woman," after quoting numerous studies Tigay and Hamilton conclude that, out of deference to the sensibilities of the locals, Hirah used a more "refined" term when in conversation with them rather than employ crude language. I have therefore chosen to render the term by the equally *genteel*, semirespectable (and archaic) designation of "courtesan" (from the Italian *courtigiane* or "female courtiers") (Jeffrey Tigay, *Deuteronomy*, JPS Torah Commentary [Philadelphia: Jewish Publication Society, 1996], 387, note 65; Hamilton, 454–455).

42. Under biblical law (see Leviticus 20:10; Deuteronomy 22:21) the penalty for adultery (which is the offense under consideration) is stoning to death. Was Judah proceeding under Canaanite law, ordering her to be burnt alive, or was he sending her to be stoned to death, and then her corpse to be burnt?

43. Note the word *send*. This has been a key term in this chapter. Judah promised to *send* the "woman" a kid from the flock; Tamar demands a pledge till he will *send* it. Judah *sends* the kid by the hand of Hirah, and when the "woman" can't be found he clears his conscience with the declaration that he fulfilled his obligation and *sent* the kid. Everything is third-hand, by indirection. But responsibility and reality can be kept at arm's length only so long. Now, comes payoff time, Tamar *sends* to Judah the items that publicly proclaim both his responsibility and his disgrace. The word also rings another bell: "And they *sent* the robe

of many colors and brought it to their father" (Gen. 37:32, emphasis added). It is payback time in more ways than one. As Judah had repudiated all responsibility for his brother's fate, *sending* his torn and bloody robe to shock his father, so does Tamar *send* his staff, seal, and cord back to him to demonstrate to him and to the world where responsibility lies.

44. *Haker-na*, the very words Judah and his brothers had used to their father when they presented him with Joseph's torn and bloody robe of many colors, pretending that they had just found it and were uncertain to whom it belonged.

45. Implied is the clause: (she did this thing) "inasmuch as...."

46. Literally, "and he knew her again no more." As in English, the Hebrew term "to know" has several meanings. Here the context clearly requires the sense of sexual intercourse, which is why we have rendered the phrase as "and he did not lie with her again." But there are several ways this idea can be rendered in Hebrew, and since the author chooses to use the verb "to know" several scholars are of the opinion that beyond the surface meaning the author is hinting to the reader several additional thoughts: "The statement ... may have more than a legal, historical referent. Throughout most of the narrative Judah has not really known Tamar. She is a brother's wife (v. 8), a daughter-in-law (v. 11), a widow (v. 11), a prostitute (v. 15), and a woman (v. 20). Most conspicuously he did not 'know' Tamar as Tamar when he thought he was consorting with a prostitute" (Hamilton, 451). Which raises the question: as he never knew Tamar, did he ever really know Joseph? Menn suggests: "Although this phrase refers primarily to the fact that Judah never again had sexual relations with his daughter-in-law, the wording seems especially appropriate given that the reader of the narrative too knows too little about Tamar following her reprieve" (Esther M. Menn, *Judah and Tamar (Genesis 38) in Ancient Jewish Exegesis: Studies in Literary Form and Hermeneutics* [New York: Brill, 1997], 33). But "knowing" aside, from a practical point of view, why does Judah abstain from further relations with Tamar? Esther Menn does not think that moral squeamishness adequately explains Judah's restraint. She continues: "The narrator's final note concerning Judah, that 'He never knew her again' (Gen. 38:26), conveys more than a concern with the morality of the patriarch. It also expresses Judah's continuing wariness of the woman he suspects in his son's deaths and his resolve to distance himself from the dangers of her embrace" (ibid., 47).

47. The text is pointedly ambiguous as to whether his motive was to save Joseph's life — slavery being the lesser of the evils when compared to brutal murder — or cupidity, the desire to turn a dirty dollar.

48. Kass, 536.

49. In retrospect it is now evident that Tamar is not a prostitute but acted solely on principle. Her refusal to accept payment underlines this fact.

50. Literally, "said."

51. Perez means "breach."

52. This position, including the relationship between Ruth and Genesis 38, is more fully developed in my *Four Biblical Heroines*, 66–67, 87–89.

53. And ultimately, according to Isaiah, the Messiah.

54. See Genesis 30:14; 34:1–31; 35:22.

55. Kass, 528.

56. See Appendix 2: "Can Judah and Tamar Be Fitted into the Joseph Narrative?" for a clarification of the temporal parameters of Genesis 38.

57. King Abimelech of Gerar is recorded as having a friend, one Ahuzzath (Gen. 26:26). And even this instance is ambiguous, for in those times there was an official court position, one of the highest offices in the Royal administration, with the title of "The Friend of the King." So Ahuzzath may not have been a friend in our sense of the term, but simply a royal counselor or adviser. As this is the probable meaning in 26:26, then Judah's friendship with Hirah is unique in Genesis, and indeed in the entire Pentateuch.

58. Legally they are the sons and heirs of Er.

59. As such they are listed in Genesis 46:12.

3

The Slave

Be still, be still, my soul; it is but for a season:
Let us endure an hour and see injustice done.
— A. E. Houseman, *A Shropshire Lad, XLIII*

Now Joseph had been taken down to Egypt and an Egyptian man bought him from the hand of the Ishmaelites who had taken him down there, [namely] Potiphar, the Head of Security,[1] a high official[2] of Pharaoh. Now the Lord[3] was with Joseph and he became successful[4] in the house of his Egyptian master.[5] And his master saw that the Lord was with him, and that the Lord caused all that he did to succeed in his hands. So Joseph found favor in his eyes, and [he made him] his personal servant[6]; he put him in charge of his house,[7] and all that he possessed he gave over into his hands. Now it came to pass from the time that he put him in charge of his house and all that he possessed that the Lord blessed the Egyptian's house because of Joseph, so that the blessing of the Lord was upon everything that was his, in the house and in the field. So he left everything that he possessed in Joseph's hands[8]; and with him there, he paid attention to nothing but the food[9] that he ate. Now Joseph had a beautiful body and was strikingly handsome[10] [Gen. 39:1-6].

After reconnecting us to Joseph, and reminding us of the situation when he paused in his story, the narrator proceeds to recount an amazing success story. First the luck of the marketplace: Joseph is purchased by a high government official. Instead of being put to the harsh and brutalizing work of a field hand, he is assigned to house duty. Then, through diligence and success in the tasks assigned, he is promoted, and then promoted again, until he becomes the Steward — in modern parlance, the Chief Executive Officer — of the entire estate.[11] The narrative moves so swiftly and so smoothly that we may fail to grasp the implications of these stages. Let us examine the path of Joseph's ascent in detail.

In the first place was it pure luck that Joseph's purchaser was Potiphar? What was it about Joseph that impelled one such as Potiphar to purchase an unskilled foreign slave, who could neither speak nor understand the Egyptian language, and designate him a house slave, a position that would require a serious investment in training? It is unlikely that prospective purchasers could make any realistic assessment of the native abilities of merchandise exhibited in a slave market except in the case of the resale of local slaves for whom there existed a track record. From among the dispirited rabble of recently enslaved Asiatics, what was it that made Joseph catch Potiphar's eye? Here we need to move along to the end of the account of Joseph's meteoric rise — to the seemingly extraneous aside: "Now Joseph had a beautiful body and was strikingly handsome" (Gen. 39:6). The translation hardly does justice to the force of the comment in the original Hebrew. In our terms the remark presents this young Asiatic as stunningly handsome in both face and form, a fit model for a classic Greek statue! He stood out as a thoroughbred stallion stands out among nags. It is reasonable to assume that it was this remarkable physical beauty that catches Potiphar's eye, and leads him to buy Joseph and assign him to house duty solely for his ornamental qualities.

The next stage is in Joseph's hands. Here attitude becomes crucial. Can he quickly get over the shock of familial rejection, kidnapping, enslavement and culture shock? After all, thrown into an alien environment, he cannot even comprehend commands, much less communicate on any serious level. Nothing in his previous life had prepared Joseph for this crisis. But amazingly the spoiled brat rises to the occasion. We are not told, but evidently he must have taken hold of himself, exhibited a positive attitude and proved a quick study. He learns the language and the duties required of him, and performs them with diligence. We can even postulate a high level of initiative; otherwise subsequent promotions become difficult to explain.

The first promotion seems to have been from general house slave to the position of Potiphar's personal servant, which would involve the duties of a valet and possibly over time expand to include some of the functions of a butler, such as the supervision of some of the household duties. Success in these tasks would have led to the next stage: preparation to take over the running of the entire household and, eventually, the entire estate.

It is necessary that we examine the implications of Joseph's promotion to Steward of the estate. We know something about Egyptian estate management. Managers had to be literate, capable of composing written reports and carrying on business correspondence. They had to have accountancy skills; estates were complex businesses that were expected to show a profit. They had to be good managers: they had large and diverse staffs under them. As their offices were situated in the Manor House, they were in constant contact with the owner's family and had to have the appropriate manners to associate with the nobility without giving offense. There were schools that specialized in the teaching of accountancy and administration for future administrators. Joseph must have been sent for this training, which included the reading and writing of complex hieroglyphics. These skills, as well as the social skills and practical experience necessary to the job, must have taken years to master. Much time, effort and money were needed to fit Joseph for his new responsibilities. Potiphar must have judged Joseph's potential very high to make such a large investment in him. He never regretted it.

Joseph proves to be a superlative estate manager. He is an instant success. Under his management things go like a charm. The profits begin to mount. Above all, Joseph proves extremely responsible. Potiphar delegates his authority and discovers that he does not need to supervise Joseph. He can safely leave everything in his hands, and so he does. Now free to focus on his governmental responsibilities, his only contact with the estate, we are informed — besides presumably semiannual or quarterly profit and loss statements — is the daily meal he takes on his estate. With Joseph as his steward, Potiphar has arrived at a situation of which most wealthy slave owners could only dream.

Before we proceed with our tale, it would be well to pause and note what the narrator claims to be the secret of Joseph's good fortune. No less than five times in the course of only four verses he insists that it is the Lord who is the author of Joseph's success. The section commences with the narrator informing us that the Lord (that is, the God of Joseph's fathers Abraham, Isaac and Jacob/Israel)[12] was with him (Gen. 39:2) and caused everything that he undertook to succeed (v. 3). The narrator then proceeds to inform us that as soon as Joseph was put in charge of Potiphar's estate the Lord blessed the entire estate because of Joseph (v. 5). More: the narrator claims that Potiphar was well aware that the lad's success was propelled by divine favor:

> *And his master saw that the Lord was with him, and that the Lord caused all that he did to succeed in his hands*[13] [Gen. 39:3].

If the repetition seems excessive, it is a measure of the strength of the narrator's insistence that this success story has its roots neither in good luck nor in natural talent, but stems solely from the direct intervention of "the Lord." What makes this insistence all the more remarkable is the fact that in the entire Joseph narrative, only in this chapter is God referred to by His personal name, traditionally rendered as *the Lord*.[14] It is only the narrator who uses this designation; all the parties to the drama, here and elsewhere, use exclusively the more general designation *elohim*.[15] The unusual intrusion of God's personal name in this chapter, as well as the narrator's insistence that it is He who is responsible for Joseph's spectacular success, are points that we will return to in our analysis of the Joseph narrative.

The Honey Pot

As Newton has taught us, though in a different context, every action produces an opposing reaction. This is true not only in physics but in the realm of human affairs as well, and Joseph's spectacular success is to have its effects. The very elements that have propelled him to success — his striking beauty and the suave daily performance of his duties in the Manor House — are to prove his undoing. Beauty and propinquity do their work: the mistress of the Manor, Potiphar's wife, becomes hopelessly enamored of him.

This is no sudden passion. Years have passed.[16] The enormous gulf between mistress and slave, between aristocratic Egyptian and despised Asiatic, prove insufficient to withstand the daily presence of this ravishing "demigod." We can picture to ourselves the vain struggle of this proud Egyptian noblewoman (strangely unnamed — to the end she remains simply "Potiphar's wife")[17] against the lure of a sordid affair with this contemptible Hebrew slave. It takes years for passion to chip away layer after layer of racial and aristocratic pride, and bring her to the point of first yearning for, then trying ever more openly to seduce, and finally to abandon all pride and openly solicit Joseph.

> *And now it came to pass after these things*[18] *that his master's wife lifted up her eyes* [longingly][19] *to Joseph and said, "Lie with me!" But he refused and said to his master's wife, "Look here,*[20] *as long as I am here my master gives no thought*[21] *to anything he has in his house*[22]*; he has put everything that he has into my hands.*[23] *He is not greater in this house than I, and he has withheld nothing from me except you, because you are his wife. How then can I do this great evil and sin against God?" And it came to pass,* [although] *she spoke to Joseph day after day to lie by her, to be with her,*[24] *he would not listen to her* [Gen. 39: 7–10].

Twice the narrator refers to her as "his master's wife;" and Joseph himself refers to her as the wife of his master. On the face of it there is total asymmetry in their positions: she is the master and he is the slave. She herself emphasizes this fact: her solicitation of Joseph takes the form of a peremptory command, "Lie with me!" Yet, as Sarna notes, there is a terrible irony in this situation: "She, the mistress of the house, is a slave to her lust for her husband's slave."[25]

Joseph's position is unenviable. To reject her demand to become her lover would be, at the very least, to make an enemy of the mistress of the house. To accede would put him into deadly danger. To be caught bedding his master's wife would be death.[26] Did Joseph see this coming? He probably did. Before she could bring herself to stoop to propositioning him, the woman must have tried to tempt him into making the first overtures. I have no difficulty in postulating months of "chance meetings," glances and hints, all of which Joseph pretended not to notice. But now he is confronted with the unavoidable. He turns her down flat. He gives his reasons: his master has entrusted everything to him, how can he betray his trust? Further, he cannot violate his master's proprietary rights over his wife, and thus affront his dignity. And lastly, there is the moral dimension: in the pagan world adultery was "The Great Sin."[27] He cannot bring himself to commit so grievous a transgression against the gods.[28]

Potiphar's wife does not take no for an answer. She keeps after him day after day, hoping to wear him down. But Joseph resolutely refuses to listen to her. It would seem that Joseph has matured. The traumas that he has undergone, the challenges he has overcome in making a success of himself in Egypt have forged in him a new moral fiber. He has found within himself the strength to overcome the twin temptations of sex and ambition (for we must never forget that binding his master's wife to him sexually could be a potent help in advancing his career). The narcissistic spoiled brat of Canaan is a thing of the past.

And yet, perhaps not so. There is another way to read this narrative — a narrative that, as we have already seen, is conspicuous for its ambivalence. Maurice Samuel focuses on the way Joseph phrases his rejection of the woman's overtures.[29] Is it really necessary to stress how important he is, as important as her husband ("He is not greater in this house than I")? Does his rejection require him to point out that if he indeed were to have an affair with her he could get away with it ("My master gives no thought to anything he has in his house")? And even the high moral-religious ground on which he concludes ("How then can I do this great evil and sin against God?") is ambivalent on two counts. On the surface it sounds like a rhetorical question, and so it is usually taken. But does Joseph have to phrase this as a question? He could just as easily state this as a definitive remark: "I cannot do this great evil and sin against God!" Phrasing it as a question leaves open in the mind of the listener the possibility that Joseph is asking a factual question: How can I be sure that I can get away with this great sin? To the woman's terse order (two words in the original Hebrew), Joseph, instead of replying with equal terseness and then breaking off the encounter, replies with a speech, long and rambling by comparison (35 words in the Hebrew), and rife with ambiguous phrasing. And due to this phrasing, it becomes possible for Potiphar's wife to understand in his refusal that Joseph is simply playing hard to get. It all depends on the tone in which Joseph answered her, something of which we have no way of judging. All we can say is that the woman does not take Joseph's response as final. In this reading Joseph, perfectly aware of his effect upon her, that she "has fallen for him," is playing with her and leading her on.

We have said that Joseph's final remark is ambiguous on two counts. The second count is his reference to God. Five times the narrator has insisted that *the Lord* is the cause of Joseph's success story,[30] yet Joseph never refers to Him. The first time Joseph is recorded as referring to the deity he uses the term *elohim*. As we have previously noted, the term is ambiguous.[31] On the assumption that Joseph is indeed referring to the Lord, God of Israel, we have rendered here *elohim* as "God." But the possibility remains that what Joseph is referring to is "the gods," the realm of the divine as understood by the pagans. After all, he is addressing an Egyptian who would thus understand the term. In this case Joseph would be referring to the concept of "the fear of God/the gods," a well-nigh universal belief in the Ancient Near East that there are minimum moral standards, sanctioned by the gods, incumbent upon all human beings. If this be the case, then Joseph's remark could be paraphrased: "How then can I do this great evil and offend against common decency?"[32]

Kass raises an even more disquieting possibility:

> We will still see several occasions in which Joseph talks about God, but in which we suspect he is really referring only to himself. It is therefore entirely possible that Joseph acts here not as an innocent who lives by piety and moral principle, but as a charismatic fellow who enjoys exploiting his good looks, exercising his powers, and attracting others while displaying his own aloofness.[33]

We will keep these alternative possibilities in mind as we proceed.

The Trap Snaps Shut

> *Now it came to pass on one such day that he came into the house to do his work, and none of the household*[34] *were there in the house. She seized him by his garment, saying, "Lie with me!" But he fled, leaving his garment in her hand, and bolted out of the house.*[35] *Now it came to pass, when she saw that he had left his garment in her hand and fled the house she summoned the men of her household and said to them, (saying): "See, he has brought us a Hebrew to insult us!*[36] *[He] came to lie with me and I screamed.*[37] *Now it came to pass, when he heard me raising my voice and screaming that he left his garment with me and bolted, and fled the house.*[38] *And she laid aside his garment by her until his master returned to the house* [Gen. 39:11–16].

The game has been going on for some time, a game of cat and mouse: she soliciting him and he refusing to respond. But which is the cat and which is the mouse? Either way the pressure builds remorselessly. It is only a matter of time before someone breaks. It proves to be the woman. Coming one day to his office (which is located, as the offices of all estate managers are, in the Manor House), Joseph finds the place deserted. Whether this was a fortuitous circumstance of which she took advantage, or whether she had engineered it, we are not told. Confronting him she forces the issue, seizing his garment she reiterates her demand.

Of what sort of garment are we speaking? Egyptian men of the period wore short linen kilts that reached to somewhat above the knees.[39] These kilts were simply a short length of cloth wound around the hips and tucked into a belt.[40] Thus the effect of seizing Joseph's kilt would probably have been to render him naked. Certainly when he panicked and bolted he fled naked, his kilt remaining clutched in her hand.[41]

Congreve's lines epitomize the situation we now confront:

> *Heav'n has no rage, like love to hatred turn'd,*
> *Nor Hell a fury, like a woman scorn'd.*[42]

This last rejection was one too many; it unleashes a storm. Come what may she will be revenged. Presenting Joseph's kilt, easily recognizable, as proof, she summons her Egyptian staff and accuses Joseph of attempted rape. She is an intelligent woman and her little speech is very clever. Look what our master has done to us, Egyptians all, by bringing this despised Hebrew among us; it is an insult to all of us Egyptians. Look what he tried to do to me. He tried to rape me but I screamed and, coward that he is, he panicked and fled. Here is his kilt, proof that I am not making this up. Then, having mobilized the staff to belief in her version, she awaits the return of her husband. To him her tale is slightly different.

> *So she told him a similar story,*[43] *saying: "The Hebrew slave that you brought to us came to me to insult me.*[44] *And it came to pass, when I screamed,*[45] *that he bolted out of the house, leaving his garment [behind] with me." Now it came to pass, when his master heard his wife's words that she told him, saying, "These are the kind of things your slave did to me," he became furious* [Gen. 39:17–19].

The focus has shifted. It's all Potiphar's fault. If he hadn't bought and brought that nasty Hebrew in the first place, none of this would have happened.

So Joseph's master took him and put him in prison, the place where the king's prisoners were held.[46] *And it came to pass that, as he was in prison, the Lord was with Joseph and was gracious to him,*[47] *and gave him favor in the eyes of the Chief Warder of the prison* [Gen. 39:20–21].

Something strange is going on here. Four times within one verse the same root (*shr*) is repeated: twice in the form of the noun "prison," once as the noun "prisoners" and once as the verb "imprisoned" (held). Then, in the next verse, it is repeated a fifth time: "prison." The author is making a point, emphasizing that Joseph was thrown into prison. We would have expected execution as the appropriate punishment for the attempted rape of an Egyptian noblewoman. True, unlike her harangue to the servants, in her complaint to her husband she does not explicitly charge Joseph with attempted rape. But if he came to "insult" her, and he left his clothing behind when he fled, at the very least he is being charged with indecent exposure. Indecent exposure by a slave before a married noblewoman would equally be punishable by death. Why does Joseph get off so lightly?

We have been told that upon hearing his wife's story Potiphar is furious, but with whom? Knowing the two principals in the matter, and perhaps not being totally oblivious to what had been going on, does Potiphar see through the frame-up? The injustice of the matter aside, Potiphar is being placed in an impossible position. On the one hand he has no choice but to save face by backing his wife. On the other hand he is being faced with sacrificing an extremely valuable estate manager and forfeiting the large investment he has made in his training. No wonder he is furious. As I see it, Potiphar compromises: he can't leave Joseph on the estate. Appearances must be preserved. But he is in charge of the state prisons. He can confine whom he will. So this becomes Potiphar's solution: he will warehouse his investment until he can find some other use for him.

So Joseph is thrown into prison. But not just any prison housing common criminals; he is incarcerated in a special prison reserved for state prisoners. This jail is undoubtedly close to the capital if not in its midst, and thus close to Potiphar's office, so he can keep an eye on things. Moreover, considering the rank of those who would be held there, the conditions would be several cuts above the average.[48]

And once again the narrator returns to his theme of "the Lord" being with Joseph. His charisma is still working; the chief Warder of the prison takes a liking to Joseph. He makes him Head Trustee.

So the Chief Warder of the prison placed all the prisoners that were in the prison in Joseph's hand, and everything that was to be done there, it was he who did it. The Chief Warder did not oversee anything that he did,[49] *because the Lord was with him* [Joseph], *whatever he did the Lord made it succeed* [Gen. 39:22–23].

Things seem to be repeating themselves. There are two ways we can look at our tale to date. The first is the standard evaluation: Joseph, once betrayed by his brothers, is again betrayed; this time by his master's wife. Naive, blameless and unblemished, more sinned against than sinning, he soldiers on, undaunted and, overcoming all obstacles, by perseverance and with high intelligence contriving to turn every disaster into a steppingstone to success. This is one take on Joseph and it has the ring of truth.

But there is another way of looking at things. Things do seem to be repeating themselves, but not necessarily in a manner we have been considering. Once again Maurice Samuel:

She [Potiphar's wife] forced the issue, to her undoing, and to Joseph's. She committed the crime, and it was Joseph who was cast into prison. Thus on the surface. In reality it was Joseph who forced the issue, as he had done in his boyhood with his brothers, forced it steadily day by day, until the explosion came. In those days he had played with his brother's hatred; now he toyed with a woman's love. In both instances he was the active agent, and set the pattern; and to make this clear, in both instances he had his coat torn off him — in a kind of unmasking — and was thrown into a pit.[50]

So in this reading Joseph remains Joseph; nothing has changed and we are back at the beginning. He is trapped in a never-ending cycle of narcissism, arrogance and collapse. And this reading also has the ring of truth. And all the while, hovering over every collapse, is the Lord, brooding over the follies of men, but nonetheless ever with Joseph.

In either reading of his character, Joseph, in the "pit," has his work cut out for him.

Notes

1. See Chapter 1, note 59.
2. See Chapter 1, note 60.
3. The "Tetragrammaton"; see Introduction, note 76.
4. Literally, "and he was a man who succeeded."
5. Reading with Syr., MT reads: "and he was in the house of his Egyptian master." It seems Joseph was utilized as a house slave.
6. Literally, "and he served him." The term *sharet* has the sense of a personal servant in Exodus 24:13 and 2 Kings 6:15.
7. Literally, "he placed him over his house."
8. Literally, "abandoned," a unique use of this idiom which normally means "to abandon to the power of another;" a highly negative phenomenon. The normal idiom would be "to give over to the hands of another," as in verse 4: "All that he possessed he gave over into his hands." But note that this word will turn up again to describe Joseph abandoning his garment when he flees from the clutches of his master's wife.
9. Literally, "bread." Bread — the "staff of life" — is often used in the Bible as a synonym for food.
10. The term *yefe toar* describes the figure while the term *yefe mareh* refers to the face. These terms are usually used to describe women; their use here to describe a man is unique. This same language was used to describe Joseph's mother, Rachel; it seems that he took after her and might be described as a "dream boat."
11. The Egyptian term is *mer-per*, which Sarna (*Genesis*, 272) renders as "comptroller."
12. Genesis 28:13–21.
13. This presents an interesting question: the narrator is perfectly aware that as an Egyptian, Potiphar neither knows nor recognizes "the Lord," that is, the God of Abraham, Isaac, and Jacob/Israel. (Centuries later another Egyptian, Pharaoh, is to put this lack of recognition into words: "Who is the Lord that I should heed his voice? I do not know the Lord" [Exod. 5:2]. Subsequently, for clarity, Moses, who is addressing Pharaoh, is forced to refer to the Lord as "the God of the Hebrews" [7:16; 9:1].) What Potiphar does recognize is the realm of the divine (in his terminology "the gods"). Normally our narrator is at pains to differentiate between the God of the Hebrews (the Lord), the realm of the divine as monotheistically conceived by the Hebrews (God) and this same realm as conceived by pagans (the gods). Here, when referring to Potiphar's understanding of Joseph's success story, the narrator is forced to blur these distinctions due to his need to emphasize that it is precisely "the God of the Hebrews" who is controlling the situation. Potiphar, of course, thinks that it is "the gods" who are responsible.
14. See note 3 above. But in the Judah narrative (Gen. 38) the Lord is mentioned 3 times.
15. Which we render as "God" when used by an Israelite, and "gods" when used by a pagan.
16. Joseph was seventeen when he was "sold into Egypt." He is twenty-eight at the time of his fall.
17. To overcome this "oversight," Thomas Mann, in his magisterial novel *Joseph and His Brothers*, Trans. H. T. Lowe-Porter (New York: Alfred A. Knopf, 1943) is forced to invent the name Mut-em-enet for her. A rabbinic commentator invented the name Zuleika.
18. An expression denoting the passage of an indefinite amount of time.
19. See Psalm 123:1–2 for this use.

20. Hebrew *hain*, an interjection calling attention to some fact upon which action is to be taken or a conclusion based (BDB; Francis Brown, Samuel R. Driver, Charles A. Briggs, *Brown–Driver–Briggs Hebrew and English Lexicon of the Old Testament.* [Peabody, MA: Hendrickson, 2001], s.v. "Hain").
21. Literally, "with me [here] my master does not know."
22. Reading with Syr. and Vulg.; MT reads "in the house."
23. Literally, "hand."
24. A euphemism for sexual congress. See 2 Samuel 14:20.
25. Sarna, *Genesis*, 273.
26. "A faithless wife could be burned alive with her paramour and their ashes scattered in the Nile — for Egyptians a punishment of particular horror which ruled out eternal life" (Johnson, 123).
27. "It is now known that this is a technical term for adultery throughout the ancient Near East.... Adultery was regarded in the ancient Near East as both a civil and a religious crime, a 'great sin' against the gods" (Jacob Milgrom, *Numbers*, JPS Torah Commentary [Philadelphia: Jewish Publication Society, 1990], 348–349).
28. The term Joseph uses, *elohim*, is grammatically in the plural. When used by a monotheist it is understood as the plural of majesty — thus "God." Pagans hearing the term would understand it as "the gods." See note 15.
29. Maurice Samuel, "The Brilliant Failure," in *Certain People of the Book* (New York: Alfred A. Knopf, 1959), 329–330.
30. And before the chapter ends he will return three more times to this theme.
31. See note 27.
32. Adultery was universally considered "The Great Sin," a fundamental breach of common decency; see note 27 above. Another example would be the murder of infants. (See Exodus 1:16–21, where "the fear of God [the gods]" is the motive for the midwives refusing to murder the infants they have delivered. Common decency forbade it.)
33. Kass, 544.
34. Literally, "men of the house."
35. Literally, "and fled outside."
36. Or, "to play with us." The Hebrew term has sexual connotations (see Genesis 26:8).
37. Literally, "called out in a loud voice," this same word used at the beginning of the verse when she summoned her servants (although without the modifier, "with a loud voice").
38. Literally, "and went outside."
39. At other periods the kilt was longer, reaching a point half-way between knee and ankle.
40. Manual laborers wore a form of loin-cloth. Some worked naked.
41. The Samaritan version reads "garments" (plural) where MT reads "garment" (singular). By thus removing any possibility of his fleeing half-clothed, the Samaritan text insists upon his nakedness.
42. William Congreve, *The Mourning Bride* (Edinburgh, UK: Hamilton, 1755) III, viii.
43. Literally, "and she spoke to him similar words."
44. See note 35 above.
45. Literally, "raised up my voice and called out."
46. Literally, "imprisoned."
47. Literally, "and extended to him *hesed*," the Hebrew term for unconditional and unearned love. *Hesed* in the Bible is first and foremost a way that God manifests Himself to mankind. His care for humanity shows itself through His *hesed*, His loving-kindness, giving people far more than they deserve. But human beings can also manifest *hesed* through acts of unconditional kindness, love, and loyalty far in excess of the normal, or what the other deserves based on his or her own behavior. In so doing they are reflecting God's grace. The Rabbinic sages, basing themselves on the principle of *Imitatio Dei*, made of this a central injunction: "As God is gracious and kind, so shall you be gracious and kind."
48. In Egypt the term "the pit" was a common term for prison. They often were just that.
49. Literally, "that was in his hand."
50. Samuel, 330.

4

The Interpreter of Dreams

I have had a dream, past the wit of man to say what dream it was.
— William Shakespeare, *A Midsummer Night's Dream*, IV

In dreams begins responsibility.
— W. B Yeats, *Responsibilities*

Has Joseph learned anything from his bitter experiences? On one level the answer must be yes. From the experience of enslavement and his period of servitude under Potiphar, he undoubtedly learned that he had it within himself to rise above adversity; when thrown into a sink or swim situation he could learn to swim. But on a deeper level — of the causes of his enslavement — he seems to have learned very little up to now.

> To this point Joseph's career has followed a familiar pattern. At home, he was the favorite of the head of the household (his father Jacob), a first among equals (his brothers) who was thus envied and hated by his peers, stripped and thrown into a pit, and sold into slavery. In Potiphar's house he was again the favorite of the head of the household, a first among equals (the slaves) who was later hated by his master's wife, stripped, and thrown into prison. In prison, we find him again the favorite of the head of the "house," once again a first among equals (the prisoners). Can the pattern of "success breeding failure" be avoided?[1]

Or to put the matter in another way: as long as Joseph remains Joseph, and the pattern keeps repeating, he will continue to snatch defeat from the jaws of victory. Either he must change himself or alter the pattern (or both) to avoid recurring disaster. Does Joseph realize this?

That Joseph is highly intelligent we can no longer doubt. In the enforced leisure of imprisonment[2] we can postulate a period of deep introspection. I am going to hazard the suggestion that Joseph does begin to realize that relying solely on his good looks, his native charm and his vaunting ambition is not enough to ensure sustainable success. At the very least he will need to develop further the ability to empathize with others; he will have to gain more insight into how people work and what levers he can use to manipulate them. Above all, he will have to learn to subordinate his ego to his career; he will have to realize that he cannot afford to casually play games with people just to enhance his sense of self. If he wants to succeed he will have to avoid getting sidetracked by ego and focus exclusively on success. In a word, Joseph will have to mature and become more serious. Moreover, he cannot expect lucky breaks. He must be ready to seize opportunities as they present themselves. It remains to be seen if events will confirm this assumption.

The Trustee

> *Now it came to pass after these things that the Cupbearer[3] of the King of Egypt and the Baker gave offense[4] to their Lord, the king of Egypt. Now Pharaoh was furious with his two officials, with the Chief Cupbearer and with the Chief Baker. And he gave them over to the custody of the Head of Security,[5] to the very prison where Joseph was imprisoned. Now the Head of Security assigned Joseph to them, and he attended them; now they were [some] days in custody[6]* [Gen. 40:1-4].

This is a strange opening to our current scene: wordy, redundant, yet at the same time vague and opaque with regard to matters of motive and background. Who are the "Chief Cupbearer" and the "Chief Baker"? What have they done? Why is Pharaoh furious with them? And most important, why does the Head of Security (who, of course, is none other then Potiphar) assign Joseph to "attend" to them? What exactly is Joseph's assignment? We are being forced to fill in gaps that have been purposely left in the text.

Let us begin with information that was part of the background knowledge of most of the original readers of our narrative: the offices of Cupbearer and Baker in the monarchies of the Ancient Near East. They were all officials of the highest rank and with the highest security clearance; they had to be because they controlled the food and drink that entered the monarch's mouth. Because they had the ongoing opportunity to poison his food and drink, they held his life in their hands, therefore the positions were filled only by persons in whom the monarch invested absolute trust. As such they had the king's ear and were enormously influential.[7]

What went wrong? Something, obviously, connected with their functions. Did Pharaoh suffer an attack of acute indigestion? Were the charges gross negligence—food and/or wine that had gone bad—or more serious: attempted poisoning? Since the Chief Cook is not included in the indictment, the suspicion seems focused on some sort of event in which the edibles consisted of baked goods and wine—a sort of Egyptian cocktail party with pastry hors d'oeuvres.[8] But if so, why incarceration? Death would seem the appropriate penalty for upsetting the royal digestion, and even more so for a suspected attempt to poison the imperial personage. Taking into account the way things spin out we can entertain the possibility that the king is uncertain as to where the blame lies. As a result both are turned over to the Head of Security, who has charge of the prisons, to be held until guilt can be determined.

So far so good. But where does Joseph come into the matter? Here Kass makes an ingenious suggestion: Potiphar, who has been "warehousing" Joseph in his "white-collar" prison, has finally found a use for him.[9] His assignment is to act as a police spy, to gain, as a fellow prisoner (albeit a trustee), the confidence of the Cupbearer and Baker and to attempt to determine which of the two is the guilty party. "For it is common knowledge that men while in prison often loosen their tongues, confessing or bragging about their deeds or otherwise betraying their culpability.... Once upon a time Joseph would report his brothers' wrongdoing to their father; now he will, indirectly, report the wrongdoing of Pharaoh's servants to their ruler."[10]

And with patience the opportunity arrives.

> *One night both of them dreamed a dream*—[that is] *the Cupbearer and the Baker of the king of Egypt who were in custody in the prison—each dreamed his own dream with its own* [separate] *meaning.*[11] *When Joseph came to them in the morning he saw that they were troubled.*[12] *So he questioned the officials of Pharaoh who were in custody with him in his master's house, saying, "Why are your faces*

downcast today?" They said to him, "We have dreamed a dream and there is no one to interpret it." And he said to them, "Do not interpretations [come] from God? Please tell them to me." [Gen. 40:5-8].

"To dream a dream:" the last time we heard this phrase it was on Joseph's lips as he recounted his dreams of grandeur in Canaan,[13] and there we stressed how out of place it was.[14] Here the phrase is in its natural setting. In the Introduction we discussed the place of dreams in the Egyptian culture, and the importance accorded to those knowledgeable in the science of dream interpretation, and skilled in applying this knowledge. We will shortly explain why the dreams seem portentous to the prisoners, even ominous.[15] Yet there is no one to whom to turn for elucidation. Here Joseph leaps into the breach. "Do not interpretations [come] from God? Please tell them to me" (Gen. 40:8). At first blush Joseph seems to be saying that dreams, and therefore their meanings, have their origins in God (or the gods)[16] and I, skilled in the knowledge of the divine, am in position to interpret them. But why should the prisoners believe such a grandiose claim from a non-Egyptian? Where could he, a Hebrew and a slave to boot, have obtained the lengthy training in this esoteric Egyptian science that would give him the required competence? Or is Joseph saying something else: that I possess divine powers and it is this that gives me the power to interpret dreams — that the term *elohim* which he uses applies to himself? "Because only God can interpret dreams, therefore tell your dreams to me!"

However this statement is meant, and however understood by his listeners, one of them picks up on the offer while the other holds back.

Then the Chief Cupbearer told his dream to Joseph. And he said, "In my dream, behold, there was a vine before me. On the vine were three branches. And as it budded its blossoms shot up and its clusters ripened into grapes. Now Pharaoh's cup was in my hand, and I took the grapes and squeezed them into the cup and gave the cup into the hand of Pharaoh" [Gen. 40:9-11].

Two things stand out in this dream. The first is the obvious connection with the Cupbearer's official duties: his dream relates to the conditions of his service to Pharaoh. The second is less obvious and much stranger: the way time is telescoped in the dream. Normally, the entire process from the budding of grape vines and their blossoming until the grapes ripen takes an entire season. Then the grapes must be pressed, fermented and aged — a process that can take anywhere from months to years. It is as though, in the dream, someone has pressed the fast-forward button. Everything is strangely compressed into a few moments. Time seems almost to stand still; everything has almost become a "now." We will come back to this point later.

How Joseph relates to this dream is instructive. With hardly a pause Joseph reacts.

Then Joseph said to him, "This is its meaning[17]*: The three branches are three days. In three days Pharaoh will lift up your head and restore you to your office. And you shall place Pharaoh's cup into his hand as was your custom formerly, when you were his Cupbearer. But remember me*[18] *when it is well with you, and do me the kindness*[19] *of mentioning me to Pharaoh, to release me from this* [prison] *house. For I was kidnapped; stolen*[20] *from the land of the Hebrews; and here also I have done nothing that they should have put me into the pit"*[21] [Gen. 40:12-15].

Joseph's little speech divides into two parts, the interpretation of the dream and a plea for help. The key to Joseph's interpretation (as indeed what will be the key to all Joseph's interpretations of Egyptian dreams) is his transposition of numbers enumerating physical objects (in this case three branches) into temporal equivalents (here three days). A static material picture has been transformed into a dynamic sequence. The transposition reveals a positive prognosis: in three days you will be out of here and back in your old position. And based on this, the plea: please, when you are back at the palace enjoying all the good things of life, don't forget your fellow unfortunate. As you have been an innocent victim, so am I — kidnapped out of my land and sold into slavery. And now I have been thrown into jail when I did nothing to deserve it. You will be in constant contact with the Pharaoh. Put in a good word for me and get me out of this place.

The Chief Baker, his initial skepticism (or was it something more?) overcome by the compelling interpretation and a positive prognosis, now can't wait to get in on the act.

Now when the Chief Baker saw how well he had interpreted,[22] he said to Joseph, "Now me; in my dream, behold, three wicker baskets were on my head. And in the uppermost basket there were all sorts of pastries[23] for Pharaoh, and the birds were eating them from out of the basket over my head" [Gen. 40:16-17].

This dream also relates to the dreamer's profession and his service to Pharaoh. He is on his way to Pharaoh with baskets piled on his head, carrying baked dainties for Pharaoh's table. But ominously, unlike the Cupbearer, he never gets there. Instead birds swoop down and eat up the pastries meant for the King's table. Once again Joseph reacts instantly, and again the key to the dream is the transposition of a material numeral into a temporal one.

Joseph answered and said, "This is its meaning[24]: The three baskets are three days. In three days will Pharaoh lift up your head from off you, and will impale you on a stake, and the birds shall eat your flesh off from you" [Gen. 40:18-19].

The Baker does not seem to be very smart. Taking note only of the good outcome of the interpretation of the Cupbearer's dream, while leaving out of account the differences in the basic nature of the dreams themselves, he has no doubt that he too will receive a positive interpretation. And until well past the halfway point of Joseph's pronouncement the two interpretations are virtually identical. Then suddenly comes the turnabout.

The phrase "to lift up someone's head" has the meaning of granting recognition, dignity, and honor to someone so that he can hold up his head with self-confidence and pride. It admirably fits the situation of the pardoned Cupbearer, head hanging low in dejection in prison, and now being returned to his former honor. And for a moment it seems to the Baker that he too is to tread that golden path, until Joseph adds the fatal words "from off you." This completely reverses the meaning of the phrase: "to lift up one's head from off one" means to decapitate. The Baker's fate is to be that in three days he is to have his head cut off, his body publicly impaled upon a stake and left for the birds to devour.[25] To this appalling prognosis Joseph does not see fit to append any personal postscript.

Why this fixation on a three day period? Now we are to learn.

Now it came to pass on the third day — Pharaoh's birthday — that he made a feast for all his servants, and he called to account[26] the Chief Cupbearer and the Chief Baker from among his servants. He restored the Chief Cupbearer to his cup bearing, so he [once again] *placed the cup in Pharaoh's hand. But the Chief Baker he impaled — even as Joseph had interpreted to them* [Gen. 40:20-22].

In three days Pharaoh is to celebrate his birthday, which is likely to be a day of reckoning for all concerned: a day of feasting, a day of pardons and perhaps a day of judgment. The "Son of the Sun" has completed another cycle with his father; the immortal god has arrived at yet another milestone in a cycle of immortality. This is the only Egyptian holiday mentioned in the Bible, and one totally alien to the ethos of ancient Israel.[27] Of course all royal officials (including the Cupbearer and the Baker) were well aware of its imminence — as of course was Joseph. Did the anxiety produced by this knowledge color the dreams of the two prisoners, or even bring on the dreams? Did it play a part in Joseph's interpretation? Probably. The fact that Joseph's dream interpretations indeed come to pass has fueled a celebration of Joseph's prophetic powers, and the main disagreements with regard to them have centered on the source of this predictive omniscience. One school of thought, basing itself on Joseph's own statements (cf. 40:8), credits divine inspiration. The second school seizes on Joseph's intelligence and wisdom as the driving force behind his uncanny insight into the unfolding of the future. To this argument Kass adds an interesting psychological spin.

We must not lose sight of the purpose of Joseph having been assigned to attend to the Chief Cupbearer and the Chief Baker. If our reasoning is correct, the Cupbearer and the Baker are under suspicion of having poisoned the king, either through gross negligence or with malice aforethought. But who of the pair is the guilty party? Joseph has been attached to them in the role of a "stoolie," to gain their confidence and elicit from them the information that will enable determination of innocence or guilt. And, most importantly, to report his findings to his boss, the Head of Security (for we must never forget that not only is Joseph under his authority as a prisoner, but he remains Potiphar's slave — his personal property). Let us reexamine the prison sequence from this perspective.

From this point of view, not only the dreams but also the behavior of the pair are highly revealing. Beginning with the Cupbearer, his actions and his dream indicate a man with a clean conscience. Having nothing to hide, he readily offers to reveal his dream. His dream is positive, showing a man focused on serving his master and actually doing so. Now contrast this behavior with that of the Baker. He does not offer to reveal his dream, and only does so when he thinks that he too can receive a positive prognosis. His dream also reveals a less than positive attitude. Unlike the Cupbearer, whose dream concludes by his placing the cup in Pharaoh's hand, the Baker in his dream never delivers his pastries to Pharaoh's table. Ominous birds swoop down and devour the goodies. He makes no effort to drive them away,[28] remaining passive. At the very least the dream does not reflect a very positive attitude to his service of Pharaoh, and taken together with his reticence in revealing the dream in the first place, it may betray a sense of guilt.[29]

Joseph's verdicts are encapsulated in his interpretations. For the Cupbearer: innocent, therefore reinstatement. For the Baker: guilty, therefore execution. When we realize that Joseph's conclusions would have been reported to his master, his prophecies become self-fulfilling.

> It is traditional to read this passage as evidence of Joseph's powers of prophecy and clairvoyance; and no one can gainsay that interpretation. But our analysis suggests a less mysterious, more ordinary interpretation: the dreams of the butler [cupbearer] and baker revealed to Joseph the true culprit, and Joseph's talebearing all by itself guaranteed the predicted results.[30]

Joseph has learned enough about the ways of those in power not to expect his freedom in reward for his signal service to the crown. He understands full well that it is in the interests of the powers that be that a successful "stoolie" be kept locked up in prison where he can be used again and again. That he places no hope in Potiphar can be seen by his appeal to his fellow prisoner: once restored to your post you will have Pharaoh's ear. Please use your influence to help me also to see the light of day. Certainly one good turn deserves another. But Joseph's reliance on his fellow unfortunate proves naive.

> However the Chief Cupbearer did not remember Joseph, but he forgot him [Gen. 40:23].

So has Joseph learned anything? That he can bend with the wind and make the best of bad situations he already knows. These present experiences merely confirm past lessons. But in the understanding of people and how their minds work he seems to have made real progress. Assuming that our analysis is correct, his interpretation of the dreams of his fellow prisoners shows real psychological insight. This newfound insight into the psyche of people in place of his former obtuseness bespeaks profound change, a change that opens the possibility of escaping the repetitive "success breeding failure" syndrome in which he has been trapped.

And there is a further lesson that will be internalized in the long months ahead as he waits in vain for the Cupbearer's aid in escaping the pit: never to rely on the good will of others. This is the last time Joseph will take that path. From now on he will rely only on himself.

The Promoter

> *Now it came to pass after two full years*[31] *that the Pharaoh dreamed, and behold, he was standing by the Nile. And behold, out of the Nile came up seven cows, beautiful to look upon and fat-fleshed, and they grazed the upon the reed beds.*[32] *And behold, seven other cows came up after them from the Nile, ugly to behold and gaunt, and they stood next to the [first] cows on the banks of the Nile. And the cows that were ugly to behold and gaunt ate up the seven beautiful looking and fat-fleshed cows. And Pharaoh started awake* [Gen. 41:1-4].

Two long years have passed, bitter with disappointed expectation. If the Hebrew idiom means, as we have surmised, that exactly two years to the day have elapsed, then Pharaoh, back in birthday mode,[33] receives an unexpected "birthday gift." His dream is unusual and it is worth our close attention. In his recounting of the dream, our narrator stresses, first and foremost, the dream's setting. *Four times* he unnecessarily repeats that the events take place on the banks of the Nile. (Pharaoh, on the other hand, when he recounts his dream does not seem to fully grasp the significance of the locale; he only refers to the Nile twice.)[34] The Nile is Egypt; the country is no more than the river and its floodplain snaking its way through an uninhabitable desert of windblown sand dunes and rocky plains. This floodplain is extremely limited. At its widest point it is no more than fourteen miles across. In some areas it narrows down with the enclosing steep bluffs washed by the waters of the river.[35] As in Egypt there is no rain, life is wholly dependent on the Nile. Rain in Central Africa, at the headwaters of the Nile, causes the river's annual rise, inundating the fields and guaranteeing bumper crops. Should the river fail to rise, or rise only moderately, the result is disaster; the crops wither and die. Everything depends on what comes out of the Nile. But surprisingly, in Pharaoh's dream it's not water coming up out of the Nile but cows! It is on the cows that Pharaoh focuses, missing the national significance of the Nile.

The sequence, a staccato series of images punctuated with the exclamation "and behold," is nightmarish. Seven fat sleek cows emerge from the waters, wade up onto the banks and begin to graze. They are followed by an equal number of scrawny, starving cows who prove to be cannibals. Instead of falling to on the lush reeds they turn upon their predecessors, attack them and devour them. The shock and unnatural violence of the scene jolts Pharaoh awake in a cold sweat.

Eventually Pharaoh gets back to sleep.

And he slept, and dreamed a second time. And behold, seven ears of grain came up on a single stalk, fat and good. And behold, seven thin ears of grain, blasted by the East wind, sprouted after them.[36] And the thin ears of grain swallowed the seven fat and full ears of grain; and Pharaoh started awake and behold, it was a dream! [Gen. 41:5-7].

The second dream, though on the surface less terrifying than the first, seems only to have acted as a multiplier to the sense of panic induced by the cannibal cows. Again Pharaoh starts from his sleep; we are informed by the Hebrew phraseology that his heart is pounding wildly.

Now it came to pass in the morning that he was in a panic,[37] and he sent and summoned all the experts[38] of Egypt and all of its wise man; and Pharaoh told them his dream. But there was no one who could interpret them for Pharaoh [Gen. 41:8].

More than the contents of the dreams, more even than their nightmare quality is the emotional coloring which gives rise to a choking sensation of pure terror. It is this, and possibly also the proximity to his birthday, that convince Pharaoh that what he has received is an omen, one that cannot but be of vital import, yet whose meaning he cannot fathom. Still not fully recovered from the terror of the night, his heart still pounding, he summons all his experts and wise men (note that *all*), the experts in the field of dream analysis and interpretation. He tells them his dream, "But there was no one who could interpret them." Note also the nouns and pronouns: the Pharaoh tells them his *dream* (singular) but no one can interpret *them* (plural). The Pharaoh instinctively lumps his dreams into one undifferentiated nightmare; his advisers insist on seeing them as two disparate "revelations." Perhaps this is the reason that they cannot come up with an interpretation that is acceptable and satisfying to their king (for it certainly stretches the imagination to conclude that these intelligent courtiers can come up with nothing by way of explanations).[39] Into this impasse steps the Chief Cupbearer.

Then the Chief Cupbearer spoke up to Pharaoh, saying, "My sins do I recall this day. Pharaoh was furious with his servants and committed me to the custody[40] of the Head of Security, me and the Chief Baker. Now the same night we dreamed a dream, I and he, each one a [separate] *dream with a* [separate] *meaning[41] did we dream. Now there was a Hebrew lad there with us, the slave of the Head of Security. And we told him our dreams and he interpreted them,* [telling] *each one the meaning of his dream. And as he interpreted so it came to pass; I was restored to my position and he was impaled"* [Gen. 41:9-13].

It is noteworthy that the Chief Cupbearer stops short of actually recommending Joseph, but simply, without comment, recounts an incident. He too is playing it safe, leaving Pharaoh to come to his own conclusions. If Joseph should bomb, well — he never recommended him. So much for the supposed solidarity of unfortunates.

Then Pharaoh sent and summoned Joseph. And they hurried him out of the pit, and he shaved and changed his clothes, and came before Pharaoh [Gen. 41:14].

Let us not hurry over this brief verse. Something very important is happening here. The Pharaoh's servants are in a rush: when the king issues his commands they must be expedited with the maximum possible speed. So "they hurried him out of the pit." But then everything slows down. It almost certainly was Joseph who put on the brakes. He cannot appear before Pharaoh as he is. It would be improper. He must wash (not mentioned but implied). He must change from prison attire into clothing proper for a court appearance. And, most significantly, he must shave.

In the Ancient Near East, all men were bearded.[42] The one exception was the Egyptians. They, and only they, were clean-shaven; their heads as well as their faces.[43] In shaving his face and head, apparently for the first time, Joseph is transforming himself. Outwardly he is no longer a Hebrew; his appearance now will proclaim him to Pharaoh as an Egyptian.[44] This is a harbinger of things to come. Thus altered, Joseph is brought before Pharaoh.

And Pharaoh said to Joseph, "I have dreamed a dream and no one can interpret it. Now I have heard it said of you that for you to hear a dream is to interpret it." And Joseph answered Pharaoh, saying, "It is not in me. God will answer for Pharaoh's well-being"[45] [Gen. 41:15-16].

As Pharaoh hears it, he takes this as an encouragement and commits himself by relating his dreams.

So Pharaoh spoke to Joseph, "In my dream, behold, I was standing on the banks of the Nile. And behold, out of the Nile came up seven cows, fat-fleshed with beautiful bodies,[46] *and they grazed upon the reed beds. And behold, seven other cows came up after them, scrawny, extremely ill-formed and emaciated, such as I have never seen so bad in all Egypt. And the emaciated and ill-favored cows ate up the first seven cows. And when they had been taken into their stomachs,*[47] *you could not tell that they had been taken into their stomachs; their appearance was just as bad as at the start. And I started awake* [Gen. 41:17-21].

Aside from interpolating a number of his impressions and reactions, the factual part of Pharaoh's account is virtually identical with what we have previously been told. The Pharaoh continues:

And I saw in my dream, and behold, seven ears of grain came up on a single stalk, full and good. And behold, seven shriveled ears of grain, thin and blasted by the East wind, sprouted after them. And the thin ears of grain swallowed the seven good ears of grain. I spoke to my experts but no one can tell me [the meaning] [Gen. 41:22-24].

One aspect of Pharaoh's account stands out: he recounts two separate and distinct dreams, yet he persistently refers to them (three times) in the singular as "a dream" or "my dream." It is on this anomaly that Joseph seizes as his opening wedge.

Were it not that we know otherwise, we might suppose from the smoothness and structure of his answer that Joseph has been composing it for days. Joseph is remarkable in his ability to think on his feet. With no appreciable pause, without any hemming and hawing, he launches into his response.

Then Joseph said to Pharaoh, "The dream of Pharaoh is one [dream]" [Gen. 41:25a].

Joseph's opening point is that Pharaoh's instincts are correct; that the two dreams are really simply separate aspects of a single revelation, in which God is revealing to Pharaoh the future.

What God [or the gods] *is* [about to] *do He has told to Pharaoh* [Gen. 41:25b].

Then Joseph immediately applies his by now familiar interpretive technique, transposing numbers that relate to material objects into temporal units.

The seven good cows are seven years, and the seven ears of grain are seven years. It is one dream. And the seven thin and ugly cows that came up after them are seven years, and the seven empty ears of grain, blasted by the East wind, are seven famine years [Gen. 41:26-27].

Having, with the single word "famine," planted the seed of what is to come, Joseph backtracks to reinforce the idea that all this is a divine revelation, direct to Pharaoh; a prediction of things to come.

It is just as I have said to Pharaoh: the thing that God is [about to] *do He has shown Pharaoh. Behold, seven years of great plenty in all the land of Egypt are coming. And after them will come seven years of famine, and all the plenty will be forgotten in the land of Egypt. The famine will ravage*[48] *the land. Nor will the abundance in the land be known due to this famine that will come thereafter, for it will be very severe*[49] [Gen. 41:28-31].

Having imparted the central message, Joseph now returns to his starting point — that of one unified revelation — elucidating the final remaining mystery: why the single revelation had to be repeated in two separate installments.

And as for the repeating of the dream to Pharaoh twice, [it means] *that the matter is established*[50] *by God, and God is hurrying to do it* [Gen. 41:32].

Ending on the reiteration of the absolute certainty of the impending disaster, and stressing its onrushing nature, its imminence, Joseph, without giving anyone a chance to react, rushes on to the key issue — *his* issue. Joseph has learned his lessons well. He will no longer pin his hopes on gratitude and goodwill. He will not leave his promotion to others. He will promote himself. He has produced a diagnosis. He now follows with the plan of action that can deal with the crisis and prevent calamity, and proposes the person who is able to implement the remedy — himself. This is what Joseph's speech is really all about: self-promotion.

Therefore, let Pharaoh seek out[51] *a discerning, wise man,*[52] *and set him over the land of Egypt. And let Pharaoh act and appoint overseers over the land and mobilize*[53] *the land in the seven years of plenty. And let all the food of the good years that are coming be gathered, and let the grain be collected under the hand of the Pharaoh, food in the cities, and let it be guarded. And the food will be a reserve for the land, for the seven famine years that shall be in the land of Egypt, so the land may not perish in the famine* [Gen. 41:33-36].

On the surface Joseph is proposing an enlightened plan to deal with an impending national crisis, one that no one would have the temerity to openly oppose. But actually he is doing much more. Joseph, the psychologist, is speaking to Pharaoh. He has been evaluating Pharaoh's personal needs and interests, and is speaking directly to them. What he is saying to Pharaoh is: my proposal is that you use this emergency to centralize all the economic resources of Egypt into the hands of the state; in other words, into your hands. With control of all the resources will go enormous enhancement of your power, and this enhancement will be permanent. Now you need someone to implement this program of concentration of power into your hands. He cannot be part of the current establishment; he must not be part of any interest group or any clique. They would inevitably resist surrender of their share of power. He must be brilliant, capable, and responsible only to you. He must be completely dependent on you, with no independent power base. That way you can be sure of his absolute loyalty. Who do you think fits this bill?

The promoter has finished his pitch and one can postulate a long and pregnant pause. Joseph and Pharaoh look at each other, and the message flashes invisibly across the space between them: they understand each other.

And this thing seemed good in the eyes of Pharaoh, and in the eyes of all his servants [Gen. 41:37].

Besides the fact that most of the courtiers have not yet had the time to become aware of all the implications of Joseph's proposal, how could anyone with the good of the nation at heart oppose so farsighted a plan? Then Pharaoh breaks the silence:

And Pharaoh said to his servants, "Could we find [another] *man in whom is the spirit of God?"* [Gen. 41:38].

Needless to say, there can be no answer to this rhetorical question.

So Pharaoh said to Joseph, "Since[54] God has made all this known to you, there is no one as discerning and wise as you. You shall be over my House[55]; by your command shall all my people be directed.[56] Only the throne will be greater than you."[57] And Pharaoh [further] said to Joseph, "See, I have set you over all the land of Egypt."[58] And Pharaoh drew off his ring from his hand and placed it on Joseph's hand; and he had him dressed in fine linen, and put a collar of gold around his neck.[59] And he caused him to ride in the chariot of his viceroy, and they cried before him "Abrek."[60] Thus he placed him over all the land of Egypt [Gen. 41:41-43].

In one fell swoop Joseph is not only appointed but also invested with the insignia and the accoutrements of power. The transfer of the royal signet ring to Joseph's hand confirms him as the Grand Vizier of Egypt.[61] New clothing appropriate to his high office ("clothes make the man") and the gold collar of office complete the transformation. Publicly parading Joseph in the second grandest chariot in Egypt not only introduces him to the public as Grand Vizier, but also drives home to the court that Joseph is in charge. The miserable slave is now, after Pharaoh, the most exalted personage in the land. The despised Hebrew has become the Egyptian par excellence.

Notes

1. Kass, 549, note 50.
2. Despite any duties involved in being a trustee, Joseph would have had ample time to brood on his lot.
3. This term (Hebrew *mashkeh*, from the root "to give to drink") is unique in the Bible. Both Jonathan, who served as his father's cupbearer (1 Samuel 20:25) and Nehemiah who held this position in the court of Artaxerxes I (Neh. 2:1) are never referred to as "cupbearers" by the biblical text. The term appears only in the Egyptian context, and then only in relation to Joseph. In much the same way the term "to interpret (a dream)," *poter*, and "interpretation (of the meaning of a dream)," *pitaron*, are unique to this narrative and reflect its Egyptian setting.
4. Literally, "sinned against."
5. Literally, "he gave them over in custody in the house of."
6. A phrase that can mean an indefinite period. Some read it as the equivalent of "a year of days," i.e., one full year.
7. In Egypt this situation was steeped in irony. The Egyptian religion insisted that the Pharaoh was a god. Yet the very existence of the god is dependent on the loyalty and good will of the mortals who feed him and sustain him.
8. The Egyptians were known for their baked goods. "No less then fifty-seven varieties of bread and thirty-eight different types of cake are known from hieroglyphic texts" (Sarna, *Genesis*, 279).
9. Can we also entertain the possibility that Joseph's trustee position is at least in part due to a suggestion to the Head Warder of the prison by his boss, the Head of Security?
10. Kass, 552.
11. Literally, "interpretation."
12. Literally, "he looked, and behold they were troubled."
13. And on his father Jacob's lips as well, as he berated his son for his pretensions (Gen. 37:10).
14. See page 44.
15. It is worthwhile to notice that in the case of the Cupbearer and the Baker (in contradistinction to the case of Pharaoh) it is nowhere stated that the dreams come from God. We are therefore free to assume that these dreams are simply dreams reflecting the anxieties and inner preoccupations of the dreamers.
16. See Chapter 3, note 13 and 15.
17. Literally, "interpretation."
18. Literally, "if you will remember me when I was with you and act kindly to me."
19. See Chapter 3, note 47.
20. Literally, "for I was stolen, stolen away." The double repetition indicates emphasis and certainty.
21. I.e., prison; see Chapter 3, note 48.
22. The Hebrew could also mean, "saw how positive the interpretation was."
23. Literally, "food, baked goods."
24. Literally, "interpretation."

25. For an Egyptian this was a horrifying fate. The preservation of one's body (as a mummy) was the passport to the afterlife. To have one's body devoured by birds was to forfeit any future.

26. Literally, "lifted up the head of." The author has been playing with this phrase. Depending on the context he has had it mean "to pardon" and "to decapitate." Now he uses it in a third meaning, one of enumeration, to take a head-count. This indeed is the most common use of the phrase in the Bible (see Exodus 30:12; Numbers 1:2, 49; 4:2, 22; 31:26, 49) (Nahum M. Sarna, *Exodus*, JPS Torah Commentary [Philadelphia: Jewish Publication Society, 1991], 260; Chapter 30, note 20).

27. No birthdays are recorded in the Bible for any Israelite, either king or commoner. The very idea was alien to the Israelite ethos. The Israelites celebrated annual remembrances of redemptive acts of God and annual seasons of thanksgiving to God. That a human should mark out milestones in what is, objectively, a seamless passage from cradle to grave would have appeared to the ancient Israelites as presumptuous, to say the least. As they saw it, only God could designate certain moments in the flow of time as possessing special significance. Pharaoh may even have agreed with this point of view; but then he was a god (at least in his opinion and the opinion of his people) and thus *his* birthday was a day of cosmic significance.

28. Compare his passivity with the active involvement of Abraham: when birds of prey swoop down on the carcasses of the animals he has slain for the covenant ceremony, he drives them off (Gen. 15:11).

29. He certainly shows no great desire to appear before Pharaoh. He remains frozen in his tracks, neither preparing (baking the pastries), protecting, nor delivering them.

30. Kass, 560.

31. Literally, "at the end of two years of days."

32. The rendition follows M. Dahood, based on Ugaritic usage ("Notes on Genesis," 80).

33. The suggestion is that of Samuel David Luzzato. See Glossary.

34. According to biblical narrative convention, when a specific event or occurrence is described by the narrator and then recounted by one of the persons in the drama, it is the narrator's account that is definitive.

35. This was true only of Egypt south of Memphis (modern Cairo). To the north lies the Delta, one hundred miles long and up to one hundred and fifty miles wide at its base, but also totally dependent on the inundation of the Nile.

36. That is, lacking edible kernels; the exact opposite of the fat ears.

37. Literally, "his spirit pounded"; i.e., his heart was racing.

38. Usually translated as "magicians"; "The term for Pharaoh's scholars or sages is *hartummim*, which goes back to the Egyptian term *hery-tep*, best translated as 'expert' and often found in combination *kheri-hab heri-tep* which means 'lector-priest and expert'" (Kitchen, *Reliability*, 350).

39. Another possible way of looking at things is that they (correctly) recognized the dreams as portends of evil and, afraid to be the bearers of bad news, simply professed puzzlement.

40. Literally, "placed me in custody in the house of."

41. Literally, "interpretation."

42. Eunuchs, of course, were not. Which was one of the reasons the beards were so important: they publicly differentiated "true men" from eunuchs.

43. Herodotus informs us that Egyptian priests, in addition to shaving their heads and faces, shaved all their body hair.

44. Was Joseph shaven while in the service of Potiphar on his estate? Possibly not. The narrator makes no mention of it there while highlighting it here. Moreover, when "Mrs. Potiphar" pointedly refers to Joseph as "a Hebrew," she is probably referring to his appearance as well as his ethnicity.

45. Literally, "the *Shalom* of Pharaoh." "By far the most common use of 'peace' (*shalom*) in the Bible is to mean 'well-being'—usually referring to the health or prosperity of an individual" (David Hazony, "Plowshares into Swords: The Lost Biblical Ideal of Peace," *Azure* 3 [Winter 1988]: 92).

46. The phrase is usually used of human beings. It has previously been used to describe Joseph. See Chapter 3, note 10.

47. Literally, "into their midst."

48. Literally, "consume."

49. Literally, "heavy."

50. Hebrew *nachon* is a legal term, which means to be established beyond the shadow of a doubt.

51. Literally, "look out for."

52. One of the terms used for Pharaoh's experts who had been called in to advise him, and who had failed so signally to give meaning to a dark dream.

53. From the word *hamush*, "to be armed, equipped, prepared."

54. Literally, "after."

55. All Egypt was Pharaoh's "House." The term "Pharaoh," the title of the Kings of Egypt, means literally, "Great House."

56. Literally, "by your mouth shall all my people be equipped, be provisioned." "Be directed" is dictated by the context.

57. Literally, "will I be greater."

58. I. e., "I have made you Grand Vizier." The formal Egyptian title of this office is "Chief of the Entire Land."

59. The collar of office, made of plaited gold wire, which covered his shoulders and upper chest. Thus, Alter, *Genesis*, 240.

60. An Egyptian word of unknown meaning, possibly something like "All Hail" or "Make Way."

61. The king's signet ring, when stamped on a document, was the Royal signature. Transferring the ring to Joseph gives him the power to sign in the name of the king.

5

The Egyptian

Let the dead Past bury its dead!
Act— act in the living Present!
  — H. W. Longfellow, *A Psalm of Life*

The quality of mercy is not strain'd...
        it becomes
The throned monarch better than his crown.
  — W. Shakespeare, *The Merchant of Venice, IV*

Before proceeding, let us pause to consider Joseph's new clothes. Clothing has had a key role to play in our story. It was Joseph's being clothed in that opulent and splendid "Robe of Many Colors" that first stoked to an all-consuming fire the smoldering enmity of his brothers. It served both as a symbol of his rise to preeminence and, when it was torn from him it symbolized his fall. Indeed, the robe dominates the first part of the story. This investiture and stripping becomes a prefiguring of the next stage of the tale. The presentation of the torn and bloody robe to Jacob, falsely testifying to Joseph's demise, prefigures the presentation of Joseph's garment to Potiphar, testifying (equally falsely) to Joseph's guilt. In both cases his stripping precedes his descent into the pit.

In our present case this new raiment symbolizes more than his elevation; it testifies to Joseph's transformation into an Egyptian. I am going to contend that this transformation is more than external and imposed from above by Pharaoh. The process was begun by Joseph himself upon his release from prison. It was he who began it by shaving his face and head, and dressing himself in clothing appropriate to an audience with Pharaoh: in Egyptian court attire. Pharaoh, by reclothing Joseph in costly fine linen, is simply setting the royal seal of approval on Joseph's self-transformation.

That Joseph's change of appearance is more than superficial will become increasingly clear. Its roots predate his descent into Egypt. We remember Joseph "dreaming dreams" in Canaan, so improper a phrase for a Hebrew but now finally finding its natural home in the pagan milieu of Egypt. We recall the strange content of his dreams, so inappropriate for a shepherd and only now finding its proper setting on the banks of the Nile. What I am suggesting is that the Egyptian way of life and thought come naturally to Joseph; he was from his youth a natural Egyptian. And it is this inherent nature, at least as much as his native brilliance and his driving ambition, that will enable him to make a spectacular success of his newly launched Egyptian career. In a deep sense, Joseph belongs; he has come home.

And Pharaoh said to Joseph, "I am Pharaoh! Without your consent[1] no man shall raise hand or foot in all the land of Egypt [Gen. 41:44].

5. The Egyptian

With this short statement Pharaoh lays down the ground rules that will govern both Joseph's powers and Joseph's relationship with Pharaoh.

We must never for a moment forget that Egypt was, at least in theory, a totalitarian society. At one time, in the Pyramid Age, it had been a totalitarian society in practice as well. The vicissitudes of civil strife and societal collapse, the growth of temple property holdings, the impoverishment of the crown, and the resurgence of the autonomy of the great nobles, and thus the enforced delegation of authority to them, had all led to a very real weakening of Pharaonic power. Great noblemen had been governing the country's nomes[2] with a high degree of autonomy, albeit in the name of the Pharaoh; the temples and their cadres of priests had become in large measure a law unto themselves; the country was a crazy quilt of small peasant landholders with a reasonable amount of economic freedom. Egypt was no longer as it was in the golden era of the Old Kingdom, when the whole land had been mobilized for the stupendous task of single-mindedly constructing monumental tombs for each succesive Pharaoh. Power — political, economic and religious — had over the years become disastrously diffuse.

The aim of Pharaoh, therefore, is not simply the imposition (or reimposition) of a command structure. Having orders rigorously obeyed is not sufficient. All areas of freedom and spontaneity must be obliterated. The goal is to be that no one is to be free to do anything except by direct order or express permission: "Without your consent no man shall raise hand or foot in all the land of Egypt." The vision is breathtaking. All the reins of power are to be gathered into one pair of hands. The hands of course are to be Joseph's. But he is not to be the ultimate beneficiary. He is to be the tool. Always — "I am Pharaoh!"

And Pharaoh now puts the final touches on the Egyptianization of his tool: name and mate.

And Pharaoh called Joseph's name Zaphenath-paneah, and he gave him Asenath daughter of Potiphera, priest of On, as wife [Gen. 41:45a].

Zaphenath-paneah means "The god speaks; he lives."[3] If clothes make the man, the name proclaims the essence.[4]

> In the psychology of the ancient Near Eastern world, a name was not merely a convenient means of identification but was intimately bound up with the very essence of being and inexorably intertwined with personality. The inauguration of a new era or a new state policy would frequently be marked by the assumption of a new name on the part of the king. A classic example is the case of Amen-hotep IV of Egypt, whose change of name to Akh-en-aten testified to the revolutionary new theology that he imposed on his people.[5]

The choice of a wife — a choice not left to Joseph but which also Pharaoh takes upon himself— raises some interesting questions. Pharaoh's intent is to enhance Joseph's position further by embedding him in the highest echelons of society. Marrying Joseph to the daughter of the Head Priest of On insures that no doors will be closed to him. The text pointedly does not comment on what might have been the Priest of On's opinion of the match between that "Hebrew nouveau riche" and his daughter. When Pharaoh commands, you comply, smiling all the way. (Of course Asenath's opinion was totally irrelevant, as all concerned would have agreed.)

But exactly who was this Priest of On? On, a city about seven miles northeast of modern Cairo, was one of the most ancient religious hubs of Egypt, the center of worship of the sun-god Re.[6] The Head Priest bore the title "Greatest of Seers." In an intensely religious society[7] such a marriage would have implications. It would be like being married to

Map 2

The Two Lands (Egypt) During the Thirteenth Dynasty (c. 1786–1633 BCE)

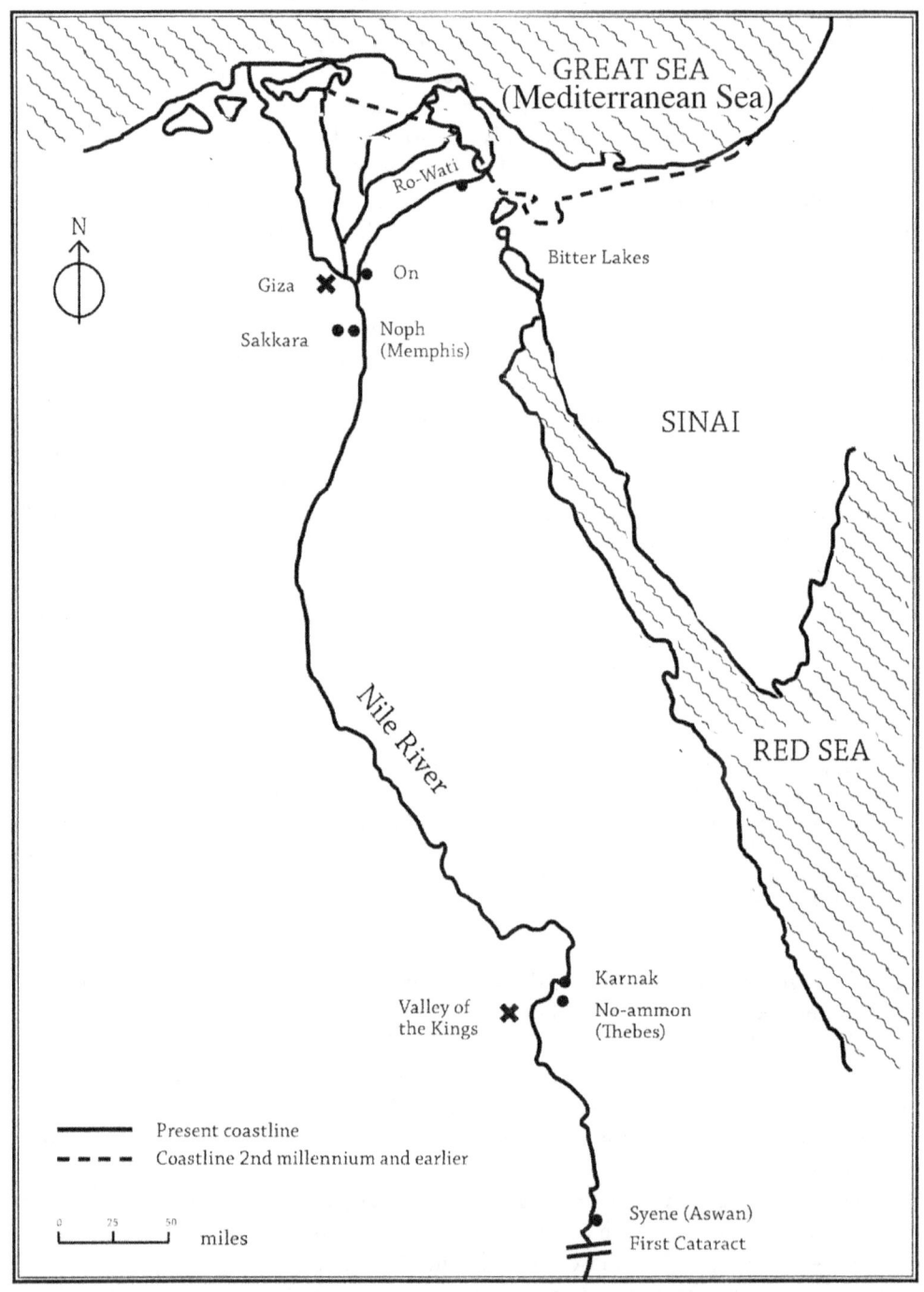

the daughter of the Archbishop of Canterbury in the England of several centuries ago. That a minimal level of public religious observance would be expected of any high state official — at the very least active participation alongside Pharaoh in the chief events of the liturgical year — would naturally apply to Joseph.[8] Obviously, more than mere perfunctory attendance would have been expected of the son-in-law of the High Priest of On.

This issue of Joseph's inevitable involvement in the pagan religion of Egypt was neatly sidestepped by noble prizewinner Thomas Mann in the most widely read version of the Joseph Story in the twentieth century: the magisterial four-volume novel, *Joseph and His Brothers*. Mann identifies the Pharaoh as none other than the heretic king Amenophis IV, better known to history by the name that he assumed, Akhenaten ("Servant of the Aten" — the sun disk). He tried to carry through a religious revolution against the traditional religion of Egypt by promoting a form of monotheism: elevating the Aten, or sun disk, to the status of a super-god while simultaneously suppressing the worship of Amun-Re, the chief deity of the then capital of Egypt, Thebes. In the process all the other deities of the traditional pantheon were also suppressed. By portraying the Pharaoh as a monotheist, and the Egyptian court as monotheist by fiat, Mann avoids any possible conflict between the faith of Joseph and that of his hosts. Indeed, he pictures Joseph and Akhenaten carrying on cozy chats on various aspects of monotheistic theology. But while this historically unsupportable fantasy might have seemed plausible to Mann, writing when he did,[9] it is not an option for us. In Joseph's time Egyptian religion was pagan, root and branch. The festivals were religious festivals centering on the worship of the various gods, and Joseph, as a court official, was obliged by his position to participate in their worship.

But things were not necessarily so cut and dried for Joseph. The public sphere was far from the only manifestation of religion in ancient Egypt. Religion was all pervasive; it permeated the private lives of individuals as well. Most people did not concern themselves with "official" religion and the temple services, except on the great feast days.

> Private worship usually took place outside Temple precincts, in small street-corner or countryside shrines, or in private homes.... Excavation of workmen's houses in the little necropolis-town of Deir el–Medina reveals that nearly all had niches for small altars and the busts and statues of gods. Very likely every house had a religious shrine of some kind. Private men created their own gods and theology.... Thus the Egyptians first set the pattern of the dual faith — a personal faith of choice combined with the public faith of duty and decorum.[10]

Thus it is perfectly reasonable to assume that Joseph could, in accord with the virtually universal Egyptian practice, participate fully in all public worship of the gods, yet feel himself at liberty to privately worship the God of his fathers, Abraham, Isaac and Jacob.[11] The question is, did he in fact do so?

And here we come face-to-face with an issue, hinted at up to now, that becomes central to the understanding of Joseph as we progress. The problem is that we are never explicitly told what Joseph's relationship with God was. We will only be able to reach any such conclusions as we do from indirect evidence. And the most important evidence comes from what is *not said* in the text. Unlike his fathers, we are never told that Joseph hears the voice of God. God, who was the ongoing companion of Abraham, Isaac and Jacob, never appears to Joseph and never speaks with him. Further, and again in contrast to his fathers, Joseph is never depicted as turning to God in prayer — even in the worst moments of his life.[12] Joseph continually talks *about* God[13] (indeed no one in Genesis speaks *about* God as much as Joseph), but he never talks *to* Him. The implications of this phenomenon, new to the biblical narrative, will be explored in due course.[14]

Perhaps some insight as to Joseph's state of mind can be gained from his reactions upon becoming a father.[15]

> *Now to Joseph two sons were born before the year of famine arrived, whom Asenath, daughter of Potiphera, priest of On, bore him. And Joseph called the name of his firstborn Manasseh,[16] "For," he said, "God has made me forget all my suffering and all my father's house." And the name of the second he called Ephraim,[17] "For God has made me fruitful in the land of my affliction"* [Gen. 41:50–52].

We remember Joseph standing speechless as Pharaoh announced his elevation to the position of power and prestige — either dumbfounded or, more likely, exhibiting glacial reserve. Years have gone by and Joseph has retained his reserve, remaining closemouthed as to his inner thoughts and feelings.[18] At long last Joseph breaks his silence and gives us a fleeting glimpse into his soul. He names his first son "he who causes to forget," giving as the reason that God has made him forget all his suffering — and here we run into an ambiguity. We have rendered his statement literally as two clauses — two separate reasons for the name: God has made Joseph forget all his suffering *and* He has made Joseph forget his father's house. On the other hand we can treat the explanation as a single idea expressed by two terms[19]: He has made Joseph forget all his suffering *in* his father's house. So does Joseph want to put all his suffering (both in Canaan and in Egypt) behind him, or only his suffering at the hands of his brothers?[20] And is it only his suffering that he wishes to forget, or is it his family as well — his father's house?[21]

The naming of his second son, Ephraim, merely shows us the other side of the same coin. He names his second son Ephraim, so he tells us, because God has made him fruitful in Egypt. After having been brought to Egypt as a slave and having suffered in prison, he has made good. Remember, when he makes this statement he has five or six years behind him of being at the top; plenty of time to have settled in and become used to power and the good things of life in the most affluent society in the world. By the names he gives both of his sons, he proclaims he has turned his back on his past, both suffering and family (and heritage?); from now on the focus will only be Egypt. The past is dead, and Joseph the Hebrew is a thing of the past. The future belongs to Zaphenath-paneah, and the Egyptian will only look forward.

But despite the best of intentions, one's past is not so easily discarded. Even as he turns his back on his father's house he gives his sons *Hebrew* names, not Egyptian ones. And the reasons Joseph gives for the names are based on *Hebrew* derivations. This is abnormal. The almost universal practice of Semites settling in Egypt was to give their children Egyptian names, even when they did not change their own. Soon his arrangements will produce their own unexpected consequences: out of his Egyptian policy his past will rise up to confront him.

The Overseer of the Granaries[22]

> *So Joseph went out over the land of Egypt. Now Joseph was thirty years old when he entered the service of Pharaoh,[23] king of Egypt. And Joseph went out from the presence of Pharaoh and went through all the land of Egypt* [Gen. 41:45b–46].

The question has been raised, considering the realities of ancient Egypt, whether the picture presented to us of a foreigner being elevated to such high office be considered even remotely possible. The answer is decidedly yes. "It was not at all extraordinary for foreigners, and Semites in particular, to be welcomed by the court and to rise to positions of responsibility and power in the government of Egypt."[24] James Hoffmeier cites an analogical case, one Aper-el who served as vizier to Amenhotep III and continued well into the reign of Amenhotep IV (Akhenaten). "In Aper-el, who was a vizier and a Semite, we have a striking parallel to Joseph in Genesis."[25]

Following a laconic remark giving us Joseph's age at the time of his appointment,[26] we are informed that Joseph immediately enters in upon his duties, beginning with an extensive tour of the country, probably to acquaint himself firsthand with the land and with the officials through whom he will have to implement his policies.

> *During the seven years of plenty the land produced abundantly.*[27] *And he gathered all the food of the seven years of plenty*[28] *that were in the land of Egypt, and he placed the food in the cities; the food from the fields around each city he placed within it. So Joseph collected grain in huge quantities, like the sands of the sea, until he ceased counting, for it was beyond counting* [Gen. 41:47–49].

The aim of Joseph is to create a command economy. This means placing all resources under state control by centralizing the storage of grain in cities where it can easily be controlled and guarded. Crops will be first collected and stored, then rationed out to the population. Inasmuch as over 90 percent of the population were peasant farmers, he was thereby inserting a layer of bureaucrats between the overwhelming majority of the people and the food they themselves had produced. Needless to say, the difference between what they had produced and what they got back is critical. Besides what was put aside for the famine, the bureaucracy created to control the economy — District Overseers and armies of clerks, accountants, collectors and guards in turn mobilized to work under their direction — siphoned off a large portion of the grain collected. Without the panic created by the looming famine — there seems little doubt that the "prediction" was promulgated far and wide to justify the radical changes taking place; Joseph seems to have cultivated the sense of a project of national salvation in a race against time — otherwise these wholesale confiscations would have produced an uprising. "And he gathered all the food of the seven years of plenty" (v. 48). Note the word *all*. Does this mean that the farmers were left without the seed grain for next years planting, and had to apply to the government even for this?

The massive collections, granary construction to hold the unprecedented supplies, and loading operations continue until (maybe about the fifth or the sixth year) the recording system breaks down, unable to keep up with the load. All pretense of accountability is now abandoned; rapacious confiscation with no pretense of a just return has become the order of the day.

> *Now the seven years of plenty that were in the land of Egypt came to an end, and the seven years of famine began to come, even as Joseph had said. Now there was famine throughout the lands, but in all the land of Egypt there was bread. When all the land of Egypt was famished the people cried out to Pharaoh for bread, and Pharaoh said to all Egypt, "Go to Joseph; whatever he says to you, [that] do." Now the famine had [spread] over all the land, and Joseph opened all the granaries*[29] *and sold food to the Egyptians. Now the famine grew severe*[30] *in the land of Egypt. And all the earth came to Egypt to buy food from Joseph, because the famine was severe in all the earth* [Gen. 41:53–57].

Two elements stand out in this section. The first is that the famine is not confined to Egypt but afflicts the entire region: Libya to the west and Syria-Canaan to the east. This is a phenomenon that is unusual, although not unheard-of, because the surrounding region depends on very different water sources than Egypt. Those regions depend on local rainfall; if the rains fail then so do the crops. But there is no rain in Egypt; the land depends on the rise of the Nile to irrigate the crops and fertilize them. And the rise of the Nile, as we have learned, ultimately depends on the intensity of rainfall in Central Africa, in the catch basin that drains into the blue Nile. A shortfall of a few inches and the Nile will not rise sufficiently to do its work in Egypt. But Central Africa is a completely different climate zone. What therefore is being reported is two simultaneous failures, a very uncommon phenomenon. The result is that Joseph, who has been squirreling away seven years of bumper crops, holds not only Egypt but also the entire region at his mercy.[31]

How Joseph deals with this situation is instructive both as to his character and to the character of the Egyptian state that he serves. He opens the granaries but does not distribute the food, which after all belongs to the farmers who grew it. He sells it to them! And probably at inflated monopoly prices as well. This is adding insult to injury. Not only have the farmers in the name of national emergency had their grain confiscated (we have not heard of any compensation), making fat a bloated bureaucracy, but they now are being forced to buy back their own grain at famine prices just to keep body and soul together. As an added benefit, the people of nearby lands will also have to purchase food at whatever price Joseph sets.

The partnership between Pharaoh and Joseph has come to pay off time.[32] As Pharaoh says: "Go to Joseph; what ever he says to you [that] do!" (v. 55). Joseph the Egyptian is the only game in town.

Notes

1. The Hebrew reads "without you." "Consent" is implied.
2. Egypt was divided into districts called nomes, a division that may go back to prehistoric times.
3. LXX seems to reflect a different name, *psontenpa-anh*, which means "the sustainer of life." But this, being a late Egyptian word, contemporaneous with the Greek translation of the Bible and suspiciously apt to the story, looks like a late interpolation.
4. "And the Lord God formed out of the earth all the wild beasts and all the birds of the sky, and brought them to man to see what he would call them; and whatever the man called each living creature, that would be its name. And the man gave names to all of the cattle and to the birds of the sky and to all the wild beasts" (Gen. 2:19–20). In the Israelite tradition God delegates His divine prerogative to man, created in His image. Pharaoh, on the other hand, a god himself, exercises his prerogative in renaming Joseph; and by bestowing upon him an Egyptian name, he proclaims him properly an Egyptian.
5. Sarna, *Genesis*, 124.
6. In Hebrew this city was known as Beth-shemesh (the House of the Sun) and in Greek, Heliopolis. The worship of Re was especially important, politically, as Egyptian theology proclaimed Pharaoh as the son of the sun-god, Re.
7. "Herodotus described the Egyptians as the most religious people on earth, and he was writing of an age when the dynamism of the Egyptian state had run down and the forms, rather than the substance, were in control. At an earlier period ... the intensity of faith was such as to exclude purely secular considerations altogether" (Johnson, 20–21).
8. As one example, in the forecourt of the principal temple at On stood the sacred stone of Re (the model for all the later obelisks of Egypt), and at its foot the great altar where sacrifices of sheep, goats, and cattle to the sun-god were carried out on an extravagant scale. On New Year's Day, Pharaoh himself presided as Chief Priest, prostrating himself before his "father" in the view of tens of thousands of his subjects. The court, as well as the commoners present, then partook of the meat of the sacrifices to Re, as well as the offerings of bread, beer, and cakes.
9. Akhenaten lived in the middle of the fourteenth century BCE While during the first half of the last century some scholars, notably H. H. Rowley, held the opinion that Joseph may have been contemporaneous with Akhenaten, more recent scholarship places him at a much earlier period. The Egyptologist K. A. Kitchen (*Reliability*, 343–359) finds the end of the eighteenth/beginning of the seventeenth century as consistent with the data reported in Genesis concerning Joseph. With this dating Joseph had been resting, mummified, in his tomb for hundreds of years before Akhenaten was ever born. For more detail on the dating of Joseph see the Introduction, page 11–13.

10. Johnson, 133, 135.

11. This would have involved continuing in the footsteps of his ancestors: offering sacrifices to God and turning to God in prayer at significant moments, and especially in times of crisis.

12. Joseph, while in prison, does deliver a heartfelt petition for succor. This one recorded plea for aid, however, is not directed to God but to a disgraced public official, a dispenser of alcoholic beverages! (Gen. 40:14–15).

13. Or "the gods;" the text is uniformly ambiguous.

14. We are speaking of the central protagonists of the Genesis narrative: God speaks to Adam and Eve (and the serpent); to Cain and Abel; to Noah; and the Fathers, Abraham, Isaac, and Jacob; as well as to Sarah and Rebecca. The absence of God in the Tamar and Judah episode (see Chapter 2) has been dealt with separately in my previous work, *Four Biblical Heroines*, Chapter 7.

15. For the purpose of a seamless exploration of our theme, we are dealing with the next verses out of their textual sequence. In Genesis the verses come in their chronological sequence: between the account of the years of plenty and the start of the famine years.

16. Meaning, "he who causes to forget."

17. Meaning either "fertile land" or "pasture land."

18. Obviously Joseph has had much to say during these years, but what he has had to say has been of a technical and administrative nature. The silence of the text implies that Joseph has avoided self-revelation; nothing that he had to say was personally significant. On the other hand, actions often speak louder than words. More on the matter of Joseph's actions later.

19. The technical term for this is *hendiadys*.

20. A further thought: does he include his father as a cause of suffering? Considering how his father doted on him, the question seems, on the face of it, preposterous. Yet it will prove, in the chapters to come, a serious issue.

21. And if so, does this imply forgetting the heritage of Abraham, i.e., the Covenant?

22. The full title of this office, which Joseph as Grand Vizier may have subsumed under his overall authority, is "The Overseer of the Granaries of Upper and Lower Egypt."

23. Literally, "when he stood before (Pharaoh)," an idiom that means "to enter into the service of." See 1 Samuel 16:22; 1 Kings 1:2.

24. Sarna, *Genesis*, 288. He gives as examples a nomad named Yanhamu and one Ben Ozen, both Semites, who rose to high office during the days of the Empire.

25. Hoffmeier, 94.

26. His age at the time of his appointment (thirty), his age at the time of his enslavement (seventeen), and the lengths of the years of plenty and the years of famine form the basis of a chronological framework for our entire narrative.

27. The Hebrew is not clear. Another way the verse has been rendered is "during the seven years of plenty he [Joseph] made storage pits for grain."

28. Reading with LXX and Sam. (Samaritan Bible, see Glossary); MT omits "of plenty."

29. Reading with LXX, Vulg., Syr.; MT reads, "everything that was in them."

30. Literally (both here and in verse 57), "strong."

31. We are not told about Mesopotamia, the far end of the Fertile Crescent. That region was also dependent on irrigation fed by the two great rivers, the Tigris and Euphrates. Were people going to Paddan-aram to buy food as well as to Egypt? We are not told. Are we not being told because it is irrelevant to our story, or is it that the river flow there too has diminished and famine is also stalking "The Land Between the Rivers?"

32. Note how Pharaoh distances himself from the actual gouging. It is Joseph's part to do the dirty work and, as front man, to be the lightning rod and take the blame. Pharaoh positions himself above the sordid world of commercial transactions; aloof and benign, the god turns his gaze to celestial matters while the cash cascades into his treasuries.

6

Cat and Mouse

Fury said to the mouse,
That he met in the house,
"Let us both go to law: I will prosecute you–

Come, I'll take no denial:
We must have the trial;
For really this morning I've nothing to do....

I'll be judge, I'll be jury,"
Said cunning old Fury:
"I'll try the whole cause, and condemn you to death."
— Lewis Carroll, *Alice's Adventures in Wonderland*

We return to the moment of Joseph becoming a father: in the act of naming his sons he has definitively turned his back on his past — his suffering and his father's house. The time has come to explore this issue further.

Not Even a Postcard

That his father's house, his family, has no idea of what has become of Joseph became evident at the time of his disappearance some twenty years previously. As will become evident in the events about to unfold, they think he is dead, resulting in a burden of guilt that the passage of time has not assuaged. That this is so is solely because Joseph has not seen fit to disabuse them of this misapprehension. Why? It is not due to any physical impediment. Even as a slave, a steward to Potiphar, he would have had ample means to send a message informing his family that he was alive[1]; how much more so these past seven years as Grand Vizier of Egypt.

That Joseph bears no love for his brothers may be understandable, but what seems incomprehensible is his callousness toward his father. His father had favored him over all his brothers, pampered and spoiled him and loved him to distraction. It is hard to believe that Joseph would have had no idea as to what his disappearance would do to his father. Yet for twenty years he has made not the slightest gesture aimed at relieving his father's sorrow. In effect, long before his declaration in the naming of his eldest son, Manasseh, he has written his father off along with his brothers. What can explain his turning his back on his father?

Let us return to Joseph's last recorded interactions with his father. After relating his self-exalting dreams to his brothers and then to his father — wherein the sun, moon and stars grovel before him—Jacob had publicly called him to order for his arrogance and slapped him down. Not long thereafter he had sent Joseph to check on his now seething brothers at Shechem. In retrospect, does Joseph blame his father for having sent him into the lion's den, abandoning him to his brothers, and thus sharing with his brothers in the responsibility for what had happened to him? Worse, has Joseph come to the conclusion that his father had been fully aware of the roiling hatred the brothers felt toward him and so, by sending him alone and unprotected to Shechem, had cold-bloodedly "set him up?" It would seem to me that some such calculation lies behind Joseph's resolute and protracted writing off of all ties to his "father's house." As his father had abandoned him, so Joseph now abandons his father. The only other alternative that appears even remotely reasonable to me is the not very nice picture of a social-climbing parvenu who is ashamed of his low origins and tries at all costs to conceal them.[2]

Joseph's motives for forgetting his father's house be what they may, events which he himself has set in motion will not allow him to disengage. With an inevitability that seems born of fate, his past reaches out and envelops him. And in confronting his brothers Joseph will be forced to confront himself: who he is as much as where he comes from.

Self-Confrontation

> *The mills of the gods grind slow,*
> *But they grind exceeding fine.*
> — Ancient Greek Aphorism

Hunger has a propellant force that is the irresistible.

Now there was a famine throughout the lands ... and all the earth came to Egypt to buy food ... because the famine was severe in all the earth. Now Jacob saw[3] *that there were provisions* [of grain][4] *in Egypt, and Jacob said to his sons, "Why do you keep staring at each other?" And he continued,*[5] *"Behold, I have heard that there are provisions* [of grain] *in Egypt. Go down there and procure* [some] *for us*[6] *from there, so that we may live and not die." So ten of the brothers of Joseph went down to procure grain from Egypt* [Gen. 41:54, 57; 42:1-3].

The family is starving and its head, Jacob, jolts his sons into action. So ten of the brothers (note: brothers of Joseph, not sons of Jacob) organize themselves to make the journey to Egypt. Joseph may be dead (they believe him so) but hardly out of mind.

The author stresses the fact that *ten* brothers went down to Egypt. His emphasis on the number *ten* was not meant as an introduction to the following verse in which we are told that Benjamin did not go with his brothers. Actually, this stress is intended to be understood in opposition to the number *Nine*. In other words the author subtly wishes to remind us that Judah has returned to his brothers.[7]

We left Judah, humiliated and deeply shaken up by his daughter-in-law, Tamar, in the lowlands, at Achzib, after having turned his back on his family for almost twenty years. And now, we are indirectly informed, he has made his peace with the family and has rejoined it. The reunion must be very recent.[8] He is very much in the background and keeping a low profile, as befits one recently readmitted to the family council. It will not be until the next chapter that he feels himself sufficiently at home to open his mouth and attempt to influence events.

> *But Jacob did not send Benjamin, the brother of Joseph,[9] with his brothers, for he said, "Lest harm befall him." So the sons of Israel were among those who came to procure* [grain], *for there was famine in the land of Canaan* [Gen. 42:4–5].

Jacob's favoritism, and his possessiveness, seems to have settled in Joseph's absence on Benjamin, sole remaining son of the beloved Rachel. Benjamin is no longer a child. At this point in our tale he must be at least in his early twenties; older than Joseph was when he vanished. A further point to ponder: it was Jacob who sends his sons, but it is as "the sons of Israel" that the brothers enter Egypt.

We remember the previous times that this shift of names — from Jacob to Israel — have taken place. The first time the name Israel was used was in the context of his open preference for Joseph (37:3). The second time was when he sent Joseph to Shechem (37:12). Now, for the first time in our narrative Jacob's sons — with Judah but minus Joseph and Benjamin — are referred to as "the sons of Israel." Once again the family is divided, the favorite excluded from the main body. The last time the favorite was sent to his brothers. Now the brothers, all unknowingly, are being sent to the former favorite.

We must not be unmindful of the crisis conditions that underlie these events. The term "provisions [of grain]," and its verbal cognate "to procure [provisions]," form a continual drumbeat throughout the chapter. Ten times the root is repeated (with an additional two times at the end of the previous chapter and three times at the beginning of the succeeding chapter),[10] emphasizing the overriding necessity that is relentlessly driving the action. The ten brothers are but drops in the flood of humanity that is being driven to Egypt by the ever-increasing pressure of starvation. Egyptian pictures realistically portray the effects of famine: gaunt figures, their ribs almost bursting from their emaciated frames, seated listlessly resigned to their grim ends. We must imagine such a horde of gaunt figures, the brothers among them, pressing on to the one locus of hope. And awaiting them is the Grand Vizier of Egypt, the dispenser of life.

> *Now Joseph was the master of the land[11]; it was he who dispensed provisions to all the people of the land. And Joseph's brothers came and bowed down to him, with their faces to the ground* [Gen. 42:6].

What is Joseph doing here? The responsibilities of the Grand Vizier were enormous. It seems that almost every branch of the State administration came under the his jurisdiction. He was the intermediary between local authorities and the king; he had to receive their reports and transmit to them the king's commands. He controlled irrigation and agriculture, the assessment and collection of taxes, the reception of foreign tribute and the entertainment of foreign envoys. He was responsible for the upkeep of roads and buildings, the police force and the army garrisons in Egypt proper.[12] And to add to all this, there is now the administration of a nationwide famine relief program. Did Joseph have nothing better to do than to personally preside over the sale of grain to hordes of starving Asiatics? Should not what was, after all, a minor sideline in the Egyptian scale of priorities have been relegated to the supervision of some mid-level member of the state bureaucracy?

Such speculation leads us to suspect that the upcoming confrontation between Joseph and his brothers will be more than a mere fortuitous occurrence. Has Joseph purposely positioned himself at the granary complex in the capital to which Asiatics are directed knowing that, with hunger driving them, sooner or later his family must turn up?[13] If so, then what is to take place will not be the result of happenstance — a cascade of spontaneous reactions to unanticipated occurrences — but rather the result of carefully considered and well-prepared programming.

6. Cat and Mouse

Now Joseph saw his brothers and he recognized them, but he treated them like strangers[14] and spoke harshly to them and said, "From where do you come?" And they said, "From the land of Canaan to procure food." Now Joseph recognized his brothers but they did not recognize him. And Joseph remembered his dreams which he had dreamt about them, and he said to them, "You are spies! You have come to see the land in its nakedness!" [Gen. 42:7–9].

The gates have been opened for the morning sale of grain to foreigners. Among the throngs pressing forward and prostrating themselves, Joseph, enthroned and in full regalia upon a podium, recognizes his brothers. Would he have so unerringly picked them out among the hundreds of similarly clad and bearded Semites groveling face down before him had he not been looking for them? He singles them out for questioning.

We are told three things by the narrator about the conditions in which the subsequent interrogation takes place. In the first place, while Joseph recognizes the brothers, they do not recognize him (hardly surprising considering that the Joseph they knew was a teenager, while the man on the throne above them is a mature Egyptian,[15] and besides they believe Joseph to be dead). Secondly, that as he confronted them, Joseph was remembering the dreams of their groveling before him that he had dreamed in Canaan.[16] And last, that he didn't let on that he knew them, and that he spoke harshly to them. Everything that now takes place is colored by these facts.

The confrontation opens with Joseph directing a perfunctory question to the brothers, and they offering a simple and self-evident reply. Then comes the thunderbolt out of the blue: "You are spies! You have come to see the land in its nakedness!" (v. 9). That is, your story of coming to buy food is a cover story. The truth is you have used that pretense to enable you to enter Egypt to uncover her military secrets (extent of border fortifications, garrison strengths, etc.)—which is what "seeing the land in its nakedness" means. You are a team of spies! The brothers, completely unbalanced both by the accusation and by Joseph's tone of voice,[17] scramble to justify themselves:

And they said to him, "No, my lord, your servants came to procure food. All of us are sons of one man; we are honest men. Your servants have never been spies." And he said to them, "No, for you have come to see the land in its nakedness!" And they said, "We, your servants, are twelve brothers, the sons of one man in the land of Canaan; and behold, the youngest is with his father this day, and one is no more."[18] And Joseph said to them, "It is just as I told you: you are spies!" [Gen. 42:10–14].

Besides sticking to their story that they merely came to purchase food, and protestations that they are honest men and no spies, the flustered brothers can come up with only one argument to support their innocence: that they cannot be spies because they are all brothers, the sons of one father. While individuals might risk the inherent dangers of espionage, no family would be so foolhardy as to risk the future of the entire family (wives and children as well) on a single joint mission. This argument, along with all their protestations, Joseph summarily rejects as unsubstantiated twaddle. This leads the brothers to further panicky protestations, fleshing out details of the original argument—that there were originally twelve brothers; that the youngest remained with their father and that one is no more—details that add nothing to the argument. As Gilbert and Sullivan were to put it:

Merely corroborative detail, intended to give artistic verisimilitude to an otherwise bald and unconvincing narrative.[19]

These, likewise, Joseph brushes aside. But now he seems to reconsider; he professes to be willing to check out their story.

> "By this shall you be tested: By the life of Pharaoh![20] You shall not go out from this place unless your youngest brother comes here. Send from amongst you one and bring[21] your brother. And [the rest of] you will be imprisoned, that your words be tested, whether they be true; and if not— by the life of Pharaoh— you are assuredly spies!" And he locked all of them up in prison[22] for three days [Gen. 42:15–17].

You claim to be brothers and that you have a little brother at home. How do I know that that was not made up on the spur of the moment? Produce him. If you can, it will tend to substantiate the rest of your story. If you can't, that will prove to me that your story is all a tissue of lies and that you are indeed spies. And then, apparently to drive home the point that he is serious and that he holds their lives in his hand, "the master of the land" claps them into prison.

And so it goes: brutal arbitrary pressure followed by partial thaw, blow followed by reprieve followed once again by blow: cat and mouse, cat and mouse.

The Name of the Game

How can we explain this ruthless game that Joseph is playing with his brothers? There seem to be only two possibilities: that Joseph, at long last having the brothers helplessly in his power, is taking his revenge for what they did to him when he was helpless in their hands. In a word, he is playing with them, torturing them; a sophisticated and drawn-out revenge. The other possibility is that Joseph is testing them to see if they have repented of their evil and reformed themselves sufficiently to merit forgiveness.

> By far the commonest suggestion for explaining Joseph's actions is some variation of the following. Joseph's intention is to test his brothers to see whether they have reformed, repented and shown loyalty to Benjamin and Jacob, as preconditions for his forgiveness and his reconciliation with them ... that Joseph has to put his brothers through such agonies if true reconciliation is to be achieved.[23]

Turner then quotes Westermann:

> The narrator wants to say that at the very moment that he saw his brothers before him, Joseph had decided to heal the breach.... The structure as a whole allows this conclusion. It is to this purpose that Joseph allows his brothers to undergo the severe trial of being at the disposition of a potentate. A quick pardon at this moment could not have led to a real solution, as the continuation shows.[24]

In other words, the pressures under which the brothers will suffer will amount to a species of "tough love." This last interpretation is the almost universal choice of commentators from ancient times down to the present.

The reasons for this choice are fairly obvious. Without some ennobling purpose behind the cat and mouse game that Joseph is playing, a game increasingly sadistic as it progresses, he risks an inevitable descent into the role of the villain of the tale. After we, as readers, have come to identify with Joseph, first as victim and then as spectacular achiever against all odds, it is almost impossible to dethrone Joseph from the role of hero. But honesty demands that we free ourselves from our natural emotional involvement in order to look at the matter from a detached point of view.

The most basic problems with the theory that Joseph is testing his brothers reside firstly in the fact that there is no hint of this in the text. When Abraham is ordered by God to sacrifice his son, Isaac, the narrator informs us at the start that this was merely a test.

Nowhere in our narrative is there any comparable statement. Second, as Mark O'Brien cogently argues, "the narrator portrays the brothers as changed men at the time of their first encounter with Joseph.... There was no need to test them."[25] Moreover, "It is difficult to see why a 'quick pardon' could not have produced a reconciliation. In fact Joseph subjects his family to such severe treatment that any reconciliation is threatened."[26]

The truth is that there are serious problems with both explanations. In the first place, the theory that Joseph is somehow testing his brothers hardly brings credit to Joseph. In some ways it is even more defamatory to Joseph's character then simple and open revenge. We have been told by the narrator that Joseph is playing with his brothers while, at the same time, remembering the dreams he dreamt[27] in Canaan. The brothers and their father had reacted to the obvious *interpretation* of the dreams[28] — that they were destined to grovel to Joseph — but neither they nor we have as yet paid sufficient attention to the *content* of the dreams, especially the second one. In the first dream Joseph appears among his brothers, a sheaf among sheaves, an equal among equals, and the other sheaves defer to him. In the latter dream Joseph does not appear; he is an unseen presence, central but invisible. All that is visible are the heavenly bodies — sun, moon and stars — and their single activity is to bow before the awesome presence of the unseen Joseph. In our preliminary analysis of this dream, we pointed out that the heavenly bodies owe obeisance only to their Creator. Joseph is receiving what is due only to God. But there is yet a further consideration: in the biblical faith all creation is visible and evident. There is but one Invisible Presence and that is God. By identifying himself with the invisible presence in his dream, Joseph was either identifying himself with God or usurping God's place — both blasphemous. If we postulate that, while remembering his dream, Joseph is "testing" his brothers, then we must conclude that he is playing the role of a deity in relation to them — for "testing" implies judgment, and who is Joseph, a mere mortal, to judge his fellow mortals? God, and only God, is capable of probing the complex motivations of a human's inner being and judging them:

> *I, the Lord, am the One who probes the heart,*
> *the One who tests the inner being,*
> *To give each person according to his ways,*
> *according to the fruit of his doings* [Jeremiah 17:10].

It is true that Joseph has an oversized ego — he could hardly have risen so fast and succeeded so well without one — and that he has always had a natural affinity for the Egyptian world and a strong tendency to assimilate into it. Yet I for one would be extremely hesitant to ascribe to Joseph the pagan belief that he himself is a god. As I hope to be able to demonstrate, even at this point Joseph is more a son of Israel, and a descendant of Abraham and Isaac, than he realizes. Deep within himself Joseph knows full well the boundary between the human and the divine, what is permitted to humans and what lies beyond the pale. As a youth Joseph may have flirted with egomania. Life has matured him. As we shall shortly learn, as a man he has put childish things behind him.[29]

So, if Joseph is not playing God with his brothers, what is driving him? We fall back on the very human desire for revenge; to get his own back at those who had cruelly stripped him, hurled him into the cistern — the first pit of the many he has endured, literal and figurative alike — and severed him from his father's house. To return he no longer desires; to make those responsible pay — yes.

Before we ourselves succumb to the temptation to play God and begin to judge Joseph, a word of caution: perhaps our reasoning to date has been too simplistic. Whatever we may think of Joseph, it would be fatal to forget that this is a person of extraordinary talent, even a genius. The locus of his genius lies not in the spiritual realm but in that of the practical: an administrator of brilliance, before he is through he will remake Egypt single-handed. To ascribe single and simple motives to him would be to misunderstand him. To pose the choice as one between "testing his brothers" and taking revenge upon them, while remaining blind to other possible factors, is to turn Joseph into a caricature. The picture we are presented is subtle and nuanced. Instead of trying to impose our categories on Joseph, let us step back and try to see Joseph and his brothers from a dialectical point of view as, I will contend, the author of our narrative presents him.

We return to that bitter moment at Dothan when, spying Joseph from afar, the brothers cease to see him as a brother and come to the decision to do away with him. By alienating themselves from him, the brothers initiated a chain of events that lead to unexpected, even perverse, results. The brothers succeed in getting rid of Joseph in the short-term, but at a disastrous price. In the long run they can't do away with him. The guilt they bear will not allow them to bury him and clear their consciences. So Joseph will come back to haunt them. Now that he is no longer with them — "he is no more" — they can empathize with his suffering.

Because the brothers had distanced themselves from him, Joseph now distances himself from them. He alienates himself from them, treats them like strangers and speaks harshly to them. And in so doing it is he who now initiates a chain reaction that breeds unexpected results. I will contend that his apparently revenge-driven games have the unanticipated result of igniting a previously unknown empathy with his brothers. From hatred is born fellow feeling.

My provisional contention is that one of Joseph's motives, though not the one uppermost in his consciousness, is to "get his own back" from his brothers. But unknown to himself other motives are stirring beneath. Just as Joseph ostentatiously proclaims through the naming of his sons that he has forgotten his father's house, yet contradicts himself by giving them Hebrew names, so when he thinks he is distancing himself from his brothers, he is actually bringing himself nearer to them. The opposite of love is not hatred but indifference. He proclaims his indifference, he pretends not to know his brothers, but he goes out of his way to meet them. Had he truly wanted to alienate himself from his family, he simply would not have been overseeing the distribution of grain to Asiatics. If our reasoning is correct, and that he prepositioned himself to be where his family would have to show up, one of the things that is driving Joseph is the desire to re-engage with his family, but on his own terms. He explains it to himself in part as a desire to make his brothers suffer for what they did to him. But his repeated bursts of empathetic emotion belie his feigned alienation.

Joseph, as I see him, is a profoundly conflicted individual. At his deepest level he loves his family; he loves his father's house. Alongside this he loves himself, and resents anything, past, present or future, that would put any limits on the scope of his place in the sun. And he will never be able to effectively reconcile these two loves. Now his conflicted self will play itself out in a game of cat and mouse. In the end the game will resolve itself, not in reconciliation but in enlightenment. And in this enlightenment Joseph will achieve greatness — not the greatness normally ascribed to him nor that we might want, but greatness of a rarer sort, not normally given to mortal man.

But perhaps even this analysis, while I believe it to be true, is also premature. Besides testing, revenge and re-engagement, there remains yet one further option. The exploration of this fourth possibility will have to wait, however, until its proper place in the tale. So until then we will suspend judgment and await the time when we will be able to reopen this issue and, perhaps, finally resolve it.

The Game Continues

> *On the third day Joseph said to them, "This do and live, for I am a god-fearing man.*[30] *If you are honest men, one of your brothers will be confined in your prison, and you go and bring provisions for your starving households.*[31] *But your youngest brother you must bring to me, that your words be verified, and that you may not die."*[32] *And they agreed*[33] [Gen. 42:18–20].

After three terrifying days, experiencing the pit in which Joseph had been immured for endless months,[34] never knowing if they would ever again see the light of day, the brothers are brought forth. Joseph ("the man" as they call him, not being privy to his identity as we are), apparently having experienced a change of heart, has reversed himself. Instead of sending one brother back to get Benjamin while leaving the nine others locked up in that horrid hole, he will merely keep one as hostage while letting nine go home. That way they will be able to take food back to keep their starving families alive while the game continues. This, moreover, may give their father the false hope that, at the price of writing off one son, the rest of the family can last out the famine until the next crop without having to go back to Egypt; Joseph knows full well that there will be no next crop, that the famine will continue, and that they will have no choice but to return to him. The brothers agree to the terms. They have no choice.

This new turn of events unleashes a storm of hand-wringing and mutual recrimination among the brothers, all unaware that everything they say is being overheard.

> *Now they said to one another,*[35] *"Truly we are guilty for our brother, for we saw the distress of his soul when he pleaded with us and we heeded not; therefore this distress has come upon us." And Reuben answered them saying, "Didn't I say to you, 'Do not sin against the boy?' But you would not listen. And behold, we are being held accountable for his blood." But they did not know that Joseph understood,*[36] *for the interpreter was between them* [Gen. 42:21–23].

The brothers are speaking freely. They must be out of earshot of the interpreter, and cannot conceive that "the man," the master of the land, understands Hebrew.

This is probably the first inkling that Joseph has had that his brothers have been suffering pangs of remorse, not only for their deeds but even more for their cruel indifference to his suffering. The fact that rather than cite Joseph by name they refer to him by the emotion-laden term of "brother" must hit him especially hard. Not having been privy to the debates among the brothers, this is probably the first time that he had any inkling that the action of his brothers, so seemingly unanimous—falling upon him, stripping him and throwing him into the cistern — was actually preceded by, and followed by, serious differences of opinion. The superstitious belief that Joseph's spilled blood (for they believe that he is dead) has come back to haunt them must be especially unnerving to Joseph. Unexpected emotions well up from his depths, emotions that he cannot control. He has no option but to turn away and leave the room.

> *And he* [Joseph] *turned away from them and wept. And he returned to them and spoke to them. And he took Simeon from them and put him in irons before their very eyes!* [Gen. 42:24].

This was unexpected. In all that Joseph has been through, we have never been told that he has wept. Stiff upper lip has been the order of the day. Yet here the iron façade cracks. This lapse must have been deeply disturbing to Joseph, revealing to him depths of feeling that he did not know he possessed. But Joseph is not made of mush. No crybaby can run the Egyptian empire. Viziers are made of sterner stuff; no temporary lapse will divert him from his carefully considered plan of action. Now he returns dry-eyed, singles out Simeon, and has him chained hand and foot. That will show them that he means business.

Why Simeon? Was it that he held a special grudge against Simeon, or was it that he was the second eldest among the brothers? Having learned that Reuben had argued against the purge of Joseph and had been overruled, perhaps following a plan that was chronologically oriented, Joseph gives Reuben the benefit of his protests and passes him over for "special attention," proceeding to the next in line.

> *Then Joseph gave orders to fill their containers with grain, to return their silver[37] to each one's sack, and to give them supplies for the road. And so it was done for them. So they loaded their provisions on their donkeys and departed from there. Now one of them opened his sack in the lodging place to give fodder to his donkey, and saw his silver; there it was at the mouth of his pack! And he said to his brothers, "My silver has been returned!" And their hearts failed them[38] and they tremblingly turned each to his brother, saying, "What has God done to us?"* [Gen. 42:25–28].

Joseph has developed into a marvelous psychologist. From the first unexpected accusation of espionage, which completely threw them off balance, the brothers have not been permitted to regain even a semblance of equilibrium. The surprises and shocking demands follow each other thick and fast. Even upon leaving Egypt they are not to be free of psychological pressure. The unexpected and the irrational pursue them, even in the sacks of grain which they have purchased. What does it mean? Will they be accused of theft? Is God playing with them? On top of the guilt they bear for leaving Simeon behind in chains, and beyond the worry of how they will break the news to their father—both of the loss of Simeon and the demand that they produce Benjamin—comes the irrational return of their money. Joseph has ensured that peace of mind will be an unobtainable blessing.

The brothers seem to have used their time on the road to orchestrate their return. While the narrator insists that they ultimately hide nothing from their father, yet the way the synopsis of events is worded and the staged "discovery" of the return of their money in the presence of their father indicates how emotionally precarious their relations with their father have become. It is as though they are navigating a minefield where one false step can trigger an explosion.

> *And they came to Jacob their father in the land of Canaan, and they told him all the things that had happened to them, saying, "The man, the lord of the land, spoke harshly to us. He made us out to be spying on the land. We said to him,' We are honest men; we have never been spies. We are twelve brothers, sons of our father. One is no more, and the youngest is with his father in the land of Canaan.' But the man, the lord of the land, said to us, 'By this shall I know if you are honest men: one of your brothers shall you leave with me, and take provisions[39] for your starving households and go. And bring your youngest brother to me that I may know that you are not spies but honest men. [Then] your brother will I give [back] to you, and you will be free to trade in the land.'"[40] And it came to pass as they were emptying their sacks, and behold, each one's money pouch was in his sack! And they saw their money pouches, they and their father, and they were afraid* [Gen. 42:29–35].

So now the recriminations begin once again; but whereas before the brothers were blaming themselves and shouldering their own guilt, here their father, in a paroxysm of maudlin self-pity, is heaping the responsibility for all that has happened on the heads of his sons while holding himself blameless. He is the innocent victim and they are the vile perpetrators.

> Then said to them their father, "Me have you bereaved! Joseph is no more; and Simeon is no more; and Benjamin you would take from me! All this has come upon me!" And Reuben said to his father, "Kill my two sons if I do not bring him back to you. Put him in my hand and I will return him to you" [Gen. 42:36–37].

Once again Reuben, the oldest, tries to save the situation. His heart is in the right place. Unless they produce Benjamin they are condemning Simeon to a lingering death in the dungeons of Egypt, and should the famine persist, only Benjamin can unlock the access to further food supplies. But his bombastic offer — trust Benjamin to me; I give you two of my sons as hostage, and you can kill them if I don't bring him back safe — falls flat. As in his clumsy attempt to save Joseph and return him to his father, so here Reuben demonstrates once again his ineptitude as a leader. His grandiloquent gesture is irrelevant and unconvincing; far from inspiring trust it produces the exact opposite. Reuben, despite his position as the firstborn son, does not have what it takes to assume the leadership role that rightfully should be his. This is his last attempt to take control of the situation. It is rejected out of hand.

> But he [Jacob] said, "My son shall not go down with you, for his brother is dead, and he alone is left. If harm should befall him in the way in which you are going, you will bring down my white hairs to Sheol in sorrow" [Gen. 42:38].

The egocentricity and blindness of the old man is mind-boggling. In his eyes he has only had two sons! One is dead, and the other is his sole surviving son whom he will not endanger. All the others are irrelevant to him and, by implication, no sons of his. That the brothers accept this without protest stands to their eternal credit. Their respect for their father, even in his dotage, overrides his rejection of them. Whatever his maunderings he will remain their father to the end.

And here, for the moment, the matter rests.

Notes

1. Jacob was living in a region that was distant only a few days journey. That there were constant communications between Egypt and Canaan is conclusively shown by the Tel-el-Amarna letters, and by subsequent events in our narrative.
2. That some elements of this second motive do exist will become evident down the line, but I find it hard to attribute his protracted estrangement from his father to this alone.
3. Not "heard," i.e., hearsay, but actually saw with his own eyes caravans returning from Egypt with food (Kimchi, see Glossary).
4. Hebrew *shever*, grain (possibly threshed grain). The term seems often to be used in emergency situations when rationing applies and may imply emergency provisions. The verbal form seems to imply the doling out or rationed purchase of limited supplies of grain.
5. Literally, "said."
6. LXX reads "a little food."
7. Sacks, 363.
8. See Appendix 2 for an analysis of the chronology and why Judah could not have rejoined the family much before the events that are now being related.
9. That is the full brother; Benjamin and Joseph are sons of the same mother as well as the same father.
10. The ubiquitous use of this root *sbr* in our narrative, in both its nounal and verbal forms, accounts for almost three quarters of all its appearances in the Bible.
11. Possibly a euphemism for vizier.
12. This catalog of responsibilities is taken from the age of the New Empire. In our earlier period they

may have been somewhat less extensive but, considering the less centralized nature of the state at that time and the much more modest administrative apparatus at the vizier's command, the burdens would have been no less backbreaking.

13. The capital, Ro-wati, was ideally sited so as to dominate the gateway between Egypt and Canaan (see Introduction, page 12). It was here that Asiatics would come for provisions. It seems likely that Asiatics were dealt with at a different depot than the ones serving native Egyptians. Under famine conditions, mixing native and foreign populations when doling out food would inevitably have led to explosive situations.

14. Hebrew *vayitnaker*, from the word *nokhri*, "a stranger, an alien." Another way of rendering this phrase would be: "he alienated himself from them."

15. Clothing aside — Egyptian men were bare-chested at this period, for a Hebrew a state of undress — the Joseph they remembered at age seventeen would already have been bearded; the Egyptian before them is clean-shaven and "made up": upper-class Egyptian men employed eye-shadow and mascara to highlight and enhance their eyes.

16. Ackerman, in pondering the syntactical connection between Joseph's recalling his youthful dreams of dominance and his immediate reaction (hurling the accusation of espionage against the brothers), "suggests that everything that follows is related to his dreams.... And somehow, from Joseph's point of view, the dreams have not been *completely* fulfilled. And as we read further it quickly becomes clear that Joseph's immediate purpose is to have the brothers bring Benjamin to Egypt. Then we recall: *all* of the brother's sheaves had bowed to Joseph's sheaf, and Benjamin is still in Canaan. The lad must join the brothers in Joseph's presence" (James S. Ackerman, "Joseph, Judah and Jacob," in *Literary Interpretations of Biblical Narratives*, ed. K. R. R. Gros Louis and J. S. Ackerman, II, [Nashville: Abingdon, 1982] 87, emphasis in the original).

17. Joseph and the brothers, as we shall learn, are conversing through an interpreter. While they can learn the content of his remarks only upon translation, they can clearly hear the tone of his voice and judge its emotional content.

18. Literally, "and one is not."

19. Gilbert and Sullivan, *The Mikado*, II.

20. This is a formal oath format. The standard Hebrew form is "by the life of the Lord." To an Egyptian, Pharaoh is a god. Joseph is swearing an oath "by god." For this understanding of the oath format, M. Greenberg, "The Hebrew Oath Particle."

21. Literally, "take."

22. Literally, "put them all together into prison."

23. Laurence A. Turner, *Announcements of Plot in Genesis* (London: Sheffield Academic Press, 1990), 156.

24. Westermann, 37–50, 107.

25. Mark A. O'Brien, "The Contribution of Judah's Speech, Genesis 44:18–34, to the Characterization of Joseph," *CBQ* 59 (1997): 436, 439. See page 103.

26. Turner, 158.

27. Note the phrase. We have already discussed the interesting phenomenon that, with the single exception of Joseph, the phrase is used in the Bible uniformly of pagans. See Chapter 1, page 44.

28. We have not as yet fully considered the question as to whether the dreams were merely wish-projections of an overinflated ego or whether they embodied true predictive power. This consideration will have to wait until a later point in our tale.

29. I thus concur with Turner when he determines, "I conclude, therefore, that the narrative provides no support for the view that Joseph treated his brothers harshly in order to ascertain or provoke their repentance" (159).

30. Literally, "for I fear God"; i.e., I am a moral man. See Chapter 3, page 71 and especially note 32 on page 75.

31. Literally, "for the famine of your houses."

32. Espionage would seem to be a capital crime.

33. Literally, "and they did accordingly."

34. But without the relative freedom Joseph enjoyed as a trustee. Moreover, the phrase we rendered as "and he locked all of them up in prison," reads literally, as we have noted, "put them all together into prison," implying that all ten were crammed together in one fetid cell. Joseph seems to have ensured that Egyptian prison conditions, horrid at best, were made especially loathsome. Did the brothers even have room to lie down?

35. Literally, "each man to his brother."

36. Literally, "was listening."

37. I. e., their money. There were no coins in those days. Lumps of silver were used as a medium of exchange, their value determined at the point of transaction by weighing them. Note that a "shekel" was not a unit of value but a unit of weight. Thus the price of Joseph when he was sold (Gen. 37:28) was silver to the weight of twenty shekels.

38. Literally, "their hearts went out of them."

39. Reading with LXX, Syr. and Targ. (see Glossary); MT lacks the word *provisions*.

40. It is not clear if the brothers are here quoting a previously unreported speech of Joseph, or if they are merely making explicit the implied terms of Joseph's conditions: bring me Benjamin and I will free my hostage and permit you to buy more grain.

7

The Entrapment

O what a tangled web we weave,
When first we practice to deceive!
  — Sir Walter Scott, *Marmion*

This impasse cannot persist. As the days lengthen into weeks the provisions dwindle and starvation once again looms. The brothers hold their peace, either out of fear of provoking another outburst from their father or in the realization that brutal necessity will, at the last, trump Jacob's intransigency. Gnawing hunger finally forces his hand.

> *Now the famine weighed heavily upon the land. And it came to pass, when they had finished eating up the provisions that they had brought from Egypt, their father said to them, "Go back and procure for us a bit of food"* [Gen. 43:1–2].

Somehow, in his dotage, Jacob seems to be pretending to himself that by adopting the stance of a beggar, whining that he wants just a *little* food ("a bit"), he can somehow circumvent the conditions imposed on them by "the lord of the land." But now, with hunger driving him, he may at last be open to reason. It is Judah who takes upon himself the task of getting their father to accept reality.

Judah Seizes the Leadership Role

In the familial and clan-based social structure of Hebrew society in the second millennium BCE primogeniture was definitive. The firstborn son was, by virtue of his premier position in the birth order, the designated leader of the next generation.[1] This position was occupied by Reuben. We have seen how, on two occasions, he attempted to assert his natural right only to fail miserably. His motives are good, but he lacks both the common sense and the personality necessary to impose his will upon either his brothers or his father. The fiasco of the endeavor to bring his father to his senses proves to be his last attempt to fill the role of leader. From here on he seems to abdicate his designated role and lapses into passivity. It is into the vacuum thus created that Judah steps.

Judah, the fourth in order of birth,[2] has at this point in his life an unimpressive, indeed largely negative, CV. He obviously participated with his brothers in the pillaging of Shechem (34:27–29). He participated in the assault upon Joseph, helping to hurl him into the cistern. He was complicit in the conspiracy to cover up the abduction of Joseph; at the very least he was present when the torn and bloody "robe of many colors" was presented to Jacob. And then, turning his back on both his family and the heritage of his fathers, he settled among the Canaanites and adapted to their norms. On the positive side of the ledger can be cited the one virtue he holds in common with Reuben: they both rejected fratricide. Each in his own way refused to stain his hands with their brother's blood.

It took Tamar to jump-start the redemption of Judah's character. Forced to confront himself and his manifold failings, he finds it within himself to publicly admit to his failures. This leads directly to the second step in his rehabilitation: he abandons the life among the Canaanites that he has painstakingly built up over two decades and returns to his family. Now he takes the next giant step: he accepts the responsibility of ensuring the survival of the family.

Up to this point Judah has held his peace. To speak up would have been futile. Jacob has been in no mood to listen. But now, sensing a crack in the stubborn wall of negativism, Judah seizes the opportunity to intervene.

> *And Judah said to him, "The man[3] strictly warned us, saying, 'You shall not see my face unless your brother is with you.' If you will send our brother with us we will go down and procure food for you. But if you will not send [him] we will not go down, for the man said to us, 'You shall not see my face unless your brother is with you'"* [Gen. 43:3–5].

Ignoring the blatant self-pity and supplicating attitude of Jacob, Judah, speaking as the spokesman of all his brothers, bluntly delivers an ultimatum to their father: face reality. Without Benjamin we will not be allowed access to food supplies. Twice he stresses this fact. Then follow the terms: we have better things to do with our waning energy than to waste it in futile excursions. If you will permit us to take Benjamin, the passport that will gain us entree to the man who controls the food, we will go. If not, we refuse to waste our time. This demarche is in effect a slap in the face to the old man, and it elicits the maudlin response:

> *And Israel said, "Why did you bring this evil upon me by telling the man that you have another brother?"* [Gen. 43:6].

This return to the self-pitying tactic of casting blame on all and sundry for his self-inflicted woes elicits a chorus of self-justification from the assembled brothers, one in which Judah wisely refuses to join.

> *And they said, "The man explicitly questioned us about ourselves and our family[4] saying, 'Is your father still alive? Do you have [another] brother?' And we answered him accordingly. How could we know[5] that he would say, 'Bring down your brother?'"* [Gen. 43:7].

This self-justifying assertion raises an important issue. The account of the brothers directly contradicts the narrator's description of the event (42:10–13). As related in the last chapter, Joseph's only question is, "*From where do you come?*" (42:7) Thereafter Joseph simply accuses the brothers of being spies, and continues to reassert this accusation. It is the brothers who blurt out the fact that they are all sons of one father, that there are two other brothers who are missing, the youngest who remains with their father in Canaan, and one who "*is no more.*" For that matter this is not the only contradiction. Judah has insisted that the man warned them, saying, "*You shall not see my face unless your brother is with you,*" but this is not how the narrator reports Joseph's speech:

> "*This do and live, for I am a god-fearing man. If you are honest men, one of your brothers will be confined in your prison, and you go and bring provisions for your starving households. But your youngest brother you must bring to me, that your words be verified, and that you may not die.*" *And they agreed* [Gen. 42:18–20].

Is Judah simply summarizing Joseph's demand, the bottom line so to speak? Yet Judah claims to be quoting Joseph verbatim; indeed he repeats the identical words twice! (43:3, 5)

There is a general rule in biblical narrative prose: the narrator is absolutely trustworthy. Anything the narrator tells us is truthful.[6] Consequently, when there is a discrepancy between the narrator's account of a specific event and that of one or more of the protagonists in the drama, we believe the account of the narrator. Thus the simple solution to our problem should be that we should believe the narrator when he tells us that the brothers simply blurted out the family data in their nervous attempt to clear themselves of the charge of espionage. We should then conclude that the brothers are simply lying (perhaps unintentionally — they may actually remember the traumatic events in the way they are presently relating them) in order to excuse themselves to their father.

But things are not that simple. Later, in his confrontation with Joseph, Judah reminds him that he had originally questioned the brothers, specifically asking them, "Do you have a father or [another] brother?" (44:19). This assertion goes unchallenged, as does his further assertion that Joseph had said to them, "Unless your youngest brother comes down with you, you shall see my face no more" (44:23), a close paraphrase of Judah's statement to his father. Thus taking into consideration that the text apparently corroborates the accounts that Judah and the brothers give to their father, it would seem that the account given in Genesis 42 by the narrator is an abbreviated version of the initial encounter between Joseph and his brothers, condensed for dramatic effect. As we continue the tale, this sparse account is amplified, the lacuna being filled in step-by-step.[7]

We return to our tale.

Judah, who has held himself aloof from his brothers' attempt to excuse themselves from any responsibility for the current impasse, refuses to be diverted from his central aim: to force their father to face facts. He treats his father's plaint as an attempt to change the subject, and he simply ignores it.

> *And Judah said to Israel, his father, "Send the lad*[8] *with me and let us rise and go, that we may live and not die; neither we, nor you nor our children. I myself will be surety for him; from my hand shall you require him*[9]*; if I do not bring him back to you and set him before you then let me bear the blame forever.*[10] *For had we not procrastinated we could have* [been there and] *returned twice over!"* [Gen. 43:8–10].

Having presented his father with an ultimatum, Judah, never deviating from either his simple language or his blunt, confrontational style, now puts the issue into a personal context. Instead of demanding that Benjamin be sent with *them*, he proposes that he be sent with *him*; that he be consigned into his personal care. When responsibility rests on everyone, it devolves on no one in particular; only when an individual takes upon himself a given responsibility does it become a serious matter.

Judah has deeply internalized the lesson so uncompromisingly taught him by Tamar. Judah's wonderfully persuasive appeal to his father resonates with echoes of his traumatic confrontation with his daughter-in-law. He first insists that whether Benjamin does or does not have leave to go is a life and death issue for them. Without Benjamin's release there will be no food, and we all will starve to death. Then Judah sharpens the focus from the general to the specific: that means you, father, will starve. But more than self-interest is at stake; at the last Judah raises his sights to encompass the future — their children. This is a rising crescendo: their responsibility to preserve their lives trumps the risk to any single one of them; then Judah insists, by implication, that the life of Israel, the head of the clan, trumps the value of the lives of any number of the brothers; finally, and above all, their ultimate responsibility is to safeguard the future, their children (and thus the future of the covenant). It is the paramount value, superseding the lives of their generation and that of their progenitor.

This had been Judah's greatest failure: worse than his callousness to his daughter-in-law had been his willingness to sacrifice the future progeny of his deceased son Er in order to avert risk to his youngest son Shelah — to sacrifice the future for the present. Tamar had risked her life to ensure the future. By so doing, she brought Judah to an understanding of his priorities. It is the future, i.e., the children, that comes first.[11] Then Judah, taking full personal responsibility, offers himself as surety — as a pledge — for Benjamin's return.[12] How seriously he means this we are soon to learn. In making this commitment, consciously or unconsciously, Judah is using the same term Tamar had used to him when, only a year or two ago, she had demanded a pledge: "[Only] if you give a pledge until you send it [the payment for her services]" and Judah had replied, *"What pledge shall I give you?"*[13] (Gen. 38:17-18). At that time the pledge had been his seal, his cord and his staff. Now, in place of objects that represent him, he offers himself. Judah then sets the seal on his commitment with a vow that should he fail in his undertaking, he will incur eternal blame. The word he uses (which we have rendered as "blame") is *het*—literally, "sin. "[14] This has a far deeper meaning than simply "taking the blame." It means that he will labor to his last days under the crushing burden of an unredeemable sense of sinfulness. This is a terrible burden of responsibility that he takes upon himself. Judah has come a long way from the crossroads at Enayim.

Judah's peroration to this powerful appeal is politic: instead of putting the blame where it belongs for the impasse that has paralyzed the family for months — their father's overprotection of his youngest son to the detriment of his other progeny — he spreads the onus to cover them all.

> *"For had* we *not procrastinated we could have* [been there and] *returned twice over!"*[15] [Gen. 43:10, emphasis added].

Unlike their father, Judah knows there is nothing to be gained by casting blame on others.[16] By the end of this little speech the leadership of the family has passed from Reuben to Judah.

Bowing to the Inevitable

In his little speech to his father, Judah has been appealing to the best in him, and it is as Israel that their father replies.

> *And Israel their father said to them, "If it must be so, do this: take some of the choice products of the land in your bags and take* [them] *down to the man as a gift—a little balm, and a little honey, gum and labdanum,*[17] *pistachio nuts and almonds. And take in your hand double the silver; and the silver that was returned in the mouths of your packs return in your hand. Perhaps it was a mistake. And take your brother and rise and return to the man. And may God Almighty*[18] *grant you mercy before the man, that he send back to you your other brother, and Benjamin. And as for me, if I am to be bereaved, I shall be bereaved"* [Gen. 43:11-14].

Judah has succeeded at the last in bringing their father around. In so doing he has cemented his position both as leader and spokesman for the brothers. His now is the persuasive voice.

Two things stand out in Israel's capitulation. In the first place, in accepting the — for him — traumatic dictates of necessity, he is simultaneously regressing to a previous time of deep stress: the confrontation with his much-wronged brother Esau. Then, as now, he had played the game of avoidance as long as possible, only biting the bullet when his hand was forced.[19] Then, as now, Jacob had labored under a heavy burden of guilt.[20] Then his approach to the danger of his advancing brother with his four hundred armed retainers had been appeasement — the dispatch of lavish gifts to temper the expected fury due to remembered wrongs. Now he reverts to the selfsame strategy, sending gifts by means of his sons, in hopes of smoothing over the impending dangers looming in the coming confrontation. Jacob seems stuck in an endless cycle of repetitions: attempts to escape the consequences of his actions, the failure of these attempts as circumstances force him reluctantly to face the consequences, and repeated attempts to "buy himself" out of an expected retribution.

Three of the items Jacob/Israel proposes — balm, gum and labdanum — we remember as part of the inventory that the Ishmaelites caravaneers were taking to Egypt when they acquired Joseph as a slave for resale in that same market. These "gifts" that Jacob/Israel has his sons take are high-value items not native to Egypt, and in high demand there. This listing, besides serving as a reminder of the Ishmaelite caravan that prompted Judah's suggestion to sell Joseph, indicates that Jacob was well aware of which foreign products were valued in Egypt.

The second matter that stands out is Jacob's resignation. The paradigmatic activist and optimist, always maneuvering, always manipulating, ever with an eye out for the main chance, has finally accepted that he can no longer control his destiny nor avoid it. What will be, will be. "If I am to be bereaved, I shall be bereaved." His half-hearted gesture, that of ordering his sons to take a gift for "the man," his specifying its contents, and his advice to return the money they found in their packs, are feeble gestures. Indeed in comparison with his past mighty efforts to carve out a life for himself, this gesture proves to be his last. After this moment Jacob, as Jacob, lapses into passivity.

Egypt Redux

> *So the men took this gift, and they took double the silver in their hand, and Benjamin, and rose and went down to Egypt and stood before Joseph. When Joseph saw Benjamin with them he sent to the one who was the over his house, "Bring the men to my house, and slaughter and prepare* [an animal], *for the men shall dine with me at noon time"* [Gen. 43:15–16].

Joseph recognizes his brothers among the crowd of Semites presenting themselves before him and takes note that there are ten of them. Counting himself and Simeon, whom he holds, the number is now complete. His condition has been met. He does not speak to them. Rather he instructs his steward, speaking in Egyptian, which the brothers do not understand, to escort the men (note the term)[21] to his home and to prepare a banquet for the noon meal — the main meal of the day. He proposes to entertain these men as his guests.

> *So the man*[22] [the steward] *did as Joseph said, and the man brought the men to Joseph's house. But the men were afraid because they had been brought to Joseph's house, and they said, "It is because the of the matter of the money that was returned to our packs the first time that we have been brought, as a pretext to attack us and to enslave us, and seize our donkeys"* [Gen. 43:17–18].

They are afraid, and justly so. Their experiences in Egypt have been brutal. The first time, upon entering the land, their reception had been to be singled out for special attention from among all the hungry horde by the awesome Egyptian official, questioned, accused of espionage, cast into prison and released only upon leaving one of their number hostage. Now, on the second visit, they are once again singled out, separated from their fellow Semites, and escorted away. Have they been told that they are being taken to the residence of "the man?" We are not informed. But what is certain is that they have no idea of the purpose. Their first panicky assessment is that they are about to be accused of theft. Having already experienced irrational accusations and the rigors of an Egyptian prison they fear for the worst: confiscation of their possessions and enslavement.

> *So they approached the man who was over Joseph's house and spoke to him at the entrance to the house. And they said, "Please, my lord, we came down at the first to procure food. And it came to pass when we arrived at the lodging place and opened our packs and behold, each man's silver was in the mouth of the pack — our silver in the full weight.*[23] *So we have returned it in our hand. And we have brought down other silver in our hand to procure food; we do not know who put our silver in our packs"*[24] [Gen. 43:19–22].

This is hardly news to the steward, as it was he who had been, on Joseph's orders, the perpetrator of the deed.

> *And he said, "Peace be unto you.*[25] *Do not fear. Your God, the God of your father,*[26] *placed the treasure for you in your packs. I have received your payment."*[27] *And he brought out Simeon to them. So the man brought the men into Joseph's house and gave them water, and they washed their feet. And he gave feed to their donkeys. And they prepared the gift against the coming of Joseph at noon, for they had heard that they were to eat bread there*[28] [Gen. 43:23–25].

The steward calms their fears; they owe nothing. He confirms that he received their money and that they are clear of any debt. He offers no explanation for the return of their money; it must have been "an act of God." He then sets the seal upon his assurances by releasing their brother from confinement, reuniting them with Simeon. He even provides food for their animals. At this juncture he must have explained to them what they are doing at the house of "the man": they have been invited to dinner.

The relief of the brothers must be immense; both the absence of any charges and the return of Simeon (in what condition after months in prison we are not told, but we can imagine) results in a collapse of tension. They enter, they wash their feet,[29] prepare their gift for presentation and with cautious anticipation await the coming of "the man."

> *So Joseph came home and they brought him the gift that was in their hand, into the house, and they prostrated themselves to him with their faces to the ground.*[30] *And he greeted them*[31] *and said, "Is your aged father, of whom you spoke, well? Is he still alive?" And they said, "Your servant, our father, is well. He still is alive." And they bowed and made obeisance* [Gen. 43:26–28].

Roughly a quarter of a century has passed since the teenage Joseph dreamed his grandiloquent dreams, and at long last the glorious moment of their fulfillment has arrived: all his brothers are groveling at his feet. But what of their aged father? It would be a bitter pill indeed should he have missed this moment by passing away in the interim between their last mission and this. No, they assure him, he is alive and well. Though absent he is yet your servant; this gift is a tribute[32] to your awesome majesty.[33]

> *And he raised his eyes and saw Benjamin his brother, his mother's son,*[34] *and he said, "Is this your youngest brother of whom you spoke to me?" And he said, "May God be gracious to you, my son." And Joseph hurried* [out] *for his feelings toward his brother overcame him and he wanted to weep,*[35] *so he came into a room and wept there* [Gen. 43:29–30].

Joseph could not have recognized Benjamin; a small child when last he set eyes on him, he now is a grown man and the father of several sons.[36] Upon confirmation that this stranger is indeed Benjamin, Joseph's reaction is twofold: at the first his response is paternal, even "god-like" in its solicitude — "May God be gracious to you, my son." But Joseph finds himself unable to sustain this pose. No sooner does he begin to address him than he is so moved that he must break off and leave the room so as to avoid breaking down in public. But why? This is the second of three encounters that lead to an unexpected upsurge of emotion that Joseph cannot control. Each apparently has different causes. We remember the first: Joseph was overcome when he overheard the brothers rationalizing their plight by saying that it was just retribution for their hardheartedness when they had turned on Joseph:

> "Truly we are guilty for our brother, for we saw the distress of his soul when he pleaded with us and we heeded not" [Gen. 42:21].

And at their reaffirming their brotherhood with him Joseph feels a wrench in his depths. Further, at that moment Joseph finds himself back in the cistern, stripped and bruised, in shock, pleading desperately for his life. And we can with ease conjecture the wave of self-pity that washes over him, pity for lost brotherhood and pity for what had befallen him. There is nothing like self-pity to induce a good cry, and Joseph indulges in one, albeit in private. It would not do to let the number two of Egypt be seen breaking down.

The current situation is different. Here the issue is not self-pity. The narrator's phrase that we have rendered as "his feelings toward his brother overcame him" is the Hebrew idiom *nikhmeru rachamav*, which means literally "his mercies were heated up." The word mercy, *rachamim*, derives from the word *rechem*, "womb," and thus denotes the feelings that a mother has for her children, the "fruit of her womb."[37] The narrator insists that Benjamin is the son of Joseph's mother, born from the same womb. Does the sight of Benjamin trigger the memory of his mother, now dead for many a year? I would suggest that, at this point, it is for his lost mother as much as for his feeling of closeness to his mother's child, his only full brother and like him an orphan, that he weeps. Kass here makes an interesting suggestion, that he is shedding tears "also for himself and the divisions within his soul."[38] Joseph's emotional makeup is not simple. Once again, when overcome, his first thought is to preserve the image of the immovable administrator, the lord of the land. And above all, the game of cat and mouse must go on. The emotional roller-coaster Joseph is orchestrating must not get derailed.

> So he washed his face, and went out and controlled himself and said, "Serve the meal."[39] Now they served him by himself, and them by themselves and the Egyptians that ate with him by themselves; for the Egyptians could not eat bread with the Hebrews — it was an abomination to Egypt [Gen. 43:31–32].

Why does the narrator digress into the details of the seating arrangements? We are told that Joseph dines at a table alone, the brothers at a separate table and the Egyptians dining with them at yet another table. Then we are given a cryptic explanation of the seating arrangements: Egypt is a racist society and it is impossible for Egyptians to bring themselves to eat at the same table as Hebrews — indeed, it would be considered an abomination.[40] So far so good. But Joseph dines apart from all of them. Why? This can hardly be the matter of rank that it is often taken to be, for then there would be no reason to mention the racial divide between Egyptians and Hebrews. But remember that Joseph is a Hebrew — all Egypt knows this basic fact. Though he dresses like an Egyptian, speaks accentless Egyptian and holds the highest appointive position in the land, he cannot cease being a racially despised Hebrew. All must bow to him and obey his least command, but none will eat with him.[41] On the other hand, in part because as an Egyptianized Hebrew of high rank (and because he cannot give the game away by admitting his relationship to these Hebrews) he cannot eat with them either. Both by the culture that he has adopted as his own, and the high pinnacle to which he has climbed, Joseph is self-alienated from his own. So we are being shown, by something as trivial as seating arrangements that, despite everything, Joseph is suspended between two worlds, belonging to neither, at home nowhere.

> *And they* [his brothers] *were seated* [at a table] *before him: the firstborn according to his birthright and the youngest according to his youth. Now the men* [stared] *at one another in astonishment* [Gen. 43:33].

The seating order is preset. The brothers are escorted to their places and find themselves sitting in their proper birth order, from oldest to youngest. How could anyone have known? It seems like magic. The element of the unknown has returned, and anxiety reigns in its wake. And the irrational continues. Despite the total reversal of roles, from accused spies to honored guests, despite "the men" being treated as men by "the man," uncertainty persists. They cannot regain their balance. The charade continues.

> *Now portions were passed to them from before him* [Joseph], *and Benjamin's portion was five times larger than the portions of all the rest* [Gen. 43:34a].

The animal that was slaughtered for the feast is being carved at the head table where Joseph sits in stately solitude, and servants pass the portions to the diners. Benjamin, though the youngest, gets a cut five times the size of those of his brothers. Why? And of course drink is passed around in copious quantities.[42] Conviviality is now the order of the day.

> *So they drank and got drunk with him* [Joseph] [Gen. 43:34b].

The Set-Up

During the siesta which follows the banquet, while the brothers are sleeping off the effects of their heavy eating and drinking, Joseph is busy.

> *Now he commanded him that was over his house, saying, "Fill the men's packs with food, as much as they can carry,*[43] *and put each man's silver in the mouth of his pack. And my goblet, my silver goblet,*[44] *place in the mouth of the pack of the youngest,* [along with] *the silver for his provisions." And he did as Joseph had spoken. With the morning, at first light, the men were sent off, they and their donkeys. They exited the city; they had gone no great distance when Joseph said to him who was over his house, "Rise, pursue the men. And when you overtake them say to them, 'Why have you* [re]*paid evil for good? Why have you stolen my silver goblet?*[45] *Is it not the one from which my Lord drinks and assuredly divines?*[46] *This is an evil thing that you have done!'"* [Gen. 44:1–5].

Joseph is setting up his brothers in general, and Benjamin in particular. The last time around, without evidence, Joseph accused his brothers of espionage. This time there will be evidence to back up his charges, even if he himself has to plant it. And once again we are confronted with a necessity of grappling with the question: what is driving Joseph to play the games with which he is torturing his brothers?

The standard explanation is that all this cat-and-mouse maliciousness is simply the stage setting for the ultimate test of the sincerity of his brothers' repentance for the crimes they have committed. The question is whether, when push comes to shove, the brothers will treat Benjamin as they treated him, and abandon him. As Sacks puts it:

> Joseph has now decided to put his brothers to the fullest test. He will place them in a position where they will be strongly tempted to treat Benjamin as they had treated him. The point of Joseph's trial is that repentance is only complete when one knows that if he were placed in the same position he would not act in the same way he had acted before.[47]

But this reasoning is spurious because the analogy won't hold. The cases of Joseph and Benjamin are in no way similar. The brothers hated Joseph because of his pretentious arrogance and because he informed on them. There is absolutely no evidence in the text that Benjamin was either arrogant or a tattletale. For that matter, there is no evidence that he was hated. Furthermore, what drove the brothers to do away with Joseph is that he was a threat to their future. By presenting Joseph with a "robe of many colors" their father had designated him as the future leader of the clan. The thought that this arrogant little monster would someday have power over them drove the brothers frantic. This was a future that had to be aborted at all costs, while it was still possible. Their purging of Joseph had been, in the minds of his brothers, essentially an act of self-preservation.[48] But their father had never presented Benjamin with a similar robe. He was not the designated heir apparent and so no threat to their future. There was indeed every reason to expect the brothers not to treat Benjamin as they had treated Joseph, and when indeed this proves to be the case nothing whatsoever is proved. The test is no test. What is more Joseph, being far from stupid, would have appreciated this only too well.

Then what is the point of the relentless hounding of his brothers that we are witnessing? We have already discussed briefly the issue of Joseph's motivations. Perhaps this is the place to shift focus and ask ourselves the question as to how Joseph understands himself and what he is doing.

We have already suggested revenge as a possible motivating factor, even though there is no overt evidence for this in the text. It is, however, extremely doubtful if Joseph would have seen himself as consciously seeking to "get his own back" from his brothers. This would have seemed too petty for such an exalted a personage as the Grand Vizier of Egypt. We will have to look elsewhere, and the narrator gives us a nudge as to in which direction to look. When Joseph first beheld his brothers the narrator informs us: "And Joseph remembered his dreams which he had dreamed about them" (Gen. 42:9). Is the narrator hinting that Joseph views himself in the context of his youthful dreams of grandeur, and sees the current situation (which, if we are correct, he himself has engineered) as part of a predestined drama in which he reenacts in reality what he previously had experienced in a dreamscape?

Let us look at the immediate outcomes of Joseph's stage-managing, and then reason backward to try to intuit the purpose. Joseph, on the flimsiest of pretexts, demands that the brothers produce Benjamin, and makes Benjamin's appearance before him a condition for future food purchase. Then he imprisons Simeon as a hostage, and generally arranges matters so that the brothers have no alternative but to bring Benjamin down to Egypt. Next, he frames Benjamin and thus provides a pretext for extracting him from the family, to be his personal slave. But what does Joseph stand to gain from all this?

We return to Joseph remembering the dreams of his youth; remembering them as his brothers are lying face down before him in the dirt of the great courtyard fronting on the granary. Here at long last his dream is being realized. But wait: in the dream *eleven* stars bowed low to him, and here only ten brothers lie prostrate. This is no true fulfillment of the dream. Only when all eleven brothers grovel before him can the dream's conditions be satisfied. Forcing the brothers to return with Benjamin makes the fulfillment of this part of the dream possible. And so it comes to pass: in his house all eleven brothers (Simeon having been liberated and rejoined with them for the occasion) prostrate themselves before Joseph.[49]

But having achieved this realization of his dream, why does Joseph continue his game? Simply because all the terms of the dream have as yet not been satisfied; his father has not yet prostrated himself before him. So now, I would suggest, it is Jacob that becomes the focus of Joseph's maneuvers. Did Joseph expect his father to accompany Benjamin, the obverse of keeping his son by his side when he originally sent all the other brothers to Egypt? If this was the expectation it was dashed.[50] So the problem becomes how to induce Jacob to come to Egypt. The answer is to use Benjamin as bait. It would seem reasonable to assume that if the brothers were to return home with the news that Benjamin had been seized and enslaved by "the man, the Lord of the Land," in due course Jacob might feel himself compelled to go to Egypt to attempt to procure the release of his beloved son. One can easily imagine Joseph picturing, in his mind's eye, his father, prostrate before him, pleading for the remittance of Benjamin's sentence, thus fulfilling another portion of the dream. Thus the framing of Benjamin becomes but one more step in the program of "dream realization." On this reading, Joseph's behavior can be only described as compulsive.[51]

Does Joseph expect the brothers to cut their losses and abandon Benjamin as they have, in effect, abandoned Simeon?[52] If so he has badly misread the situation.

The trumped up charges to be brought against Benjamin are more than simple theft. They are, first, the theft of a precious object (silver), a cup of high, even magical significance which enables its owner to discover hidden mysteries,[53] and second, gross ingratitude; repaying open-handed hospitality with larceny. The range of the charges is designed to shock.

> *So he* [the steward] *overtook them and spoke to them in these words. And they said to him, "Why does my Lord speak words such as these? Heaven forbid*[54] *that your servants would do such a thing. Behold, the silver*[55] *that we found in the mouth of our packs we returned to you from the land of Canaan. How then should we steal from the house of your Lord either silver or gold?"* [Gen. 44:6–8].

The brothers respond with shocked indignation that such an accusation could ever be made, citing as proof of their honesty the fact that when they had discovered their silver in their packs, fearing some mistake, they had brought it back all the way from Canaan. So certain are they of their innocence that they proceed to a rash commitment:

> *"With whomsoever among your servants it be found, let him die; and we also,*[56] *we'll be slaves to my lord." And he said, "Let it be according to your words. He with whom it is found shall be a slave to me, and you shall be blameless"* [Gen. 44:9–10].

In effect what the steward says is: for so heinous a crime, the punishment you suggest is appropriate. But I am impressed by your protestations of innocence and am convinced by them that this is no conspiracy. Most of you are indeed ignorant of the theft and thus innocent. But one of you has perpetrated this deed, and he alone shall bear the guilt. Then, with a display of magnanimity (but in reality acting on Joseph's instructions), he commutes the sentence from death to slavery.

> *So they hurried, and each man lowered his pack to the ground and opened it. And he searched, beginning with the oldest and ending with the youngest, and the goblet was found in Benjamin's pack* [Gen. 44:11–12].

The steward, possibly from having observed his master's maneuvers, now enters into the game of cat-and-mouse with gusto. Having planted the goblet, he, of course, knows exactly where it is. But he begins where it is not, leaving the discovery to the very end, allowing their confidence to build before shattering it. In the process he is once again demonstrating to the bewildered brothers the mysterious knowledge possessed by the Egyptians of their birth order; nothing is hidden from these Egyptians! Note also that nothing is said about the silver in the mouth of their packs, the existence of which provides a further shock to the brothers. This silver has become a motif of their troubles; wherever they go it follows them. They can't seem to get rid of it. The steward contemptuously ignores the silver in a single-minded search for the goblet, and the brothers keep their mouths shut, by this time terrified of drawing attention to what may get them deeper into trouble. And then comes the final shock — the discovery of the goblet.

> *Then they tore their garments*[57]*; each man reloaded his donkey and they returned to the city* [Gen. 44:13].

What is not usually noted at this point is that only Benjamin is under arrest. The other ten brothers are under no compulsion to return to Egypt. It is their spontaneous decision not to abandon their brother that leads them to accompany him back to "the scene of the crime" and the terrifying "man" that awaits them.

> *So Judah and his brothers arrived at Joseph's house, he still being there,*[58] *and they threw themselves on the ground before him* [Gen. 44:14].

Something has happened. Up to now we have been thinking in terms of Joseph and his brothers. But the ground has been shifting as the tale progresses. Judah's presence, at first only hinted at, then becoming overt, has been increasingly prominent. Now it has become official. Judah has now been accepted by his brothers as their leader and spokesman, and thus is in direct competition (although no one yet knows it) with Joseph for ultimate leadership of the covenanted family and the people yet to come.

> *And Joseph said to them, "What deed is this that you have done? Didn't you know that a man such as I would surely divine?" And Judah said, "What can we say to our lord? What shall we speak and how can we justify [ourselves]? God has found out your servants' transgression.*[59] *Behold we are my lord's slaves, both we and him with whom the goblet was found in his hand." And he [Joseph] said, "Heaven forbid that I should do so!*[60] *The man in whose hand the goblet was found will be my slave; as for you, go up in peace to your father"* [Gen. 44:15–17].

Behind the façade of almost obsequious abasement and confession, Judah is laying the basis for making a stand. In the first place, in the name of all the brothers he accepts collective responsibility for the crime. He makes no claim of innocence; the goblet being found in Benjamin's possession, no profession of ignorance or non-involvement will hold any weight. We were caught red-handed and must accept the responsibility. On one point only does he obliquely contradict his accuser. Joseph had boasted that it was through his more than human, occult powers of divination that he had been able to identify the thief, while Judah quietly insists that it is God who is the source of hidden knowledge.[61] This amounts to a subtle critique of the charge. Only God is infallible; all human activity (including divination) is open to human error. Of course Judah can have no certainty that Benjamin did not somehow appropriate the cup. In the nature of things he was not watching him every moment that they were in the Grand Vizier's house. But his conviction of the potential fallibility of divination will give him the courage to stand his ground against Joseph's implied claim of omniscience. If God revealed to Joseph who it was that stole the cup, then Judah has nothing to say. But knowledge from any other source is open to challenge. Beyond that, speaking as spokesman for the entire family, Judah insists that they will not abandon Benjamin. If slavery is the fate that awaits him, than this will be the fate of them all.

This will not suit Joseph. If we are correct in our supposition that he may be intending to use Benjamin as bait to lure his father to Egypt, then he needs the other brothers as messengers to bring the news of Benjamin's seizure to Jacob. He expresses shock and horror at the injustice of Judah's offer; only the guilty should suffer. He reiterates the stance of the steward: the brothers are free to abandon Benjamin and leave.

The brothers, despite the fearful pressures upon them, have made their gesture of solidarity with Benjamin. Now Joseph has reminded them that their father is starving. Go, he tells them, and save the life of your father. He has given them an "out." The question now becomes, will they take it?

Notes

1. Jacob, by designating Joseph as the future leader of the family (by clothing him in a "robe of many colors"), was clearly flying in the face of long-established custom. There seems to me little doubt that this flouting of tradition was as much a factor in provoking the vehement animosity of the brothers as Joseph's arrogant personality.

2. Simeon and Levi, respectively the second and third in birth order after Reuben, seem to have been non-contenders. Their one moment of prominence was to initiate a massacre of the men of Shechem in order to rescue their kidnapped sister, Dinah, and avenge her rape (Gen. 34, especially vv. 25–31). This exploit did not lead to a leadership role in the family. At any rate, at this juncture Simeon is out of the picture, being detained in an Egyptian prison. Of Levi we hear nothing; he makes no protest when his younger brother Judah pushes himself forward.

3. Originally referred to as "the man, the lord of the land" (Gen. 42:30, 33), now and henceforth shortened to "the man."

4. Literally, "emphatically asked us about ourselves and our kin." The phrase that we have rendered as "explicitly questioned" consists of the verb *to ask,* repeated twice for emphasis (technically termed "the infinitive absolute"). This grammatical usage, employed when an author wishes to place unusual emphasis upon a particular act, is extremely difficult to render into idiomatic English. This problem is usually coped with by adding an adverb to replace the infinitive form of one of the verbs; thus instead of "the man warned warned us" in verse 3, the phrase is rendered "the man strictly warned us." So here "the man questioned questioned us" is rendered as "the man explicitly questioned us." In all such cases the adverb does not appear in the original Hebrew but is a replacement for the repeated verb, necessitated by the demands of idiomatic English translation. The term we have rendered as family, *moledet,* has the meaning of kindred, i.e., relatives that are not necessarily limited to the immediate nuclear family.

5. Yet another instance of a verb repeated for emphasis. Literally, "knowing could we know?"

6. "The Bible always tells the truth in that its narrator is absolutely and straightforwardly reliable.... In context his remain accounts of the truth communicated on the highest authority.... The reader cannot go far wrong even if he does little more than follow the statements made and the incidents enacted on the narrative surface.... But follow the biblical narrative ever so uncritically, and by no great exertion you will be making tolerable sense of the world you are in, the action that unfolds, the protagonists on stage, and the point of it all" (Sternberg, 51).

7. Meir Sternberg, following his assertion that the narrator always tells the truth, immediately modifies this affirmation: "On the other hand, the narrator does not tell the whole truth either. His statements about the world — character, plot, the march of history — are rarely complete, falling much short of what his elliptical text suggests between the lines. His *ex cathedra* judgments are valid as far as they go, but then they seldom go far below the surface of the narrative, where they find their qualification and shading" (ibid.).

8. Hebrew *naar,* a term that can be used for any male from infancy to marriageable age (Sarna, *Genesis,* 298) Although the youngest of the brothers, as noted in the previous chapter, Benjamin at this point must be, at a minimum, in his early twenties.

9. An idiom meaning "I shall be held responsible," and used primarily with regard to matters of bloodshed.

10. Literally, "I will have sinned against you for ever," i.e., the guilt for my failure will never leave me.

11. It is in this, even more than in his steadiness and persuasiveness, that Judah far surpasses Reuben in qualification for leadership. Reuben, by his grandiloquent and ultimately unconvincing gesture, "Kill my two sons if I do not bring him back to you," is proposing to sacrifice the future to safeguard the present generation, Benjamin. Reuben is where Judah was before Tamar taught him where his priorities should lie. More, while Reuben only offers to sacrifice his two sons, Judah has already lost two. Reuben and Judah are a contrast between immaturity and hard-won maturity.

12. "The Hebrew stem '-r-v [arev] is most frequently used in reference to the acceptance of legal responsibility for a debt contracted by another. The guarantor may undertake to ensure that the borrower will not disappear, or he undertakes to repay the loan should the borrower default" (Sarna, *Genesis*, 298).

13. In the case of Tamar, she demands a pledge (*eravon*)—an article of value to hold against the payment for her services. In our case the term Judah uses, *eervenu* (I will be surety, a pledge), is the same word in a different grammatical construction.

14. *Het* is a sin that is committed unintentionally, inadvertently. Needless to say Judah will do everything within his power to avoid committing it.

15. I am indebted for much of the above analysis to Kass, 584–586.

16. Implied in this remark is the fate of Simeon. They should have returned at once to free him. Because of their procrastination he has been rotting in prison all this time. Their father has been sacrificing his second son due to his fears for the youngest—yet Judah pretends that the *sin* is due to them *all*.

17. See Chapter 1, note 45.

18. Hebrew *El Shaddai*: an appellation for God most common in the Age of the Fathers and in pre-monarchial Israel. The term *Shaddai* is probably cognate to the Akkadian *shadu* which means mountain, and thus would be parallel to the divine epithet "The Rock" (cf. Psalm 18:3, 32, 47; 92:16; 2 Samuel 23:3; etc.). The Vulgate renders *Shaddai* as "Omnipotens" from which we derive the traditional English translation of "Almighty." In Genesis the appellation *El Shaddai* is always connected either to a promise of fertility or the preservation of life. Here the reference is to the lives of both Benjamin and Simeon.

19. During the years that Jacob had spent "abroad" he had been the "guest" of his uncle Laban—in effect in the power of a double-dealer who shamelessly exploited him. In the end Jacob proved himself the sharper dealer of the two and got the upper hand of his uncle, enriching himself at his expense. This engendered such fierce enmity on the part of Laban and his kin that Jacob felt that he had no alternative but to flee Paddan-aram, forcing him to return to Canaan where he would have to confront the brother whom he had cheated.

20. It was Jacob's theft of his brother's blessing that led to his flight, fearing Esau's revenge.

21. Just as Joseph has become "the man," so have the brothers ceased to be referred to as "brothers" and have been depersonalized, becoming simply "the men."

22. An abbreviation of "the man who was over the house," i.e., the steward. Note how all the actors are being stripped of their individual attributes and are being reduced to their basic common denominator: simply "men."

23. I.e., all the money we had paid. See Chapter 6, note 37.

24. Is the steward multilingual that they can converse with him, or is an interpreter present at the house? This may explain why only now, at the entrance to the house, the brothers speak.

25. I.e., rest easy, have peace of mind.

26. The God of your father: a common expression in the Ancient Near East to designate a deity of whom the speaker does not know either name or attributes.

27. Literally, "your silver came to me," a legal formula confirming receipt of full payment and implying renunciation of any claim (Sarna, *Genesis*, 301).

28. I.e., to dine there; bread is being used as a synonym for food.

29. Wearing sandals in a dusty environment would leave one's feet extremely dirty. Thus the first act upon entering (or prior to entering) any abode would be to wash one's feet.

30. Reading with LXX and Vulg.; MT lacks the word *faces*.

31. Literally, "and he inquired as to their peace."

32. The Hebrew term, *mincha* (repeated four times), which we have rendered as "gift," is actually a technical term referring to an offering brought in token of submission. By far the most common use of this term in the Bible is to designate an offering to God. Is the repeated use of this term a hint that this offering is deemed by Jacob and his sons as being consigned to one of virtual semidivine status? It could well be taken as such by Egyptians.

33. Joseph receives the news in silence. "Nothing is said about his feeling any relief at the news that his father is alive and well" (Kass, 588).

34. I.e., his full brother, as opposed to all the others who were half brothers.

35. Or, "he was on the verge of weeping."

36. See Chapter 9 for a discussion of the sons born to Benjamin prior to the descent into Egypt.

37. The only other place in the Bible where this exact idiom is used is in the story of Solomon's judgment, when two women claim the same infant. Solomon decrees that, as there is no objective evidence that can differentiate between the two claims, the child be cut in half and each woman receive one half. The true mother cannot bear to see her child killed; "her mercies were heated up" (1 Kings 3:26), i.e., her compassionate feelings overcome her and she renounces her claim. Better the child should live even if he belongs to another. (On the basis of her renunciation, Solomon declares her the mother and awards her the child.)

38. Kass, 589.

39. Literally, "place bread."

40. This is the first use of the term "abomination" in the Bible, a term that is critical to the understanding of the Israelite ideal of purity, especially in Leviticus. Its use in this context underlines the strength of Egyptian feelings of racial and cultural distance from the Hebrews, as well as highlighting the contrast between Egyptian and Israelite values. More on this point later.

41. And Joseph is far too wise to attempt to break this taboo.

42. Egypt, as a grain-growing country, had a large brewery industry. Beer was the national drink. Aristocrats, on the other hand, drank wine, much of it imported.

43. That is, with no relation to the amount they have paid.

44. The Hebrew word *geviah*, probably a loan word from the Egyptian term for a "libation vessel," seems to denote a bulbous-shaped cup of larger than usual size; hence our rendering of "goblet."

45. Reading with LXX. Syr. and Vulg. reflect a similar reading. MT lacks this question.

46. Literally, "divining he will divine"; another example of a verb repeated for emphasis. For the significance of this remark see note 53 below.

47. Sacks, 379.

48. This explains why Judah's proposal was so readily accepted by his brothers; if the primary aim was to remove Joseph from the succession to leadership of the clan, selling him into slavery in a foreign land would be as effective as killing him, and further would have the advantage of enabling them to avoid fratricide.

49. It must be kept in mind that at this point the brothers are unaware that it is Joseph who is the object of their obeisance. It is to the "Lord of the Land" that they are bowing.

50. Perhaps this might explain the first words Joseph addresses to his brothers on their second visit: "Is your aged father, of whom you spoke, well? Is he still alive?" Working on the assumption that Jacob and Benjamin are inseparable, and expecting therefore to see them both, Jacob's nonappearance would raise the fear of illness or death as the most likely causes for his absence.

51. Turner, to whom I owe the above scenario, takes the matter yet one step further. He reminds us that not only the sun but also the moon (Joseph's mother) bowed to him in his dream. But Rachel is dead. "The reader, however, is left to ponder whether Joseph considered this to be impossible. Does he attempt to fulfill only those parts of the dream which can be fulfilled, or has he become so intoxicated with power that he believes he is capable of anything, and if his plans to get Jacob had not been thwarted, would have plotted even the fulfillment of the element concerning his mother?" (Turner, 163).

52. It is brutally clear that it was hunger, and not the desire to free Simeon, that led the family to produce Benjamin.

53. The purpose of divination, treated as a science in Egypt, was to gain knowledge of the future as well as other matters normally hidden from human eyes. This was accomplished by reading the omens. This in turn is "predicated on the assumption that the course of events is predictable: its advance notices are imprinted in natural phenomena" (Milgrom, *Numbers*, 472). While it is impossible to tell exactly what kind of divination is meant here, it is probable that the particular method referred to (technically termed hydromancy or oleomancy) involves interpreting water or oil patterns in a cup. Drops of oil would be put into a cup full of water, or drops of water into a cup of oil, and the future was foretold from the shapes assumed by the drops.

54. Hebrew *Halilah*, an idiomatic expression often rendered as "far be it from me that...." It expresses shock and indignation at the very idea.

55. Reading with LXX; MT lacks the word *the*.

56. I.e., the rest of us.

57. In demonstrative mourning for the doom hanging over Benjamin; he is as good as dead, as is their father when they are to return without him. See Chapter 1, note 52.

58. I.e., he has not left for work and is waiting for the denouement of their return.

59. Hebrew *avon*; a wrong deed, known to be wrong yet committed nevertheless.

60. Joseph expresses shock, in this case feigned, at the very suggestion that he should lend a hand to so disproportionate, indeed so unjust a procedure. See note 54 above.

61. This is a fundamental divide between monotheism and paganism. Pagans believe that human beings, using divination and magic, can acquire both knowledge and power beyond that apportioned to ordinary mortals. Thus these practices are intrinsic to paganism. It is the conviction that omnipotence and omniscience are unique to God that led Israelite monotheism to declare both divination and magic as no more than manifestations of human hubris, and to ban their practice.

8

The Unmasking

The loathsome mask has fallen, the man remains
Sceptreless,
— Percy B. Shelly, *Prometheus Unbound, II*

Up to now we have tended to view "the brothers" as a unified and villainous corporate mass as opposed to Joseph, the hero of the tale; and so indeed Joseph has viewed both them and himself. But the term "the brothers" is an abstraction, a generalization. The fact is that every group is comprised of individuals, each one a unique personality. While it is true that the majority of "the brothers" remain mere names, devoid of personality and individual attributes until almost the end of the tale,[1] some of them have been progressively emerging from anonymity to individual and differentiated treatment.

The first to do so was Reuben when he took a stand against fratricide. Because of his stand Joseph was not murdered outright but rather thrown into the cistern. This was the most that Reuben was able to accomplish, and under the circumstances it was no small accomplishment. We know he was opposed to the assault upon Joseph from the start, and did all he could to reverse its outcomes.[2] His overheard I-told-you-so reminder to his brothers—"Didn't I say to you, 'Do not sin against the boy?' But you would not listen. And behold, we are being held accountable for his blood" (42:22)—was an eye-opener to Joseph. The revelation that at least one of his brothers had been on his side on that terrible day at Dothan is probably a prime cause of Joseph's loss of self control.[3] And, as already mentioned, it was also the probable cause that Reuben, despite being the obvious choice as hostage, was passed over and spared months of incarceration in an Egyptian dungeon. Along with Joseph, we too are beginning to differentiate between the brothers, singling out some for special assessment.

The next to take note of is Benjamin, the youngest in the family. We have been watching with ever increasing unease the special treatment accorded him by Joseph. First, his presence is made the condition of future food supplies; then, at a banquet in which the brothers are guests of honor, he is served a portion five times that of his brothers.' Finally, it is he who is chosen to be the "fall guy," framed and consequently reduced to slavery.[4] We have speculated that it is the fact that Benjamin is Joseph's only full brother that accounts for this "favoritism." But we can mention another factor that makes Benjamin unique in the eyes of Joseph: he was the only brother that was not involved in the attempted murder of Joseph. A mere child at the time, he was neither with them at Dothan nor privy to their intent. There is far more than his father's favoritism that sets Benjamin apart from all his brothers.

Lastly, we have been watching Judah increasingly standing out from his brothers. The process begins with that morally ambivalent suggestion that they sell Joseph into foreign slavery rather than kill him.[5] Then Judah voluntarily separates himself from the family for over two decades — a period during which he grows in moral stature — to return a changed man. Now we have been observing him by stages assuming the leadership of the family. All this lengthy process is unknown to Joseph. He has no warning that the Judah standing before him in the midst of his brethren is not at all the Judah he knew over twenty years before. He is due for an even bigger surprise than that accorded him by Reuben.

The game that Joseph has been playing with his brothers has the aspect of a carefully choreographed drama. In this drama the parts are carefully delineated: "the brothers" are cast in the role of the collective villain of the piece, while Joseph has reserved for himself the role of victim-hero. With the framing of Benjamin the drama has reached its planned climax.

We have not been told how the climax was to have played itself out; we can only speculate. Upon the "discovery" of the "purloined goblet" the steward annulled the rash sentence the brothers had imposed on themselves. He then arrested Benjamin, decreed a verdict of enslavement on the "guilty party," and freed the ten remaining brothers to continue on their homeward journey. It is plain that he was not acting on his own initiative. Even though we are not specifically told, he could not be other than acting on Joseph's explicit instructions to arrest only Benjamin. This is the whole point of the exercise: to possess Benjamin. This line of reasoning leads me to conclude that Joseph assumed that "the brothers," running true to form, would abandon Benjamin and seize the opportunity to hurry off with the grain in obedience to the twin imperatives of getting themselves far from danger and getting food to their starving families.[6] And it is just here that things begin to go wrong.

Foregoing their chance to get away, with one accord Benjamin's brothers refuse to abandon him, and voluntarily return with him to Egypt — to the house of "the man." Upon their arrival in Egypt Judah is differentiated from "the brothers," being delineated as their spokesman.

"So Judah and his brothers arrived at Joseph's house" (Gen. 44:14). The decision to formally designate Judah as their leader, with the task of speaking for them, must have been taken during this short trip. Someone would have to present their case and, after the demonstration of Judah's skill in bringing their father around, it must have seemed obvious to all that Judah was their best bet. If our reasoning is accurate, Joseph must have been surprised to find himself confronting all his brothers, and not just Benjamin. Based on what was to follow not so far in the future, I think that Joseph was planning a warm, although perhaps private, reception for Benjamin. With all the brothers present he has no choice but to continue to play the game: harsh, accusatory and trumpeting his omnipotence. But instead of the expected denials and protestations of innocence, Judah admits all. Further, speaking for all his brothers, he makes explicit what had been implicit in their return: they would not abandon their brother. If his fate is to be slavery, then it is there that they will join him.[7]

Though the brothers cannot know this, their declaration is deeply unsettling to Joseph. It reverses the terms of his drama. By sticking to their brother at any cost rather than abandoning him, the brothers have transmuted themselves into the hero-victims, while Joseph has been transformed into the oppressor-villain. Considering that it is he who had framed Benjamin, this reversal is deeply embarrassing and cannot be tolerated. Joseph rejects it categorically, attempting to regain the moral high ground by insisting that the very suggestion is unjust and that he would never accede to it.

"Heaven forbid that I should do so! The man[8] in whose hand the goblet was found will be my slave; as for you, go up in peace to your father" [Gen. 44:17].

Joseph is saying, categorically, that he will not allow the brothers to stick together. If they won't abandon their brother voluntarily, he will force them to abandon him. Besides, he continues, think of your father (who is also his father, though of course he cannot mention this). You are free and I will not hold you; go and take food to him before he dies. It is Joseph's mention of their father that provides the fulcrum for Judah's appeal, enabling him to gain the leverage to break, once and for all, Joseph's game plan.

Judah Steps into the Breach

And Judah drew near to him and said, "Please, my lord, please allow your servant to speak a word in the ear of my lord. And do not be angry with your servant, for you are like the Pharaoh himself" [Gen. 44:18].

It is worth pausing to consider this opening. Judah's wording recalls that used in the incident when his great-grandfather, Abraham, pleaded for the doomed cities of Sodom and Gomorrah. God had charged that the moral turpitude of the cities had exceeded all tolerable boundaries, and had passed a verdict on them of destruction. The account continued:

Abraham remained standing before the Lord and Abraham drew near and said.... "Please, I venture to speak to my Lord ... please, let not my Lord be angry that I speak" [Gen. 18:22–23, 31, 32].

Being recalled by the wording to that ancient incident, we are led to recall the basic principle undergirding Abraham's plea:

"Heaven forbid[9] that You should do such a thing.... Heaven forbid! Shall not the Judge of all the earth deal justly?" [Gen. 18:25].

The central contention of Abraham is that one representing high moral standards, and holding the responsibility of administering high affairs, is obligated to maintain those standards and not abrogate them. Being reminded of this principle we are being invited to read Judah's plea in its light.

A further point: the interview begins with the brothers, Judah among them, prostrate on the ground and at a distance from Joseph. Judah drawing near to Joseph implies that he has risen to his feet. Drawing near indicates that the distance between them has lessened. The request, "Please allow your servant to speak a word in your ear," suggests intimacy; a private as opposed to a public communication. Thus we have two men standing, no distance between them, holding a private conversation. With the exception of the deferential, even obsequious language—*"for you are like the Pharaoh himself"*—Judah has managed to establish a situation of near equality between them. In these conditions Judah commences his appeal.

"My lord asked his servant, saying, 'Do you have a father or [another] brother?' And we said to my lord, 'We have an old father, and a young child of his old age, and his brother being dead he is the only one by his mother who remains, and his father loves him.' Now you said to your servant, 'Bring him down to me that I may lay my eye on him.' And we said to my lord, 'The lad cannot leave his father; should he leave his father he would die.' And you said to your servants, 'Unless your youngest comes down with you, you shall see my face no more'" [Gen. 44:19–23].

Up to this point Judah is simply summarizing the course of events which both we and Joseph know well. Beyond a certain pathos in the way the situation is described, Judah has added nothing to Joseph's understanding.[10] Now Judah enters into territory that lies beyond Joseph's ken.

> *"And it came to pass, when we went up to your servant, my father, we related to him the words of my lord. And our father said, 'Go back and procure for us a bit of food.' And we said, 'We cannot go down unless our youngest brother is with us; then we will go down, for we may not see the face of the man unless our youngest brother is with us.' Your servant our father said to us, 'You know that my wife bore me two [sons]. Now one went out from me, and I said: Surely he has been torn to pieces,[11] and I have not seen him since. And you would take this one also from me![12] Should harm befall him you will bring down my white hairs to Sheol in grief'"[13]* [Gen. 44:24–29].

Judah's recounting of the events in Canaan, while informing Joseph of nothing that he could not have assumed, is nonetheless extremely revealing. His account once again expands that of the narrator, adding nuances that deepen our understanding of both the Jacob and Judah. Jacob is quoted as saying, "You know that my wife bore me two [sons]." This tells us nothing new. We have already been made aware that as far as Jacob is concerned he only had one wife, Rachel, and consequently only two true sons, Joseph and Benjamin. All his other wives and their sons are irrelevant to him. Up to now the brothers have passed over these inferences in silence. It must be very hard for Judah to admit publicly that his father does not consider him a real son. It is a mark of his maturity that he can publicly admit to such deeply humiliating treatment and accept it out of an unqualified love for his father.

In passing he reveals (perhaps inadvertently) something about his father: Jacob has never really accepted Joseph's death. He remains highly ambivalent. While on an intellectual level he accepts, on the basis of the evidence of the torn and bloody robe, that Joseph "is dead" (42:38) and "no more" (42:36), yet now Judah quotes him as saying, "I have not seen him since" (44:28). Emotionally he cannot accept Joseph's death, which is probably why Jacob has been unable all these years to achieve closure and to go on with his life. For twenty-two years he has been frozen in this ambivalent posture, alive and yet not alive, which is what makes his dependence on his one remaining "son" so precarious.

With this as preparation Judah comes to the essence of his plea.

> *"And now, should I come to your servant, my father, and the lad—whose life is bound up in his life—is not with us, now it will come to pass when he sees that the lad is missing he will die; and your servants will have brought down the white hairs of your servant our father to Sheol in sorrow. Now your servant has pledged himself*[14] *for the lad to my father, saying, 'If I do not bring him back to you then the sin* [that I have sinned] *against my father shall stand for ever.'*[15] *Therefore please let your servant remain as a slave to my lord in the place of the lad; and let the lad go up with his brothers. For how can I go back to my father and the lad not be with me? Let me not see the evil that would befall*[16] *my father"* [Gen. 44:30–34].

Joseph's attempt to regain the high ground has failed. All unbeknownst, Judah has opened Joseph's eyes to the full enormity of the sadistic games he has been playing. Beyond the psychological tormenting of his brothers, beyond willfully perverting justice by planting false evidence and bringing false charges, Joseph is committing patricide. He, the beloved son, is about to murder his father. All the long-suppressed love of father and family, and all the values of his ancestors rise up in revulsion. Contrasted to the nobility of his brother Judah, who is offering to exchange his freedom for that of Benjamin, and so save the life of a father that has in effect rejected him, Joseph sees himself for what he is—despicable.

In the face of this shattering self-discovery, Joseph's façade crumbles and he completely breaks down. The game has ended.

The Mask of Joseph and the Mask of God

Volcanic eruptions do not come unheralded; they are preceded by preliminary earth tremors. Joseph's previous breakdowns have been minor and controllable; by removing himself from the vicinity, crying a bit in private, and then readjusting his mask, as it were, he could return to continue the game. This time the breakdown is total. There is no question of replacing the mask and continuing; the façade of the aloof and unapproachable "man," the lord of the land, is forever shattered. All that Joseph can manage, before irretrievably dropping the visage of the persona that he has built over most of his life, is to clear the room of spectators to the disrobing of his soul.

> *And Joseph could no longer control himself before all those in attendance on him, and he cried out, "Everyone clear out!"*[17] *Thus there was no one standing with them when Joseph made himself known to his brothers. Now he burst into sobbing,*[18] *and the Egyptians*[19] *heard; and it was heard* [in] *the House of Pharaoh.*[20] *And Joseph said to his brothers, "I am Joseph; is my father is still alive?" And they could give him no answer because they were in shock*[21] [Gen. 45:1–3].

Joseph manages to hold himself in check while his startled Egyptian staff troops from the room, before bursting into hysterical sobbing (weeping would be too mild a term). Needless to say his attendants do not stray far. Avid ears are listening at every door and under every window, and relaying what they hear to others. In no time, word of these happenings has reached the palace. As Joseph fully knows, events such as these cannot be kept secret. It is just that he cannot bear to have strangers present at the moment when he bares his soul and declares himself once again part of the family.

Joseph, the master diplomat, is anything but diplomatic with his brothers. The emotional eruption he is undergoing allows him no time for a gentle build up. The self-revelation bursts upon the startled brothers with shocking abruptness. As soon as he can bring his torrent of sobbing under partial control, he gasps out, "I am Joseph!" And then, almost as an afterthought, "Is my father still alive?"[22] Note the *my*. Jacob is the father of everyone in the room, yet Joseph cannot bring himself to refer to *our* father. At the very moment of his reuniting with the family a yawning gap separates the parties[23]; small wonder that his brothers are struck dumb.

The word the narrator uses when he speaks of Joseph "making himself known" to his brothers, *behitvada*,[24] appears in only one other place in the entire Bible. In Numbers 12:6, in the context of an extremely dramatic incident,[25] God uses this term to describe His self-revelation to prophets. The verse reads as follows:

> *And He said, "Hear these My words:*
> *When a prophet of the Lord arises among you,*
> *I make myself known to him in a vision,*
> *I speak to him in a dream* [emphasis added].

That the author should select for use in our case a rare term which God uniquely uses to describe His mode of revealing Himself to man suggests that there is something more going on than merely a person dropping his mask at the end of a masquerade — something revelatory, even prophetic. Alerted by the author, we are prepared to take extremely seriously remarks that are often devalued as being little more than self-congratulatory bombast.

We return to Joseph. Sensing the chasm separating him from his brothers, he continues:

And Joseph said to his brothers, "Please, come close to me," and they came close. And he said, "I am Joseph your brother, whom you sold into Egypt. And now, do not be sad or angry with yourselves that you sold me here, for God sent me before you to preserve life. For it is now two years that there has been famine in the land, and there are yet five years in which there will be neither plowing nor harvest. Now God has sent me before you to ensure for you a remnant on earth, to save you alive for a great deliverance. So now it was not you who sent me here, but God. And He has made me a father to Pharaoh,[26] *and the lord of all his House, and ruler over the whole land of Egypt* [Gen. 45:4–8].

This is a remarkable statement from a man who is, within the context of Genesis, demonstrably secular. Son, grandson and great-grandson of men whose lives centered on God and who regularly and routinely worshiped Him, yet Joseph is never recorded as either praying or engaging in an act of worship to the God of his fathers.[27] To be sure, Joseph constantly talks *about* God (no one in Genesis talks *about* God more).[28] But he never talks *to* God, never prays *to* God, and never worships God. And of course God never talks to him as He continually communicated with his father, grandfather and great-grandfather. His is the first generation to whom God is silent!

Because of the overt secularism of the Joseph narrative there is a tendency among some commentators to treat Joseph's words as part and parcel of Joseph's usual self-justifying rhetoric, yet the author has tipped us off that such is not the case. We are being directed to treat Joseph's words as revelatory; something on the level of prophetic truth. Is Joseph's revolutionary self-understanding, his insight into his place in the cosmic scheme of things, the result of a long process of introspection or rather a sudden unexpected insight, the pieces suddenly coming together as a function of the emotional crisis he is undergoing? We are not told. Yet at this particular climax in his emotional life, Joseph is able to articulate a vision of breathtaking insight with vast theological implications. In four short sentences this self-made man — superlative manipulator, administrator, fixer and achiever — has come to the realization that his life is not about himself at all, but rather that he has been serving a purpose of transcendental scope. Far from being the prime player in life's drama, he is but a pawn in a game played on a vast board whose purpose he but fleetingly glimpses and whose end is beyond his comprehension. But now he does understand the purpose of his life: to save his family from starvation. It is this that he spells out to his still dumbfounded brothers and, I believe, to himself as well. Thus what is taking place is a dual process: Joseph is dropping his mask and revealing himself to his brothers, and God, using Joseph as a vehicle, is dropping His mask and revealing His workings to mankind.

We shall go into greater detail and explore the implications of this revelation at a later point. At present we return to Joseph's efforts to re-affiliate with his family.

Part of the shock the brothers are experiencing is due to the fact that the Egyptian "lord of the land" is speaking Hebrew! "I am Joseph; Is my father still alive?" were the first Hebrew words he has spoken to them. An interpreter no longer stands between Joseph and his brothers. The distance between them has narrowed, linguistically as well as physically. But despite this real attempt to set his brothers at ease, and to bridge the gap created by time, hatred and guilt — "And now, do not be sad or angry with yourselves that you sold me here, for God sent me before you to preserve life ... it was not you who sent me here, but God." (5, 8) — Joseph's greatest moment is tainted by ego; he can't stop himself from boasting.

"He [God] *has made me a father to Pharaoh, and the lord of all his House, and ruler over the whole land of Egypt"* [8].

This effort to alleviate feelings of guilt, and to build bonds of brotherhood falls far short of success, for now the attempt to open a conversation among putative equals degenerates into a series of preemptive commands.

> *"Hurry, go up to my father* (note the *my*) *and say to him, 'Thus says your son Joseph*[29]*: God has made me the lord of all Egypt! Come down to me; do not delay! And you shall dwell in the land of Goshen, and you shall be near me, you and your sons, and your son's sons, and your flocks and your cattle, and all that is yours. I will sustain*[30] *you there, for there are yet five famine years* [coming], *lest you be impoverished—you, your House and all that is yours'"* [Gen. 45:9–11].

Having dictated to his brothers the message they are to deliver, verbatim, to their father, Joseph continues:

> *"And behold, your eyes see,* [as well as] *the eyes of my brother Benjamin, that it is my mouth that speaks to you. And you shall recount to my father all my glory in Egypt, and all that you have seen. Now hurry and bring down my father here." And he fell on the neck*[31] *of his brother, Benjamin, and he wept. And Benjamin cried on his neck. And he kissed all his brothers and wept on them. Now after this his brothers spoke to him* [Gen. 45:12–15].

The significance of the preemptory tone of these fiats, as well as their long-term ramifications will be discussed at some length in the next chapter. For the present it will be sufficient to note that Joseph is finally taking steps to fulfill his mandate as he sees it: he will save the family by bringing it down to Egypt where he will take it under his care. He orders his brothers to convey this message to *his* (Joseph's) father, again using the first person singular. His conspicuous disinclination to use the inclusive "our" is probably not intentional. In his mind he has always set himself apart from his brothers; they are two separate but related species within the larger ambit of "the family." The one and only development seems to be in his new attitude to Benjamin. In the adult Benjamin he seems to see another member of his particular species, which he expresses in his special relationship to him and by distinguishing between him and the rest of his brothers. His comment, "Behold, your eyes see, [as well as] the eyes of my brother Benjamin, that it is my mouth that speaks to you" in which he authenticates the truth of his pronouncements by pointing out that they can see that it is his very own mouth that is speaking Hebrew to them[32]—arbitrarily differentiates between Benjamin and his other brothers. All the brothers have eyes and ears; the phrase "behold your eyes see" is all inclusive. The only purpose that can be served by the phrase "and the eyes of my brother Benjamin" is to drive a wedge between Benjamin and the rest of his brothers. From now on the family will consist of two unequal groupings: Joseph and Benjamin, and "the others."

One final comment on Joseph's exposition: four times Joseph refers to God, the general term used by Israelites and pagans to refer to deity.[33] However, when the narrator refers to Divine Providence as directing Joseph's destiny, it is the Lord, the God of Israel that is named. Thus when Joseph arrives in Egypt and lands in the house of Potiphar, we are informed that "the Lord was with Joseph" (39:2), an assertion that is repeated a further four times.[34] When Joseph subsequently lands in prison we are again informed that "the Lord was with Joseph" (39:21), an assertion repeated twice. Yet Joseph never mentions the Lord, only God. Is this a sign of Joseph rejecting the particularism of a special relationship between the descendants of Abraham and Abraham's God? It is too early to speculate. We will simply keep these facts in mind.

His exposition concluded, Joseph gives way once again to a display of emotion: beginning with Benjamin he weeps on the necks of his brothers, one at a time. He also kisses them. Instructively, while Benjamin reciprocates and weeps along with Joseph, we are not informed of any of the other brothers breaking into tears. And while Joseph kisses each in turn, we are not informed that the brothers return his kisses. The whole description leaves the impression of a very one-sided emotional display. The episode concludes with the enigmatic remark: *Now after this his brothers spoke to him* (Gen. 45:15). This calls to mind the comment at the beginning of our tale, how Joseph's brothers related to him: *They hated him and could not speak peaceably to him*[35] (Gen. 37:4). There we were specifically told how his brothers felt toward Joseph and how they articulated their feelings. By contrast here we are pointedly left in the dark as to how his brothers feel about him and his treatment of them; nor are we given any indication as to either the tone or the contents of their speech. Despite this evident reluctance on the part of the narrator to elucidate or comment, I think that we can safely assume that, considering the circumstances, the brothers were both polite and extremely careful in their remarks. The gap between Joseph and most of his brothers remains daunting.[36]

Aftermath

Our author leaves the brothers to their difficult task of sounding each other out and trying to establish lines of communication after a hiatus of twenty-two years, and turns the spotlight on a palace buzzing with gossip of the dramatic happenings we have been witnessing.

> *Now the report was heard in the House of Pharaoh, to wit*[37]: *the brothers of Joseph have come. Now [the matter] found favor in the eyes of Pharaoh and his servants.*[38] *And Pharaoh said to Joseph, "Say to your brothers, 'This do: load up your beasts and go; come to the land of Canaan and take your father, and your households and come to me, and I will give you the best the land of Egypt [has to offer], and you will eat the fat of the land.' And now you command them,*[39] *'This do: take wagons from Egypt for your children and for your wives, and convey your father and come. Don't bother about your personal possessions,*[40] *for the best of all the land of Egypt shall be yours"* [Gen. 45:16–20].

Apart from the revelatory segment of his exposition, Joseph's speech to his brothers has been extremely bombastic and egotistical. He self-importantly informs them that he is "a father to Pharaoh, and the lord of all his House, and ruler over the whole land of Egypt," and in the verbal epistle that he directs his brothers to deliver to *his* father, he informs Jacob that he is "the lord of all Egypt." This boasting[41] may be understandable as having its origins in the wish to overawe his family, but objectively it is simply not so. The Lord of all the land of Egypt is Pharaoh. The grandiose promises Joseph makes to his family are empty unless Pharaoh confirms them. The narrator, by shifting the scene to the palace, intervenes to set the record straight by showing where the real power lies, thus puncturing Joseph's pretentiousness.

Pharaoh summons Joseph and gives him orders. Why doesn't Pharaoh leave Joseph to handle his own family affairs? Is it that he suspects that, left to his own devices, Joseph may do less than he should, short-changing his family? As it happens, both Pharaoh and Joseph have the same idea: rather than leaving the family where it is and sending food to them as needed to tide them over the next five years, their solution is to relocate the family to Egypt, i.e., bring them to where the food is. This is the simple administrative solution to an immediate problem which gives scant thought to long-term consequences.

8. The Unmasking

The offer seems generous and, from the family's point of view, it assuredly is. They would be satisfied with much less. But from Pharaoh's point of view it amounts to, as we would say, chicken feed. As we shall learn, the entire family comes to a total of no more than seventy souls — not even a statistical blip within the masses of Egypt's population. For Pharaoh the offer amounts to no more than a gesture of appreciation for the sterling achievements of his prize administrator. And what is this proposal for Joseph? At the best evaluation, it is a way of reuniting himself with his family (we remember his remark, "And you shall live in the land of Goshen[42] and you shall be near me"). In the alternative view, it could be seen as a way of imposing his domineering influence over the family, a virtual impossibility were they to remain in distant Canaan. We must never forget his early dreams; we have been warned that he never has (42:9). Most probably his motives are mixed; we will have to see how things develop before coming to any conclusions.

> *And so the sons of Israel did[43]; Joseph gave them wagons as Pharaoh had commanded,[44] and he gave them provisions for the journey. To all of them, to each one, he gave a change of clothing, but to Benjamin he gave three hundred [shekels of] silver and five changes of clothing. And to his father he sent as follows: ten donkeys bearing [some of the] best [products] of Egypt, and ten she-asses bearing grain, and bread and food for his father for the journey. So he sent off his brothers and they went, and he said to them, "Do not be in turmoil on the way"[45]* [Gen. 45:21–24].

This is an offer that can't be refused. Joseph, at once, expedites Pharaoh's command (was it original to Pharaoh or is it an idea that Joseph had had some hand in?). Laden both with basic staples and goodies, and accompanied by ox-drawn wagons to transport their aged father, as well as those incapable of making the journey on foot — the sick, pregnant women, and little children — the brothers set out for Canaan. Joseph's parting admonition is instructive: "Do not be in turmoil on the way," that is, keep calm, keep cool. Is the admonition ironic, a reaction to the notably reserved attitude adopted by the brothers to Joseph's self-revelation? Or is he concerned that, once out of his presence, all the emotions that they have been repressing will break out uncontrollably? Either way, Joseph seems to have doubts as to the depth of the reconciliation he had hoped to effect.

> *So they went up from Egypt and came to the land of Canaan, to Jacob their father. And they told him, saying, "Joseph is still alive; and he is ruler of all the land of Egypt." His heart froze for he didn't believe them* [Gen. 45:25–26].

It is obvious to all, even before the brothers open their mouths, that something dramatic and unexpected has happened. Besides the ten donkeys they had taken with them from Canaan, now loaded to the maximum, are another twenty similarly laden, and ox-drawn wagons of Egyptian manufacture to boot! If they were wearing the new fancy Egyptian clothing Joseph had given them, the effect would have been more dramatic still. And then, even before the starving women and children can fall upon the food, the brothers blurt out the news: Joseph is alive and ruler of all Egypt! Their father goes into shock.[46]

We are informed by the narrator that the reason for Jacob's collapse is that "he didn't believe them." What didn't he believe? Here, contrary to the general opinion, I rely on the reasoning of Maurice Samuel:

> What does the narrator mean to tell us here? Thomas Mann assumes, as every one else seems to do, that Jacob fainted with the pain of his joy. But "if he believed them not" why should he have fainted with joy? The narrator is driving at something else. *Jacob did not believe that Joseph could have behaved with such savagery toward himself and toward his brothers.* That is the shocking point, and I insist that we have here the most damning comment in the story.[47]

The narrator continues:

And they spoke to him all the words that Joseph had said to them, and he saw the wagons Joseph had sent to carry him, and the spirit of Jacob their father revived. And Israel said, "It is enough! Joseph my son yet lives. I will go and see him before I die" [Gen. 45:27–28].

Maurice Samuel comments:

> "It is enough." The wagons convince him that the "ruler over the land of Egypt," the cold jester who had said: "Ye shall not see my face except your brother be with you," has decided to end the cat-and-mouse game, and the Joseph of old, the Joseph the father believed in, is yet alive. It is enough and more than enough. Nothing matters but that Joseph is alive; and the old man prepares for the last journey of his long life.[48]

Notes

1. This is largely due to the concise style of the narrative, driven by the author's desire not to get bogged down in side issues.
2. We remember being told that his aim was to return Joseph, unharmed, to his father (Gen. 37:21–22).
3. Three times the iron façade cracks, and Joseph cannot control the tears that well up. At each instance we speculate on the proximate causes of the breakdowns.
4. We have speculated that this might just have been a ploy to get Benjamin away from the family and into Joseph's hands.
5. Morally ambivalent because we are not told Judah's motivation: to save Joseph's life or to turn a dirty dollar?
6. This assumption on the part of Joseph would be eminently reasonable; after all, self-interest and the pressure of necessity had in the past led his brothers not only to dump him but also to abandon Simeon.
7. Note that, though not spelled out but implicit in this stance is that, by it, they are condemning their families to death by starvation.
8. Note that, despite having been "introduced," he does not refer to Benjamin by name. Benjamin also has been depersonalized into simply "the man."
9. This is the very phrase that Joseph has just used—implying outraged high moral standards. See Chapter 7, note 54 and 60.
10. The same cannot be said for us. In reminding Joseph of his cross-examination of them on the occasion of their initial interview in Egypt, and of his decree, "Unless your youngest brother comes down with you, you shall see my face no more," we are being informed that the narrator's account of that original interview was no more than an abbreviated summary in which much was left unsaid. See page 109–110.
11. Literally, "mauled he has been mauled"; once again a verb repeated for emphasis. The Hebrew root *trf* refers specifically to the mauling and mangling of prey by vicious carnivore, especially lions.
12. Literally, "from [before] my face"; i.e., from my presence.
13. Literally, "in evil." For Sheol see Chapter 1, note 55.
14. Literally, "has become surety."
15. See Chapter 7, note 10.
16. Literally, "find."
17. Literally, "Remove every man from off of me!"
18. Literally, "he gave his voice in crying."
19. Reading with LXX; MT reads, "Egypt."
20. Reading with LXX and Syr.; MT reads "and the House of Pharaoh heard." I.e., the news reached the Palace. In effect everyone in Egypt, high and low, is privy to what is taking place in Joseph's house.
21. Literally, "they were terrified before him." The term here rendered "were terrified" also has the sense of "struck dumb."
22. In the deepest sense this was no afterthought. More than anything else, it was the thought of his father, forced upon him by Judah—the word *father* repeated 14 times (!) in his appeal—that, penetrating his façade, triggered the eruption.
23. Much ink has been spilled trying to reconcile this question with the fact that Joseph has already been told that their father is still alive (Gen. 43:27–28). No reconciliation is necessary considering the

explosive emotional pressure under which Joseph is laboring, not to mention the newly awakened guilt he is experiencing over what he has been doing to his father. Indeed, to expect rational self-consistency at a time such as this is not to take seriously the emotional crisis through which Joseph is passing.

24. This is the reflexive form of the verb *yadoah*, to know.

25. The incident involves Miriam and Aaron, sister and brother, respectively, of Moses, who have been spreading racist slander concerning their brother's marriage to a black woman. It is God who is calling Miriam and Aaron to task for their offense.

26. I.e., Grand Vizier. "This phrase was applied to viziers as far back as the third millennium." (Speiser, 339)

27. And this despite, as we have previously indicated, the fact that, by virtue of his position as a high official of the court and government of one of the most intensely religious peoples of the Ancient World, he would have had to participate routinely in the worship of the deities of Egypt. See pages 89–91.

28. We have already called attention to the ambiguous nature of many of these references to deity. It is often far from clear if Joseph is talking about the God of his fathers or "the gods" (the term *Elohim* is a plural form and can mean "the gods"), or simply "the realm of the divine" recognized by pagans. At times Joseph may have been talking out of both sides of his mouth, meaning God while knowing his pagan listeners would understand him to be referring to "the gods." And perhaps there were times when Joseph himself was not sure to whom or to what he was referring.

29. There are various attempts to explain the use of his opening phrase as being a standard preface, or "messenger formula," that would precede any letter or communication in the Ancient Near East. To my way of thinking, this attempt to excuse Joseph of hubris does not work. Within the context of the Bible, the use of this formula is restricted almost exclusively to use as a preface to the Word of God ("Thus says the Lord") and, to a much lesser degree, it is used for the edicts of kings. It is to this ubiquitous biblical usage that Joseph's words must be compared and in this context the words "thus says your son Joseph" sounds, at the very least, pretentious; at the worst it borders on the blasphemous (we remember Joseph's second dream where he all but usurped the place of God).

30. I.e., provide for you.

31. Hebrew *tzavar*; this word refers not only to the neck but also to the shoulder blades. As the word, in both its appearances in this verse, is in the plural it might be better to render it as "shoulders."

32. Ibn Ezra, ad loc.

33. See Chapter 3, notes 13 and 15, and pages 69–70, 71–72.

34. See pages 69–72, 73.

35. See Chapter 1, note 16.

36. Or, as Herbert E. Ryle, *The Book of Genesis* (UK: Cambridge University Press, 1914), 403, puts it: "Joseph's brethren were evidently slow to believe that they might rely on his sincerity."

37. Literally, "saying."

38. The biblical text constantly draws a distinction between Pharaoh and the Egyptians. They are to be seen and judged separately.

39. Reading with LXX and Vulg.; MT reads, "You are commanded."

40. Literally, "Your eyes shall not have pity on your personal possessions."

41. It is this boasting tone that leads some of the most perceptive modern commentators to suspect that Joseph's remarks as to God's plan and his place in it is simply part and parcel of his self-promotion, even his self-deception. For example: "Though it may seem uncharitable to mention it, we do not even know if Joseph believes what he is saying, or, perhaps, what he believes, since he all too often appears to us inclined to conflate himself with deity" (Kass, 607–608).

42. Goshen: a fertile district in the northeast corner of the Nile Delta, lying athwart the direct route between the Egyptian capital and Canaan, long a haunt of Semites and well-suited to pasturing cattle and sheep.

43. I.e., all the sons of Jacob, Joseph included.

44. Literally, "according to Pharaoh's mouth."

45. In the sense of being agitated, flustered. The basic meaning of the term *regez* is to be excited, emotional. "Strangely enough several translations have 'quarrel' for *regez*: 'In an unusual instance, Joseph uses this term when ordering his brothers not to argue or quarrel while traveling home' (NIDOTE [New International Dictionary of Old Testament Theology & Exegesis], III, 1045–46); I can see no reason for translating 'quarreling' or regarding this an 'unusual instance'" (Ron Pirson, *The Lord of Dreams: A Semantic and Literary Analysis of Genesis 37–50* [London: Sheffield Academic Press, 2002], 118, note 72).

46. Commentators have debated endlessly whether the phrase *vayapag leebo* (which I have rendered "and his heart froze" from the Syriac cognate which means to grow cold — other renditions are "went

numb," "stopped," "fainted," etc.) refers to a fainting spell, to a mini-seizure or to a minor heart attack ("a physical syncope"). I feel that the description of the "symptomatology" is so vague and metaphoric as to make all attempted diagnoses speculative. The author was not a graduate of a modern medical school (and not even a contemporary witness of the events depicted), and to treat what is obviously a poetic depiction of shock and collapse as a clinical diagnosis is to miss the point entirely.

47. Samuel, 326 (emphasis in the original).
48. Ibid.

9

The Long Farewell

Fair these broad meads, these hoary woods are grand;
But we are exiles from our father's land.
— Sir Walter Scott, *Canadian Boat Song*

Before accompanying Israel and his sons on their descent to Egypt,[1] let us return one last time to the decisive face-to-face confrontation between the two premier sons of Israel, Joseph, the favorite and Judah, the recently emerged contender for primacy. They have much in common, yet what divides them ultimately overrides that which unites them. Both depart from the family, only to reunite with it after a hiatus of approximately twenty-two years, deeply altered by their experiences. But it is at this point that the similarity ends.

In the first place the reasons for their departures are radically different. While both departures are termed "descents,"[2] Joseph's departure is involuntary; he leaves because he is kidnapped, or, as he puts it, (reading literally) "for I was stolen, stolen away from the land of the Hebrews"[3] (Gen. 40:15). Judah's departure, on the other hand, is purely on his own initiative. As their departures differ, so do their homecomings. Judah's return mirrors his departure. As he "went down" from the highlands to the lowlands of Achzib, so on his return he "ascends" back to the highlands to rejoin his family on the family's own terms; and it is on these terms that he rises to the leadership of his brothers. Joseph, for his part, does not reascend to his family: he brings his family down to join with him in Egypt, and this on *his* terms. While Judah shucks off the Canaanite identity he assumed in the lowlands, Joseph remains "the Egyptian Lord" to the end, his relationship with his family largely confined to providing material support.

It is when we become sensitive to the implications of the words placed by the author in Judah's mouth at the pinnacle of his finest moment that we become aware of the gap that separates the two brothers. At the climax of his plea Judah declares:

> *Therefore please let your servant remain as a slave to my Lord* in the place of the lad (*tachat hanaar*) and let the lad go up (*vehanaar yaal*) with his brothers [Gen. 44:33, emphasis added].

These words call to mind similar expressions that form the climax of that terrible trial when their ancestor, Abraham, was called upon to sacrifice his son. This tale, one of the central traditions of the family and known to them all, concludes:

> *A messenger of the Lord called out to him* [Abraham] *from the heavens and said, "Abraham! Abraham!" And he said, "Here am I." And he said, "Do not stretch out your hand against the lad, and don't do anything to him...." And Abraham raised his eyes, and saw, and behold, a ram, caught by his horns in a thicket! So Abraham went and took the ram,* and offered him up as a burnt offering (*vayaalehu leolah*)[4] in the place of *his son* (*tachat beno*).[5] [Gen. 22:11-13, emphasis added].

There, in that ancient tale, a ram is sacrificed, taking the place of the lad (Isaac); here Judah offers himself as the ram — offers to sacrifice himself— to take the place of the lad (Benjamin), and so to save him that he might go up to his father unharmed. This offer to sacrifice himself for his brother, and even more, for their father, forever raises Judah to a level that Joseph cannot even aspire to. Thus does Judah keep his pledge to his father, and thus does he earn the blessing that will be his.

Beyond the nobility of Judah's offer to sacrifice himself for brother and father, his speech highlights the differences between Joseph, the Egyptian, and Judah, son of Israel, and what each represents. Kass comments:

> [The speech obligates the reader] to ponder the difference between the Egyptian way of mastery, magic, and bureaucracy and the Israelite way of honoring one's father (and mother), between a way of life in which supreme obligations and obedience are to the god-king Pharaoh, channeled through his ministers ("thy servants"), and a way of life in which supreme obligations and obedience are to God, channeled through the father as the head of the clan.... Judah's mother, at his birth, named him well: Judah (*Yehudah*) — Praise (*hodah*) the Lord.[6]

We return to father, Jacob, preparing for his journey to see his beloved son before he dies. If the tale of the almost-sacrifice of Isaac backgrounds the confrontation between Judah and Joseph, another tale, also part of the tradition of Abraham, weighs upon old Israel at this fateful juncture. This — the land in which he was born, the land in which he has been living for decades — is the Promised Land: the land promised by God Himself to Abraham in a moment of darkness and dread. The tale has been passed from father to son, told in hushed voice in solemn gatherings as dusk would pass into night: how father Abraham had entered into a formal covenant with the Lord whom he had followed from Ur of the Chaldees to Canaan.

> *Now the Lord said to him, "I am the Lord who brought you out from Ur of the Chaldees[7] to give you this land to inherit." And he said, "O my master, Lord, how shall I know that I shall inherit it?" And He said to him, "Take Me a three-year-old heifer, and a three-year-old she-goat, a turtledove and a young pigeon." So he took all of these and cut them in two, and placed each part opposite the other, but he did not cut up the birds.[8] Now falcons[9] swooped down on the carcasses and Abram[10] drove them off* [Gen. 15:7-11].

Having made all the preparations for the formalization of a covenant or treaty, Abram waits, driving away carrion birds that are attracted to the bloody carcasses.

> *Now it came to pass, as the sun was about to set, a deep sleep fell upon Abram, and a deep dark dread came falling upon him. And He said to Abram, "Know well that your seed shall be strangers in a land not theirs and they shall be enslaved and oppressed four hundred years! But upon the nation for whom they slave will I execute judgment, and afterward they shall come forth with great wealth...." And it came to pass, as the sun set that there was deep darkness, and behold! a smoking brazier with a flaming torch appeared which passed between these pieces. On that day the Lord made a covenant[11] with Abram, saying, "To your seed do I give this land"* [Gen. 15:12-14; 17-18].

In a deep trance, Abram is subject to a terrifying dream/vision in which he sees flame and smoke, symbolizing God, passing between the halved carcasses, thus ratifying the covenant. And hears its terms: this land will be given as an ineradicable inheritance to his descendants. But this will come at a price; a window opens into the future, revealing to Abram that these same offspring are fated to descend into the pit of bondage. Four hundred years will they slave in some foreign land under bitter oppression, and only after this sentence is served to its full term will they be freed and enter into their inheritance.

This grim prophecy — centuries of suffering looming before Abraham's descendants — and offsetting them, the promise of the land of Canaan as an inheritance, these are the two halves of the tradition passed on within the family. And it is this tradition that presses remorselessly upon the aged Israel. His grandfather had abandoned the Promised Land; so, for that matter, had he in his younger years. But in both cases the departure was, from the start, meant to be temporary. There was never any question in their minds that as soon as the temporary impetus to their departure ended they would return. And so they did; this land was their permanent abode. Abraham, his hand forced by famine, had departed to Egypt (Gen. 12:10-20). Young Jacob had also departed the land for Paddan-aram under the pressure of necessity for what had been intended as a short cooling-off spell; a brief hiatus that unexpectedly had stretched out for twenty years. In the end he also had returned.[12] But this time Jacob/Israel knows with a certainty that brooks no denial that this departure is a one-way ticket. Should he leave he will die on foreign soil.

There is a deeper dread that burdens Israel's soul. The preparations to depart Canaan are not for a trip of short duration. This is a migration. Joseph's imperious "invitation"— an invitation that will brook no denial — is not for a period of a year or two but for permanent residence: You shall dwell in the land of Goshen. (Gen. 45:10). From personal experience he himself knows how easy it is to make a new life for oneself and become part of a new environment. Will his children and grandchildren ever come back to Canaan once they become acclimatized to the good life of Egypt, living off "the fat of the land?" Will they even want to return? And then what will become of the Promise? Then there is the deeper fear, the dread fate foretold:

"Know well that your seed shall be strangers in a land not theirs, and they shall be enslaved and oppressed four hundred years!" [Gen. 15:13].

Is this what will become of their migration to Egypt? It is with a deep sense of foreboding that Israel begins his journey.

The Oracle at Beer-sheba

So Israel set out[13] *with all that was his and came to Beer-sheba; and he offered sacrifices*[14] *to the God of his father Isaac* [Gen. 46:1].

Leaving Hebron, his home for more than two decades, the first leg of the journey to Egypt brings Jacob/Israel and his extended family to Beer-sheba, twenty-five miles to the south. Here his ancestors had dwelt for extended periods. Here his father Isaac had built an altar which was still standing.[15] And it is here, on his father's altar, that Jacob feels the need to propitiate his father's God, the deity that had forbidden his father to take the very step that he is now taking: to go down to Egypt.[16]

We are confronting a deeply conflicted man. On the one hand, as Jacob, he wants to go to Egypt with every fiber of his being. Not only is he, the ever practical man of the world, being driven by the reality of famine, but, as the father who, despite all, still loves his son with a consuming passion, he is being drawn to Egypt by a force he cannot resist. That is undoubtedly one reason for his sacrifice: an offering of thanksgiving to God that his son is yet alive. But there is another side to the coin. In his role as Israel, he is committed to keep alive in the hearts of his children and grandchildren God's Promise. He fears that in entering Egypt, the brilliant high culture there will wean them away from the New Way of God. And worse, he is consumed with the fear that he may be inadvertently leading his children into the centuries of slavery foretold to his grandfather, Abraham. Is he doing the right thing in turning his back on the Promised Land? Jacob/Israel is in desperate need of guidance. His sacrifice is a plea for direction, and that night direction comes.

> *Now God spoke to Israel in visions of the night, saying, "Jacob! Jacob!" And he said, "Here am I." And He said, "I am God, the God of your father. Fear not*[17] *to go down to Egypt, for there I will make you into a great nation. I Myself shall go down with you to Egypt, and I shall also most certainly bring you back up,*[18] *and Joseph shall place his hand upon your eyes*[19] [Gen. 46:2-4].

Far from ordering Jacob to retrace his steps, God, after identifying Himself as indeed the God of Isaac, and thus the God who had forbidden Isaac to leave the Promised Land, sets his stamp of approval on the course Jacob is taking. More, He reassures Jacob/Israel that He will not abandon him but will accompany him on his way, that from a family his descendants will grow into a great people, that he personally would return to the Promised Land and that his beloved son Joseph will be present at his death. All this must have been profoundly reassuring and comforting to Israel. And yet, reading between the lines, there are in this revelation profoundly disturbing elements. Considering that Joseph has never left Egypt, and that he will be present at Israel's deathbed, the implication is that Jacob was right in his intuition that he will never return but will die on foreign soil. This will not be due to his advanced years, his life drawing to a close before the famine comes to an end. Surprisingly, and contrary to all expectation, Jacob has yet seventeen years ahead of him — meaning that he will find himself with a window of twelve years in which to return to Canaan after the end of the famine. But he will never be able to extricate himself, nor will his children. Egypt will have proved to be a trap, and the trap will have closed on all of them.

We remember old Jacob wailing, "I will go down to Sheol to my son, mourning" (Gen. 39:35). And now, in a sense, his lament has become prophetic. He is going down to his son, not in mourning but with very mixed feelings; and not to Sheol, the realm of the dead, but to Egypt, land of tombs, graves and mummies. Sheol and Egypt have become analogous in the story.[20] And just as there is no exit for those who go down to Sheol, so will there be no escape for those descending with Jacob. The earth and her bars will have closed over them forever.[21]

There is one further implication: the stay in Egypt will be a long one. The promise that in Egypt the family will grow into a great (that is, multitudinous) nation implies a time span not of generations but of centuries. None of those now in the process of going down to Egypt, even the infants among them, will ever set eyes on the Promised Land again. The chosen family of God is now entering a cocoon where it will slumber, only to reemerge centuries hence, as the Chosen People and to then resume its programmed destiny. The belly of Sheol will have proved to be a nurturing womb. Does Jacob realize any of these implications? Probably not. Now that his fears have been stilled by God's assurances he can think of nothing but "Joseph my son yet lives. I will go and see him before I die" (Gen. 45:28).

The oracle at Beer-sheba proves to be the last time God speaks to Jacob/Israel.[22] More than half a century before, as Jacob began his first journey and received his first communication from God, it was from Beer-sheba he set out. It is fitting that his final journey should start from the same place.

The dawn breaks,

> *and Jacob arose from Beer-sheba, and the sons of Israel transported Jacob their father, and their children and their wives in the wagons that Pharaoh sent to convey them. And they took their cattle and their goods which they had acquired in the land of Canaan, and they came to Egypt, Jacob and all his seed*[23]

with him. His sons, and his son's sons, his daughters and his daughter's daughters[24] *and all his seed did he bring with him to Egypt* [Gen. 46:5-7].

With the descent to Egypt the Age of the Fathers draws to a close.

The Enumeration

Closing the book on the Age of the Fathers, the author pauses in the narrative flow to give us an accounting of how the family has grown from its meager beginnings — the single couple of Abraham and Sarah — only three generations before. The general rule governing this list is that only males are listed (the exceptions will be specially noted). But despite the exclusion of females, the males are grouped by their mothers, in the following order: Leah, Zilpah her maid, Rachel, Bilhah her maid.

Now these are the names of the children of Israel[25] *who came to Egypt,*[26]
Jacob and his sons:
Jacob's first born, Reuben.
Now the sons of Reuben [were] *Enoch, and Pallu, and Hezron, and Carmi.*
And the sons of Simeon [were] *Jemuel,*[27] *and Jamin, and Ohad, and Jachin, and Zohar,*[28] *and Saul the son of the Canaanite woman.*
And the sons of Levi [were] *Gershon, Kohath, and Merari.*
And the sons of Judah [were] *Er, Onan, Shelah, Perez and Zerah — now Er and Onan died in the land of Canaan — and the sons of Perez* [were] *Hezron and Hamul.*[29]
The sons of Issachar [were] *Tola, and Puvah,*[30] *and Iob,*[31] *and Shimron.*
And the sons of Zebulun [were] *Sered, and Elon, and Jahleel.*
These are the sons of Leah whom she bore to Jacob in Paddan-aram, and [also] *Dinah his daughter. All the souls of his sons and his daughters were thirty-three.*

Now the sons of Gad [were] *Ziphion,*[32] *and Haggi, and Shuni, and Ezbon,*[33] *and Eri, and Arodi, and Areli.*
And the sons of Asher [were] *Imnah, and Ishva, and Ishvi, and Beriah, and their sister Serah.*[34]
Now the sons of Beriah [were] *Heber and Malchiel.*
These are the sons of Zilpah, whom Laban gave to Leah his daughter.
And she bore to Jacob sixteen souls.

Now the sons of Rachel, Jacob's [favorite] *wife*[35] [were] *Joseph and Benjamin.*
Now to Joseph were born in the land of Egypt, whom Asenath, daughter of Poti-phera, priest of On, bore to him: Manasseh and Ephraim.
And the sons of Benjamin [were] *Bela, and Becher, and Ashbel, Gera and Naaman, Ehi and Rosh, Muppim and Huppim, and Ard.*[36]
These were the sons of Rachel which she bore to Jacob, fourteen souls in all.
Now the sons of Dan [were] *Hushim.*[37]
And the sons of Naphtali [were] *Jahzeel, and Guni, and Jezer, and Shillem.*
These were the sons of Bilhah, whom Laban gave to Rachel his daughter, and she bore these to Jacob, seven souls in all.

All the souls who came with Jacob to Egypt, issue of his loins, not counting the wives of Jacob's sons, were sixty-six souls.[38] [To this add] *the sons of Joseph who were born to him in Egypt were two souls;* [thus] *all the souls belonging to] the House of Jacob that came to Egypt* [come to] *seventy*[39] [Gen. 46:8-27].

This list is inherently problematic: the head count and the given totals can be made to match only through more or less convoluted manipulation. To make matters worse, two totals are given. Probably the most perceptive treatment of the questionable nature of the figures is that of Kass:

> Many interpreters have sought to solve the apparent contradictions and reconcile the numbers, while others think that sixty-six has been rounded out to a symbolic approximation, one that conveys "fullness ... ten times sacred seven." [Alter, p. 279] But readers alert to the problem that lies beneath the cheerful surface of the impending family reunion will notice that the heart of the numerical difference concerns the proper place of Joseph and his Egyptian-born sons. Sixty-six souls *came with Jacob* into Egypt; counting Jacob, Joseph and his two sons, there were seventy souls of the house of Jacob *now present* in Egypt. Will Joseph and his sons go with the sixty-six others? Or will the latter Egyptianize and go with Joseph? Will Jacob remain with the sixty-six who came with him? Or will he become most attached to Joseph, his favorite?[40]

The coming episodes, while seemingly concerned with family reunion, problems of location and settling, and preparations for the coming demise of this last of the Fathers, are, underneath the surface froth, focusing on these central issues.

The Immigrants

Our tale takes up where it left off for the mini-census of the migrants. The caravan — family, possessions, cattle and sheep — reach "The Walls of the Ruler" which mark the Egyptian frontier.[41] On the other side of the "Walls" lies Goshen.

> *Now he* [Israel] *sent Judah before him to Joseph, to inform him of their imminent arrival in Goshen*[42]; *so they came to the land of Goshen. And Joseph harnessed his chariot and went up to meet Israel his father in Goshen; now he appeared before him and fell upon his neck. And he wept on his neck a long time* [Gen. 46:28-29].

The words that we have rendered "now he appeared before him" (Hebrew *vayaira ailav*), is a phrase that is exclusively used in the Bible for God revealing himself to human beings.[43] It can hardly be an accident that the author chooses to use this term to preface the meeting of father and son after twenty-two years. What is the author implying? Is it Joseph's ostentation? From numerous Egyptian illustrations we can picture the scene: Joseph in his chariot[44] decked out in all his finery, with fans of colored ostrich plumes shading him from the sun and all his splendid escort in attendance, presenting a stunning tableau to the eyes of old Israel.[45] In this reading Joseph presents himself as a demi-god; a veritable epiphany. Or is the author hinting at Joseph's attitude, one of godlike condescension to his lowly family? Or perhaps a bit of both? What we can be sure of is that the author is calling our attention to the huge gap in the standing and status of the two parties.

Unlike his several meetings with his brothers, Joseph here has nothing to say; neither, for that matter, has his father. After twenty-two years of callous indifference on the part of Joseph, what is there to say? His silence has already said it all. Joseph simply throws himself on his father's neck and cries, and cries, and cries.

We are not told that Israel cries. For twenty-two years he has cried and mourned for his beloved son. There are no tears left. Dry-eyed and silent he stands while Joseph dissolves in tears. At last Israel breaks the silence.

> *And Israel said to Joseph, "Now I can die, having seen your face, for you are yet alive* [Gen. 46:30].

This is hardly a cry of joy or thanksgiving. There is infinite sadness and resignation behind this simple remark.[46] Israel has been granted his dearest wish, to see his son yet alive,

Map 3

The Eastern Delta During the Thirteenth Dynasty

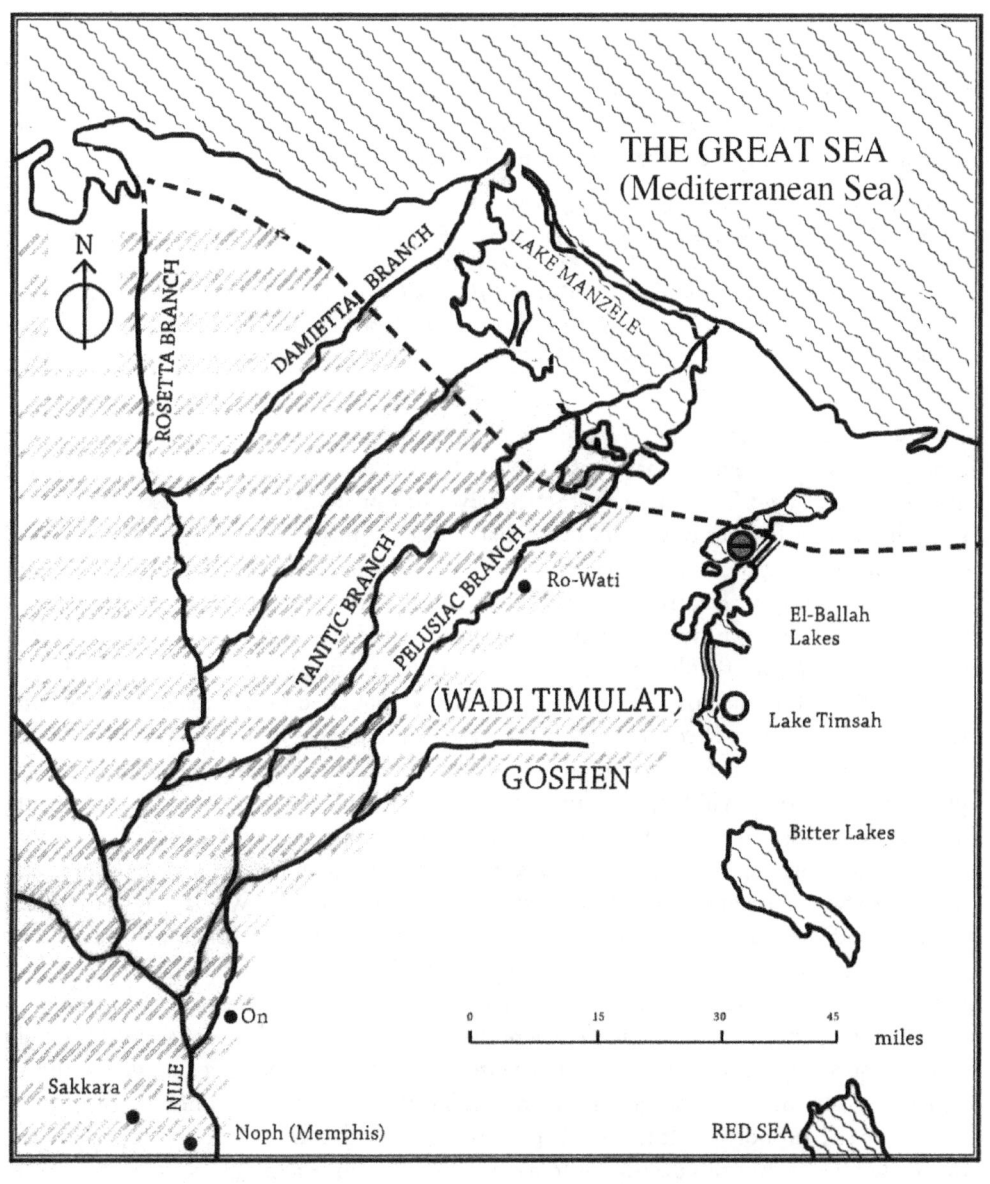

but this wish has turned to ashes in his mouth. This Egyptian lord, this stranger who has left him in sorrow for twenty-two years, who has toyed with his brothers, thrown Simeon into prison and framed Benjamin is anything but the son of whom he had dreamed. But in this life one must take what one can get. "It is enough. Joseph my son yet lives. I will go and see him before I die" (Gen. 45:28). And now, having seen Joseph and what he has become, Israel is resigned to his death.

The silence broken, Joseph finds his voice and takes charge. The master manipulator now gets to work and begins arranging things. And in the process this Lord of the land reveals indirectly to his family a fact of which we already had been made aware, that he is far from being in charge. He cannot make decisions. Only Pharaoh makes decisions. He has power only to the extent that he can manipulate Pharaoh.

> *And Joseph said to his brothers, and to his father's House,*[47] *"I will go up and tell Pharaoh, and say to him, 'My brothers, my father's House, who were in the land of Canaan, have come to me. Now the men are shepherds; for they have always been keepers of livestock,"*[48] *and they have brought their sheep, and their cattle, and all that is theirs.' Now it shall be, when Pharaoh summons you and says,' What do you do for a living?' You shall say, 'Your servants are keepers of livestock,*[49] *from our youth until now, both we and our fathers,' in order that you may dwell in the land of Goshen. For all shepherds are abhorrent in Egypt"* [Gen. 46:31-34].

Joseph the director, in the course of handing out the lines to be spoken by the brothers in the presentation ceremony that he is scripting, makes a strange remark: *"For all shepherds are abhorrent in Egypt."*[50] It cannot mean that livestock breeding in and of itself is taboo in Egypt; in another few verses we will learn that Pharaoh himself owns large herds of cattle. Its probable implication is that Egypt, a society built on agriculture, holds those who tend livestock, a profession largely associated with Semitic nomads, in deep contempt, even loathing. Its practice in Egypt was mainly confined to the Delta and left largely in the hands of Semites. This means that by arranging for his family to reside in Goshen, an outlying and peripheral district on the border of Egypt (and largely populated by Semites), while keeping them nearby[51] Joseph is effectively segregating them in a largely non-Egyptian district and thus is isolating them from the Egyptian mainstream. This is to have long-term ramifications. On the positive side it will help the family maintain its traditions and lifestyle, minimizing the pressures to assimilate to an Egyptian style of living. But balancing this is the fact that the family is being consigned to a pariah status. Are these Joseph's intentions? Probably not. His motives would seem to be largely personal and administrative. We have already noted Joseph's stated wish to keep his family close to him. Settling them in Goshen will accomplish this purpose: near but not too near (Joseph probably has no desire for his "primitive" and uncouth family — as they would have appeared to his peers — to be constantly dropping in on him). Also, settling them in a place where they can continue their occupation — the only one they know — will save the effort and expense of personally supporting a mass of indigent relatives, or, alternatively, the expense of retraining them to other livelihoods. In Goshen they can be self-supporting. It is doubtful whether Joseph thinks forward much beyond the immediate present. But this decision is to have serious consequences centuries down the line.

> *And Joseph came and told Pharaoh, saying, "My father, and my brothers, their sheep and their cattle, and all that is theirs have come from the land of Canaan, and behold they are in the land of Goshen"* [Gen. 47:1].

Pharaoh, in his gesture offering Joseph's family asylum in Egypt, specifically instructed them to leave their possessions — which to nomadic Semites meant primarily livestock —

behind (45:20). It was Joseph who instructed them to bring their cattle and sheep (v. 10). Now he informs Pharaoh that they have arrived with all their cattle and their sheep despite Pharaoh's instructions. Does he affect surprise at the situation? At any rate, he has halted their progress toward the capital and they at present are on hold in Goshen, just this side of the frontier. We are not informed of Pharaoh's reaction to this development. But certainly everyone agrees that they cannot be allowed to proceed to the capital as they are.

Joseph, sequestering most of the family and all the livestock in Goshen, arranges for an audience for a few selected family members, obviously those that can put on the best face for the family.

> *Now from the pick of his brothers he took five men and presented them to Pharaoh. And Pharaoh said to his brothers, "What do you do [for a living]?" And they said to Pharaoh, "Your servants are shepherds, both we and our fathers." And they said to Pharaoh, "We have come to sojourn in the land, for there is no pasture for the sheep of your servants, for famine is severe in the land of Canaan. And therefore, please [allow] your servants to dwell in the land of Goshen"* [Gen. 47:2-4].

The brothers, following the lines scripted by Joseph, openly admit to their abhorrent status, semi-excusing it by pleading a family tradition that unfits them for anything else. They plead for asylum in Egypt due to the duress of famine, do not ask to enter Egypt proper to partake of the promised "fat of the land"—i.e., high living—but to settle down in Goshen, isolated from the Egyptians who abhor them. In a word, they are saying that they know their place and will in no way presume to impose upon Egyptian sensibilities.

Pharaoh does not answer them. His reply is directed to Joseph, possibly in private after the brothers have been dismissed.

> *And Pharaoh said to Joseph, saying, "Your father and your brothers have come to you"* [Gen. 47:5].

In other words, this is a fait accompli and there is nothing to do but to accept it as such. I won't go back on my promise.

> *"The land of Egypt [lies] before you. Settle your father and your brothers in the best part of the land; let them dwell in the land of Goshen. And if you know any able men among them, now place them as Master herdsmen*[52] *over [the livestock] belonging to me"* [Gen. 47:6].

The manipulation succeeds. The problem, artificially created when Joseph told his family to bring all their livestock, has been contained. (And now we begin to understand why Joseph dictated the *exact wording* of his invitation, to be repeated verbatim to his father.) The family is to reside only in Goshen. Give them holdings on some of the best pasture land there, Pharaoh instructs Joseph. And to grant them extra economic support, if any have administrative ability (not unlikely as they are Joseph's brothers, and the apple never falls far from the tree), give them supervisory positions administering my herds.[53] It is important here to notice what Pharaoh does not say: give them jobs in the government. There are plenty of Semites who hold positions in the bureaucracy. Being a Hebrew was no bar to office, even high office; note Joseph himself. Was Pharaoh protecting himself against the danger of nepotism? Did he want to insulate the bureaucracy from the potential creation of a family clique promoted and advanced by Joseph himself? Best to leave the family encapsulated in Goshen.

The Man of God Meets the Man-God

The last several weeks have been among the most eventful in the long life of Jacob/Israel. From the soul-shattering announcement that Joseph is yet alive and the invitation to settle in Egypt, to the decision to turn his back on the Promised Land and to migrate to Egypt; from God breaking His wall of silence, once again revealing His will (including a tantalizing glimpse of the future), to the shock of reunion with his son, the period has been both an emotional roller coaster and the beginning of a profound reevaluation on the part of this last of the Fathers. This in turn will lead to the final maturation of Jacob into the true Israel, and to his finest moments. The first step in this process is taken in a meeting between Jacob and Pharaoh.

This meeting is purely pro forma. The business has already been done and the basic decisions made during and subsequent to the presentation of the delegation of brothers. Now, probably a few days later, Pharaoh, as a gesture to his Grand Vizier, grants an audience to his father. The audience is designed to last only a few minutes. Jacob will be introduced, Pharaoh will say a few words, Jacob will mouth some platitudinous compliments, will express his gratitude for benefits received, and then be dismissed — all very routine. That the audience turns into something very different comes as a surprise to all concerned.

To fully appreciate what takes place, we must digress for a brief excursus into the ways of life and death as they were understood by Egyptians. The Egypt of three and four thousand years ago, the land of tombs and mummies, is generally perceived by the denizens of the modern West as obsessed by a culture of death. Yet this understanding profoundly misinterprets the point of view of the ancient Egyptian. It was not death that dominated his horizon but rather the opposite: life. Egyptians of those days were, by our lights, remarkably optimistic. It has been speculated that this was due to the consistent way in which the Nile River rose each year, flooded the fields, and thus guaranteed continual bumper crops.[54] Food was plentiful and one could reasonably look forward to a full stomach tomorrow, next week, and next year. Life was good, and the longer one could enjoy it the better.

With this kind of attitude, the central cultural thrust became the denial of death and a desire to prolong life indefinitely. This was true from the earliest times.

> Very early Egyptian religious texts, in so far as we understand them, do not make absolute distinctions between life and death. At death one "moved to the West," that is passed from the fertile strip to the edge of the desert on the west bank of the Nile, where the dead were buried. Since the body remained, or could be made to remain, incorruptible, and since the gods and divine activities were all around on earth anyway, the moment of death was not a transcendental change but an episode in a continuum ... Egyptologists deny that ... the Egyptians were morbid. They were, so far as we can judge, a lively, extrovert, cheerful people, greedy for the pleasures of the senses and all the good things of the world. It was, it is argued, the very fact that they cared for life so much — and that life in Egypt was so rich — which made them so anxious to prolong it.[55]

The ideal lifespan in Egypt was one hundred and ten. Beyond this the Pharaoh and his nobles could expect to live on forever.[56] With this as background we now turn to the episode of Jacob's audience with Pharaoh.

> *And Joseph brought Jacob his father and presented him to Pharaoh, and Jacob blessed Pharaoh. And Pharaoh said to Jacob, "How many are the days of the years of your life?" And Jacob said to Pharaoh, "The days of the years of my sojournings are one hundred and thirty years; few and evil have been the years of my life, and they have not attained the days of the years of my fathers in their days of their sojournings." And Jacob blessed Pharaoh, and went from the presence of Pharaoh* [Gen. 47:7-10].

Joseph brings his father into the throne room, into the presence of the ruler of Egypt who is a god.[57] And Jacob, who not so many days before had been personally addressed by God in "visions of the night," far from being awed sees before him not a god but a man.

Having experienced the revelation of the true God, Jacob has the basis to make a comparison. And not merely a man, but, Jacob intuits, a pathetic human being beset with delusions of grandeur and false values, a creature in need of blessing. And so, amazingly, Jacob takes command of the situation and blesses Pharaoh![58] In whose name does he bless him, God (*elohim*) or the Lord of Abraham? We are not told, but probably the former; it is not likely that Pharaoh will ever have heard of the latter and will not understand what is going on. But either way Jacob has imposed a set of values upon the situation: the man who calls himself a god and who thinks he is a god is desperately in need of blessing, and so Jacob, the man of God, to whom God has just recently spoken, blesses him in His name.[59]

What Pharaoh makes of all this we are not told. He probably assumes that Jacob is calling down the blessings of all the gods upon him, even though in his eyes he is in little need of them. But it is likely that he pays scant regard to the blessing because of his preoccupation with his own agenda. Pharaoh is aware of Joseph's age; Joseph at this time is around forty. He has seen some of Joseph's brothers, most of them between ten and fifteen years older than he, with grown children of their own. That means that their father must be at least seventy-five. And here this ancient man stands before him, looking about a hundred! With the Egyptian preoccupation with longevity Pharaoh asks, "How many are the days of the years of your life?" The question simply means, "How old are you?" But Jacob sees fit to focus on the way the question is idiomatically structured, mirroring the Egyptian preoccupation with life. His reply inverts the question, putting the idiom first while changing the terms of reference: "The days of the years of my sojournings." Sojourning means wandering; a sojourner is a person with no fixed or permanent abode. Unlike the Egyptians who have (or think they have) a permanent place in this world, a life that is not only rooted but unlimited, Jacob knows that human beings are temporary residents in a world not theirs, here today and gone tomorrow. Life, to the Fathers, has no permanence to it. It is a journey, and one of limited duration. No tomb, no mummification can prolong that journey in this world. Not for nothing did one of the earliest Israelite liturgical pronouncements, recited by every Biblical Age farmer bringing his first fruits to the sanctuary, open with this description of Father Jacob: "A wandering Aramean was my father." (*Deut.* 26:5). The self-portrait of Jacob as a sojourner will become the paradigm for the self-understanding of the human condition by his descendants.

The second concern Jacob raises in his short answer is equally pointed: "Few and evil have been the years of my life." Life, Jacob instructs Pharaoh, is not a soft bed of roses. Roses there may be, but life's predominant feature is thorns. This journey is beset by obstacles and characterized by struggle. It is through pain and struggle that we become what we become. Then, almost as an afterthought, Jacob answers Pharaoh's question: I am one hundred and thirty years old! But don't think that is such an achievement; my ancestors' wanderings lasted even longer.[60] In the light of their longevity, my one hundred and thirty years are indeed few.

Pharaoh is in shock. He can only aspire to one hundred and ten years before he "moves to the West." Does Pharaoh want to learn the secret of such longevity? We do not know because at this point the audience ends. Having, in effect, rejected some of the central assumptions of the theology and lifestyle of the Egyptians, and having sketched the outlines of an alternative — indeed almost the exact opposite of the Egyptian — Jacob peremptorily once again blesses Pharaoh, and then, without any by-your-leave (we are not told that he was formally dismissed) he picks up and departs.[61] "And Jacob blessed Pharaoh, and went out from the presence of Pharaoh." While Joseph accompanied his father when he entered and presented him, we are not told that his father took him with him when he departed.

In the entire audience Jacob displays an enormous independence and self-confidence. We are not told that he bows. He tellingly refrains from the use of obsequious language: he never refers to himself as "your servant," the normal form of address of an inferior to a superior (note Judah's speech to Joseph). He takes the initiative of blessing Pharaoh (twice!), opening and closing the interview and thus dominating it. And he imposes his agenda, implicitly rejecting Pharaoh's worldview while presenting his own. Above all, in the face of the majesty, power and glory of Imperial Egypt he maintains his dignity. It is a mark of how far he has come from the callow young man who matched wits with his uncle Laban in Paddan-aram, seeing who could con the other, and to what degree he has outgrown the maudlin old man moaning that his white hair is being sent down to Sheol in grief. This was his finest hour to date. There are yet more such moments to come.

Settling In

> *So Joseph settled his father and his brothers, and he gave them a holding in the land of Egypt, in the choicest part of the land, in the land of Ramses, as Pharaoh had commanded. And Joseph sustained his father and his brothers, even all the House of his father, with bread according to the number of their dependents*[62] [Gen. 47:11-12].

"The land of Ramses" is a synonym for the land of Goshen. But this name was not applied to the northeast Delta until the reign of Ramses II in the early thirteenth century BCE, who reestablished the Egyptian capital near the site of the old and now abandoned Hyksos capital of Hat-waret (Avaris).[63] This is at least 250 to 300 years after the events we are chronicling. This fact is recognized by virtually all scholars nowadays who routinely call the reference to "the land of Ramses" an anachronism. But, as Kitchen points out, "This datum is *not* put in the mouth of any of the actors (Pharaoh, Jacob, Joseph, etc.), but comes either from the narrator of the story or a later modernizer."[64] The latter is unlikely, for why should a "later modernizer" update one reference to Goshen while leaving a score of other references unaltered? If we accept the likelihood that the use of the phrase "the land of Ramses" is that of the narrator, then the question becomes: why precisely at this point in the story does the narrator wish to call to our attention that sometime in the future, the land of Goshen where the children of Israel are being settled will be known as the land of Ramses?

To ask this question is to be made privy to the answer. Ramses will be the Pharaoh of the oppression; his capital, Pi-Ramesse, will be built in large measure by the forced labor of the Israelites. Thus by referring to the new "holdings" of the children of Israel, the "choicest part of the land" as being in "the land of Ramses," the narrator is warning us not to be too enamored of the good fortune of the Israelites. The short-term windfall that Joseph drops in their laps will prove, over the longer term, to work to their detriment. By being settled on the periphery of Egyptian society, out of the mainstream, the Israelites are being marginalized. Their good fortune in being endowed with the "best" in Egypt will only breed envy and discontent among the mainstream population. The seeds are being sown for the eventual demonization and enslavement of their descendants.

But this lies in the future, far beyond the horizon of the children of Israel. For the present life is good; they turn their backs on the Promised Land and settle down in Egypt.

Increasingly Egypt will be seen as home. Their farewell to the Promised Land will not be a short one. Centuries are to pass before their descendants will evince a desire to return. But by that time things will have altered radically.

So Israel dwelt in the land of Egypt, in the land of Goshen, and they acquired holdings in it, and were fruitful and multiplied greatly [Gen. 47:27].[65]

NOTES

1. In Hebrew, to travel to the Promised Land is "to ascend," to leave the Promised Land is "to descend." This helps explain the "going up" and "going down" terminology of the text.

2. In Joseph's case *hurad* (Gen. 39:1), "had been taken down"; in Judah's case *yarad* (38:1), "went down."

3. The question of who did the kidnapping is dealt with in Appendix 1. At the very least, even if the brothers are not directly complicit in the actual kidnapping, they certainly set him up for it.

4. Literally, "to send up a going up," the technical terms for offering a sacrifice, the same word used in the phrase "let the lad *go up*" in Judah's plea.

5. I.e., Isaac. It is not without significance in our context that twice in the narrative Isaac is referred to as "the lad" (*hanaar*) as, of course, is Benjamin.

6. Kass, 603–604.

7. Abraham's birthplace in Mesopotamia.

8. The ritual described here, a formal means of solemnizing a treaty, was common in the Ancient Near East. The animals are cut in half and arranged into rows with a space between the pieces (the two birds, being too small to halve, are simply placed opposite each other). "Covenants in which the two parties step between cloven animal parts are attested in various places in the ancient Near East as well as in Greece. The idea is that if either party violates the covenant, his fate will be like that of the cloven animals" (Alter, *Genesis*, 65).

9. Carrion-eaters.

10. Abram was Abraham's original name. Only later in his life was his name changed to Abraham. See the account in Genesis 17:4–5.

11. Literally, "cut a covenant," an expression referring to the cut-up carcasses used in the ceremony.

12. Abraham and Isaac had each been forced by famine to relocate to Gerar in Philistia; for them a foreign jurisdiction but nonetheless situate within the future borders of the Promised Land. Both finally left Philistia and returned to Canaan proper. See Genesis 20:1–18; 26:1–22.

13. Literally, "journeyed," apparently by donkey. Conveyance by wagon is first mentioned when he leaves from Beer-sheba for the desert journey to the Egyptian frontier (Gen. 46:5).

14. Literally, "he sacrificed sacrifices." The term rendered as sacrifices (Hebrew *zevach*) refers to a specific type of sacrifice, a free-will offering of which but a small portion is burnt on the altar while most of the animal is consumed by the worshiper and his family in a communion meal "before the Lord."

15. See Genesis 26:25. We do not hear that Jacob needed to repair it.

16. "Now the Lord appeared to him [Isaac] and said, 'Do not go down to Egypt; remain in the land.... Reside in this land and I will be with you and I will bless you, for to you and to your seed will I give all these lands, and I will fulfill the oath that I swore to Abraham your father'" (Gen. 26:2–3).

17. "This same reassurance was given to Abraham and to Isaac; it will be given to Moses as well. It is never preceded by a statement revealing their disquiet. The idea is that man's inner anxieties and fears—although unexpressed—are known to God" (Sarna, *Genesis*, 313).

18. Literally, "I will bring you up, even bringing you up."

19. I.e., it will be your son Joseph who will close your eyes upon your death.

20. Ackerman, 107.

21. Cf. Jonah 2:7.

22. Indeed, centuries of divine silence will now ensue. The tale of God speaking to man will take up where here it leaves off only with the words out of the burning bush: "Moses! Moses!" And Moses will, as Jacob, reply, "Here am I" (Exod. 3:4).

23. I.e., descendants.

24. "That is, his daughter Dinah, his daughters-in-law, and his granddaughters" (Sarna, *Genesis*, 314).

25. The Hebrew term, *B'nai Yisrael*, up until this point rendered "the sons of Israel," here undergoes a subtle shift of meaning. Previously referring literally to Jacob/Israel's sons, it here begins to be used as a

collective term to refer to Israel's descendants, including grandchildren and great-grandchildren; thus it will be henceforth rendered as "children of Israel."

26. This phrase, "Now these are the names of the children of Israel who came to Egypt," serves the function of dropping the curtain on the dynamic Age of the Fathers. When, after the sleep of centuries, the curtain will rise again, the rising of the curtain will be signaled by the exact same words (Exod. 1:1).

27. Jemuel: in the parallel lists in Numbers 26:12 and 1 Chronicles 4:24, he is listed as Nemuel. "The difference may be a matter of dialect" (Sarna, *Genesis*, 314).

28. In Numbers 26:13 and 1 Chronicles 4:24, he is listed as Zerah. Both names have the same meaning: "brightness."

29. Who were born in Egypt. See Appendix 2 for a detailed treatment.

30. In 1 Chronicles 7:1 he is called Puah.

31. LXX and Sam. (as Numbers 26:24 and 1 Chronicles 7:1) read Jashub.

32. Listed as Zephon in Numbers 26:15.

33. In Numbers 26:16 he is called Ozni.

34. As women were usually excluded from genealogical lists there must have been some unusual reason for including Serah. What it was we do not currently know.

35. Leah is pointedly not called a wife; neither are Zilpah and Bilhah (although at the very start of our tale they are specifically called such [Gen. 37:2]!). Even in the dry genealogy the narrator is reminding us of Rachel's status of favorite, and of the implications of this favoritism that are to follow: the unique status of Joseph and Benjamin in their father's eyes.

36. This list contains many problems. Of the ten sons, four are listed as grandsons in 1 Chronicles 8:3, 5; Numbers 26:38–41; and LXX. Moreover 1 Chronicles 7:6 lists only three sons, 1 Chronicles 8:1ff lists five sons, and Numbers 26:38–40 records five sons. Inasmuch as the purpose of all these lists is to establish the progenitors of the future clans of Israel — the true building blocks of the Israelite social order — where grandsons founded clans they too are listed, c.f. the case of Judah (see Appendix 2). However we choose to split the list between sons and grandsons, considering Benjamin's age at the time of the descent to Egypt, most of them had to have been born in Egypt, as were all of Joseph's sons and grandsons, and several of Judah's.

37. Despite Dan's single son, the narrator persists in the use of the same formula, beginning, "Now the sons of X [were]...."

38. This total, on the simplest reckoning, amounts to adding the totals of each matriarch as listed, while excluding those who died (Er and Onan) and those born in Egypt (Manasseh and Ephraim). Thus Leah (33–2=**31**) + Zilpah (**16**) + Rachel (14–2=**12**) + Bilhah (**7**) = 66.

39. This total would seem to be reached by taking the above 66, adding Manasseh and Ephraim, as well as Dinah and Jacob himself. Some commentators leave out Dinah and include God, who promised Jacob to "go down with you to Egypt" (Gen. 46:4).

40. Kass, 621.

41. "The Walls of the Ruler" was the Egyptian name for the line of fortifications that guarded the northeastern frontier of Egypt. It consisted of a moat 210 feet wide (70 meters), backed by an earthen rampart and strategically sited forts, which stretched from Lake Timsah (present day Ismailia) to the El-Ballah Lakes, and from there to the Mediterranean (see Map 3). Its purpose was to limit and control the flow of Asiatics into Egypt. See Hoffmeier, chapters 3 and 7 for the identification of the "canal" discovered by the Israel Geological Survey in 1971 with the "Walls of the Ruler," and aerial photographs of the "canal."

42. This rendition follows Flavius Josephus (*Antiquities of the Jews*, 2:184), who relied on a different text than the one we possess. This is in line with the various ancient versions which indicate that Judah is sent ahead to arrange "that he [Joseph] should appear before him" (Sam., Syr.) or "come to me came" (LXX); i.e., Jacob. MT reads, "to instruct before him to Goshen." But beside the defective grammar, this makes little sense geographically. Goshen was just beyond the entry point. They didn't need instructions to get there. Once they entered Egypt they were already in Goshen. They would have to traverse Goshen to get to anywhere else in Egypt.

43. For example: "Now the Lord appeared to him (*vayaira ailav*) by the terebinths of Mamre" (Gen. 18:1), re God appearing to Abraham.

44. Remember that this is the number two chariot of Egypt, the fanciest chariot after that of Pharaoh.

45. We must try to imagine the feelings produced by Joseph's appearance upon Israel: face and head clean-shaven, bare-chested, face "made up" with cosmetics. The brothers had already gotten used to the appearance of the Egyptian lord who later proved to be Joseph. For Israel, expecting to see the son he remembered, to be confronted with *this*, the shock must have been overwhelming. Was this *his* son? What had become of the son he once knew?

46. Kass remarks on the significance of the fact that in Canaan, before having seen Joseph, he refers to him as "my son" (Gen. 45:28). Now, having seen him, he no longer calls him "my son" (46:30) (Kass, 623).

47. I.e., to the entire family, including his brother's wives, children, grandchildren, etc.

48. Literally, "men of livestock."

49. See previous footnote.

50. This is only the second appearance of the word *abhorrent* in the Bible — from Exodus onward it is to become a critical term. It first appeared (Gen. 43:32) when we were informed that it was an abomination for an Egyptian to eat at the same table with a Hebrew. Was this taboo purely racial, or was it also due to the fact that the Hebrews were shepherds?

51. The capital, where Joseph resided, was located in the heart of the Eastern Delta. Goshen was between the region of the capital and the frontier. See Map 3.

52. Literally, "officers of cattle."

53. "The careful reader notices that Pharaoh's welcome of the Israelites into Egypt depends entirely on his ties to Joseph; when this tie breaks, so will the welcome" (Kass, 627).

54. It is true that there were lapses; our tale revolves about one such catastrophic failure. But in comparison with neighboring lands, dependent on irregular rainfall, and so where famine was a regular phenomenon, the failures of the Nile were so infrequent that they could be dismissed as rare and aberrant occurrences. They did not undermine the overall confidence in the blessed consistency of good times.

55. Johnson, 137–138.

56. This restricted immortality is true of the period about which we are writing. Later, during the Age of the New Empire, Egyptian religion was further democratized to allow even the common man the prospect of individual eternal life.

57. According to Egyptian theology Pharaoh was the son of Re, the sun-god, and thus a god himself. Not only did every Egyptian believe this implicitly, so did Pharaoh.

58. Some commentators are disinclined to render the Hebrew word *vayevarech* in accordance with its primary meaning, "and he blessed," preferring a secondary meaning of "he greeted." They thus interpret our verse to mean that Jacob deferentially "greeted" Pharaoh with some platitudinous statement such as "Long live the King," citing 2 Samuel 16:16 and 1 Kings 1:31 as authority. But in neither of these examples is the word *vayevarech* used, and, as we shall see, Jacob is anything but deferential. I prefer to stick to the primary meaning of words and not defer to rarely used secondary meanings unless forced to do so by context. To my way of thinking, neither the narrative context nor the textual structure requires Jacob to utter platitudes.

59. With this act Jacob commences the culmination of his life-work. "Previously Jacob has either received blessings, or failing that, stolen them. Never before has Jacob *given* a blessing" (Turner, 172, emphasis in the original).

60. Jacob is not boasting but is being simply factual: Isaac is recorded as dying at age 180 (Gen. 35:28) and Abraham at 175 (25:7). But beyond mere longevity, what is significant is that the narrator sums up the lives of Abraham and Isaac as follows: for Abraham, "a good ripe age, old and contented" (25:8); for Isaac, "in ripe old age" (35:29). A similar comment is pointedly lacking in the case of Jacob's death, underlying his own pessimistic evaluation of the years of his pilgrimage on this earth as "few and evil."

61. We are not told that the brothers departed at the end of their audience. This is understood; at the end of an audience one is dismissed and then leaves. My assumption is that the reason the text takes the trouble to highlight Jacob's departure is that it was unusual; i.e., he did not wait to be dismissed and also possibly he leaves without Joseph.

62. Understanding the unique Hebrew phrase, *lefi ha-taf*, as meaning "per person." The Hebrew literally reads, "by the mouth of the little ones," or "according to the little ones."

63. See Introduction, page 12.

64. Kitchen, *Reliability,* 348 (emphasis in the original).

65. This summary verse finds its place in the text at the very end of chapter 47. We have advanced it to its present position to round out the account of the settling of the Israelites in Egypt. We will return to this verse and analyze it when we reach the point in the narrative where the author placed it.

10

The Egyptian Trajectory

Fear can never be the soul of a well-organized society; it is not order—it is only the veil over chaos. Where liberty is lacking, soul and truth are lacking.
— Astolphe de Custine, *Russia in 1839*

L'Etat c'est moi.
— Attributed to King Louis XIV

In Chapter 4 we quoted Kass' analysis of the trajectory of Joseph's career. In his summation Kass notes a recurring pattern of success breeding failure,[1] and we then posited that to achieve sustainable success Joseph would have to either change himself or alter the pattern, or both. The question thus became: was either alternative within Joseph's power?

Self-transformation is one of the most difficult challenges that can face a human being. Since his prison days we have been observing a partial maturation of Joseph. He has not outgrown his disastrous penchant for playing games with people, but he has managed to contain the practice, relegating it to the sidelines. In his role as Egyptian official, he seems to have become completely focused and mature. We have no reports of other than serious behavior. Only with regard to his family, and his brothers in particular, does he allow himself the luxury of continuing his old sport. But it is with regard to the pattern itself that Joseph has achieved a radical break with his past. In contrast with his past in which he was always the first among equals, he has managed to promote himself into a situation where he has no peers. He is unique. He remains the favorite of the head of the House (Pharaoh). But in his position as second to the king of Egypt, he stands alone. The deck has been reshuffled. By a fundamental change in his external condition, and by acquiring a greater measure of control over himself, the terms of Joseph's existence have been altered. Joseph has dealt himself a new hand.

Over the last four chapters we have been observing Joseph's relations with his family, and in these little seems changed. But no matter how central this relationship may be to his emotional life, in terms of time and energy expended, in contrast with his professional life — that is his Egyptian career — his interactions with his family assume minimal proportions, probably less than 5 percent of the total. We are now about to readjust our perspective and see Joseph where he lives 95 percent of the time as the faithful servant of Pharaoh. The focus shifts to Joseph the Egyptian.

The Despot's Manager

Joseph's preoccupation with his family is over. From his point of view his problems with them appear satisfactorily resolved. His primary responsibility to them has been fulfilled—the family's physical survival has been assured. The family is now confined to Goshen, properly cowed and respectful, where he can benevolently patronize them. The struggle for dominance, it seems to him, is over. He is now free to be fully himself and to pursue his destiny. That destiny is Egyptian.

We have constantly stressed his Egyptian appearance. Joseph's external self-transformation into an Egyptian personage has been astonishingly rapid and complete. Yet only in this surface sense has Joseph assimilated to the Egyptian way of life. His inner self needed no metamorphosis. From the very start of our tale, in Canaan, we found his "soul" to be "Egyptian." His ambitions were grandiose and his will to power gargantuan. Canaan, along with the new way of life his ancestors had initiated and which his family was trying to incorporate and transmit, was "too small" for him. He yearned for the power and the glory that was Egypt long before he ever set eyes upon it. Upon his arrival he found himself at home. With a sense of shock he recognized his natural habitat. On Egyptian soil he could flourish—and he did.

In the current section the narrator focuses on Joseph the Egyptian; what he is and what he becomes. By his deeds do we come to know him. And through Joseph the narrator is opening our eyes to where the "Egyptian trajectory" leads. We will watch as Joseph, ruthlessly and systematically, reengineers the socioeconomic structure of the land, re-creating the totalitarian state of the Old Kingdom,[2] the era when Egypt was most truly itself. From the feudal society he found upon arrival composed mostly of free farmers, owners of their own homesteads, under Joseph's forced engineering Egypt emerges a slave state, with power concentrated in a single pair of hands—those of Pharaoh.[3] It is this totalitarian state that will eventually enslave the descendants of Joseph and his family. From the long perspective of history, it will emerge that it is Joseph who is the father of the foretold "oppression."[4]

Exploiting a Crisis

The famine is now in its third year; Egypt and neighboring Canaan are desperate.

Now there was no bread[5] in all the land,[6] for the famine was very severe,[7] and the land of Egypt and the land of Canaan were helpless[8] before the famine. And Joseph gathered in all the money[9] that was to be found in the land of Egypt and in the land of Canaan, in return for the provisions that were being procured; and Joseph brought the money into Pharaoh's house [Gen. 47:13–14].

We have already discussed Joseph's method of exploiting the crisis to make windfall profits: selling grain to the populace and, although we are not told, most probably at inflated, famine prices—the very grain that he had gathered up from them only a few years before.[10] Had Joseph simply confiscated the grain or had he bought it up at the rock bottom prices of a market glutted by oversupply? Again we are not told. Either way Joseph has carried out a speculator's classic coup: he has cornered the market. Being the only game in town, he can charge any price he wants.[11] But now we learn something interesting. We have known that Joseph was not acting on his own behalf but rather as Pharaoh's agent, his broker if you will. And now we learn that he did not take a commission. "And Joseph brought the money into Pharaoh's house." Not some of the money, but *the money*, is deposited in the Department of the Treasury in the Royal Palace. Joseph does not see himself as a partner with Pharaoh in this stupendous speculation (with a rightful share in the profits) but as a devoted public servant, implementing a far-seeing plan of social engineering which he himself has formulated.[12] There is something almost inhuman about the disinterested and cold-blooded way in which Joseph proceeds, step by step, to execute his carefully thought-out plan for restructuring the state.

The first phase of the plan has come to its inevitable end as the wholesale gouging of the public soaks up all available funds. The well runs dry.

> *Now the money that was in the land of Egypt and in the land of Canaan ran out, and all Egypt came to Joseph saying, "Give us bread! Why then should we die right before you, for there is no more money?"*[13] *And Joseph said, "Bring your livestock and I will give you bread*[14] [in exchange] *for your livestock if you have no more money. So they brought their livestock to Joseph, and Joseph gave them bread* [in exchange] *for the horses, the flocks of sheep, the herds of cattle and the donkeys; so he provided them with bread that year* [in exchange] *for all their livestock* [Gen. 47:15–17].

It is Joseph's purpose to impoverish the population, not the country. Livestock is capital, and Joseph aims at a transfer of wealth and not its destruction. Joseph must have arranged for the rate of exchange to be such that it was worthwhile for the farmers to exchange their animals for food rather than to kill and eat them.

> *And when that year ended they came to him the following year*[15] *and said to him, "We will not hide from my lord that the money has run out, and the herds of cattle* [are] *my lord's; nothing remains before my lord except our bodies*[16] *and our farms.*[17] *Buy us and our farms in exchange for bread, and we and our farms will be the property*[18] *of Pharaoh. And give us seed* [for planting] *that we may live and not die, and that this soil not turn into a wasteland. So Joseph acquired all the lands of Egypt for Pharaoh, for every Egyptian sold his farm, for the famine was too much for them*[19]*; and the land became Pharaoh's. And as for the people, he* [Joseph] *transferred them to the cities,*[20] *from one end of Egypt's border to the other* [Gen. 47:18–21].

The policy of pauperization proceeds to its grim dénouement. First the people are stripped of their possessions — their money, their livestock[21] and their land — and, at the last, their freedom. The Egyptian peasants are hereafter to be state slaves, assigned to work state land. And just as Joseph went to the considerable trouble and expense to build fortified granaries in the major cities and to transfer all the surplus grain to them before the outbreak of the famine — physically removing the grain from the region where it was grown, and thus severing all connection between the peasants who grew the produce and the grain that they had produced, so now Joseph acts to sever the peasants from the soil that had been theirs. He initiates a huge population transfer, uprooting the peasantry from their ancestral properties and shipping them from one end of the country to the other, to cities far removed from their home locales.[22] The suffering, both physical and emotional, for those transferred must have been immense. One thinks of the horrors undergone by the peasants of the Ukraine and the Crimea who had to endure the terrible social engineering of Stalin during the 1930s. Joseph's program could never have succeeded had not the Egyptians been so enfeebled by starvation that they were too weak to resist the well-fed soldiers who implemented the mass expulsions and resettlements.

So the vision has been achieved: the wealth of Egypt — money, livestock, land and people — has been concentrated into the hands of one man, the god-king. And with the wealth, the power has gravitated to those same hands. Egypt, a totalitarian society in theory, has been transformed into a totalitarian state in reality. The Golden Age of the Old Kingdom has, under the wand of the Hebrew magician Joseph, been reborn.

Only one anomaly mars the perfection of the resurrection — the priesthood, a corporate group too entrenched and too powerful to confront.[23] Unlike the days of old when the priests were essentially powerless and subservient to the Pharaoh, here an exception will have to be made.

Only the lands of the priests he [Joseph] did not buy, for the priests had a fixed allowance from Pharaoh; they ate from their allowance that Pharaoh gave them; therefore they did not sell their lands [Gen. 47:22].

Now Joseph decrees the rules that are to govern the lives of the peasantry under the new order:

Then Joseph said to the people, "Behold, I have this day acquired you and your lands for Pharaoh. Here is seed; now sow the land. At the harvests you shall give one-fifth to Pharaoh, and four-fifths shall be yours as seed for the field and food for you and those of your households, and as food for your little ones."[24] And they said, "You have kept us alive. May we find favor in the eyes of our lord; we have become Pharaoh's slaves." So Joseph made it a law to this very day concerning the farmland of Egypt: one-fifth belongs to Pharaoh. Only the land of the priests, it alone did not become Pharaoh's [Gen. 47:23–26].

Let us examine this decree and its implications, a decree which set the parameters for the coming age and which persisted down the centuries, so we are informed, right down to the days of the biblical writer who penned these words. Crop yields in the ancient world were tiny in comparison with the ones to which we are today accustomed. In those days a good wheat harvest would yield between 8 and 12.5 bushels per acre.[25] Of this yield approximately 2.3 bushels had to be put aside for seed for next year's planting. "In good years grain yields of slightly under four times seed grain sown were the norm."[26] When from this gross yield 20 percent is subtracted for Pharaoh, and then the seed grain for next year's planting is removed from the remainder, what is left would be barely sufficient to get the average family through to the next year's harvest. Pharaoh's 20 percent cut, far from being "moderate" as so many modern commentators assume, was actually the safety margin that in good years would allow the peasants to build up a reserve against emergencies — crop disease, locusts, fluctuation in the flow of the Nile river, etc. Lacking this margin, the specter of hunger now permanently hovers over every peasant hovel. Control of this suitably cowed population has been immensely simplified.

The response of the people to Joseph's decree is ironic. They are grateful for being allowed to live. When considering the alternative, slavery becomes the lesser of the evils. But being granted their lives is no act of mercy on Joseph's part. Pharaoh now owns all the land; without peasants to work it the land becomes, as the peasants themselves have phrased it, "a wilderness," that is, worthless. The peasants fully understand this; they are necessary tools. Note well that they never appeal for mercy or the fellow feeling owed by one human being to another. They expect neither, from the state or from Joseph who embodies it. Their appeal is purely utilitarian: let us die and your whole investment becomes worthless. That is not in your interest. The peasants, Joseph and Pharaoh all understand one another perfectly.

The Ethical Issue

Many modern commentators profess themselves horrified by Joseph's ruthless engineering. Among the milder of the denunciations is the following example:

The measures adopted by Joseph for the relief of the famine might be thought to strike a discordant note in his character. To appropriate the surplus produce of the seven years of plenty, and then compel the Egyptians to *buy back*, even to their own impoverishment, what they had themselves previously given up, does not seem consistent with our ideas of justice and equity.[27]

The general approach of these condemnations is to contrast Joseph's actions with either "enlightened" modern standards or with the ethical standards of the Bible itself. By either of these standards Joseph's actions emerge as repugnant. Well, one might contend, Joseph was not a "modern" and he had distanced himself from the Abrahamic heritage. He cannot be held to standards inappropriate to his time and place. As an Egyptian he should be measured against the Egyptian standards of his day. But the uncomfortable truth is that Joseph comes off poorly even by Egyptian ethical standards, as the following tomb declaration of one Ameni, the nomarch or governor of the Nome (province) of Oryx, demonstrates.

> There was no citizen's daughter whom I misused, there was no widow whom I oppressed, there was no peasant whom I repulsed, there was no herdsman whom I repelled, there was no overseer of serf-labourers whose people I took for [unpaid] time. When years of famine came, I plowed all the fields of the Oryx-nome, as far as its southern and northern boundary, preserving its people alive, furnishing its food, so that there were none hungry therein. I gave to the widow as to her who had a husband; I did not exalt the great above the small in all I gave. Then came great Niles rich in grain and all things, but I did not collect the arrears of the field.[28]

Even after allowing for a certain amount of exaggeration, this was how, in the Egyptian view of things, an administrator was expected to behave.

The attempts to find excuses for Joseph's behavior are legion.[29] They all fall into four categories:

1. *They asked for it*. Instead of standing on their rights the Egyptians offered themselves as slaves, an expression of their servile natures. They got exactly what they asked for.
2. *Joseph is protecting his own kin*. His family is landless and alien. By impoverishing the Egyptians and removing them from their holdings, he is equalizing the conditions of Israelites and Egyptians; now neither have any claim to the land.
3. *Its all God's doing*. Joseph's life is controlled by predestination.
4. *Relativism*. There were different standards in those days and Joseph lived and acted by them. To expect Joseph to live and act by current moral standards would be anachronistic.

These rationalizations are all extra-biblical. When we turn to the text itself, we find that the narrator neither overtly excuses nor condemns. He simply relates the facts and leaves us to draw our own conclusions. Rather than analyze the various excuses, it may be more productive to follow the lead of the narrator. For while he eschews overtly passing judgment, for good or for ill, and apparently only presents the facts, by his choice of facts and the way they are presented he seems to be pushing us in a particular direction, and that direction is not commendatory. The bottom line is that the Egyptian people are stripped of their possessions, lands and freedom; these are acts abhorrent to the biblical principles of personal liberty, economic autonomy and landed rights.

The structure of the society in which Joseph finds himself is hierarchical.

> One of the defining characteristics of a hierarchy is that the parts are taught to sacrifice for the whole.... But when Joseph ... made serfs out of the Egyptian peasantry, the whole of Egypt was being made to sacrifice for a single part, the Pharaoh and his entourage.... Joseph left the system into which he was elevated less humane than it was by making Pharaoh more powerful than he had been. In cultural terms, Joseph helped change an inclusive hierarchy, in which there was place for a multitude of landowning farmers, into an exclusive hierarchy, narrow and steep, in which only a single hierarch rules.[30]

And while there are those, largely of a Marxist bent, who deem this "progress," in the biblical scheme of values, it is clearly the opposite.

In attempting to analyze the moral content of Joseph's actions, however, I think we are missing the narrator's main thrust. The real question should be, why did the narrator pen this tale of the socioeconomic reconstruction of Egypt in the first place? It is clearly a digression from the main focus of the story which, from start to close, is not on Joseph alone but on the family — the family of the covenant — and especially on the issue of who is to lead them forward into the future. And one of the answers to the question of why this section was included relates to the issue of outcomes.

The consequences of Joseph's actions are to prove as catastrophic as they are unintended. Joseph has enslaved the Egyptian people and created a slave state. In this state there is a striking exception to the norm: an alien people who are free and prosperous: the Israelites. Totalitarian states cannot long abide exceptions. It will only be a matter of time before this deviation is rectified. Ivan Caine sums up the big picture: "Since Joseph had, in effect, sold the Egyptians while protecting his family, it is poetic justice that his family's seed should be sold, in effect, into slavery. He who had himself been sold, then sold others, had his people sold."[31] We are being prepared for the future. It is to be understood not as a natural disaster imposed by external forces upon the hapless Israelites but as the organic and inevitable outgrowth of the actions of an Israelite addicted to the Egyptian way.

But I think the text is telling us more than how counterproductive for his family and his descendants Joseph's supreme accomplishments prove to be. I suggest that the reason for this lengthy digression from Joseph's interaction with his family and from the issue of who will lead the descendants of Abraham, Isaac and Jacob into the future is that the narrator is revealing to us one possible path: the way of Egypt, and where the "Egyptian way" ultimately leads. Egypt is a paradigm of the path of power and glory, whether it be situated on the banks of the Nile, on the banks of the Tigris and the Euphrates rivers, the Ganges or the Yellow rivers. The whole point of the New Way founded by Abraham is to lead to a way of life founded on the principles of the inherent dignity of every human being and on the freedom of the individual. This Abrahamic way is the exact antithesis of the way of Egypt, and it is this Abrahamic destiny that Joseph abandons when he embraces the way of Egypt.

In another sense Joseph stands out as a paradigm: he is the first of a long series of sons of Israel yet to come who will find their métier in turning from the path of Abraham (who himself turned away from the glory that was Ur of the Chaldees and Haran), to pursue the game of power in the service of the great civilizations in which they found themselves.[32] Their paths, and the outcome of their endeavors, when they were successful, were to prove distressingly similar to those of Joseph. In this sense our tale not only describes a central turning point in the development of the faith of Abraham, but also marks the beginning of a recurrent phenomenon of talented Israelites, born into the New Way, who backslide into the old. Joseph is still with us today.

Notes

1. See page 76.
2. The Old Kingdom, sometimes known as the Pyramid Age, is the way Egyptologists delineate the period of the third through the sixth dynasties (c. 2686–2181 BCE). This was the quintessential Egyptian society in its purest form, and the "Golden Age" of Ancient Egypt; the ideal of all subsequent Egyptian periods — ever looked back to with nostalgia and longing.

3. The single exception being the religious establishment; the priests were too influential to touch. All land and most of the population were now the property of either the Crown or the Temples.

4. Genesis 15:13; see Chapter 9.

5. Bread, "the staff of life," is used here and in all this section as a synonym for food.

6. The word *land* is here used to designate the larger region, the Near East. In the latter part of the verse this same term, *eretz*, suitably modified, is used to designate specific areas within this larger region.

7. Literally, "heavy."

8. The root of the term *va-taila* means "not to be able" (Sarna, *Genesis*, 136 [ad loc.; also on Gen. 19:11], and Sarna, *Exodus*, 38, on Exod. 7:14).

9. Literally, "silver."

10. Genesis 41:47–49. See Chapter 5.

11. "Why did they run out of money so soon? Was the surplus of the first seven years bought at a discounted price? Did Joseph use his position to buy low and sell high? ... [T]his elementary economic analysis does suggest that market forces could not have been all that were at work to make Egyptian landholders into serfs to Pharaoh" (Aaron Wildavsky, *Assimilation versus Separation: Joseph the Administrator and the Politics of Religion in Biblical Israel* [New Brunswick, NJ: Transaction, 1993], 142).

12. Joseph is apparently content with his salary, which is undoubtedly generous in the extreme. Joseph, after all, has to live up to his position if he is to be able to function in his role as CEO of Egypt. But nowhere is there any hint of him personally profiting from the systematic pauperization of the Egyptian populace. The proceeds all go directly to Pharaoh.

13. Note that at this point Canaan and its inhabitants disappear from the narrative. Having skimmed off all the ready cash in Canaan, and having no intention of incorporating Canaan into Egypt, Joseph loses interest in them. They can all starve as far as he is concerned. Now we can appreciate the importance of Joseph's intervention for his family. Without his special interest, nothing could have saved them. They would not have even been able to barter their livestock for food. That option was only open to Egyptians.

14. Reading with LXX, Sam., and Vulg.; in MT the word *bread* is missing but implied.

15. Literally, "the second year." Possibly the meaning is: the second of the remaining five years of the famine.

16. Literally, "our corpses, our carcasses." They are already half-dead, walking skin and bones.

17. Literally, "our farmlands."

18. Literally, "slaves." Many commentators contend that the Egyptians were reduced to serfdom, and soften the rendition accordingly. But I agree with von Rad that the stronger term — slaves — better conveys the intention of the author. Both land and humans have become the sole property of Pharaoh (von Rad, *Genesis*, 410).

19. Literally, "was too strong for them."

20. In place of "he transferred them to the cities" (LXX, Sam., and Vulg.), read, "he made slaves of them."

21. For the Egyptians, livestock was a capital investment, the only significant one available besides the land. As we remember, Pharaoh was heavily invested in livestock (Gen. 47:6).

22. The text indicates that they were sent to cities. These could only have served as temporary catchments until the peasants could be assigned to the new state lands that henceforth they are to farm for the state.

23. This was probably a wise decision. Of all the later Pharaohs, only Amenophis IV, c. 1379–1362 BCE (better known to history as Akhenaten), had the temerity to fling down the gauntlet to the religious establishment. Despite the full power of the state — immeasurably stronger in Amenophis' time — arrayed against them, and their opponent being accepted by everyone, themselves included, as a god, and thus the object of their worship, the priests won the contest hands down.

24. LXX omits this final phrase.

25. Today in North America the yield is routinely above 47 bushels per acre. Thus ancient yields were only between 17 percent to 25 percent of current yields; and this in a good year. Currently, due to genetically modified seed, the yields are becoming significantly higher.

26. Brian Fagan, *The Great Warming: Climate Change and the Rise and Fall of Civilizations* (New York: Bloomsbury, 2008), 5. These figures are for preindustrial Europe, but all preindustrial agriculture was equally inefficient. While not fully applicable, the data here can give a rough idea of agricultural realities in ancient Egypt. Due to the unique conditions of the Nile valley — irrigated fields and the fertilization provided by annual flooding — the higher end of the yield range would probably be more representative of the norm. But only in the good years. "Contrary to popular belief, the summer Nile inundation is unpredictable and varies from year to year, as drought or plentiful rain affect Ethiopia.... A flood that was 6 feet below average could leave up to three quarters of some provinces of upper Egypt without irrigation water.

At the other extreme, an exceptionally high flood would rise precipitously and sweep away everything, even entire villages, before it" (ibid., 196).

27. S. R. Driver, *The Book of Genesis* (London: Methuen, 1904), 401, (emphasis in the original).

28. A. E. Bailey, *Daily Life in Bible Times*, (New York, C. Scribner's Sons, 1943), 64, 66, as quoted in Wildavsky, 141.

29. A good sampling can be found in Wildavsky, 146–158.

30. Ibid., 145, 143.

31. Ivan Caine, "Numbers in the Joseph Narrative," In *Jewish Civilization: Essays and Studies, Volume I*, ed., Ronald A. Brauner (Philadelphia: Reconstructionist Rabbinical College, 1979), 11. This future has already been hinted at by the substitution of the phrase "land of Ramses" for land of Goshen (Gen. 47:11). See the last section of Chapter 9.

32. A prime example of this phenomenon would be Tiberius Julius Alexander (nephew of the great Jewish philosopher and Bible commentator, Philo of Alexandria) who became Prefect of Egypt and one of the highest ranking generals in the Roman army. He was Titus' chief of staff in 70 CE and directly involved in the destruction of Jerusalem. Another example would be Benjamin Disraeli, baptized at age 13, popular novelist, politician, and Prime Minister of Great Britain; the outstanding proponent of British imperialism.

11

The Write-Off

> *Now hollow fires burn out to black,*
> *And lights are guttering low:*
> *Square your shoulders and lift your pack,*
> *And leave your friends and go.*
>
> *O never fear, man, nought's to dread,*
> *Look not to left or right:*
> *In all the endless road you tread*
> *There's nothing but the night.*
> — A. E. Housman, *A Shropshire Lad, LX*

> *So Israel dwelt in the land of Egypt, in the land of Goshen, and they acquired holdings in it, and were fruitful and multiplied greatly* [Gen. 47:27].

After the digression of the last chapter, with its focus on Joseph's career path and his remarkable success in reengineering Egyptian society, our author returns us to the main thread of the narrative. As such, the verse above can be seen as a bridge sentence, connecting the isolated description of the transformation of Egypt with the tale of the seed of Abraham. But to see this sentence as only a bridge would be a mistake. When we remember how the preceding episode concluded — that of Israel and his children getting permission to settle in Egypt — we begin to see a pattern.

> *So Joseph settled his father and his brothers, and gave them a holding in the land of Egypt, in the choicest part of the land, in the land of Ramses, as Pharaoh had commanded. And Joseph sustained his father and his brothers, even all the House of his father, with bread according to the number of their dependants* [Gen. 47:11–12].

Stepping back, we realize that the tale of the impoverishment and enslavement of the Egyptians is bracketed by announcements of the contrasting good fortune of the Israelites. Unlike the Egyptians who are forced to trade everything they have, including their freedom, for the bread that keeps them from starvation, the Israelites, like the priests, receive their daily bread as a gift of the state. More — during the five remaining years of the famine, an inverse dynamism is unfolding. As the Egyptians lose their land holdings, the Israelites increase theirs. Note that at the time of settlement Joseph gave his family "a holding"; now after dwelling some years in the land of Egypt they have "acquired holdings (plural) in it." The declining fortunes of the Egyptians and the rising fortunes of the Israelites are being both contrasted and emphasized. And Joseph is the cause of both. We have already commented on the long-term implications of this state of affairs. These implications are not simply our retrospective judgment superimposed on the text. The author, by his emphasis, is insisting on them.

The Oath

The years pass, the famine ends; but we are not told of any move on the part of the family to return to the Promised Land. The children of Israel, and Israel himself, seem to have settled in. Life in Goshen is good. A full decade and a half will pass before our tale renews.

What is the state of the relations between Jacob and his son? While we are not explicitly informed, much can be gleaned from the little that we are told. We have already speculated on the deep disillusionment of old Israel with Joseph, and its causes: his years of disengagement from the family, never allowing his grieving father even a hint that he was alive; his cruel treatment of his brothers when they came before him in Egypt and the vicious games he played with his family; and not least the total Egyptianization of his lifestyle, all these made blatant by his appearance. But we have not pondered what we can deduce about how Joseph himself viewed the same matters.

Joseph can hardly have been unaware of his father's coldness and reserve upon their first meeting after twenty-two years. While he had thrown himself on his father's shoulders and wept, his father had simply stood there tearless and silent. Then had come the fateful audience with Pharaoh. We have discussed the probable motivations and frame of mind of the two protagonists in the audience, Jacob and Pharaoh. But until now we have avoided considering Joseph. We are told nothing about Joseph except that it was he who escorted his father into Pharaoh's presence and (probably) introduced him. But what was his reaction to the surprising turn of events that ensued: older Jacob's refusal to conform to protocol, his seizing control of the meeting, blessing Pharaoh, in effect lecturing Pharaoh on proper values and then taking the initiative to terminate the audience by blessing Pharaoh once again and departing? Would we be that much out of line to suggest deep embarrassment on Joseph's part? While we were informed that he escorted Jacob in, we are not informed that he accompanied his father out. Is this mere oversight on the part of the author, or is the silence a weighted one? Is Joseph, by his non-accompaniment, distancing himself from the gaucheries of his "provincial" father? There seems ample reason to suspect a certain coldness, of mutual disillusionment, growing between father and son; a distancing between the two. The events now to be narrated hardly seem to evidence closeness and mutual empathy born of common outlook and frequent convivial contact.

His end felt to be approaching, Jacob considers that it is not too soon to put his affairs in order. Normally the occasion to broach such matters would be one of the regular family get-togethers. But this assumes that Joseph attended family events or visited his father on a regular basis. Neither seem to have occurred, because Jacob finds it necessary to schedule a special meeting, inviting his busy son to visit him. As the meeting takes place in Jacob's bedroom this may indicate that old Israel is now bedridden. He is, after all, a very old man.

> Now Jacob lived seventeen years in the land of Egypt, thus the days of Jacob, the years of his life, were one hundred and forty-seven years. Now when the time[1] of Israel's death drew near, he called his son, that is Joseph, and said to him, "Please, if I have found favor in your eyes, please put your hand under my thigh [as a pledge][2] that you will act toward me with loyalty and truth. Please do not bury me in Egypt. When I lie down with my fathers, carry me from Egypt and bury me in their burial place." And he said, "I will do as you have said" [Gen. 47:28–30].

What stands out first and foremost is the excessive politeness of Jacob's language, politeness to the extent of verbal groveling. Three times in a single sentence old Jacob feels the need to say "please," and this in addition to the fawning "if I have found favor in your eyes." Jacob did not feel the need to address Pharaoh in an obsequious matter; he spoke to him as to an equal. That he finds the need to couch his request to honor his choice of burial spot in such an abject manner speaks volumes about the relations between father and son. Joseph, with a curt (in the Hebrew) three-word reply, promises to do so. But this proves insufficient. It seems that Jacob does not trust his son to keep his promise. He demands that Joseph bind himself with a formal oath.

> *And he said, "Swear to me." And he swore to him. And Israel bowed at the head of the bed* [Gen. 47:31].

As we shall learn, Israel has good reason to fear the way his Egyptianized son will dispose of his body once he dies. He is so grateful that he has managed to elicit from Joseph a binding oath that, despite being confined to bed, he bows in thanksgiving to God. He now can rest secure that when his time comes he will be laid to rest beside the bones of his father, Isaac, his grandfather, Abraham, and, not least, his wife Leah.[3]

The whole episode reeks of a fundamental lack of shared values and mutual trust. From favorite son, Joseph seems to have dwindled in his father's eyes into an object of suspicion and distrust.

The Leap into the Future

Three times toward the end of his life Jacob is recorded as confronting his son Joseph over matters seen by him as vital. Twice it is he who initiates the meeting, and once it is a turn for the worse in his deteriorating condition that brings matters to a head. In the first confrontation Israel resolves to his satisfaction the question of his funeral arrangements. In the second face-off he will take a stand on an issue that has been a concern of his since his entry into Egypt.

> *Now it came to pass after these things that it was told to*[4] *Joseph, "Behold, your father is ill." So he took his two sons with him.*[5] *And it was told to Jacob, saying, "Behold, your son Joseph has come to [see] you." So Israel summoned his strength and sat up in bed*[6] [Gen. 48:1–2].

The news that his father is sinking rouses Joseph into action. He suspends his work for the day and, considering the gravity of the situation, decides to bring his two sons with him to see their grandfather, perhaps for the last time.[7] It quickly becomes evident that the old man's condition has indeed deteriorated. The last time Joseph was reported to have visited, he found his father, while bedridden, still able to turn himself over and make obeisance unaided. Now it takes all the energy Jacob can muster just to sit up in bed.

Despite his decrepitude Jacob's mind is clear, and it is obvious that he has been doing some serious thinking. He has come to a remarkable decision, and he knows exactly how he will deliver it when the occasion presents itself. The unexpected appearance of Joseph, far from throwing him off balance, is exactly the opportunity he has been awaiting.

> *And Jacob said to Joseph, "God Almighty*[8] *appeared to me in Luz,*[9] *in the land of Canaan, and blessed me and said to me, 'Behold, I will make you fruitful and will multiply you, and will make you an assembly of peoples; and I will give this land to your seed after you as an everlasting possession.'*[10] *And now your two sons, who were born to you in the land of Egypt before I came to you in Egypt, shall be mine; Ephraim and Manasseh shall be mine just as are Reuben and Simeon* [Gen. 48:3–5].

It is far from certain that Joseph grasps the implications of what his father is saying, much less any hint of what he is about to do. Jacob opens by relating a piece of family history. This is not new to Joseph. It can be taken for granted that Joseph, while still a boy, had heard some version of this account while yet in Canaan. It is the tale of Jacob's theophany at Beth-el (formally known as Luz) upon his return from Paddan-aram.[11] Israel reminds his son that at that time God had spoken to him, granting him the land of Canaan as the permanent possession of himself and his seed. Jacob's retelling of the tale of this grant is not a direct quote but rather a paraphrase of what God had said, which itself was a renewal of the original land-grant made to his fathers, Abraham and Isaac.[12] The purpose of this prologue is to establish the right of Jacob to dispose of what is his. Having been granted the land of Canaan by God gives Jacob the right to assign its parts as an inheritance as he sees fit. Jacob now implements this right by specifying who exactly shall be his heirs; he designates his grandsons Ephraim and Manasseh as his beneficiaries. He does this by formally adopting them as his sons. This is his meaning when he declares that they "shall be mine; Ephraim and Manasseh shall be mine just as are Reuben and Simeon." This declaration raises Ephraim and Manasseh to the same status as Jacob's oldest sons.[13]

In all probability, Joseph takes this surprise adoption of his two sons as an act meant to especially honor him. It is doubtful whether he grasps the practical long-range implications of what is taking place.[14] When the children of Israel will cash in on God's Promise and take possession of the land, the descendants of Ephraim and Manasseh will be considered tribes in their own right, each entitled to a full share of the land as the equals of the tribes founded by each of the sons of Jacob. However — and here lies the sting — Israel continues:

Now those born to you[15] after them shall be yours; they shall be called by the name of their brothers in their inheritance [Gen. 48:6].

To whom is Israel referring? We have not been informed of any further offspring, nor in the entire Bible is there any record of such.[16] There are those who therefore see this statement as anticipatory: should you have any more sons then.... But the grammar argues against such an interpretation, as does the law of probability. Joseph at this point is in his late fifties. If he has not had any children in the last twenty years, further progeny, while not impossible, would seem highly unlikely, and hardly worthwhile for Israel to take into account. Either way in fact there were none that we know of, so the issue is moot.

Therefore what is Israel saying? Here we come to the nub of the matter: Joseph has been stripped of his inheritance in Israel. He has been denuded of his two sons; they are now legally the sons of their grandfather. In the unlikely case that there should be other sons, "they shall be called by the name of their brothers in their inheritance," that is, become subsumed into the descendants (and hence the tribes) of their brothers Ephraim and Manasseh. There is to be no tribe of Joseph.[17]

As we have already speculated, Joseph probably takes the adoption of his sons by his father as an honor, and as putting him "one-up" over his brothers: he is getting a "double portion" of the inheritance, symbolically supplanting Reuben as the *behor*, the firstborn.[18] His father gives him little time to ponder any further implications. He quickly hurries along:

And as for me, when I was coming from Paddan-aram[19] your mother[20] Rachel died, to my sorrow, in the land of Canaan on the way, when there was some distance to go to Ephrath, and I buried her there on the way to Ephrath, which is Bethlehem [Gen. 48:7].

What in the world does Rachel's death and burial have to do with adoption and inheritance, the subject of Israel's startling announcement? This digression, rambling, verbose and emotion-laden is, both in content and in style, completely at a varience with what came before and what will come after. Yet I for one reject any suggestion of maudlin senile maundering. Old as he is, I contend that Israel has his wits about him. He has planned carefully what he will say and knows exactly what he is doing. I wish to suggest that these remarks have been cold-bloodedly inserted by Jacob in his presentation as part of his game plan. They serve two purposes: tactical and strategic.

The first purpose, tactical, is one of distraction. We must never forget the position Joseph holds as Viceroy of Egypt. He is more than simply the benefactor of his family. He holds them in the palm of his hand. As we shall yet learn, for seventeen years his brothers have been living in terror of him.[21] Jacob, the man who maintained his dignity in the presence of Pharaoh, has deemed it necessary to virtually grovel before Joseph when making his legitimate request in his choice of funeral arrangements.[22] How will Joseph react if he realizes that his most deeply felt personal interests are being compromised? For this is the entire purpose of the charade: Joseph must not suspect that by raising the status of Ephraim and Manasseh to the status of inheritors, Israel is thereby disinheriting Joseph, ejecting him from the "heritage of Jacob." Joseph must not be given the chance to think matters through too deeply. So Jacob digresses, recalling the tragic circumstances surrounding the traumatic moment of Joseph's mother's death. I suggest that he is playing on Joseph's emotions to distract him from thinking through the long-term implications of his adoption of his sons.

But why should Jacob want to disinherit his favorite son? Here we come to the core of Israel's tragic disillusionment with Joseph. Love him as he still does, he can no longer hide from himself what Joseph is and what he is not. Both by nature and by willful career choice Joseph is a quintessential Egyptian, in many ways the antithesis of what his fathers stood for, and thus not a true son of Israel.[23] Such a one cannot be permitted to impose himself as leader upon the children of Israel, and thus draw them onto the path of Egypt. I suggest that Jacob realized this from the moment he first set his eyes upon his Egyptianized son. For seventeen years he has been torn between his love of his son and his duty to his destiny — and he has temporized. Now, with his end in sight, he can temporize no longer. He has written off Joseph as a lost cause, and has made the decision to try to salvage the next generation. This is the entire point of the exercise.

At this point we come to the strategic, or ideational, level of Jacob's remark. This is not the first time that love and duty have clashed in his life, and he has had to steel himself and write off one closest to his heart — his beloved Rachel. What do we know about Rachel? Actually very little. We are told that physically she was stunning[24] (Gen. 29:17) and that Jacob loved her (v. 30) — though we are never told that she loved him. We are told that when Jacob and his family left Paddan-aram, Rachel stole her father's idols and carried them off with her (31:19, 30–35).[25] And we know that of all the Fathers and their wives, she alone was not buried in the family sepulcher. Why was her body not brought to Hebron for burial? Bethlehem is only fifteen miles from Hebron. Yet Jacob seemingly abandons her, burying her by the roadside (35:16–20). Kass suggests that Jacob wrote her off, just as later he was to write off his son.

> Jacob is not so much wallowing in his grief as he is reminding himself ... that Joseph is now lost to him, in the same way that his mother, Rachel, was lost to him long before.... Jacob may now understand the symbolic meaning of his decision not to bury Rachel with the other patriarchs and matriarchs (though she died not far from the cave at Machpelah). Rachel's burial "in the way to Ephrath" had left her on the outside of the new way. Now her preeminent son has chosen to assimilate himself to outside ways. Rachel had clung to her father's idols; Joseph now clings to

the land of the idolaters. Jacob who has only recently insisted on being buried with "his fathers" (please note: not with his beloved Rachel) sees that — like mother like son — the beautiful Rachel and her beautiful Joseph are both detours on the way to the promise that God Almighty has made to him. Jacob revives and purifies the meaning of Rachel, reclaiming her grandsons for himself, even as he recognizes that she and her son are both lost to the way of Israel.[26]

Israel has cut his losses. Joseph has been written off and will fade from the record in Israel.

The Blessing

And Israel saw Joseph's sons and he said, "Who are these?" [Gen. 48:8].

Noticing two adult figures standing in the background, Israel inquires as to their identity. This short and cryptic statement gives rise to a number of questions: has Jacob just now noticed their presence or has he been aware of them from the moment of their entry but has ignored them? Has he only now, when he has completed his main business with Joseph, been willing to acknowledge their presence? Is he truly unaware of their identity, and if so why?[27] We will shortly be informed that his sight has dimmed with age.[28] I posit that while he may not be able to make out features, Israel was perfectly aware that three persons had entered the room, and he may have had a shrewd suspicion as to who were the two who had accompanied Joseph, but he needed confirmation. On the other hand, if Joseph was not in the habit of bringing his sons with him on his possibly infrequent visits to his father, the only previous contacts may have been when they were but children — hence his lack of recognition. They are currently young men; nineteen and twenty years old at the very least.

And Joseph said to his father, "They are my sons whom God has given me here." And he said, "Please bring them to me and I will bless them." Now the eyes of Israel were dim[29] with age; he could not see. So he brought them to him, and he kissed them and embraced them. And Israel said to Joseph, "I never expected to see your face again, and behold, God has shown me your seed." Then Joseph took them out from [between] his knees, and they bowed down to him, with their faces to the ground[30] [Gen. 48:9-12].

The entire purpose of bringing his sons with him had probably been to receive the blessing of their dying grandfather; their elevation by adoption to the status of sons of Jacob was an unexpected bonus. Now, taking into consideration his father's infirmities (which the author has been at pains to call to our attention), Joseph takes matters in hand. Jacob is sitting on the edge of the bed, his grandsons standing between his spread knees as he embraces them. Their father now draws them back a bit, they bow, and then he positions his sons to receive their blessings. The positioning is by seniority: the eldest, Manasseh, is placed on Israel's right, the premier place, while his younger brother, Ephraim, is placed on Israel's left. His father, however, does not accommodate himself to his son's scenario.

Then Joseph took the two of them, Ephraim with his right hand to Israel's left, and Manasseh with his left hand to Israel's right, and brought them[31] close to him. And Israel stretched out his right hand and placed it on Ephraim's head, though he was the younger, and his left hand on Manasseh's head, crossing his hands, though Manasseh was the firstborn. And he blessed them[32] and said:

> *The God before Whom my fathers walked–*
>   *Abraham and Isaac–*
> *The God who has shepherded me*
>   *From my birth[33] to this day,*

> *The angel who has redeemed me from all evil,*
> * [May he] bless the lads;*
> *In them may my name be recalled,*
> * And the name[s] of my fathers Abraham and Isaac,*
> *And let them teem multitudinous*[34] *in the midst of the earth* [Gen. 48:13–16].

Crossing his hands and placing his right hand on Ephraim's head and his left on Manasseh's, Israel breaks into poetry to bless them. This was normative in the ancient world. All momentous and portentous pronouncements were couched in poetry. Even as his father[35] and God[36] had blessed him in poetry, even so does he word his benediction poetically: divine protection, multitudinous descendants and, above all, that they follow in the footsteps of their fathers Abraham and Isaac, remaining with their brethren as children of Israel.

True to his nature as an administrator, Joseph is preoccupied less with the content of the blessing than with the breach in his arrangements.

> *Now Joseph saw that his father had placed his right hand on Ephraim's head, and it was wrong in his eyes. So he took hold of his father's hand to move it from Ephraim's head to the head of Manasseh. And Joseph said to his father, "Not so, my father, for this is the firstborn; put your right hand on his head." But his father refused and said, "I know, my son, I know. He too shall become a people, and he too shall be great. But his younger brother shall be greater than he, and his seed shall become a multitude of nations." And he blessed them that day, saying:*
>   *"By you shall Israel bless, saying:*
>   *'May God place you as Ephraim and Manasseh.'"*
> *And he placed Ephraim before Manasseh* [Gen. 48:17–20].

The institutionalization of primogeniture in the ancient world was an expression of its acceptance of biological determinism; the defining factors that fixed one's place in the world being parentage and birth order. The native abilities of the individual and his or her preferences (that is, the will of the unique individual) counted little. One's biology was one's destiny. This was a value system categorically rejected by the emerging religion of ancient Israel. It is this rejection of biological determinism that lies behind the ongoing polemical preference of younger siblings over their seniors that runs through the Bible.[37] Here it is ironic that Joseph, the beneficiary of the willingness of his father to override precedence and to favor him over Reuben, has become the champion of primogeniture. It can be seen as just one further mark of his Egyptianization. Jacob, on the other hand, has remained constant within the emerging Israelite ethos. What he saw in Ephraim we are not told, but he was not going to allow birth order to determine his priorities.

Israel strongly resists Joseph's attempt to interfere. Probably as a result of his son's meddling, in the coda to the blessing Jacob once again skips over a generation. It is in the name of Ephraim and Manasseh that the future generations will bless their sons,[38] *not* in the name of Joseph. Joseph, as well as most subsequent commentators, preoccupied with the switch and priority between the two brothers, pay scant if any attention to the fact that once again Joseph has been consigned to the status of a nonperson. Not by him shall the future people bless; his way will not be the way of the future. Egypt is for the Egyptians but Israel will be for the Israelites.

This final pronouncement is especially portentous. As von Rad has noticed, this is the first time that Israel as a nation is mentioned[39]: "By you shall Israel bless." It is this vision of the future that dominates the ancient Father. He who can but dimly see in the present has unrivaled clarity as he envisions the coming destiny of his descendants, and therefore his unwavering exertion to bind his grandsons to this destiny.

A Cryptic Summation

Then Israel said to Joseph, "Behold, I [am about to] die. And it shall come to pass that God will be with you, and he shall return you to the land of your fathers [Gen. 48:21].

To whom is Israel referring? We are told that he is addressing Joseph, so we must assume that his words are intended first and foremost for him. Yet the pronouns (you, twice) are in the plural. Who besides Joseph is included in this avowal of either faith or hope? The most logical assumption would be Joseph's two sons, Ephraim and Manasseh, and/or their descendants.[40]

On the face of it the statement is remarkable, and it cannot be understood to have been made purely for effect. I am dying, Israel says, and this is no time for platitudinous evasions but only for the unvarnished truth. I insist that your destiny will, in the end, prove too strong for you; that despite your persisting on the path of Egypt your end shall find you in the land of your fathers, the very land to which you promised to return me. This will not be your doing or even mine. You have recognized that it is God who controls our destinies; is He who will bring this to pass.

Israel now concludes by bequeathing his legacy to his favorite son.

And as for me, I have given you one shechem *above your brothers, which I took from the hand of the Amorites with my sword and my bow* [Gen. 48:22, emphasis added].

This verse is maddeningly obscure. The key to the verse is the Hebrew word *shechem*, which has been left untranslated. The word means *shoulder*, "and in no other passage [in the Bible] does it vary from that meaning."[41] It is also the name of the city of Shechem. Many translators and commentators render the word as *portion*. It is easy to see why: it fits the context, depicting Jacob, by bestowing a double portion on Joseph ("one portion above your brothers"), anoints him as "the firstborn."[42] There is no philological support for this rendition whatsoever, and moreover, as I will attempt to demonstrate, it contradicts the clear meaning of the narrative. The term *shechem* has been interpreted by some, metaphorically, to mean the "shoulder of a mountain," and thus "a mountain ridge." There is no support anywhere in the Bible for this usage.[43]

Having exhausted the current attempts to understand the word *shechem* in its plain or metaphorical meanings,[44] we join the majority of scholars who, by default, fall back on seeing the term as referring to the city of that name. Speiser, attaching the word *one* that precedes *Shechem* to Joseph, reads the verse as follows: "As for me, I give you, as the one above your brothers, [the city of] Shechem...."[45] Despite this reading he admits the verse to be "a laconic and obscure allusion."[46] Grammatically this may work but historically it does not. Shechem did not belong to Jacob and was not his to give. Moreover, Jacob is nowhere recorded as taking anything from the Amorites "with his sword and his bow."[47] The only holdings that Jacob possesses in Canaan that are in his power to legally bequeath are the cave and field of Machpelah, the family sepulcher which is his by inheritance, and a parcel of land outside of Shechem, which is his by purchase. Are these what Israel has in mind?

The patriarchal sepulcher is the patrimony of all the seed of Abraham; it is not Jacob's to bestow. Only the holding he purchased on the outskirts of Shechem is in his power of gift. Having disinherited Joseph, and thus having removed the possibility of his founding a tribe, could the bestowal of this plot of land at Shechem be intended as some sort of consolation prize? In the next section we will suggest that this is indeed the case. For the present we must admit, along with the overwhelming majority of commentators, that beyond guesswork there is currently no real understanding of this "obscure" verse.

In the Fullness of Time

The attempt of the dying Israel to reclaim Joseph's sons — the next generation — would seem a desperate gamble with scant chance of success. Born and brought up in Egypt as part of a privileged aristocracy by an idolatrous mother, and with only fleeting contact with their foreign grandfather, uncles and cousins, their future would appear predetermined. Yet, strangely enough, it was with these despised shepherds that they ultimately cast their lot. Centuries later their descendants are to exit Egypt along with the offspring of the other sons of Israel, forming two of the premier tribes of the People of Israel.

Jacob will receive his dying wish and be buried in the soil of the Promised Land, by the side of his ancestors and his first wife. And amazingly, the prediction of the dying patriarch will prove accurate: Joseph's destiny as a son of Israel will prove stronger than his predilection for the Egyptian way of life. Disinherited he is. He will found no tribe to bear his name, and his presence will be eclipsed in the saga of the Chosen People. After almost a third of Genesis which he dominates, for all his glory his name will fade from the pages of the Bible.[48] Egypt also will provide him no lasting heritage. The man who once acquired almost the whole land will end with nothing to bequeath. Even his memory will not so much be forgotten as rejected by his adopted land. Only his physical remains — his bones — will linger on, and these will ultimately come to rest, not in Egypt, but in that plot of land outside of Shechem that his father bequeathed to him.

We leave the final word to Ron Pirson:

> From the remainder of the Hebrew Bible it is clear that Joseph does not inherit any land.... Would it not be possible that in 48:22 Jacob gives Joseph the only piece of land he will ever get?[49]

Israel, who but recently had made arrangements for his own interment, has prepared the gravesite of his son.

NOTES

1. Literally, "the days."
2. "The practice of swearing with the hand on or near the genitalia — there was no Bible on which to swear an oath — was apparently practiced in other ancient societies.... [The one taking the oath thus] symbolically agrees to permit the man's progeny to exact retribution from him should he swear falsely" (Kass, 368, note 18).
3. This reading of the ambiguous statement, "And Israel bowed at the head of the bed," is not universally held. There are commentators who see the object of Israel's obeisance as Joseph, a continuation of his fawning attitude and obsequious language when making his request of this son who is capable, on a whim, of disposing of his corpse in any way that he might desire. These commentators also see this scene as the fulfillment of the prophecy in Joseph's second dream; the prophecy that his father would prostrate himself before him (Gen. 37:9–10). I find this scenario unacceptable. I cannot see the man who would not bow to Pharaoh bowing to any other human being. More, when entering Egypt, and confronted with Joseph in all his splendor in his golden chariot, he did not bow but remained upright and unmoved. As to fulfillment of the dream-prophecy, I will attempt to demonstrate, in due course, that this view of Joseph's dreams is mistaken.
4. Reading with LXX, Syr., and Vulg.; MT reads [someone] "said."
5. LXX adds, "and they came to Jacob."
6. Literally, "sat on the bed."

7. We have no idea where in Goshen Israel resided, but it is not unreasonable to assume a journey of at least several hours between the capital and the Israelite dwelling complex in Goshen.

8. *El Shaddai*; see Chapter 7, note 18.

9. Otherwise known as Beth-el. See Genesis 28:16.

10. Literally, "holding," the very term used of the portion of territory in Goshen given to the family of Jacob at Pharaoh's command. See Genesis 47:11. Joseph gives a part of the land of Goshen to the family as a possession, but it is God who gives the *entire* land of Canaan to Jacob and his seed as an *everlasting*, i.e., permanent, possession. The contrast implies the impermanent nature of the Israelite hold on Goshen.

11. Jacob had two encounters with God at Beth-el. The first and more famous occurred when, as a youth, he fled his home to seek refuge in his uncle's home. This revelation included the famous dream of a ladder connecting earth with heaven (Gen. 28:13–14). The second, that took place after his return from Paddan-aram, involves God's confirmation of the change of name from Jacob to Israel. From the wording of Jacob's account, it is clear that it is to the second revelation that he is referring.

12. The original episode is related as follows: "Then Jacob came to Luz, which is in the land of Canaan, that is, Beth-el, he and all the people that were with him. And there he built an altar and he called the place Beth-el.... And God appeared to Jacob once again when he came from Paddan-aram and he blessed him, and God said to him, 'You whose name is Jacob, no longer shall your name be called to Jacob, but Israel shall be your name.' And He called his name Israel." (Gen. 35:6–7, 9–10).

> And God said to him: "I am God Almighty (El Shaddai)
>   Be fruitful and multiply,
> A nation, and an assembly of nations will [come forth] from you,
>   And kings shall come forth from your loins,
>
> And as to the land that I gave to Abraham and Isaac,
>   To you will I give it,
> And to your seed after you will I give the land" (vv. 11–12).

13. There are those who go further and claim that the actions that follow this declaration (verses 12–20) constitute a formal adoption ceremony.

14. Would he particularly care even if he did? Joseph sees his arena of action and his future in Egypt. Inheriting a piece of land in Canaan would hold little interest for him. His personal prestige and his standing vis-à-vis his brothers, however, are a different matter entirely.

15. Literally (in archaic English), "And [as to] your progeny, those whom you begot [i.e., fathered] after them, they shall be yours." The phrase is in the past tense.

16. Some commentators propose that this is "a fragment of a lost tradition" that Joseph had additional children (Sarna, *Genesis*, 326). There are some who opine that, as a high official and in accord with the standards of that time, he "must have had a large harem" and consequently many children. This is pure speculation, lacking any corroborative evidence.

17. Raymond de Hoop strongly argues this position: "Commonly the adoption of Ephraim and Manasseh is interpreted as a positive event for Joseph but this point of view must be seriously questioned.... The consequence of Jacob's action is that now Joseph has no sons any more, and unless he would beget one later he would be childless. His name is wiped out completely because it will be the patriarch's name which will be called in them" (*Genesis 49 in Its Literary and Historical Context* [Leiden: Brill, 1999], 338).

18. Under later Israelite law, the *behor*, or firstborn son, inherited a double share of the estate, twice as much as the shares of the other brothers (Deut. 21:15–17). This may already have been established clan custom at this period.

19. Reading with LXX; MT omits "*aram*."

20. Reading with LXX and Syr.; MT omits "your mother."

21. See Chapter 13.

22. The fear seems to have been that Joseph would find a Hebrew funeral (interment in a burial cave, and beyond the borders of Egypt no less) as low class and demeaning, and hence socially embarrassing. This would lead Joseph to insist on an Egyptian funeral.

23. For example, it is really impossible to reconcile what Joseph has done to the Egyptians with biblical ethics and values.

24. She is described as *yefat toar* (a phrase that refers to the body and that might be rendered as "a gorgeous figure") and *yefat mareh* (a phrase which refers to facial beauty). Taken together as a package, the description denotes astounding beauty. Only Esther, among all the other women in the Bible, is accorded a similar description (Esther 2:7). And significantly, Rachel's son, Joseph, is described in identical language (Gen. 39:6).

25. Years later Jacob forced her to bury and abandon them at Shechem (Gen. 35:2). We also know that she nagged Jacob to distraction (30:1–2).

26. Kass, 641–642.

27. Sarna is insistent that our narrative is a description of a formal adoption ceremony, and that this question is no more than a legal formula required by law to establish the identity of the adoptees (Sarna, *Genesis*, 325).

28. Many commentators take verse 10 to mean that Jacob was sightless, but the text does not say this. There is a perfectly good Hebrew term for total loss of vision, "blind." However, the author does not see fit to use it. Rather, he uses a lesser term to indicate impaired vision.

29. Literally, "heavy." See previous note.

30. Reading with LXX and Syr.; MT reads, "he bowed." It makes little sense for Joseph, in this context, to bow to Jacob. But if we persist in reading with MT, the effect is deeply ironic. Joseph had dreamed that his father (the sun) would bow to him. The text never records Jacob doing so. But if we read with MT, it is Joseph that ends by bowing to his father. Turner (165–166) makes much of this ironic reversal.

31. Reading with LXX, Syr., and Vulg.; MT omits "them."

32. Reading with LXX.; MT reads, "Joseph." Vulg. reads "the sons of Joseph."

33. Literally, "as long as I have been"; LXX and Syr. read, "from my youth."

34. Hebrew *ve-yidagu larov*; literally, "may they spawn multitudinously like fish."

35. Genesis 27:28–9; 28:3–4.

36. Genesis 35:10–12.

37. For example, Isaac over Ishmael, Jacob over Esau, David over his older brothers, etc.

38. The practice of placing one's hands on the heads of one's sons and in evoking this blessing persists to this day among the descendants of Israel.

39. von Rad, *Genesis*, 413. He sees the mention of Israel in Genesis 34:7 as an anachronism, as indeed it is.

40. Another possibility, adopted by some commentators, is that Jacob is addressing, through Joseph, the entire House of Israel. Considering the context this seems a bit far-fetched.

41. Sacks, 407.

42. See note 18 above.

43. The word *katef*, a synonym of *shechem*, does have this metaphoric use in Numbers 34:11; Joshua 15:8; 10–11; 18:12–13; and probably Isaiah 11:14, where it means slope or side. But any assumption that this metaphoric usage extends to its synonym is totally unwarranted.

44. The phrase *shechem ehad* (one shechem) appears one other place in the Bible, Zephaniah 3:9, "where it is used *adverbially* in an idiomatic sense made clear by the immediate context" (Alter, *Genesis*, 291, emphasis in the original). The only difficulty is that applying the supposed "clear" meaning in Zephaniah (actually no clearer than *portion* is in our text) to our verse creates as many problems as it solves. Alter quotes the King James Version, "with one consent," and the Revised English Bible and the NJPS translation, "with one accord," i.e., unanimously, in an attempt to understand the term. Recognizing that neither of the above fit our context, he changes the wording and renders as follows: "as for me, I have given you *with single intent* over your brothers what I took from the hand of the Emorite" (sic), thus papering over the fact that the subject in Zephaniah is plural whereas in our verse it is singular. If one uses the translation in the NJPS, "with one accord," the contradiction becomes blatant. Basically, it makes even less sense than its alternatives.

45. Speiser, 358.

46. Ibid.

47. The massacre of the adult male population of Shechem (Genesis 34) was perpetrated by his sons Simeon and Levi (more on this later). Jacob had no part in the massacre and indeed denounced it vigorously. Moreover, the family did not take possession of the city but, quite the opposite, fled.

48. Only two recurrences in Exodus, six in Numbers, three in Deuteronomy, six in Joshua, three in Judges, one in Samuel, one in Kings, eight in the Prophets, five in Psalms, and twice in Chronicles — a mere 37 in all! His nonentity of a brother, Issachar, gets almost as many (35) while Dan gets 43 and counting. Contrast this with at least 219 for Judah (the person and/or the tribe he founded). This virtual erasure of Joseph's memory from the pages of the Bible after Genesis cannot be accidental.

49. Pirson, 121–122.

12

Legacy

*I loved you, so I drew these tides of men into my hands
and wrote my will across the sky in stars....*
— T. E. Laurence, *Seven Pillars of Wisdom*

As the twig is bent, so grows the tree.
— Proverb

From our brief survey of what the future holds in store for Joseph, we return to father Jacob. What a change has come over him since learning that his favorite son is alive, and since joining him in Egypt. From an ineffective and self-pitying dodderer, he has metamorphosed into the quintessence of his alternate identity — Israel. More and more he has stepped into the role of the responsible Father. Increasingly he has focused on transmitting the spiritual heritage of his forebears Abraham and Isaac, and has been obsessed with the destiny of his offspring. He has at long last faced and overcome his disastrous bias in favor of the son of his favorite wife, Rachel, and has had the courage to accept what Joseph is: an Egyptian at heart, a stranger and a digression from the path demanded by God of their forbearer, Abraham: "I am God Almighty; walk before Me and be wholehearted" (Gen. 17:1). And Israel has found the strength within himself to write off his son. We have followed his protean attempt to secure the allegiance of his grandsons, the next generation, for the path of Abraham — an attempt that will ultimately prove successful. Now one last task remains for the dying Father: to designate the future leadership of the family and to point the direction to be taken in the time to come. This will be the legacy Israel will leave to his sons.

The legacy will take the form of a deathbed Final Testament.[1] It is this Testament that forms the burden of the 49th chapter of Genesis. But before we can begin to probe into the content of Israel's last words, we have to contend with the surprising fact that they are presented in the form of a poem. Further, we must address certain specific concerns relating to both the provenance of the poetry that lies before us, and the precise relationship between the poem and the narrative we have been following.

We begin with a basic assumption: that the poetry comprising Genesis 49, verses 2–27, is a unified composition.[2] There is a general agreement that the poem is very old, dating well before the establishment of the monarchy.[3] This means that the author of the dramatic tale we have been reading and the author of the poem cannot be one and the same person. The poem had long been in circulation and was familiar to the public.[4]

The poem is in the first person, the speaker being Father Israel. Jacob's authorship is assumed and was unquestioningly accepted by ancient Israelites. This poem was very much a part of Israel's cultural heritage, and it may have served as one of the prime inspirations for the composition of the Joseph saga. It certainly was employed by the author as the centerpiece and climax of the narrative. In a word, this line of reasoning raises the possibility that it was the poem that set the agenda for the entire Joseph narrative.

The Poem Itself

If we are correct in our assumption that the "Testament of Israel" was in existence long before the composition of the narrative we know as "The Joseph Story," then our next step must be to understand the poem in isolation. Only when we have come to an evaluation of the poem on its own will we be in a position to put the poem and narrative together and see how, and to what extent, the pieces fit.

The poem is framed as an address by the Father Jacob/Israel directed to his sons. In the main (with the exception of a few digressions) he addresses each son separately. The order of these separate addresses is not random, but is structured in a matrilineal order. Jacob opens by speaking to the sons of his first wife, Leah, while reserving his remarks to the sons of his second and favorite wife, Rachel, to the last. Between these two groups the sons of the concubines are sandwiched in, grouped as follows: a son of Bilhah, followed by two sons of Zilpah, followed once again by a son of Bilhah.[5] Within each group of sons, Jacob addresses them in order of birth.[6]

It is important to understand the agenda of Jacob/Israel as it can be inferred from the poem. The central issue is to award the prize of the future leadership of the family (and of course of the tribes the sons would father) to the most worthy among the various contenders for the role. Included in this purpose will be the issue of how to deal with the losers. But inasmuch as the format of the poem is that of a deathbed last will and testament, it becomes necessary that every son be given some recognition. Thus we end with three categories of sons and three categories of address: the important sons, i.e., the two main contenders (Judah and Joseph); the less important sons, i.e., the also-rans (Reuben, Simeon and Levi); and the unimportant sons, i.e., all the rest.[7] This last category only rates pro forma mention. Having examined the poem structurally, it is time to consider it from the standpoint of content. This content must include the context of not only the Joseph Story but also of the larger background of the saga of the last of the Fathers, Jacob. As previously suggested, Jacob has two related issues before him: to make public his choice of the future leader of the "House of Israel," and the problem of how to mollify the main loser. The central problem lies in the fact that the big loser will be Joseph.

As we have already pointed out, we must never lose sight of Joseph's position in Egypt and the raw power at his disposal. Jacob by now has lost any illusions he once had with regard to his son. He is fully aware of what Joseph is capable of should he realize that his most deeply felt personal interests are being compromised; it was this awareness that determined Israel's delicate orchestration of his adoption of Ephraim and Manasseh. Joseph would never tolerate the slap in the face of being publicly supplanted by one of his brothers.[8] Joseph has already demonstrated his capacity for cruelty in the sadistic games he played with his brothers. Should he feel himself slighted — "done dirty" — he has it in his power to wreak terrible vengeance, and especially upon the brother who supplants him. With the fear of such a reaction uppermost in his mind, yet adamant in his decision that under no circumstances may Joseph assume the leadership of the Children of Israel, Jacob must find some way of softening the blow and lessening the hurt that rejection will entail. It is this issue that determines Israel's tactics.

Most obvious to Jacob is that he cannot choose Judah because he has shown himself to be the most worthy of all his sons; that would be a slight too wounding to be tolerated. Nor would relying on the fact that Judah has risen to preeminence among his brothers (that is, all the brothers except Joseph) and is accepted by them as their spokesman[9] be an improvement. This also would be calculated to provoke a violent reaction from Joseph. Only some neutral and ostensibly objective method of choice would have any chance of defusing this potentially explosive situation. In this impasse Jacob falls back on the universally accepted principle of primogeniture.

This is hardly a principle sacred to Jacob. We remember how casually he flouted it in the case of his two grandsons, reversing the birth orders of Manasseh and Ephraim. But we also remember, as old Israel undoubtedly did, how Joseph forcibly attempted to correct his father and preserve the sanctity of primogeniture. This is a principal dear to Joseph's heart and one which he might find it difficult to contend against. If Jacob can seem to base his decision on the right of the eldest, this is a decision that would not be seen as a personal slight, but simply the act of a father functioning within the mandate of immemorial binding tradition. It is this, I suggest, that determines the method Israel adopts.

Jacob begins with his oldest son, and then proceeds down the line rejecting numbers one, two and three for heinous moral transgressions. Then, seemingly by default, the mandate falls to his son number four, the next in line. This method at least does not impute moral failure to Joseph, the real reason for his rejection. In addition, he reserves Joseph to the last,[10] laying it on thick and heavy with multiple material blessings; in fact everything but the one thing that counts. Israel is also careful to accord to Joseph the longest of the "testaments."[11] In this manner, his father tries to leave Joseph with a good taste in his mouth. In is in light of this analysis that we will now approach chapter 49 of Genesis.

But before we proceed, a caveat is in order: due to the antiquity of our poem a fair portion of the terminology is obscure, as are many of the references. On numerous phrases there is no agreement as to the meaning. As a result a considerable amount of the translation is no more than guesswork.[12] In these instances we have tried to go with the current consensus view where possible, and failing any consensus with the most promising opinion among those available. But like Robert Sacks I wish to assert that "this commentary makes no pretense of having completely understood these rather cryptic passages but will try to shed some light wherever it can."[13]

For Moral Turpitude Rejected

And Jacob summoned his sons and said, "Gather yourselves and I will tell you what will befall you in days to come"[14] *[Gen. 49:1].*

This opening verse is a continuation of the prose narrative and serves as a bridge, connecting the following poem with the main body of our tale. It presupposes Jacob's statement, "I am about to die" (48:21) and thus sets the scene for what is to follow as a deathbed testament addressed directly to his gathered sons; and not only to them but to their descendants as well.[15] In a word he states that he intends to impart to them what their future holds in store for them, both as a result of the decisions he is about to announce and on the basis of their own characters and actions.

Assemble and listen, O sons of Jacob;
And listen to Israel your father.

> *Reuben, you are my first-born,*
>   *My strength and the first-fruit of my virility,*
> *Pre-eminent in rank and pre-eminent in power.*
> *Uncontrollable as water*[16]
>   *You shall be pre-eminent no more;*
> *For you went up to your father's bed,*[17]
>   *Then you defiled [my couch];*
> *Onto my couch he went up!* [Gen. 49:2–4].

The poem begins with its own introduction, calling upon the sons to gather and heed the words of their father. Jacob/Israel is the speaker.[18] Reuben, by right of primogeniture, should have inherited the leadership of the family. But due to a fatal character flaw, he has performed an abominable act of incest.[19] Taking advantage of the death of Rachel, which left her maid Bilhah unsupervised, Reuben commenced an affair with her. But Bilhah was more than just Rachel's maid; she had also been given to Jacob as a concubine. A concubine was a legal wife (albeit of low status) as well as a bed partner.[20] Within the confines of even a large family such things cannot be kept permanently secret. Eventually Jacob hears of what is going on.

> *Now it came to pass, while Israel dwelt in that land, that Reuben went and lay*[21] *with Bilhah, his father's concubine, and Israel heard* [of it] [Gen. 35:22].[22]

The language used, "and Israel heard [of it]," is preparatory to a reaction,[23] but strangely none ensues; the verse breaks off in mid-stride.[24] Only now, decades later, does the issue resurface.

In unconcealed fury, unabated by the passage of time, Jacob goes public with this long-ago affront to his honor, declaring this offence an abomination justifying his deposing his oldest son from preeminence. Then, having uncrowned the crown prince, he throws off all restraint. Up to this point the address is in the second person, directed to Reuben. Now he adds a coda, in the third person—an exclamation of fury directed to all his sons and, metaphorically, to the entire world: "Onto my couch he went up!" Reuben is finished.[25]

We move on to sons two and three:

> *Simeon and Levi are brothers,*
>   *Weapons of violence are their knives!*[26]
>
> *O my soul, come not into their council,*[27]
>   *Let not my honor be joined to their assembly;*
> *For in their fury they kill men,*
>   *And at will hamstring oxen.*
>
> *Cursed be their fury, for it is fierce,*
>   *And their rage, for it is relentless.*
> *I will divide them in Jacob,*
>   *And scatter them in Israel* [Gen. 49:5–7].

As in the case of Reuben, the curse upon Simon and Levi is incomprehensible without explanatory background. This has been provided in Genesis 34. In short, at a time when the family had settled in the vicinity of Shechem,[28] the son of the Headman or Chief of the territory raped Jacob's daughter, Dinah, then kidnapped her and held her captive, intending eventually to marry her. In negotiations between Jacob's sons and the Headman, Hamor, an agreement is proposed stipulating that if the Shechemites circumcise themselves all will be forgiven, agreement will be given to marriage between the rapist and the victim, the Shechemites will then give their daughters in marriage to the Israelites and everyone will live happily ever after. The Shechemites proceed to circumcise all their adult males. When they are thus incapacitated, Simon and Levi, Dinah's full brothers, treacherously fall upon the helpless Shechemites and, massacring them, free their sister from the condition of sex-slavery to which she had been reduced.[29]

In this case also Jacob's response is problematic. Apparently he had no forewarning as to what his sons planned, and was caught by surprise. He remonstrates with them after the fact, though not on the grounds that their act was immoral but on the grounds of expediency — that the massacre will stir up the country against them and endanger them. Simeon and Levi reject his reproof out of hand and stand on their honor and that of the family: rape of a member of the family cannot be tolerated, their sister must be freed and her violation avenged no matter what the cost! It is they who have the last word.

Now, again after several decades, Israel resurrects an ancient atrocity to justify his rejection of his second and third oldest sons from any leadership roles. Ever the incompetent and impotent father when his children were growing up and needed good parenting the most, Jacob now rakes up old sins by his wild and undisciplined sons (moral trespass he could and should have prevented) as excuses for removing them from "the line of succession."

Simeon and Levi are unique among the brothers in not receiving individual pronouncements but are treated as a pair. Indeed the opening line could justifiably be rendered: "Simeon and Levi are a pair!" as in "a pair of rascals," equal in their rapacity. In disassociating himself from them, Jacob refers to his soul (*nafshi*) in parallel with his honor (*kevodi*). *Nefesh* is the biblical term that expresses the essence of one's life and animation.[30] *Kavod*, "usually translated as 'honor,' is the God-endowed quality that distinguishes humans from other forms of life. "[31] Thus not simply the physical being called Jacob, he is saying, but the very essence of his being revolts from what his two sons are and what they stand for. They kill, cripple and destroy without restraint.[32] Their rage is an unceasing, ravaging fire. Sons such as these have forfeited not only any right to leadership but to life as well. As murderers they deserve to die — a sentence that he is both constitutionally and physically unable to carry out — so instead he curses them with the curse of division (being cut to pieces) and scattering (the pieces being strewn over the countryside); that is extinction. Needless to say, while a powerful expression of Jacob's loathing for his sons, a moral outrage long repressed and now explosively released, this curse had neither effect nor consequence in the lives of the brothers or their descendants. The destinies of the tribes these brothers founded followed courses very different from those of tribes accursed.[33]

There can be little doubt that father Jacob felt very deeply about the depravity of his three oldest sons. But considering the time that had been allowed to lapse between the commission of the outrages and their denunciation, one can't but wonder whether there might be a gnawing sense of guilt stemming from his over-permissive parenting and the lack of firm oversight that allowed his sons to reach the nadirs that they did, and this is what stoked the vehemence of Israel's denunciation. But however one reads the record, the outcome of the Testament is clear: the three oldest sons of Jacob have been disowned.[34] Which leaves son number four, Judah.

Judah Vindicated

At the very beginning of our tale, when young Joseph was flaunting his dreams of dominance over his brothers — that they all would eventually grovel before him — the brothers reacted: "What! Do you mean to reign over us! Do you mean to rule us!" (Gen. 37:8). Framed as a rhetorical question its sense in context was wholly negative: under no circumstances! But a question it nonetheless is, and as a question it has been hovering in the background of the entire narrative. Seemingly the answer has been *yes*. In Egypt, by dint of the power afforded him by his position, Joseph holds sway over his family. But this is a domination externally imposed, not a rule by the consent of the governed. Now the issue is to be settled, once and for all, within the confines of the family by the one with the authority to settle it, their father. And when the issue becomes not one of power but one of right, the answer becomes *no*. Joseph's ascendancy will be merely short-term. It is Judah who has earned the mantle of leadership; the future of the children of Israel will belong to him.

What follows is not a blessing; nowhere is it referred to as such. It is an investiture: Judah is being named as the head of the family, a leadership that will be the permanent possession of his descendants.

> [As for] *you, Judah, your brothers shall extol you*[35]*;*
> *Your hand shall be on the neck of your enemies.*
> *Your father's sons shall bow down before you* [Gen. 49:8].

Were this all that Jacob had to say to Judah it would still be definitive: triumph over all enemies and the praise and homage of his brothers. It is important to recognize how clearcut and definitive this declaration is before we begin to get bogged down in luxuriant poetic imagery and obscure allusions. Everything that follows is, at best, no more than elaboration on the opening statement. Expanding on the image of triumph over enemies, the poet shifts from the image of a warrior gripping his enemy by the neck prior to delivering the death blow (an image already present in earliest Egyptian art) to the picture of a lion sated from gorging on his prey, going up to his lair to sleep the heavy slumber of repletion. Who dares to disturb him or encroach on his territory?

> *A young lion is Judah;*
> *From prey, my son, have you risen.*
> *He crouched down, he lay down like a lion,*
> *Like the king of beasts*[36]*;*
> *Who dares rouse him?*
> *The scepter shall not depart from Judah,*
> *Nor the ruler's staff from between his feet;*
> *Until he comes to Shiloh*[37]
> *And the obedience of peoples is his* [Gen. 49:9–10].

The two words, rendered here as "scepter" and "ruler's staff," are interchangeable and refer to the same item, a staff or pole of indeterminate length which, in ancient times, was the symbol of authority. Everyone from tribal chiefs to emperors had one.[38] The picture, a continuation of the depiction of Judah as the acclaimed leader of his brethren in verse 8, is that of a seated chieftain, with staff held upright between his legs proclaiming his authority. This authority, Jacob informs the assembled sons, is no temporary matter but will pass along to his descendants.[39] As the family transforms itself into a nation, Judah's predominance and leadership will endure.

For several thousand years readers have taken this oracle as referring to David, or at least to future kingship. This reading is purely a product of hindsight and completely unwarranted by a literal reading of the text. Judah is not being invested with either the prerogatives or the trappings of royalty. There is not a single unambiguous reference to either. Judah is being given the mandate of being the first among equals, and this by the consent of those whom he is to lead ("your brothers extol you"). In this Jacob is simply placing the seal of approval upon an existing reality, and declaring it permanent. To read more than this into the text is to unhistorically read back a later and unanticipated reality into the utterance of an earlier era.

It is at this point in Israel's pronouncement to and about Judah that clarity ends, and confusion reigns supreme. (Notes 12, and especially 37 below, begin to give some small idea of the variety of interpretation and a lack of consensus for just one word in the MT.) As to the remainder, while a more or less literal translation results in coherent images, meaning eludes us.

> *He tethers his ass to the vine,*
> *The son of his she-ass to the grape-vine,*[40]
> *Of wine he washes his garment,*[41]
> *His robe in the blood of grapes.*
> *His eyes are darker than wine,*
> *His teeth are whiter than milk* [Gen. 49:11–12].

We will rest content with the essence of the statement which is understandable, and leave the significance of the poetic imagery to others, perhaps better qualified to interpret these obscure phrases.

The Others

Having disposed of the main business, Jacob now gives recognition to each of his sons. The operative principle here seems to be that one's character is one's destiny. The character of an individual not only shapes what he will make of his life, but its effects will reverberate down the generations determining the general shape of the family future. In the words of the proverb: as the twig is bent, so grows the tree. This, of course, leaves little room for free will. We will not spend overmuch time on these brief "predictions" as they have little bearing on our central themes; Jacob himself gives them short shrift. It is interesting to note, however, that like most fathers, Israel got his estimates of his sons and his prognoses of their futures as often wrong as right.

We begin with Judah's two younger brothers, sons of Jacob and Leah:

> *Zebulun shall dwell by the seashore,*
> *He shall be a haven for ships;*
> *His flank shall rest on Sidon.*[42]
>
> *Issachar is a big-boned ass,*
> *Crouching among the sheepfolds.*
> *When he saw that his resting place was good,*
> *And the land was pleasant,*
> *He bent his back to the burden,*
> *And became a willing serf*[43] [Gen. 49:13–15].

In Appendix 3 we deal with the incongruity between the futures depicted here for the descendants of these two sons of Jacob and the historic reality, to the extent that we know it. Either Jacob didn't really know his sons, a not improbable conclusion considering how wrong he was about Joseph, or biology is less determinative than Jacob thought.

Having concluded the sons of Leah we now turn to the sons of the concubines; first Dan, son of Bilhah, Rachel's maid:

> *Dan will vindicate*[44] *his people,*
>   *As one of the tribes of Israel.*[45]
> *Dan shall be* [like] *a snake on the road,*
>   *A viper on the path,*
> *Who bites the horse's heels,*
>   *So that its rider falls backward* [Gen. 49:16–17].

The idea seems to be that the tribe, though small, will be able to justify its existence by its toughness, holding its own even though overmatched by its adversaries.[46]

The series of pronouncements is suddenly interrupted by an incongruous interjection:

I await your salvation, O Lord[47] [Gen. 49:18].

Of all the explanations for this interjection the one I like the best is that of Maurice Samuel:

> This effort on Dan's behalf seems to have exhausted Jacob, for an interpolated phrase, a gasp, occurs here:
>
> "I wait for Thy salvation, O Lord."
>
> And thus the seven outsiders are disposed of, each in its turn, with Jacob's mind obviously elsewhere.[48]

If we keep in mind the setting, a deathbed Testament followed almost immediately by Jacob's death, such an exclamation makes literary sense.[49]

The disposal of the "disposable sons" resumes, but at an accelerated rate. Time is running out for Jacob and he must save sufficient energy to end with a bang.

> *Gad — raiders shall raid him,*
>   *And he raids on their heels!*
> *Asher's food shall be rich,*
>   *And he shall bring forth kingly dainties.*
> *Naphtali is a prolific hind,*
>   *Bringing forth lovely fawns*[50] [Gen. 49:19–21].

And finally Benjamin[51]:

> *Benjamin* [is a] *ravening wolf,*
>   *Devouring prey from morning,*
>   *Dividing spoil till evening*[52] [Gen. 49:27].

Perhaps Jacob read the character of his youngest son better than those of his older brothers. As things were to turn out, a vicious wolf makes not a bad depiction of the tribe as it came to be; a tribe brought to the very edge of extinction in a civil war, brought on by its infamous behavior.[53]

And now to the last, but hardly the least, item on Israel's agenda: the defusing of the time bomb that Joseph represents.

The Consolation Prize

> *The son of a wild she-ass is Joseph,*
>   *The son of a wild she-ass by a spring,*[54]
> [The son of] *wild asses by a rocky rim.*[55]

> *They harassed and shot at him,*
> *   The archers who hated him.*[56]
>
> *But his bow remained firm,*
> *   Flexible his arms and hands*[57];
>
> *By the hands of the Mighty One of Jacob,*
> *   By the name of*[58] *the Shepherd, the Stone of Israel*[59] [Gen. 49:22–24].

Up to this point (assuming the translation — especially of the first three lines — has any touch of accuracy) the picture seems to be that of a wild ass by a spring or drinking hole being ambushed by hunters who shoot at him. The image then shifts to that of an outnumbered warrior, who standing his ground, shoots back, and with God's help manages to hold his own. This interpretation suggests a poetic picture of Joseph's tribulations and the trials that he overcame. Jacob is insisting that he triumphed not only by his courage but by God's assistance. The last two lines, stressing God's help, are the only part of the poem up to now which, while hardly free of problems, are relatively unambiguous.

The poem now moves on to blessings, the only time blessings are mentioned in Jacob's Testament. Five times in five consecutive lines the word "blessings" is repeated,[60] emphasizing and re-emphasizing what is being here uniquely conferred.

> *From the God of your father, may He help you,*
> *   And Shaddai,*[61] *may He bless you:*
> *With blessings of heavens above,*
> *   With blessings of the deep that lies beneath,*
> *Blessings of breasts and womb.*
> *The blessings of your father*
> *   Surpass the blessings of the eternal mountains,*[62]
> *   The bounties of the everlasting hills.*
> *May they rest on the head of Joseph,*
> *   On the brow*[63] *of the one set apart from*[64] *his brothers* [Gen. 49:25–26].

This blessing — for the first time we can with justice use the term — is different in degree as well as in kind from what has been conferred on all the other sons of Jacob. Comparable in content and poetic style in its beginning to the previous pronouncements, it takes off, and soars poetically into exalted realms. For all the obscurity of many of its phrases and images, the "Blessing of Joseph" is the equal to the best of the early poetry in the Bible. Jacob has reserved his absolute best to eulogize his favorite son. The torrent of blessings: those of the heavens above (rain) and the deeps below (perennial springs gushing forth from the earth) are the promises of bumper crops and continual well-being[65]; the blessings of breasts and womb (fertility; large numbers of children and grandchildren, an ideal in ancient Israel, but not necessarily in Egypt).[66] These blessings metaphorically encompass all the material blessings hoped for by ancient man in general, and by the children of Israel in particular. Joseph has been granted everything but that which, in his father's estimate, is the most important — the blessings of the spirit, the blessings of leadership and of moral authority.

In my reading of the poem, and of the narrative framework that grew up around it, Israel bestowed upon his son exactly that which Joseph valued the most, emphasizing that they were blessings, and dressing the whole in rich and luxuriant poetic imagery — all to befog the critical fact that the true blessing (although not named as such) has eluded him and has been conferred upon another. Did the ploy work? From Joseph's reaction I believe that it did. Joseph will show neither dismay nor anger. He will consider himself the main beneficiary of his father's legacy and will hold no grudge against either father or brothers. After all, in his eyes what blessings there are go to him alone, and practical dominion is his anyway.

The concluding words of the blessing, when Israel defines Joseph as "the one set apart from his brothers," in both their honesty and their ambiguity exemplify the sure hand of Jacob, even in his final moments. As the Egyptian at heart, Joseph has always been an isolate among his brothers; and as the one who followed the way of Egypt, he has consciously charted a path different from theirs. In the eyes of his brothers, and at the last in the eyes of his father as well, this is negative. Joseph, however, while accepting that he is set apart, obviously sees the phenomenon as highly positive, and undoubtedly takes the designation as a compliment; one that is special and elite. And, interestingly, so do many commentators who choose to render the term *nazir,* without warrant, as "elect." Joseph over the years has managed to charm myriads of those who never got close enough to know him well. It is a cautionary lesson to us that those who did get to know him—his family in particular—without exception eventually turned from him. This includes, I contend, the author of our tale.

In the last major act of his life, Jacob has lain to rest the ingrained habit of half a lifetime and risen above his compulsive love for his son. He has bestowed the leadership where it belongs, ensuring that the family will not be diverted from the path of Abraham, and he has prevented a backlash. He deserves a mark of A.

Notes

1. Many commentators over the years have correctly rejected the definition of Israel's final words as "blessings" (based on an assumed parallel with "The Blessings of Moses," Deuteronomy 33). The majority of his pronouncements are far from blessings; some may even be defined as curses. This reevaluation has been behind the tendency to increasingly drop the title "The Blessings of Jacob" and to substitute "The Testament of Jacob."

2. In this I depart from the majority of contemporary commentators. My reasons for doing so are explained in Appendix 3: What Is a Poem Doing in the Joseph Narrative?

3. See the Introduction for a discussion of the dating of our narrative.

4. The poem was originally transmitted orally for centuries before having been translated into written form, at the earliest sometime during the Age of the Judges. I am willing to admit to some minor "modernization"—some minor alterations in syntax, grammar, and spelling to accommodate more recent speech patterns—and possibly a few minor glosses, but contend that the poem as we have it today has not been "updated" in content in any serious way, and is essentially the same as it was when originally composed. See Appendix 3. For another view regarding the poem's transmission see Introduction, note 49.

5. Bilhah was the maid of Rachel, Zilpah the maid of Leah.

6. With the possible exception of Zebulun and Issachar; but see note 42 below.

7. These categories of priority are reflected in the number of verses accorded to each: both Judah and Joseph are accorded five verses each, or together ten verses out of a total of twenty-five. The three also-rans (Reuben, Simeon, and Levi) get five verses between them. The left over ten verses are divided among the seven remaining sons, an average of one and a half verses each.

8. We must remember that for seventeen years Joseph, by virtue both of his government position and his support and patronage of the family, has arrogated to himself the position of de facto head of the family. On the death of their father, Joseph obviously expects to succeed to the formal title as well.

9. It is Judah that, by unanimous consent, served as spokesman of the brothers in their climactic confrontation with the Viceroy of Egypt, and it was Judah that shamed Joseph into revealing his true identity, ending the cruel game of cat and mouse he was playing with his family.

10. Or, due to the necessity of birth order, the next to the last. This may help to explain why the beloved Benjamin gets such paltry treatment at the end—his mention must not in any way detract from the accolades heaped upon his brother. More on this later.

11. While Joseph's "testament" is equal in number of verses to that of Judah (five each), when counted in words Joseph's exceeds Judah's (61 words to 55).

12. "Differences of interpretive opinion are such that in two instances there is no agreement about whether the language refers to animal, vegetable, or mineral! At such junctures, a translator can do no more then make an educated guess" (Sarna, *Genesis*, 292).

13. Sacks, 408.

14. Literally, "in the end of days." "Hebrew *be-'aharit ha-yamim*, like its Akkadian counterpart *ina ahrat ume*, means simply 'in the future'" (Sarna, *Genesis*, 332). Neither prophecy nor eschatology are here intended. Speiser renders the phrase "in the days to follow" (364).

15. There is an inherent ambiguity in the translation. Twice the word *you* appears, but in the Hebrew original two separate terms are used: the first, *lachem*, is directed to the sons, while the second, *etchem*, has a wider range and refers to their descendants—specifically the tribes they will father.

16. Literally, "frothy as water" or "foaming like water." I take the rendering of *pahaz* in the sense of "uncontrollable" from Hamilton, 645.

17. Literally, "the lying place of your father," a phrase with explicit sexual connotations. "The phrase is probably elliptical for 'the bed of your father's wife'" (Sarna, *Genesis,* 333).

18. The use of the two names of the patriarch in parallel assumes the knowledge, on the part of the audience of the poem, of the episodes, related in Genesis 32:23–33 and 35:10–15, of Jacob receiving his second name. Likewise the contents of 49:4 presuppose the knowledge of 35:22.

19. Leviticus 18:8 and 20:11 forbids a son to have sexual relations with a wife of his father. Deuteronomy 27:20 lays a curse on any son who does so.

20. This point is emphasized in Genesis 37:2 where Bilhah and Zilpah are specifically referred to as wives of Jacob.

21. The root of the word for "my bed," *mishkavi*, in Genesis 49:5 is the same as the verb [he] "lay with" in the account of Reuben's sin above. This is no accident; but which prompted the other depends on our understanding of which came first: in our reading the poem came first, and the short prose account in 35:22 was written later to give the background needed to understand Jacob's dispossessing of his oldest son.

22. It has become commonplace in recent years to understand this incident as a political act—in copulating with his father's wife, Reuben was attempting to usurp his father's role as the head of the family. This, to my way of thinking, is taking the currently popular slogan "everything is political" more than a bit too far. As C. G. Jung once remarked about Freud's fixation on sexual symbolism: "Sometimes a cigar is just a cigar." In the same way, sometimes lust is just lust, and fornication is simply fornication.

23. See the identical usage in Numbers 12:2 where it is followed by a strong reaction.

24. The MT contains the note, "Paragraph ending in the middle of a verse." Does this indicate that something, possibly an explosive confrontation between father and son, has been deleted? Or is the purpose to draw attention to Jacob's failure to react?

25. The demotion of Reuben had effects that rippled down the centuries. While all the earliest lists of the brothers, and the tribes to which they gave birth, list Reuben in first place, suddenly, in the Book of Numbers, when the marching order of the tribes in the wilderness is given, we find Judah in the lead of the first division (Num. 2:3–10). The demotion rankled. Reubenites, Dathan and Abiram, joined with the Levite Korah in spearheading a revolt against Moses (16:1–3). On the eve of the entry into the Promised Land, Reuben opted to trade its inheritance there for the land east of the Jordan (Num. 32). From this point onward Reuben's influence continued to decline. The tribe did not take part in the war of national liberation under Deborah (Judg. 5:15–16). In all the Biblical Age, they failed to produce one notable figure. Not one judge, not one prophet hailed from the tribe of Reuben. Undiluted mediocrity proved to be the norm. Character runs true: as Reuben was insignificant as a person, so were his descendants insignificant as a tribe. Yet to the end they labored under the sense of a long-standing injury.

26. The word *mekarotaihem* is unique and all translations are guesses. I prefer Dahood's suggestion that the root of the word is *karet*, "to cut," therefore to be rendered as "knives." Based on the background account in Genesis 34:25–29 and Exodus 4:25 where the term *karet* is specifically used for circumcision, he holds the noun *makret* to be the technical term for a circumcision knife. (M. J. Dahood, "MKRTYHM in Genesis 49,5," *CBQ* 23 (1961): 54–56.

27. Literally, "their secret."

28. This was the time that Jacob acquired by purchase a plot of land that he deeded to Joseph, and which ultimately was to serve as Joseph's burial ground. See the conclusion of chapter 10.

29. This summary does not by any means do justice to this sordid episode. It is strongly recommended that the full original be read. See also chapter 7, note 2.

30. Ethan Dor-shav, "Soul of Fire: A Theory of Biblical Man," *Azure* 22 (Autumn 2005): 90.

31. Sarna, *Genesis*, 334.

32. "To hamstring" means to cripple or disable an animal by cutting the hamstring, the large tendon in the upper part of the animal's rear legs.

33. See Appendix 3.

34. In light of the vehemence of the denunciation of his three oldest sons, it might be worthwhile to revisit Israel's adoption of his grandsons, Ephraim and Manasseh, and his raising them to the status of Reuben and Simeon (Gen. 48:5). There are commentators who view the comparison positively, Jacob conferring a sort of "first-born" status upon them. Yet at the time of the adoption, the decision to "disinherit" both Reuben and Simeon had undoubtedly already crystallized — the events of chapters 48 and 49 are closely connected in theme and in time. So singling out Reuben and Simeon, as opposed to any of his other sons, can be neither coincidental nor positive. I agree fully in this matter with de Hoop: "The equation with Reuben and Simeon contains, from a strictly synchronic point of view, a very clear message. If the sayings concerning these two tribes in Genesis 49 are considered regarding the position of Ephraim and Manasseh the message is obvious: 'you shall have no superiority'" (338).

35. The use of the word extol (*yoduha*), while a pun on Judah's name (*Yehuda*), is excessive, even extreme. "Here, quite unusually, a man is being praised; usually God or his name is the object of praise. There are only three other passages [in the Bible] where human beings are said to be praised (Job 40:14; Pss. 45:18 [17]; 49:19 [18])" (Gordon J. Wenham, *Genesis 16–50*, World Biblical Commentary, vol. 2 [Dallas, TX: World, 1994], 476).

36. "This English kenning is necessary for the poetic parallelism because there are no English synonyms for 'lion,' whereas biblical Hebrew has four different terms for the same beast" (Alter, *Genesis*, 295).

37. This phrase is notoriously obscure. This is the literal translation of the phrase as it stands. On the other hand many of the ancient versions take the term "Shiloh" to be a compound word meaning "which is to him." If so, then the line should be translated: "Until he comes whose it is," i.e., "Until the owner of the scepter comes." Another possibility: with a modest change of the vowels we get: "Until tribute is brought to him." Yet another possibility: the prophet Ezekiel seems to allude to our verse (Ezek. 21:32) as: "Until he comes whose right it is." See also Ezekiel 19.

38. Even Judah, as head of family, had one when he propositioned Tamar and left it with her as a pledge of payment for her "services" (Gen. 38:18, 25). This same staff is probably still in his possession. On the other hand, it is well to note that the Hebrew terms for "staff" used in Genesis 49:10 are neither one identical with the term used in 38:18 and 25.

39. Note how this pronouncement has shifted from second person to third person in the middle of verse 9. Jacob begins by addressing Judah. Then, from speaking *to* Judah, Israel shifts to speaking *about* Judah to the assembled audience.

40. Literally, "a vine of the Sorek variety"; a vine that produces a choice grape. (Why one would tie one's donkey to a valuable vine when the donkey would immediately eat it is a question that has engendered endless monographs with convoluted answers, none very satisfactory.)

41. Reading with Dahood, "Notes on Genesis," 81.

42. A major Phoenician port-city about 25 miles north of Tyre. On the other hand Sidon could here be used as a metaphor for all Phoenicia, as often it was in the ancient world. See Appendix 3 for a discussion of the significance of the anomaly of these "predictions" in contrast with the actual historical outcomes. The order of the two brothers is also strange: according to Genesis 30:17–20 Issachar was born first, yet not only is Zebulun listed ahead of Issachar in Deuteronomy 33:18 ("The Blessing of Moses"), but in the commission appointed by Moses to oversee the division of the Promised Land (Numbers 34:25–26) and in the actual division of the land (Joshua 19:10–17) Zebulun likewise takes precedence over Issachar. All these references testify to a very ancient and persistent tradition.

43. Following Speiser, 362.

44. A word play: *Dan yadin*; or alternatively, "Dan will judge his people."

45. The first mention in the Bible of the "Tribes of Israel."

46. Historically, the tribe never made much headway in settling its allotted territory, being confined to a small segment of it by Philistine pressure. Eventually forced out of even this, the tribe was to migrate to the far north, eventually becoming the northernmost of the tribes; hence the expression "from Dan to Beersheba," meaning "from one end of the land to the other."

47. This is the one and only time in our narrative (Genesis 37–50) that the name of the Lord, the God of Israel, is mentioned by one of the actors (Jacob/Israel). Likewise the narrator is remarkably sparing in the use of the Tetragrammaton (Gen. 39:2–3 [twice], 39:5 [twice], 39:21 and 39:23 [twice], 38:7 [twice], 38:10. The present occurrence in Jacob's words makes twelve times in fourteen chapters; an average of less

than one time per chapter. "Contrary to the stories about Abraham, Isaac and Jacob, God is hardly ever present in Gen. 37–50" (Pirson, 118).

48. Samuel, 355.

49. This, incidentally, is the first use of the term "salvation" in the Bible, a reminder of Jacob's focus.

50. Reading with Dahood, "Notes on Genesis," 81–82.

51. I am taking the liberty of moving last-place Benjamin up a notch. As I have previously contended, birth order dictated that he come after his full brother, Joseph. But here we employ a different model: despite Jacob's bias in his favor, he is not in the running and so should be grouped with those who are irrelevant to our tale.

52. Reading with Dahood, "Notes on Genesis," 82. "It is rather remarkable that Jacob only directs nine words (in the Hebrew) to his youngest son" (Pirson, 133), despite his strong emotional bias toward him. But see note 10 above.

53. See Judges 19–21.

54. No one appears to know what this verse means. Hamilton seems to offer the least improbable suggestion, based on uses in Ugaritic, which we have adopted (Hamilton, 678).

55. For want of a more attractive alternative, I continue to follow Hamilton (ibid.), but with little confidence. Literally MT reads, "daughters stride on a wall." From this to Hamilton's "[The son of] wild asses by a rocky rim" is more than a bit of a stretch, but other alternatives are even worse. Beyond the fact that everyone is trying to interpret the verse metaphorically, there is no agreement as to translation, much less meaning.

56. Or "bore him a grudge," a possible reference to the brothers. If so, does this mean that Jacob now knows what took place at Dothan? See Chapter 13, pages 188–189.

57. I.e., he proved able to overcome the assaults and even prosper. The rendition of these lines follow (Westermann, 326).

58. Reading with Syr.; MT reads "From there."

59. A unique metaphor for God; the usual epithet is "Rock."

60. Not to mention the initial verbal form in "may He bless you," which precedes the cascade; a total of six, all the more remarkable when set against the lack of any blessing up to now.

61. Usually rendered as "The Almighty." See Chapter 7, note 18.

62. Reading with LXX.; MT unclear.

63. Literally, "head." English lacks a current synonym for head (" pate" is archaic, while "bean" and "noggin" are both slangy and unsuitable in their connotations). The Hebrew term used here means literally the top of the head, and is often used with "head" in poetic parallel.

64. Reading with Targ.; The MT Hebrew, *nazir,* is here used in its basic meaning of one separated from, one set apart from. The term's technical meaning of "Nazarite," one who did not cut his hair and abstained from alcoholic beverages, obviously does not apply to Joseph. "Indeed, Joseph was apart from his entire family physically for twenty-two years and apart from them emotionally from the time of his youth (Feder, 421). And "contrary to his brothers, Joseph will not share in the inheritance of the land ... yet another way in which he is set apart from his brothers" (Pirson, 133),

65. But note: the blessing does not apply to Egypt, which does not depend on rain or groundwater but on the Nile River and the extensive irrigation systems based on it. Joseph would have to relocate to Canaan to reap its benefits. Is Joseph alert to the hint he is being given?

66. Joseph, unlike most of his brothers, has only two sons, and these are not even his anymore since their adoption by Jacob.

13

The Closing of Accounts

I am tired of tears and laughter,
And men that laugh and weep;
Of what may come hereafter
For men that sow to reap:
I am weary of days and hours,
Blown buds of barren flowers,
Desires and dreams and powers
And everything but sleep.
—Algernon C. Swinburne,
The Garden of Proserpine

To the extent that it is given mortal man to do, with this last great effort on his part, Israel has set his stamp upon the unknown and unknowable future. He is now free to depart this world, his work accomplished. The author appends a colophon to the poetic Testament, a summary and, by referring to the recipients not as sons but as tribes, a glance into the future.[1]

These are the tribes of Israel, twelve in all. And this is what their father spoke to them as he bade them farewell,[2] addressing to each a parting word appropriate to him [Gen. 49:28].

This colophon returns us to our tale, serving as a bridge between the poetry, now ended, and the prose of the narrative (much as verse 1 bridged the transition at the beginning of the poem).

The End of an Era

The author now takes up the threads of his story.

And he charged them, saying to them, "I am being gathered to my people.[3] Bury me with my fathers in the cave that is in the field of Ephron the Hittite, in the cave of the field of Machpelah, which is opposite Mamre in the land of Canaan, the field that Abraham bought from Ephron the Hittite as a burial plot. There Abraham and Sarah his wife were buried; there Isaac and his wife Rebecca were buried; and there I buried Leah. There in the field and cave that belongs to it that was acquired from the Hittites" [Gen. 49:29–32].

What does it say of the trust reposed in Joseph that, after promising and then being made to swear that he will carry out his father's wishes as to his funeral arrangements, Jacob feels it necessary to publicly repeat his request to all his sons?

These prove to be his last words. He has been seated on the edge of the bed. Now, all used up, he pulls his feet back into the bed, lies down, and assuming a quasi-fetal posture breathes his last.

So Jacob ceased charging his sons, drew his feet into the bed, expired, and was gathered to his people [Gen. 49:33].

The Age of the Fathers has come to a close.

State Funeral

Now Joseph fell on his father's face, and wept over him, and kissed him [Gen. 50:1].

This is the fifth time Joseph is said to have wept, virtually the only expression of emotion to break through the iron reserve he imposes upon himself.[4] We have previously briefly speculated on the causes of his emotional breakdowns, but as we are never explicitly informed by the narrator of the reasons, all speculations remain just that — speculations. Here we will refrain from even venturing a guess as to what feelings prompt the tears, and whether — and if so to what degree — the outburst here is simply a formal public display expected in the face of parental death. We will only draw attention to his first public exhibition (before Egyptians) of emotion[5]: when Joseph "appeared" before his father in full regalia, riding in his chariot and surrounded by his retainers.[6] There he "fell on the neck" of his father," and he wept on his neck a long time" (Gen. 46:29). His father's response had been instructive. We are not told that he also wept or reacted in any way. Erect, silent and evidently dry-eyed, he had outwaited the cloud-burst. Only then had he responded: "And Israel said to Joseph, 'Now I can die, having seen your face, for you are yet alive.'" (46:30)

This time Jacob is dead, and as such is deprived of the option of responding.[7] It is hard at a moment such as this to charge Joseph with simply putting on a show for the sake of public appearances. There must have been feeling behind this display, but what level of feeling we are not told. The display itself— throwing himself on his father's face (a unique expression in the Bible),[8] publicly weeping (but not too long, certainly nothing equivalent to his outburst upon his reunion with his father), followed by a final kiss of farewell — has to it a histrionic air. By these actions Joseph has taken command of the situation, completely upstaging his brothers.[9] It is a control he will not relinquish until after the conclusion of the lengthy funeral proceedings.

Having exhibited his filial emotions, and, incidentally, fulfilling God's promise to Jacob that "Joseph shall place his hands upon your eyes" (46:4), that is, Joseph will be present at your death and will close your eyes, Joseph now takes charge of the arrangements.

And Joseph commanded his servants the physicians to embalm his father, and physicians embalmed Israel. It required forty days,[10] for such is the full period of embalming; and Egypt bewailed him seventy days [Gen. 50:2–3].

Embalming, the lengthy and complex procedure of turning a corpse into a mummy,[11] was a process designed to ensure eternal life for the individual. This was a religious ceremony central to the faith of ancient Egypt. It was bound up with the cult of Osiris, god of the underworld, and performed by its priests. One wonders what Israel would have felt about such treatment of his corpse.

Yet none of this is allowed to intrude upon our narrative. In line with the author's policy of keeping the tale "religiously neutral," and never permitting the least mention of the religion of "the most religious people on earth"[12] to intrude, no priests are mentioned, only "physicians."[13]

And now we come to the announcement of a public mourning period that lasted seventy days![14] Hamilton makes the following observation:

> Are we to believe that the entire nation of Egypt went into mourning for two-and-a-half months for a transported Hebrew living in Goshen? This must be something mandated by Pharaoh.[15]

He is undoubtedly correct. Only Pharaoh could have imposed a national period of mourning. Diodorus of Sicily informs us that, in Egypt, at least in late–Hellenistic and early–Roman times, the period of mourning on the death of a king was seventy-two days.[16] If this also held true millennia previously, that is in Joseph's days, then Pharaoh was according to Jacob an honor just short of that accorded to royalty! But why? As a gesture of appreciation to Joseph? As a mark of respect to an old man who had blessed him in a never-forgotten interview? Our text gives no hint of an answer.

> *Now when the days of bewailing him*[17] *were past, Joseph spoke to the House of Pharaoh, saying, "Please, if I have found favor in your eyes, please speak* [these words] *in Pharaoh's ears: 'My father laid me under oath, saying: "Behold, I* [am about to] *die. In my tomb which I hewed out for myself in the land of Canaan, there shall you bury me." And now, please let me go up and bury my father; and I shall return.'" And Pharaoh said, "Go up and bury your father, even as he made you promise under oath"* [Gen. 50:4–6].

The nation-wide period of mourning finally comes to an end; the time has come to entomb the mummy that once was his father. But Joseph had promised his father, and then he had been forced to confirm that promise under oath, that he would inter his father only in the family sepulcher in Hebron, and not in Egypt. For an out-of-country burial, permission will be needed. Even Joseph may not leave at will the totalitarian state that is Egypt. But Joseph does not turn directly to Pharaoh for the necessary leave. Instead we find "Mr. Number Two of Egypt," the man who not so long ago had unrestricted right of access to the person of the Pharaoh, "going through channels." This, and the obsequious language that he employs, are eye-opening. They bespeak a serious erosion in status and authority.[18] The man who started with the mandate: "You shall be over my House. By your command shall all my people be directed. Only the throne will be greater then you.... See, I have set you over all the land of Egypt.... Without your consent no man shall raise hand or foot in all the land of Egypt" (41:41–44), now has to virtually beg persons who are formally his inferiors to transmit a message to his boss. Shall we posit that, crisis past, the great famine-that-wasn't now no more than a memory and himself no longer vital to the survival of the state, the new broom is finding itself getting progressively more and more worn down? Still holding the position of second only to Pharaoh, Joseph is increasingly finding his position a wasting advantage.

How Joseph words his appeal tells us a lot about the man. He makes no mention to Pharaoh that the terms of the oath he had taken forbid him to bury his father in Egypt, or that this is a family sepulcher. He phrases his request in positive and simple terms, terms any Egyptian would at once understand: "In my tomb which I hewed out for myself ... there shall you bury me" (Gen. 50:5). Upper class Egyptians spent the better part of their adult lives preparing their tombs, furnishing them and stocking them with all the appurtenances to supply their needs in the afterlife. The terms Joseph uses, especially the word *hewn*, would convey to Pharaoh's mind a picture of a tomb like those cut into the cliffs opposite Thebes. Oh, by the way, Joseph casually slides in, the tomb his father allegedly spent so many years preparing is situated in Canaan. This is really a request that Pharaoh cannot in all decency deny. Even so, Joseph feels it necessary to close with a promise to come right back, yet another indication of a deteriorating situation. Why the need to promise if all is well?

> Any reader who knows what lies ahead will be struck by the contrast between Joseph's timid "Let me go up" and that of the next Israelite who stands before Pharaoh, Moses' bold demand "Let my people go." In the contrast between Moses (and earlier Jacob) and Joseph we see the difference between the man who knows who he is and the man who is willing and able to be all things to all people, a difference that turns ultimately on how each man stands in relation to God.[19]

Permission in hand, the funeral procession gets under way.

> *So Joseph went up to bury his father, and all the servants of Pharaoh, the elders of his House, and all the elders of Egypt went up with him, [along with] all the House of Joseph[20] and his brothers, and his father's House; only their little ones, and their flocks and their herds they left in the land of Goshen. Also chariots and horsemen went up with them; it was a very large procession[21]* [Gen. 50:7–9].

This is a state funeral with all the trappings: the highest government officials and representatives from all the Nomes (which is possibly what the phrase "the elders of Egypt" refers to) in attendance, along with a large military escort. And all the family, of course, is present; wives as well as husbands. But note, small children and all the brothers' capital—their flocks and their herds—are left behind; not so subtle hostages to their return.[22] And as to Joseph: Pharaoh, ever the gentleman, in his permission makes no mention of Joseph's promise to return. He doesn't have to. The hundreds of soldiers escorting the funeral procession will see to it, should Joseph get it into his head to decamp.

> *And they came to Goren ha-Atad,[23] which is beyond the Jordan,[24] and they lamented there a great and solemn[25] lamentation; and he [Joseph] observed a mourning period for his father of seven days. Now when the Canaanite inhabitants of the land saw the mourning in Goren ha-Atad they said, "This is a grievous[26] mourning for the Egyptians." Therefore it was named Abel-Mizraim,[27] which is beyond the Jordan* [Gen. 50:10–11].

Having arrived at an appropriate resting spot (whose location is currently unknown),[28] the procession halts, and a formal and prolonged ceremony of lamentation takes place, making a strong impression on the local population and giving a new name to the site. It is there that Joseph observes the Hebrew seven-day mourning period that Jews practice to this day. The bier then moves on to its final resting place in the vicinity of Hebron.

Up to this point Joseph has been center stage, exactly where he planted himself. It was he who made the scene at the deathbed; it was he who ordered the mummification of Jacob's body; it was he who engineered a magnificent Egyptian funeral—a state funeral at that—and it was he who choreographed it. Israel's other sons have been reduced to nonentities. But they remain his sons, and Jacob's charge to bury him in the family sepulcher was made to them all at his deathbed. Now the narrator calls a halt to this extravaganza of Egyptian pomp and grandeur, and restores a Hebrew perspective; simple and austere.

> *Thus his sons did for him, even as he had commanded them. His sons carried him to the land of Canaan, and they buried him in the cave in the field of Machpelah, the field facing Mamre that Abraham purchased as a burial site from Ephron the Hittite. Now after they had buried his father, Joseph returned to Egypt, he and his brothers, and all that went up with him to bury his father* [Gen. 50:12–14].

And so God's last remaining promise to Israel at Beer-sheba has been fulfilled:

> *I Myself shall go down with you to Egypt, and I shall also most certainly bring you back up* [Gen. 46:4].

Jacob/Israel has come home, and Joseph, his duty to his father fulfilled, now dutifully shepherds his kin back to the place he sees as his home: Egypt.

The Lurking Fear

Back in Egypt the narrative rushes to its denouement.

> *Now the brothers of Joseph were afraid because their father was dead,*[29] *and they said, "If Joseph bears a grudge*[30] *against us, he will* [now] *certainly pay us back for all the evil we did to him." And they drew near to Joseph,*[31] *saying, "Before his death, your father commanded, 'Thus shall you say to Joseph, "I beg you, please forgive the transgression*[32] *of your brothers and their sin,*[33] *for they have done you evil."' And now, please forgive the transgression of the servants of the God of your father." And Joseph wept when they spoke to him. Now the brothers also went and threw themselves down before him and said, "Behold, we are your slaves"* [Gen. 50:15–18].

What the brothers reveal, by both word and deed, is unnerving, and puts paid to any notion that a reconciliation has been effected between them and Joseph. For seventeen years they have lived in terror of this awesome Egyptian overlord who is their brother, and who holds them in his power. For seventeen years they have been convinced that only their father's presence stood between them and the terrible vengeance that their guilty consciences insisted was their due. And now their father is gone, and the long-dreaded moment of payback has arrived. Rather than wait passively for the ax to fall, the brothers take the initiative to lay before Joseph a plea for mercy voiced by their dead father; a voice from the grave, as it were, begging his favorite son to be lenient with his brothers despite the severity of the wrongs that they have done him. To this the brothers confess that they have sinned against him, beg for forgiveness, throw themselves at his feet and offer themselves to him as his slaves.[34] They are pleading for their lives; they are convinced that their lives are hanging by a thread.

Is this scenario psychologically credible? Maurice Samuel faces the question directly:

> For seventeen years they lived in dread of their father's death, secure only in the thought of his presence. The reader will object: "That was not Joseph's fault; they could not get rid of their guilt complex." Did Joseph ever try to help them? It was not a good start, even the most biased reader will admit, to have staged for the reunion in Egypt those dramatic scenes with which half the world is familiar, and in which all who know them take such delight. If their effect has persisted on a hundred generations, what must it have been on the brothers, participant-victims? Think how, through the seventeen years before their father's death — and afterwards too, in spite of Joseph's reassurance — they woke in night-sweats, reliving the accusation that they were spies, the days of imprisonment, the discovery of the money in their sacks, the horror of their return without Simeon, old Jacob's anguish, the long wait in Canaan with the dwindling rations, the return to Egypt with Benjamin, the "theft" of the goblet: reliving the sick, bewildered memory of the hungering ones at home, and the fantastic behavior of the Governor of Egypt. This was what Joseph had rubbed into them, and to wash it out was now impossible. We may say, literally, that he had rubbed it into them with a vengeance.[35]

Considering what they had gone through and the guilt that tormented them, the brothers are certainly justified in their fears.[36] But is their evaluation of Joseph valid? Joseph's response is revealing: he weeps! Then he speaks to the brothers, who remain face down in the dust before him:

And Joseph said, "Fear not, for am I in the place of God?" [Gen. 50:19].

Joseph professes shock; how could his brothers so misjudge him? Referring to the deep-rooted tradition that vengeance belongs exclusively to the realm of the divine, and that its usurpation by man amounts to hubris,[37] Joseph says to them in effect, "What! Do you take me for a god?[38] I may seem to you godlike, but I am merely a human being with no right of vengeance. You have nothing to fear from me." And if we set aside the grandiloquent and self-flattering language, Joseph is being sincere. He intends no revenge; he has long since put aside all thoughts of vengeance, not because of a sense of humility but because of the very opposite. He is far above such petty things; he has put the wrongs done to him behind him. His renunciation of revenge is based not on forgiveness but on indifference. Joseph now continues, putting matters into perspective — God's perspective — which he now appropriates as his own:

"Now you intended me evil, [but] *God intended it for good, in order to bring about that many people should be kept alive, even as they are today. And now, fear not: I will provide for you and your little ones." So he comforted them, and spoke to their hearts* [Gen. 50:20–21].

Joseph returns to the declaration he had made to them seventeen years previously when he had first revealed himself to them.

"I am Joseph your brother, whom you sold into Egypt. And now do not be sad or angry with yourselves that you sold me here, for God sent me before you to preserve life.... Now God has sent me before you to ensure for you a remnant on earth, to save you alive for a great deliverance. So now it was not you who sent me here, but God" [Gen. 45:3a, 4b-5, 7].

In Chapter 8, on the occasion of this pronouncement, we called attention to the language used by the author as marking Joseph's words as revelatory, and thus to be taken with the utmost seriousness.[39] There is in Joseph's tone, as he addresses his brothers after the lapse of seventeen years, almost an element of sadness in that they seem not to have appreciated the significance of what he had said to them; that he now has to repeat himself. "Don't you remember what I said to you? I told you that it was not you who sent me to Egypt but God. And I told you what God's purpose was: to save you and all the family alive through the terrible famine. So why have you been torturing yourselves?"

But putting aside for a moment the brothers and their feelings, and concentrating on Joseph's words, we realize that he is not simply paraphrasing his previous remarks. In the intervening years Joseph's thinking has progressed in bold leaps. Seventeen years before he had spoken of actions — the brothers "selling him into Egypt" — and in insisting that the real actor was God: it was He who sent him to Egypt and not the brothers. But now Joseph's thinking has moved beyond acts to motives. Are good and evil only connected to actions, or do one's motives also have a role to play in the moral arithmetic of souls?

And here Joseph immeasurably deepens his radical theological understanding: yes, your motives were evil. You meant to do me harm. But behind everything you thought and did, God was hovering. And God's intentions were that the outcomes should be good. God's intentions always trump human intentions, so while your intentions were evil the outcomes turned out to be good: the saving of life. Not only do human acts lead to the outcomes that God wants, but so do human motives, evil though they may be, taken in their own terms. Inevitably they lead to good results.[40]

But with regard to the good, here too Joseph's thoughts have moved on. Seventeen years ago Joseph saw his purpose in the divine scheme of things as that of saving his family.

The phrase he used was *pelaita gedola*, which we rendered as "a great deliverance." This sense is purely physical, keeping the members of the family from death. There seems to be no cognizance of a larger purpose for the family, that the family is the seed of Abraham and that the family is thus covenanted to the task of bringing blessing to all mankind.[41] The spiritual destiny of the children of Israel is starkly absent. Fast-forward seventeen years and this picture has not changed. Blessing and bringing blessing to mankind is still conspicuous by its absence. But on the other hand, the field of vision has widened. Years of dealing with the Egyptian and regional economies has broadened Joseph's horizons. Deliverance, once restricted to the family, now has become "that many people should be kept alive." Joseph now sees his mission as saving the Egyptians, as well as hordes of Canaanites, Libyans, Syrians, etc.,[42] and among all these multitudes, also his family. Joseph's family has shrunk in his estimate into an insignificant grouping among the "many people," the masses of humanity for whom Joseph now feels responsible. He is far above such petty things as personal revenge. He continues: "So now fear not: I will provide for you and your little ones." So he comforted them, and spoke to their hearts[43] (v. 21).

So with this dose of radical theology, and Joseph's reassurances, the brothers will have to make do. Do they accept his novel theological interpretation of the events through which they have all been living? We have no idea, for the text is silent, even as it is silent as to the effect on the brothers of Joseph's reassurances. But to whatever degree Joseph's words may have quieted the immediate fears of the brothers, it is doubtful in the extreme that any reconciliation has occurred.[44] Joseph remains the Egyptian viceroy with all the power in his hands. His attitude remains that of the paternalistic master ("I will provide for you and your little ones"),[45] the brothers remain the powerless suppliants dependent on his whim and largesse. Jacob, in his Testament, had defined Joseph as "the one set apart from his brothers" (49:26).[46] At the last, his father understood him well. Not only is Joseph set apart by nature and position, but he holds himself apart by his reserve and lack of empathy as well. The gap remains unbridgeable.

Before we leave the scene, the climax of the entire tale,[47] we must not be satisfied with Joseph's point of view only. So far the brothers have remained silent. In all fairness we must let them have their say. This means examining in some detail their plea: "Before his death your father commanded, 'Thus shall you say to Joseph, "I beg you, please forgive the transgression of your brothers, and their sin, for they have done you evil"'" (50:17). After quoting Joseph's father (note they refer to *your* father, not *our* father), the brothers rush on: "And now, please forgive the transgression of the servants of the God of your father" (v. 17).

Several aspects of this plea for mercy beg for clarification. Let us first focus on the latter part of the petition, the personal plea of the brothers. This simple statement contains two elements: public admission of both the enormity of their crime coupled with an appeal for forgiveness, and the redefinition of themselves in theological terms. Note that the brothers do not appeal to Joseph on the grounds of brotherhood; they are convinced that family feeling creates no common ground between them. They will have to look elsewhere for something to serve as the foundation for forgiveness. That common ground can only be the God of their father.[48]

When we turn to the first part of the petition, the "voice from the grave," we cannot avoid pondering the question, did Jacob really leave this message for Joseph? We have only the brothers' word for it. But why should one doubt them? Either way we turn the implications are serious.

If the brothers are telling the truth, that means that they have made complete confession to their father; before his death Jacob had been made privy to the full atrociousness of what had taken place at Dothan, as well as the subsequent cover-up that caused him such misery. Indeed, the fact that he did not throw this transgression against himself into the faces of his sons in his final Testament implies that he has forgiven them, and is now begging Joseph to follow suit and also forgive them. If, on the other hand, this story is false, and the "message from the grave" is no more than "a desperate fabrication"[49] born of terror, then we must assume that Jacob met his end in blissful ignorance of what his sons had done, and his sons, unconfessed and unabsolved, remain bowed under a double measure of guilt: for what they did to Joseph and what they did to their father.

I am not willing to go as far as Pirson when he says, "I do not understand why commentators doubt the truth of the brothers' message to Joseph."[50] I can fully understand a distrust of an obviously self-serving and unsubstantiated claim. Yet on the whole I believe that Pirson is right; that we should take the brothers' statement at face value.[51] True, the text does not *force* us to believe the brothers, but then nowhere does the text give us a reason to doubt that they are speaking no less than the truth.[52]

The brothers have confessed their evil deeds (and by the terms they use[53] their evil intentions as well), and they beg forgiveness. If their story is true, then they have also confessed to their father and he has forgiven them. And while Joseph never actually forgives his brothers,[54] he does make clear that he has put the past behind him; for him it is a closed book.[55] Admonitions meant to still their fears, promises of continued paternalistic support and some kind words (he "spoke to their hearts") are far short of absolution of sin, but with these the brothers will have to be satisfied. At least the brothers have, by their repentance, succeeded in mitigating their crushing sense of guilt. While far from reconciliation, it is a step in the right direction. The asymmetry between Joseph and his brothers will persist to the end, as will the strained deference (and possibly recurrent nightmares) on the part of the brothers, and the essential indifference to them on the part of Joseph. Only a fundamental change on the part of Joseph could alter this equation, and by the time this change takes place — and it does — the brothers are dead.[56]

The Lord of Dreams

Having reached this point in our narrative, the time has come to address a question raised at its very beginning: were Joseph's dreams prophetic?

Joseph's life has been enmeshed in dreams, his own and those of others. We must be careful to differentiate between the two. J. A. Soggin wisely notes:

> [It is wrong] to connect Joseph as a dreamer with Joseph as an interpreter of dreams, as is often done. The dreams of the former are perfectly clear to those concerned and need therefore no interpretation.... The latter dreams need, on the contrary, to be interpreted, something which in the ancient Near East was usually performed by means of certain techniques, officially prohibited in Israel [cf. Deut. 13:2 and 18:10, 12].[57]

The latter case, the interpretation of the dreams of others, we have already discussed. The former, the subject of the present discussion, amount to a total of two dreams of an adolescent nature, dreamed up by a lad of seventeen. They are related by him in two different verses as follows:

> *Behold, we were binding sheaves in the field, and behold, my sheaf arose and stood upright, and behold, your sheaves gathered around and bowed low to my sheaf* [Gen. 37:7].
>
> *Behold, the sun, and the moon and eleven stars were bowing low to me* [Gen. 37:9].

The brothers interpreted the first as follows: "What! Do you mean to reign over us? Do you mean to rule us?" (37:8). His father interpreted the second: "Is it possible that I, and your mother and your brothers will come and bow low before you?" (v. 10). The meanings lie plain on the surface. It was this understanding of Joseph's dreams that led the brothers to sarcastically dub him *baal hahalamot halazeh*: "this Lord of Dreams."[58]

A hundred generations of readers of this tale have been almost unanimous in attributing the source of the dreams to God, and their content as prophetic portents of the future rise of Joseph to the leadership of his family. Is this view justified?[59]

At first glance the answer appears obvious. The dreams come to pass in later reality; the brothers end up face down in the dirt, groveling before Joseph. The proof of the dreams' origins is contained in their outcomes. But a closer look at the narrative begins to disclose problems with this simplistic understanding. In the first place, the second dream is never realized: his father never bows down to Joseph. When they are at last reunited in Egypt, Israel pointedly remains erect and does not bow.[60] And of course his mother never bows to him. Rachel was dead long before he began dreaming. Which leaves his brothers.

When the brothers first arrive in Egypt, it is true that they prostrate themselves before Joseph. But as far as they know, they are bowing to "the Man, the Lord of the land," the Egyptian Viceroy who controls the distribution of grain. This is something very different from acknowledging Joseph as their leader. This becomes plain when we contrast this scene with Jacob's formal investiture of Judah in his Testament:

> [As for] *you, Judah, your brothers shall extol you....*
> *Your father's sons shall bow down before you* [Gen. 49:8].

This is the role of leader bestowed with the consent of the governed, an acclaim earned by virtue of character and achievement. In contrast, what Joseph receives is an enforced ceremonial empty of content or meaning.[61] Moreover, inasmuch as the brothers have no idea that in prostrating themselves before the Egyptian official overseeing the grain distribution they are bowing to Joseph, it is only the accident of his presence that makes the act seem providential.

But was his presence indeed accidental? In our analysis of the arrival of the brothers in Egypt, and Joseph's recognition of them, we discussed the improbability of the Viceroy of all Egypt presiding over grain distribution to starving Asiatics, a relatively low-level job. We there came to the conclusion that the confrontation was stage-managed by Joseph: by positioning himself at the granary designated as the distribution depot to which Asiatics were assigned, it was inevitable that, sooner or later, starvation would force the brothers' appearance. And as etiquette required all applicants for food to prostrate themselves before the senior Egyptian official present, the brothers would have no choice but to bow before him.

This amounts to a superficial, technical compliance with the terms of the dreams; a realization engineered by Joseph himself. And this, as we have noted, explains Joseph's insistence that the brothers produce Benjamin. The second dream depicted eleven stars (brothers) bowing to Joseph. Ten brothers were insufficient to "realize" the dreams. Only when all eleven brothers would be prostrate before him (Gen. 43: 26, 28) would Joseph be satisfied.[62]

What I am proposing is that the conscious purpose of the entire cat-and-mouse charade that Joseph played with his brothers was not a desire for revenge[63] (which, although present below the surface, could not be admitted), as much as an elaborate forcing to "fulfillment" of his dreams.[64] That such an artificial "bringing to pass" of his dreams resulted, at best, in a partial external compliance while missing the essential inner meaning is what usually results from human attempts to force the hand of history. While Joseph succeeded in stage-managing his brothers into unknowingly bowing to him, he was never able to gain their acceptance as the leader of the family.

One cannot but marvel at the amount of time and energy, not to mention ingenuity, which this exceedingly busy man expended on this project. It must have meant a lot to him. His early dreams seem to have had a formative impact on his life. His brothers obviously saw them as the wish fulfillment of a super-inflated ego. I think that Joseph desperately wanted to believe that the dreams came from God, that they were prophetic and that therefore he was a man of destiny. But at the same time he was plagued with a sneaking suspicion that perhaps his brothers were right, which resulted in a lifelong compulsion to "prove" that his dreams were indeed portents of destiny, by using his power to force events into an outward replica of the dreams. But despite all his efforts the inner substance ever eluded him. In the end he had to be content with outer compliance based on fear; spiritually he forever remained "the one set apart."

Before we leave this subject of dreams, let us indulge in one final comment. When we think of dreams, our thoughts fly directly to Joseph. But the true dreamer was his father, Jacob. Unlike those of his son, Jacob's dreams are unquestionably "prophetic." In each one God appears to Jacob, directly addresses him and confers upon him divine commitments for his future and the future of his descendants.[65] These dreams bracket Jacob's life, coming to him as a young adult, in mid-life, and finally in his waning years. When contrasted with these portentous visions, Joseph's dreams shrink to insignificance. It was Jacob/Israel who was the true "Lord of Dreams."

The Fading of the Light

The climax reached, with a few deft strokes the author winds up his tale. But more, he also prepares us for what is to come. This little epilogue, on the surface so warm and congratulatory, is, at closer examination, heavy with foreboding.

So Joseph dwelt in Egypt, he and his father's House; and Joseph lived one hundred and ten years. And Joseph saw Ephraim's children of the third generation; also the children of Machir, the son of the Manasseh, were born on Joseph's knees [Gen. 50:22–23].

An idyllic picture is being drawn for us. Joseph, having buried his father, returns and settles down in his adopted homeland. Many years lie ahead of him. He lives to see his grandchildren, his great-grandchildren and even great great-grandchildren. Only after one hundred and ten years does his life draw to a close.[66]

And Joseph said to his brethren, "I [am about to] die. Now God will most assuredly take notice of you,[67] and bring you up from this land to the land He swore [to give] to Abraham, Isaac and Jacob."[68] And Joseph placed the children of Israel under oath, to wit: "When God has indeed taken notice of you, you shall carry my bones up from this [place]" [Gen. 50:24–25].

What has happened? Fifty-four years — more than half a century — have been passed over in silence, and we find ourselves in a different world. Hints of erosion in the Israelite condition that we have previously noted have mushroomed into a bitter reality. Egypt has ceased to be welcoming to the House of Jacob. The change of attitude on the part of Joseph is nothing short of astounding. He who made his career in Egypt and saw his family's future there, now recognizes it as a dead end. The very fact that he sees it necessary to encourage his kin[69] to put their hope in the certainty of God's future rescue from Egypt can only testify to the level of precariousness into which the family has descended. He can no longer help them and they are no longer free to leave. Too late Joseph realizes the trap into which he has maneuvered the family: what he has done to the Egyptian peasants will now be visited upon his own descendants. The dark night of slavery and oppression foretold to his great-grandfather, Abraham, stands revealed before him.

> *"Know well that your seed shall be strangers in a land not theirs, and they shall be enslaved and oppressed four hundred years!"* [Gen. 15:13].

Too late the truth is penetrating: there is no security and no future for the House of Israel as an alien minority in a land not theirs. The only future lies in the land promised by God to their ancestors, and to them:

> *"But upon the nation for whom they slave will I execute judgment, and afterward they shall come forth with great wealth"* [Gen. 15:14].

Trust in God. He will keep His word.

And now Joseph becomes personal. The land that he now realizes has no room for the children of Israel as free and prosperous residents has no room for him either. Despite his having become Egyptian in outward appearance and inner psyche, despite his many services to the state,[70] Joseph remains an outsider. He now knows that Egypt has never accepted him. It has used him and now it has no place for him.

And in this moment of truth, face-to-face with his end, Joseph seems to revert fifty-four years back to the death of his father, and his father's prophecy, addressed to him:

> *Then Israel said to Joseph, "Behold, I* [am about to] *die. And it shall come to pass that God will be with you, and He shall return you to the land of your fathers"* [Gen. 48:21].

Then he had shrugged off these words as the maunderings of an old, and perhaps semi-senile man. A half-century of increasingly bitter experience has taught him that his father was right after all. Life has proved too strong for him. His place was not in Egypt but in the Promised Land. Now that he has no future left, his final thought is to at least try to ensure that his body will end up where it should be. So his last act is to exact a promise from his kin — no, more than a promise, an oath[71] — that when they are redeemed, as God has promised, they will not leave him behind on the alien soil[72] to which he had brought them.

> *So Joseph died at the age of one hundred and ten years; and they embalmed him, and he was put into a sarcophagus in Egypt* [Gen. 50:26].

No rites are mentioned, no mourning, and certainly no state funeral. Joseph is well on his way to becoming an Egyptian nonperson.

And with this somber notice of entombment, Joseph at the last becomes the paradigm of his people: as he is entombed in Egypt, so are they; and as, due to mummification, his body will endure to be redeemed, so will the House of Israel endure the long night of enslavement to see the light of day. But that tale must await the Book of Exodus. For us the curtain now drops.

13. The Closing of Accounts

NOTES

1. This is the first time the twelve tribes of Israel are mentioned in the Bible.

2. The usual meaning of the term *barech*, "blessing," is here inappropriate; many of Jacob's remarks are hardly blessings, some are outright curses. We therefore fall back on a secondary meaning of the term — a formula of farewell; so Speiser on Genesis 26:31 (note, 202) and on Genesis 49:28 (375).

3. "This idiom ... is reserved for Israel's forefathers.... It is the act that takes place *after dying but before burial* ... it means 'be reunited with one's ancestors,' and refers to the afterlife" (Milgrom, *Numbers*, 170).

4. Joseph is never recorded as laughing, rejoicing, or loving. The only display of emotion reported, in addition to six instances of weeping, is the (secondhand) report of the cries and entreaties issuing from the cistern into which his brothers had thrown him, prompted, we can assume, by pure terror.

5. Joseph concealed his first two breakdowns by leaving the room. The third time he was only able to restrain himself long enough to clear the room of all Egyptians; only the brothers were witnesses. The fourth time Joseph permits himself to weep openly in front of his entourage.

6. See Chapter 9, page 140.

7. Most of the brothers had been equally silent and unresponsive when Joseph had "revealed himself" to them. Of all the family, only from Benjamin did Joseph elicit an emotional response to his display of feeling. See Genesis 45:14–15.

8. Probably the equivalent of the usual "throwing oneself on the neck of," but here impossible to use as the recipient is horizontal, not vertical. Possibly a modern equivalent might be: to throw oneself on the body of.

9. One wonders at the feelings of Joseph's brothers, all eleven of them. They were as much their father's sons as he was. Yet they have been eclipsed.

10. Literally, "and forty days were fulfilled for him."

11. The procedure involved removing the brain and eviscerating the corpse (the contents of the body cavity — the intestines, liver, etc. — were stored in separate jars which were entombed at the side of the body), essentially reducing the body to its outward shell. This was treated with natron, a carbonate of soda, and a combination of substances and spices which had the effect of turning the skin and flesh into a form of a leather. The mummy would then be adorned with jewelry and wrapped in layers of bandages impregnated with preservatives. Amulets and scraps of magic prayers were wrapped up in the bandages. The final result would be encased in a highly decorated wooden coffin, covered with hieroglyphic spells. This was the minimum procedure. For exalted personages many more stages and trappings could be added.

12. Herodotus, *Histories*, II, 37. See Chapter 5, note 7.

13. The "physicians" were, of course, priests who were specialists in the arts of healing, and attached to Joseph's household in that capacity. As priests Joseph could turn the body over to them and make them responsible for overseeing the procedures. The actual embalming was performed by other priests who specialized in the preparation of the dead.

14. The seventy days probably included the forty day embalming period.

15. Hamilton, 692.

16. Diodorus, *Bibliotheca Historica*, I, 91.

17. Literally, "his days of weeping."

18. There are those who explain this processing of his request through intermediaries (the House of Pharaoh refers to the courtiers and the upper-level bureaucrats that make up the entourage that surrounds the Pharaoh) rather than addressing the Pharaoh himself as due to his still being in mourning. But we have been expressly informed that the mourning period had ended before he presented his request. Others suggest that he may not approach the Pharaoh due to being in a state of impurity due to his contact with the corpse. But his father's body has been in the hands of the "physicians" lo these seventy days. More than two and a half months have passed since Joseph's contact with his father's body. Neither of these excuses sounds very persuasive.

19. Kass, 653.

20. That is, Joseph's nuclear family, and especially Ephraim and Manasseh.

21. Literally, "now behold, the body of people was very heavy."

22. The ease with which Joseph leaves their little ones, their sheep and their cattle behind as hostages to their return, should be compared with the reaction of Moses to a similar offer by a later Pharaoh: "With our young and our old will we go, with our sons and our daughters, with our sheep and our cattle will we go" (Exod. 10:9). And on this he stood fast, making clear that they intended to shake the dust of Egypt from their sandals and go home.

23. A place name; literally, "The Threshing Floor of the Bramble."

24. I.e., on the other side of the Jordan River.
25. Literally, "heavy."
26. Literally, "heavy."
27. *Abel-Mizraim* literally means "Meadow of Egypt," but due to the massive display of Egyptian lamentation, the meaning of the similar-sounding word *abel*—mourning—permanently supersedes the original connotation; the site now becomes known as "The Lamentation of Egypt."
28. Large quantities of ink have been employed in an extended, and at times acrimonious, dispute over possible locations for this site, both east and west of the Jordan River (the significance of the phrase "across the Jordan" depends on which side of the river you are standing). The oldest tradition we possess, dating at least from Jerome, locates the site in the Jordan Valley in the vicinity of Jericho. I am not inclined to become involved in this dispute as the matter is essentially irrelevant to the story. They came to Canaan, they stopped, they mourned, they continued to Hebron and there, in the cave of Machpelah, by the side of his ancestors where he wished to be, the mummy of Jacob was interred. In biblical times the place where the procession halted was known. Now it is not. Much more important information has been lost in the passage of millennia. This loss is minor and affects little.
29. This phrase is usually rendered as: "Now the brothers of Joseph *saw* that their father was dead," but "MT *wayyir'u* is an ambiguous form. If from r'h, it means 'they saw'; but if from yr,' it means 'they were afraid' (1 Samuel 4:7; 7:7; etc.)" (Hamilton, 699). Rendering the term as "they saw" makes little sense to me. Hamilton continues: "Here see must have the sense of 'knowing'; it cannot mean 'to observe with the eye,' for the brothers have already been present at their father's internment" (ibid.). But even the sense of "knowing" lacks coherence; *almost four months have passed* since Israel's death (two and a half months of an embalming and mourning, several weeks organizing the state funeral, and the funeral itself—the procession to Hebron, a week at Goren ha-Atad, and the return to Egypt—at least three weeks). To contend that only now the "full reality of their father's passing dawned on them" (Hamilton, 702), that only now the brothers "saw" the implications of their father's death, must assume that the brothers were mentally profoundly challenged.
30. This is the same word that their father Jacob had used in his Testament to describe Joseph's enemies, they "who hated him" (Gen. 49:23). The root *satam* means "to bear a grudge, to cherish animosity against." There it was the brothers who hated Joseph. Now the brothers fear that they will be paid back in kind.
31. Reading with LXX.; MT reads "they ordered for Joseph," "apparently elliptical for 'they ordered someone to inform Joseph'" (Speiser, 376).
32. Hebrew *pesha*, literally, "rebellion," "a word whose use originated in the political sphere, where it referred to the rebellion of a vassal against an overlord.... By extension it is applied to the religious realm, where it denotes Israel's rebellion against God" (Hamilton, 702, note 21). *Pesha* therefore denotes persistent, conscious, and extended evildoing.
33. Not a synonym for transgression. Sin (Hebrew *het*), literally *missing the mark* (as when shooting at a target), refers to wrongdoing committed in error, ignorance, or carelessness. For a fuller catalogue of the Hebrew terminology of wrongdoing see Millgram, *Invention of Monotheist Ethics*, 548, note 13.
34. Seventeen years before, Judah had offered himself as a slave in place of his youngest brother, Benjamin, for the express purpose of sparing their father the shock that would have killed him. Here all the brothers are offering to exchange their freedom for their lives, certain that, considering the alternatives confronting them, slavery is the lesser of the evils.
35. Samuel, 348–349.
36. Note that even Benjamin, Joseph's "favorite," is among those groveling before him in terror.
37. Note Deuteronomy 32:35, Psalm 94:1, Nahum 1:2, Leviticus 19:18, etc. "The root *nqm* [vengeance] implies extralegal retribution, which, although forbidden to men, may be exacted by God" (Milgrom, *Leviticus 17–22*, 1,651).
38. Note the parallel rebuke of Jacob to Rachel in Genesis 30:2, also a rhetorical question.
39. See page 127.
40. *Good* being defined, for the purposes of this argument, as conforming to God's will.
41. "Now be a blessing. I shall bless those who bless you, and those who damn you will I curse. And through you shall all the families of the earth be blessed" (Gen. 12:2–3). "And through your seed shall all the nations of the earth be blessed" (22:18). And especially Jacob: "through you and through your seed shall all the families of the earth be blessed" (28:13–14); etc.
42. We rendered the Hebrew phrase *am rav* (Gen. 50:20) as "many people." In Job 36:28 the context determines that the kindred expression, *adam rav*, means "all mankind;" or, as Gordis renders it, "all men" (Robert Gordis, *The Book of God and Man: A Study of Job* [IL: University of Chicago Press, 1965], 295).
43. The phrase "So he comforted them and spoke to their hearts" can best be understood in the light

13. The Closing of Accounts

of Ruth's remark to Boaz: "May I find favor in your eyes, my lord, for you have comforted me, and because you have spoken to the heart of your maidservant" (Ruth 2:13). Ruth, an alien with no rights, and expecting rank discrimination at the hands of the Israelites, has just been addressed by Boaz as a human being; more, he has made it clear that he respects her. Ruth is overwhelmed and expresses gratitude for his decency and encouragement that gives her new hope for the future with these words. For the full context see my *Four Biblical Heroines*, 47–49.

44. See note 55 below.

45. The famine is long past. The family, having had a portion of the best land in Goshen settled upon them, and having expanded that original holding into *holdings*, should be thoroughly capable of taking care of themselves. Is Joseph arbitrarily keeping them dependent on him, or is there here a hint that the conditions of the family in Goshen have taken a turn for the worse?

46. See Chapter 12, note 64.

47. "The statement about the brothers' evil plans and God's good plans now opens up the innermost mystery of the Joseph story. It is in every respect, along with the similar passage in ch. 45:5–7, the climax to the whole" (von Rad, *Genesis*, 427).

48. Note the adjective pronouns. Does the fact that the brothers do not speak of *our* God or *your* God, but only of *your father's* God imply a doubt as to whether the Egyptianized Joseph still is a worshiper of their God? If so, by his first statement Joseph lays any doubt on this matter to rest. The brothers had guessed right. For all their estrangement, it is the God of their father (and fathers) who provides the common ground between them. Joseph's reply begins from this point: "Am I in the place of God?" And then he proceeds to reiterate his theological understanding of their situation.

49. Sternberg, 379. Hamilton also is disinclined to believe the brothers' story, mainly because the text does not corroborate it (Hamilton, 703).

50. Pirson, 135.

51. "That the appeal to an order of Jacob relating to this should be considered a lie on the part of the brothers (v. 17) is an ancient but certainly quite false assumption" (von Rad, *Genesis*, 427).

52. As in most matters, the author crafts his tale in a way as to deny us absolute certainty. Certainty belongs only to God. We, as mortals, must grapple with uncertainty and choose what seems to us to be the most reasonable of the alternatives.

53. See notes 32 and 33 above.

54. Walter Brueggermann, "Genesis L 15–21: A Theological Exploration," in *Congress Volume: Salamanca, 1983*, ed. J. A. Emerton (Leiden: E. J. Brill), 1985, insists that no reconciliation ever takes place and that Joseph never forgives his brothers, and he makes a strong case to support his assertion. If so, Joseph's response amounts to the stance that since it was all God's doing, there is no need for forgiveness on his part. This is simply an evasion of human responsibility. Riven with guilt, the brothers are in desperate need of forgiveness.

55. Perhaps the reason Joseph never responds by overtly forgiving his brothers is that he realizes that to forgive them, he would have to admit to his part in the events that led to Dothan. This he seems unwilling or unable to do. The brothers (under duress, it is true) beg his forgiveness; he can never bring himself to beg theirs.

56. Considering Joseph's longevity, and the fact that he was so much younger than most of his brothers, only Benjamin was likely to have still been alive during Joseph's last years, and even this is far from certain.

57. Soggin, 337–338.

58. Genesis 37:19. "They [the dreams] would be interesting also to a modern psychologist, who could interpret them not necessarily as an indication of future events but as signs of boundless ambition" (Soggin, 337–338).

59. Turner, in what is probably the most comprehensive analysis of Joseph's dreams, draws attention to the fact that unlike the dreams reported in Genesis up to this point, which are unambiguously of divine origin, Joseph's dreams do not feature God at all, either as an actor or as being acknowledged as the source of the dream by the dreamer (144–146). The dreams do not even make any mention of God, a point that Westermann (39) considers decisive in rejecting any suggestion of divine origin. Turner comes to the opposite conclusion, due to his committing the very error Soggin warned against: confusing Joseph the interpreter of dreams with Joseph the dreamer. Because Joseph claims Pharaoh's dreams come from God, and seems to intimate the same for the dreams of his fellow prisoners (claims nowhere confirmed by the narrator and, by their very nature, suspect — when one is busy promoting oneself it is wise to take all claims with a pinch of salt), Turner then assumes that Joseph's assertions of divine origin should be transferred to his own dreams, and his statements accepted as incontrovertible truth. I, however, find every step in Turner's rea-

soning flawed and, like Westermann, can find from Joseph's accounts of his dreams no intimation whatsoever that they emanate from God. To me the decisive fact is that Joseph himself never makes the claim that God sent him the dreams.

60. For that matter he also refuses to prostrate himself before Pharaoh. See Chapter 9 for an analysis of these two incidents. Some commentators contend that when, upon hearing Joseph take his oath that he will bury his father with his ancestors in Canaan as requested, Jacob then bows on his bed, he is bowing not in thanksgiving to God but in thanks to Joseph. For a man who refused to bow to Pharaoh, this interpretation does not sound credible. See Chapter 11, note 3.

61. In the incident following the death of their father, which we have just read (Gen. 50:18) — the only time the brothers are depicted as knowingly groveling before Joseph, the author insures that the careful reader will not make the mistake of taking it as a fulfillment of Joseph's dreams. He does this by pointedly distinguishing between the terminologies used in each case. In the accounts of his dreams, Joseph twice uses the word *hishtahave* (to bow down), and his father confirms this term by repeating it (37:7, 9–10). Instead of returning to this term so as to link our incident to the dreams, the author here uses a completely different idiom, *vayiplu lefanav* (which we rendered as "[they] threw themselves down before him.") (50:18).

62. See Chapter 6, note 16; Chapter 7, pages 116–117.

63. And certainly not "testing." See Chapter 6, pages 100–101; Chapter 7, pages 115–116.

64. This may also explain Joseph's "revelatory" appearance in his chariot before his father. Was he attempting to overawe old Israel into prostrating himself before the glorious Imperial Presence? If so, the attempt proved a failure; Israel wouldn't bow. With his father, Joseph hit a stone wall. Reality could not be reengineered to conform to the dream.

65. These are: the dream in Beth-el of the ladder connecting heaven and earth, along with God's promise to Jacob that He will protect him and bring him back to the land He promised to Abraham and Isaac, and that He will give it to him and his seed (Gen. 28:12–15); in Paddan-aram he reports to his wives that in the midst of dreaming of stock breeding, an Angel of God intrudes in the dream to order him home to his own land (31:10–13); and the dream in Beer-sheba, where God authorizes Israel to go down to Egypt where his family will become a great nation, and then promises him that He will bring him back to the land of his father Isaac (46:2–4).

66. Joseph remains the quintessential Egyptian to the last. In Egyptian culture 110 was considered the ideal lifespan.

67. "The Hebrew stem *p-k-d* connotes the direct involvement or intervention of God in human affairs. This can be of a providential nature, or it can be judgmental or redemptive. The verb is a leitmotif of the divine promises of national redemption from Egyptian slavery" (Sarna, *Genesis*, 145).

68. This is the first time in the entire narrative that Joseph refers to his ancestors by name. This is yet one more sign of the revolution of consciousness that has transpired in his inner being. More, Sarna points out that "this clustering of the three patriarchs for the first time sets the pattern for all such subsequent citations in the Torah, which are invariably in a context of the divine promises of national territory for the people of Israel" (ibid., 351).

69. With the exception of Benjamin, all of Joseph brothers were significantly older than he, and it is unlikely that they are yet alive. Joseph is addressing their descendants, including his own great-grandchildren.

70. These include not only saving Egypt from disastrous famine, but also the enslavement of the peasantry and the reengineering of society, turning it back to the totalitarian model of the Old Kingdom. Everything in Egypt now bears the stamp of Joseph's inspired restructuring.

71. As Israel had not been content with a promise and bound Joseph with an oath, so now Joseph does not trust promises and insists on a solemn oath to ensure his final resting place.

72. It seems to me significant that Joseph can no longer bring himself to refer to his beloved Egypt by name. Rather than say: "carry out my bones from Egypt," he substitutes the word *mizeh*, literally, "from *this*," an expression redolent with deep disillusion, even possibly loathing.

14

Conclusion 1: Between God and Man

We are no other than a moving row
Of Magic Shadow-shapes that come and go
Round with the Sun-illumined Lantern held
In Midnight by the Master of the Show.
— Edward Fitzgerald, *The Rubiyat of*
Omar Khayyam, LXVIII

The heart of man chooses[1] his path [in life],
But it is the Lord Who directs his steps.
— Proverbs 16:9

Almost one hundred years have passed since our story began. It opened in Western Asia and it draws to its close in East Africa; a tale that spans close to a century and two continents. It is a strange saga of struggle and strife, highlighted against the background of a contest between two disparate ways of life. The time has arrived to draw some conclusions from this remarkable account.

This task will prove far from simple. Our tale is a sophisticated and complex one, woven from many different strands. It is not given to a quick summary in a pat formula. Being multi-faceted, it must be looked at from different angles. A plan of attack will be necessary.

We make a beginning with one of the strangest aspects of the Joseph Story: though a biblical drama, when opening the playbill we discover to our surprise that the hero is missing from the cast of characters. God is nowhere to be found. This is the first and most vital issue that we face, and thus our quest begins with an exploration of the religious significance of the work, discovering in the process a radical theological approach to human life on this planet, one far removed from what we normally think of as the way the Bible pictures God's ways with man. We will then conclude this chapter with an investigation of the way the story is written, discovering in the process that the very style of writing has far-reaching theological implications.

The second part of the Conclusion will focus on Joseph the man, both as a son of his people and his place in the Egyptian scheme of things. To do this we will have to draw back and look at Joseph in the context of the entire Biblical Age, taking into account what lessons both the Bible and the descendants of the family — the People of Israel — will learn from his life. And lastly, as a prelude to our final summation, we will have to explore how succeeding generations have interpreted our tale, speculating as to why they came to the conclusions that they did.

We begin with our first topic of consideration: the religious and theological dimensions of the Joseph Story.

A Secular Story

The most unusual aspect of the Joseph saga is its secular nature. In contrast to all that has gone before in the Bible and all that is yet to come, where God is the central protagonist in all that transpires, in Genesis chapters 37–50, God seems to have taken a vacation. The Joseph saga is well-nigh unique in that God never appears and He never speaks. What is more, as we emphasized in Chapter 5, while there is much chatter *about* God (no one in Genesis talks *about* God more than Joseph), no one talks *to* God. No one prays to Him or worships Him.[2] What is even more remarkable, not only is all practice of religion expunged from the lives of the protagonists in our tale who are the descendants of Abraham, but the pagans, Canaanites and Egyptians alike, are afforded the same treatment. A world that was religious to its core and in which life revolved around religious ritual and worship of the divine is inexplicably and unhistorically depicted as religion-free. Any exposition of the religious dimension found in this book has had to be externally injected. It is not explicit in the text. This is hardly the usual the way the Bible depicts its world.[3]

A direct outcome of the absence of God and the neutering of religion in our narrative is that the various protagonists are depicted as being driven solely by secular concerns. Love, hate, jealousy and fear are the prime motivators. Only old Jacob/Israel, and this primarily at the very end of the tale, seems to take seriously the heritage of Abraham and Abraham's God — the lingering patrimony of an earlier and now vanishing era. It is in this sense that I refer to our narrative as secular. Any understanding of the tale as a whole must be able to provide a compelling reason for the strange way the author sees fit to frame his narrative.

The Missing God

When we examine this phenomenon of secularism that makes the Joseph saga virtually unique in the Hebrew Bible, we realize that at its heart lies God's absence. As opposed to the mighty sweep from creation at the beginning of Genesis and onward to the end of the Bible, in which it is God who is the Initiator, Prime Mover and Main Actor — ever at center stage — in our narrative God does not initiate. God neither speaks nor acts; center stage is vacant, and God remains on the missing list for twenty-two years. Then, at the climactic confrontation when the Viceroy of Egypt reveals his true identity to his brothers, Joseph opens his mouth and proclaims a revolutionary theological doctrine. And with the force of a seismic shift in the crust of the earth, our entire perspective alters. We suddenly realize that what we have taken to be a secular family drama, or perhaps a rags-to-riches tale, is actually a tiny piece of a larger whole, vaster than anything the family could ever have conceived:

> *And now, do not be sad or angry with yourselves that you sold me here, for God sent me before you to preserve life.... So it was not you who sent me here, but God* [Gen. 45:5, 7].

With these words the missing God, absent from the stage, is now found to be backstage, directing the drama and stage-managing all the players therein. The Dramatist and His purpose stand revealed before us.

What emerges now before our eyes is a world in which God is not overtly present; He is present but hidden. He does not have a "speaking role" in the drama but rather hides behind the scenes, directing the action from offstage, and intervening, if at all, only when it is absolutely unavoidable.[4] As von Rad sums up: "Even when no man could imagine it, God had all the strings in his hand."[5] This is not the God Who is so familiar to us from the first 70 percent of Genesis: the God who Acts. This is something new; this is the Hidden God who goes by the name of Providence.

The Hand of the Hidden God

Up to now we have been looking at the Joseph Story as a humanistic drama, as indeed it has been presented to us. But now, in the light of Joseph's startling pronouncement, a pronouncement repeated for emphasis, at the very end of the tale, we can no longer continue to look at this tale from the purely human perspective:

Now you intended me evil [but] *God intended it for good, in order to bring about that many people should be kept alive, even as they are today* [Gen. 50:20].

If, as we are being informed, it was all God's doing, we must attempt to look at the data presented to us in our story through God's eyes, and to broaden our perspective to take in the entire sweep of Genesis (and of the rest of the Biblical Era as well).

We propose the following understanding:

God's faces a problem. He has chosen Abraham to be his vehicle to initiate a process that will bring redemption to mankind. He has promised him that his descendants will become a great people, that they will inherit the Promised Land, and will become a blessing to all mankind.

I will make you a great nation, and I will bless you, and I will make your name great, [therefore] *be a blessing. And I will bless those who bless you, and he that curses you shall I curse, and in you shall all the families of the earth be blessed.... To your seed will I give this land* [Gen. 12:3–4, 7].

This promise has been reconfirmed to his son Isaac:

To you and to your seed will I give all these lands, and I will fulfill the oath that I swore to your father Abraham, and I will multiply your seed like the stars in the heavens ... and all the nations of the earth shall be blessed through your seed because Abraham heeded My voice and has kept My charge; My commandments, My statutes and My teachings [Gen. 26:3–5].

and reiterated and confirmed to his son Jacob:

I am the Lord, the God of Abraham your father and the God of Isaac. The land upon which you lie, to you will I give it, and to your seed. And your seed shall be as the dust of the earth [for multitude]; *and you shall burst forth to the west and to the east and the north and the south, and through you and through your seed shall all the families of the earth be blessed* [Gen. 28:13–14].

The Promise would seem triply assured but for one fatal flaw: in the natural order of things, there is a catastrophic drought in the offing, and in the course of the ensuing famine, Jacob and all his children will inevitably starve to death. What then will become of the Promise?

Now God, after all, is God. Why doesn't He just miraculously provide the family with the needed food or cause rain to fall on their area of residence? But that is not the way the author of the Joseph Story understands how God works. God seems to prefer to let the natural physical order run uninterrupted, and to achieve His ends within its parameters rather then abolish or circumvent it.[6] God achieves His purposes through the natural interplay of human motives and human activity. Joseph struts, brags and infuriates his brothers. Jacob pampers and spoils his son and makes him a robe of many colors. Goaded beyond all endurance the brothers decide to get rid of Joseph. Sold to a merchant caravan he is dragged off to Egypt.[7] The first move in God's game plan has been completed: God's designated instrument, the most talented of Jacob's sons, has been moved out of the backwater of Canaan onto the big board—Egypt.

Move two: Potiphar purchases Joseph to utilize him as a house slave on his estate. Or, to look at the transaction from God's point of view, Joseph has been sent to training school. He will there master the Egyptian language and Egyptian customs. As he works his way up, his ability and motivation earning him repeated promotions, he will of necessity become literate, be taught to read and write, be taught accountancy and basic principles of administration—requirements for the position of Steward of a large Egyptian estate. In the course of his duties, he will also learn acceptable manners, due to constant contact with the aristocratic family he serves. Once this training is complete it becomes time for move number three.

Move three: Joseph is moved from the position of Head Administrator of Potiphar's estate to prison. Joseph, of course, sees this as a calamity (although he is undoubtedly grateful, considering the circumstances, that he was not summarily executed). How can he know that it is in prison that he will make the critical contact with the person—the Royal Cupbearer—whose recommendation will one day open the door to greatness? The contact made, Joseph is once again put in a holding pattern until the time comes for the next move.

Move four in God's game plan: Joseph moves from prison to the Royal Palace. Fully prepared, Joseph is able to seize the opportunity and become the Grand Vizier of Egypt, second only to the Pharaoh. What is more, he has the tools to make good in the unprecedented situation in which he finds himself. And in saving Egypt from disaster, he has the possibility of saving his family. This leads directly to move number five.

Move five: His brothers show up in Egypt, driven by famine to the only place one can buy food. When Joseph accepts his familial responsibilities and arranges for his family to settle in Egypt under his protection, God's game plan has been successfully concluded.

It is at this point that Joseph attains greatness. The usual view focuses on Joseph's courage, talent, brilliance and spectacular flair that allow him to triumph over adversity and to reach the pinnacle of success—the classic Horatio Alger story. But this is not the way the Bible sees it. In the Bible's view, what sets Joseph head and shoulders above most of humankind is that, looking back over the trajectory of his life, he is able to glimpse a larger picture—God's drama and his role in it. He realizes that he has been God's pawn and that, throughout his turbulent life, in trying to keep his head above water and make a success of himself, he unknowingly has served a greater purpose. In retrospect he understands the greater meaning of his life, and so in revealing himself to his brothers he is not mouthing pious platitudes but telling the unvarnished truth when he says:

> *"Do not be sad or angry with yourselves that you sold me here, for God sent me before you to preserve life.... So now it was not you who sent me here, but God"* [Gen. 45:5, 8].

Despite its secular appearance, the Joseph Story is revealed as a drama of God's governance of human affairs. It is the Hand of the Hidden God that is the force shaping the destiny of mankind.

Under the Shadow of the Puppet-Master

Joseph's startling insight into God's covert intervention in the course of his life does more than illuminate the nature of God's relation to the unfolding of human affairs in a seemingly secular world, it also raises a series of very disturbing issues. It posits that we are not the prime actors in the dramas of our lives, choosing our own roles and ad libbing the parts that we have chosen to play — but rather that we are no more then bit players in a vast drama of whose plot we are ignorant and whose parts are scripted for us. If this is indeed so, human beings are no more than puppets manipulated by a Celestial Puppet-Master. Human freedom would then appear to be no more than an illusion. And if we are not free, then to what extent can we be held responsible for our actions or be held accountable? These questions inevitably become central to Joseph's theology of Providence.[8]

Joseph, it would seem, is not blind to the tension between his deeply felt sense of having had freedom of choice in the decisions that propelled him to the commanding position he attained and the realization that God has been covertly directing the course of his life. In the seventeen years that separate his original pronouncement from his follow-up statement to his brothers, he appears to have given serious thought to this issue as well. Let us return to his second statement:

Now you intended me evil [but] *God intended it for good, in order to bring about that many people should be kept alive, even as they are today* [Gen. 50:20].

We have already discussed the progress in Joseph's thinking from a narrow focus on his family to a wider field of vision — the Egyptians and neighboring peoples — and his advance from a preoccupation with deeds to an awareness of the role of intentions. It seems to me that this latter shift in Joseph's thinking points to how he came to resolve this contradiction in his own mind. Human beings have an intrinsic area of freedom of choice with regard to their intentions and the acts that flow from them. But this is, at best, only in the short-term. The long-term outcomes are in the hands of God. This is why the unintended results of our actions so often surprise us, the distant consequences of our deeds deviating far from those which we intended and expected.

This also, by implication, confronts an issue, so far unaddressed, that underlies Genesis as a whole and the second section of Genesis—"The Travails of the Fathers"—in particular. We have been assuming that God's promises are unquestionably reliable, especially the promise to Abraham and his descendants that has proved to be the underlying foundation of the entire Joseph tale. But why? In a world of free agents with conflicting intentions and the freedom to act upon them, there can be no certainty as to how things will turn out, and whether any given promise will be able to be fulfilled. Yet contradictorily, if God controls outcomes, then despite the realms of human freedom God's promises are absolutely reliable and one can depend on their being realized.[9] Further than this Joseph does not proceed, according to the evidence available to us. Nor should we be surprised. He was not, either by training or by inclination, a systematic philosopher. His insights remained insights, food for the speculations of future generations.

And on his insights we are forced to rest. Unlike the Book of Ruth, where the narrator leads us to a definitive understanding of God's role in human affairs, in our case the narrator remains silent, neither overtly or covertly expressing an opinion in the matter.[10] The author, by putting these insights in the mouth of one of the fallible characters in his drama, rather than assigning them to the narrator, is refusing to close the issue definitively, leaving it to the reader (also a fallible human being) to decide whether to accept Joseph's understanding of the meta-meaning of the tale or to reject it. Once again, as in so many other questions in the Joseph Story, both great and small, the ball is left in our lap.

It is not my intention to examine what I believe to be Joseph's reasoning in this matter. The issues surrounding the polarity of free will and determinism have exercised the best thinking of countless theologians and philosophers for more than two thousand years. The literature is immense, and those interested in the subject will have no dearth of material for their perusal.[11] My purpose here is simply to indicate one of the starting points of what is to become a central problem of Western theology and philosophy, and what seems to be the first real attempt in the Bible to grapple with the issue.

An Ambiguous Tale

Thus far we have centered our attention on some of the major theological dimensions of the Joseph Story, and on some of its sociopolitical and human implications. It is now in order to turn our attention to the form in which the tale has been written. Far from being a relatively minor matter, the issue of style will prove an area of major concern. The focus of our problem lies in the fact that the tale, while penned by a master storyteller, has been written in a maddeningly ambiguous manner.

It is important to be clear as to what exactly we mean when we use the term ambiguous. What we are saying is that the story as a whole, and virtually all of its several episodes, are capable of being understood in either of two or more possible senses; that the tale is deeply unclear, leaving us again and again mired in uncertainty as to exactly what has occurred and what meaning to place upon the events described. This ambiguity is so all-pervasive as to exclude any possibility of accident, much less of sloppy writing. The ambiguity can be nothing else than deliberate; a studied indeterminacy by a master writer intending to avoid clarity and to leave us guessing. Some examples will make this plain.

We will take all our examples from the first chapter of the Joseph Story, but they could just as well be taken from any other chapter. The story opens with a statement designed to set the scene for the entire tale by opening our eyes to the relationship between Joseph and his brothers. We rendered this opening verse (Genesis 37:2) as follows:

> *Joseph, seventeen years of age, was shepherding the flock with his brothers; he was helping the sons of Bilhah and the sons Zilpah, his father's wives.*

We then spent more than a page commenting on the implications of this reading. But the Hebrew text is ambiguous. It can also, with equal justice, be rendered:

> *Joseph, being seventeen years old, shepherded* [that is, supervised] *his brothers along with the sheep though he was* [but] *a lad, that is, the sons of Bilhah and the sons of Zilpah, his father's wives.*

And if so, the implications are the exact opposite of the first reading.[12] So which is it? Is Joseph an apprentice serving under his older brothers or is he their boss, they serving under him? We can interpret it either way. This verse did not have to be ambiguous. It could have been written in a simple and unambiguous matter, but the author chose to write it in a convoluted style that is capable of being understood in two very different ways. This is far from the only verse in our story that is designedly unclear.

Beyond the verses being susceptible to different meanings, there are situations where questions arise that we are unable to answer due to withheld information. For example, Joseph, sent by his father to check up on his brothers who are pasturing the flocks at Shechem, arrives only to find that they have left for parts unknown. He is at an impasse and probably on the point of returning home when he meets a stranger who tells him which road the brothers took (37:12–16). Who is this mysterious stranger who appears from nowhere and so unerringly points Joseph down the road to meet his destiny? Was this merely a chance encounter, or was the stranger lying in wait for the express purpose of sending Joseph to his fate?[13] We can only speculate; the author has not seen fit to supply us with information that would allow an assured choice.[14]

A third area of ambiguity lies in the realm of motives. For example, whatever motivated Jacob to send Joseph so far away from home to check on his brothers? Was Jacob really so obtuse as to be unaware of their roiling hatred of Joseph? Or did he recognize the danger signals, yet decided to send him anyway? Why? We are left to speculate as we are given no information. Or again, we are told of Reuben's motives in persuading his brothers to throw Joseph into the cistern — to save his life and give Reuben the chance to return him to their father (37:21–4). But what were Judah's motives for counseling selling Joseph as a slave to the Ishmaelite caravaneers: to save him from a slow death in the cistern or to make a fast buck (vv. 37:26–27)? We can take our pick for we are not told.

One further area of uncertainty lies in the significance of events that, on the surface, we have been given full knowledge of: let us use as example Joseph's dreams (37:5–11). Were they simply a revelation of his not so hidden wish to dominate his family (as his brothers thought), or were the dreams prophetic, sent by God to foretell his destiny? Once again we are given no way of knowing.

If we are correct in concluding that all this obfuscation is being performed with malice aforethought, what can be its purpose? The first and foremost result of multiple ways we can understand the story, and the various segments and events that make it up, is that it forces choice upon us. Willy-nilly we have no option but to choose between alternative understandings, a reality driven home to me, for example, by the writing of this book. Another way of putting this is to adopt an operative definition of ambiguity: ambiguity in a narrative means, in practice, leaving interpretive choices open to the reader.

But why should the reader be left to thrash around in a fog of uncertainty and make choices, usually on the basis of insufficient data? It is exactly here that we come to the crux of the matter: because that is the way life is. We are constantly forced by life to make choices and we never know all the facts. Choice in life is always based on insufficient data. And this returns us to the realm of theology. According to the biblical view, all human knowledge is imperfect and incomplete. Only God has perfect knowledge. Human beings, by the very fact of being limited and mortal creatures, are fated to live their lives in a cloud of irresolution. The events that surround us are, at best, imperfectly understood and their outcomes uncertain. We can only guess at the motives of those with whom we deal; we can never be sure and often are proven wrong. It is within this haze that we must make our choices, never able to see clearly, never able to be sure. The only time human beings can be certain of anything is, the Bible insists, when the divine grace of a revelation cuts through the haze; an event rare at best, and in most lives non-existent. We as human beings have no option but to live our lives, and make the choices we must, from what we can see of this world.

There is one critical qualification to what we have said, and that is that it applies to human relations with one's fellow humans. It does not apply to what we nowadays refer to as the natural order. In the biblical view the natural order alone is exempted from ambiguity. The laws that govern reality as a whole are seen as clear and unambiguous.

> Only one sphere, and the most comprehensive at that, remains essentially outside the Bible's operations of ambiguity: the world order itself, the laws governing reality as a whole ... in order to inculcate an objective frame of reference.[15]

While human life is shrouded in uncertainty, we can accept what we would call natural law as the sole certainty in our experience. This biblical insight of the fixed nature of what we would call natural law was well understood by the ancient rabbis who reduced it to a principle: "The world functions according to its natural pattern."[16] In this view God's primal pledge to humanity,

> *So long as the earth endures,*
> *Seedtime and harvest,*
> *Cold and heat,*
> *Summer and winter,*
> *Day and night*
> *Shall not cease*[17] [Gen. 8:22],

becomes a given that can be taken for granted, creating a backdrop of certainty to our otherwise unsure lives. As for the rest, we move through our lives as through a fog, uncertain of all.

Biblical narrative incorporates this fundamental insight into the very structure of its narrative style. All narrative in the Bible employs ambiguity as part of its rhetoric; the Joseph Story takes this common technique to an extreme. By leaving interpretive choices to the reader in a way that mimics the interpretive choices open to each of us in our lives, we are being made to experience the biblical view of human reality in all its starkness. As Meir Sternberg puts it:

> Ideology and aesthetics ... join forces to originate a strategy of telling that casts reading as a drama, interpretation as an ordeal that enacts and distinguishes the human predicament.... God is omniscient, man limited, and the boundary impassible. But how to expound and inculcate this new doctrine? ... The solution devised was ... to build the cognitive antithesis between God and humanity into the structure of the narrative. Not the premises alone but the very composition must bring home the point in and through the reading experience.... With a narrative become an obstacle course, its reading turns into a drama of understanding.[18]

By mimicking the reality of human life in the style and structure of the narrative itself, the Joseph Story forces the reader to confront what it means to be human from the biblical perspective.

Understanding the biblical view of the limited nature of human knowledge and how this perception shapes biblical narrative, we now turn to the specifics of the Joseph Story. The first issue that presents itself is: is it the intent of the author to leave us floundering, uncertain as to what is taking place and what is the meaning of it all, with no possibility of definitive resolution, or is some resolution possible? I would suggest that the strategy of the author was to design the work so as to be a cooperative venture. The reader is expected to make choices as to how to understand the designedly ambiguous text. By the choices the reader makes, he or she is being led to a conclusion, hopefully the conclusion intended by the author — but not necessarily. As no one can guarantee that the choices one makes in life will not lead to perdition and necessitate reevaluation, so wrong choices made in interpretation will lead to a complete misunderstanding and a dead end.

An example of misreading would be to see Joseph as the hero of a Horatio Alger rags-to-riches success story. This way of reading the story will bring one up short when Joseph himself tells us at the end what the truth, as he sees it, is. In a sense, even as life is often self-correcting, so is our narrative; but only to a limited degree. Again, just as in life one can be obtuse and fail to heed the signals that you are going wrong, so can the reader commit to a given preconception as to the meaning of the text and hold to it in the face of all contravening evidence. This again reflects the perils of freedom.

A second issue can be posed as follows: radically differing interpretations and understandings of the Joseph Story are possible. In the light of currently popular literary theories, does this imply that all readings are equally sound? The author would reject such a conclusion. Intrinsic to the biblical understanding is the conviction that just as in nature one can reach unambiguous conclusions that we term truth, so in the realm of human strivings. This truth, however, is known only to God because only He knows all; humans can only grope toward it. But truth does exist and our author drops hints periodically, and gently nudges us toward the truth. It takes careful reading to catch the hints, just as, in life, it takes real insight, often based on much experience, to gain perspective and grasp the implications of the chaotic day-to-day phenomena. But a definitive point of view and definitive answers to questions arising out of our narrative exist. Whether we have reached them, or are even able to reach them, is a different story.

Two examples of hints I think we are being afforded are: in Chapter 13 the incautious reader may easily jump to the conclusion that the act of the brothers prostrating themselves before Joseph is a fulfillment of the dreams of Joseph's youth, yet by the differentiated use of terminology, the author hints to the careful reader that this assumption is flawed (see Chapter 13, note 61). A second example of a hint might be the way the author portrays the reactions of, first the brothers and then the father, to Joseph's revelation of his identity. Joseph weeps copiously. He is evidently deeply moved and cannot stop weeping. Yet of all his brothers only Benjamin responds to Joseph's display of emotion. The ten others stand dry-eyed and silent, as does their father when first he confronts his son in Goshen on the border of Egypt.[19] This portrayal, I believe, is meant to nudge us away from any thought of reconciliation.

Reading the Joseph Story is an exercise in learning the limitations of understanding. "The only knowledge perfectly acquired is the knowledge of our limitations ... to make sense of the discourse is to gain a sense of being human."[20]

Notes

1. Literally, "intends."
2. The one exception to this generalization is Genesis 46:1–4. We are told that Israel offers sacrifices to the God of his father, Isaac, in Beer-sheba and that God appears to him in a dream and speaks to him. However, this short episode really belongs, thematically, to the life story of Jacob, and is structurally the conclusion to the second section of Genesis, "The Travails of the Fathers," in which God routinely speaks with Abraham, Isaac, and Jacob, encouraging them and giving them directions. It is only chronological necessity, the fact of the overlap between the lives of Jacob and Joseph, which prevents the author from putting this episode at the end of the second section of Genesis where it belongs, and forces him to breach the thematic integrity of the Joseph Story.
3. Only two other narratives in the entire Bible share this strange phenomenon with the Joseph story: the Books of Ruth and Esther. I have dealt at some length with these in my previous work *Four Biblical Heroines*. Much of what I say there can apply with equal force to the Joseph narrative.
4. Twice, the narrator hints to us, God intervenes (but only covertly) to give things a nudge in the right direction: once during Joseph's service on the estate of Potiphar and once while in prison. "Now the Lord was with Joseph and he became successful in the house of his Egyptian master" (Gen. 39:2 ff). "And it

came to pass that, as he was in prison, the Lord was with Joseph and was gracious to him, and gave him favor in the eyes of the Chief Warder of the prison ... because the Lord was with him [Joseph], whatever he did the Lord made it succeed" (39:21, 23). These two instances are the only times the Name of the Lord is mentioned in the Joseph narrative. It is this that makes these remarks significant. (The one remaining mention, 49:18, is not part of the narrative but an exclamation embedded in the "Jacob's Legacy" poem.)

5. von Rad, *Genesis*, 427.

6. This is a point that was insisted upon by, among others, the thirteenth century biblical commentator, Nahmanides: "Since the world came into existence, God's blessing did not create something new from nothing. Instead the world functions according to its natural pattern" (*Commentary on Exodus 25:24*). This point of view is shared by the authors of the Books of Ruth and Esther. Some of the implications of this position will be discussed later in this chapter.

7. Even if we accept my reading of the text that it was not the brothers who sold Joseph into Egypt (see Appendix 1), by throwing him into the cistern they set him up to be seized and sold. For the purposes of the present line of reasoning this amounts to the same thing.

8. In my previous work, *Four Biblical Heroines*, I explored what I consider the birth of a theology of Providence in the Book of Ruth. Ruth and the Joseph story, in the form we have them today, are in my estimate roughly contemporaneous, the products of the first half of the tenth century BCE The focus of Ruth, however, seems to lie in the question of why a God-dominated world seems to human beings to be secular, and finds its answer in the short life span of human beings. God's purposes work themselves out over such long periods of time that human beings never live long enough to be able to perceive them in their totality. Only in the historical retrospect of hindsight, often covering centuries, can one begin to perceive the workings of the hand of God. The question of the compatibility of free will with the working of Providence is not considered; it is simply assumed. In this sense I see Ruth and Joseph as complementary works: both ostensibly secular narratives preoccupied with the problem of the nature of God's relationship to a world which seems to function independently of Him, and each grappling with a different aspect of the problem. See *Four Biblical Heroines*, 70–75.

9. This implication of Joseph's thesis that God controls outcomes is made the foundation of the crisis theology that climaxes the Book of Esther. The author of Esther refers us specifically to Joseph's culminating theological declaration (Gen. 50:20) as the source of the bedrock article of faith that God's promises are absolutely reliable, despite all contrary indications in an unstable and contingent world. For a fuller development of this thesis, see *Four Biblical Heroines*, 180, note 11; and 201–203.

10. The only apparent exception to this stance is Genesis 38:27–30 (where Tamar, by giving birth to Perez, becomes the progenitress of David). Here our narrator seems to be endorsing the conclusions of the Book of Ruth. If so, he is preparing the way for Joseph's insights and pre-endorsing them. See page 62; and also *Four Biblical Heroines*, 87–89.

11. Two somewhat dated but respectable works that might serve as an introduction to the literature for those interested are Bernard Berofsky, ed., *Free Will and Determinism* (New York: Harper and Row, 1966), and Gary Watson, ed., *Free Will* (UK: Oxford University Press, 1982). For a very readable overview of the way the problem of determinism has been seen in modern (i.e., post-Descartes) times one might try the first chapter of Hilary Bok's, *Freedom and Responsibility* (NJ: Princeton University Press, 1998).

12. There are commentators, both medieval and modern, who understand the Hebrew text in this manner. See Chapter 1, note 13.

13. This is a valid question. Biblical style does not admit to irrelevant digressions. If the text sees fit to introduce this episode into the narrative, we may accept it as significant.

14. For example, some commentators suggest that the question has been wrongly framed. It should be: what is the mysterious stranger? The implication is that he may be not a man but an angel, and that this episode may portray a supernatural intervention in the course of events to ensure that the confrontation between Joseph and his brothers takes place.

15. Sternberg, 233.

16. See for example Babylonian Talmud, Tractate *Avodah Zarah* 54b.

17. "The ordered processes of nature will never again be interrupted. The rhythm of life, reflected in the rhythmic quality of the language, is here presented through four pairs of merisms — the expression of totality by means of opposites. These describe three environmental phenomena: agricultural, climatic, and temporal" (Sarna, *Genesis*, 60).

18. Sternberg, 47–48.

19. See Chapter 9, pages 140–142, for a description of the confrontation between Israel and his son after twenty-two years of separation.

20. Sternberg, 47.

15

Conclusion 2: Joseph's Place in History

> *The grey sands curve before me ...*
> *From inland meadows,*
> *Fragrant of June and clover, floats the dark, and fills*
> *The hollow sea's dead face with little creeping shadows,*
> *And the white silence brims the hollow of the hills.*
> *Close in the nest is folded every weary wing,*
> *Hushed all the joyful voices; and we, who held you dear,*
> *Eastward we turn, and homeward, alone, remembering ...*
> — Rupert Brooke, *Day That I Have Loved*

Joseph in Retrospect

Turning from God and His doings to the realm of human beings and their affairs, what are we to make of Joseph the man? Beyond his startling ability to triumph over adversity, to rise in an alien environment to the highest governmental position and to maintain his grip on it, and his demonstrable genius in administration, his true significance in the biblical view lies in his role in furthering God's agenda. By saving his family from death by starvation, and thus preserving the future of the Promise, Joseph has fulfilled his purpose in the larger scheme of things. His greatness lies in the fact that he is able to comprehend intuitively the part that he has played in the grand panorama of history. It is given to few human beings to grasp the greater picture within which their lives unfold and the strategic purposes that they serve. To discover God and His purpose for himself in a seemingly secular world amounts to a greatness that is essentially unique in the Bible, a vision often denied even to prophets who acted as God's spokesmen. But Joseph's insight pertains solely to his place in God's scheme of things, and this only to his role as a savior of his family. His understanding does not extend to the long range consequences of his actions — his being the instrument of the eventual enslavement of his people. Joseph's vision is strictly limited to the short-term. Only at the very end of his life does he begin to expand his horizons to take in the future redemption of the family from Egypt by God, but we are given no indication that he sees himself responsible for the conditions that will make redemption necessary.

Moreover, his vision, while unerring in its veracity, is too narrow by far. He perceives his mission in the restricted terms of preserving the physical existence of his family. He never broadens his horizon to take in the spiritual dimension of his task: the purpose of his family's survival.[1] Not once do his pronouncements give any hint of recognition that the descendants of Abraham are covenanted to a destiny of becoming a blessing to mankind.[2] For Joseph, preserving life seems an end unto itself. He does not seem capable of seeing beyond the physical. Walking with God and being wholehearted[3] apparently does not resonate with him.

This obtuseness on Joseph's part to the spiritual aspect of the destiny of the children of Israel is directly connected with his greatest failing: his abandonment of the Way of God and his fascination with the way of Egypt. The two paths are mutually incompatible. And due to this surrender to the lure of the splendor, the power and the glory that is Egypt, Joseph becomes an ever-present danger to the future of the Promise; the danger that he will lead his kinsman, the nascent Children of Israel, away from the Way of God into the way of Egypt. To prevent this from happening, Joseph must be prevented from assuming the role of legitimate leader of the family. Once Israel, his father, has recognized the danger, the final years of his life are devoted to checkmating Joseph's pretensions in this realm. To this end he removes him from the leadership succession and anoints Judah in his place. To this end he adopts his grandsons, bypassing Joseph's paternity and saving Ephraim and Manasseh for the destiny of Abraham. All unbeknownst to himself, Joseph's spiritual authority has been short-circuited, and he himself has been removed to a place outside the spiritual borders of the covenanted family. The danger to the Promise has been averted.

Rooted in Joseph's adoption of the way of Egypt as his own can be found a large part of the reason for his failure as a human being, first and foremost in his relations with his family and his emotional disengagement from it. He saves his family, yes; but the way he does it is hardly designed to re-engage with them in the way Judah did after some twenty years of absence. And he plays with his brothers (for whatever reasons we assign), the trauma of those nightmare months doing permanent damage to the family. And when he finishes, he leaves them with two theological pronouncements and some promises of physical sustenance. No re-engagement, no participation in family events or family councils on the pattern of Judah.[4] At root, I would suggest, Joseph is bored with his family. Having done what was minimally necessary to guarantee their physical survival, and having concluded the ego-satisfying games he was playing, Joseph loses interest. He has so many more fascinating and demanding things to do running the Egyptian state and reengineering Egyptian society. And so reconciliation, healing and becoming part of his family once again are, if even considered, tasks put on the back burner, and there forgotten.

And here lies the nub of the matter; the difference between Joseph the Egyptian and Joseph the son of Israel. As an Egyptian he devotes himself to the state and to Pharaoh with all his heart; as a son of Israel he serves his family negligently. As an Egyptian he displays only that degree of ruthlessness his program demands, no more; as the son of Israel he is superfluously ruthless. And the trauma engendered by this unnecessary ruthlessness is to leave psychic scars that will promote future fractiousness in the tribes that will grow out of the family — fraternal divisions that will make a stable polity ultimately impossible to maintain.

> We are dealing here with matters which go far beyond the errors and sufferings of certain individuals, far beyond, into the past and the future of Joseph's people. He was play-acting not only with his brothers, but with the destiny of the folk of the blessing. A tradition of fratricidal strife had dominated the seed of Abraham since the time of the bond with God, an inheritance from primitive times. Here was the opportunity to bring the tradition to an end, to bury the hereditary hatchet in a magnificent act of family statesmanship. But Joseph gave all his understanding and statesmanship to Egypt; he ignored the opportunity nearer home, and confirmed the tradition of the folk division which, centuries later, under another form, led to the splitting of the kingdom.[5]

In sum, Joseph, despite his clairvoyant insight, fails as a human being. He never forgives his brothers and never asks for their forgiveness for the harm he has done to them. He never becomes one with the family; to the end he remains "the one set apart from his brothers" (Gen. 49:26). His "social reengineering" of Egyptian society is a manifestation of state tyranny at its worst. At heart Joseph remorselessly trod the way of Egypt.

But in the end possibly even the vast task of running the Egyptian state lost its luster after the challenge of the first fourteen years of glut and then famine. After successfully reorganizing Egyptian society so as to concentrate wealth and power in the hands of the Pharaoh, Joseph would have had to settle down to the humdrum task of managing the state: the mind-numbing detail, the staff relations problems, the endless mini-crises, the nonstop intrigues. By the time of the events that precede and surround his father's death, it appears more a lack of interest in the family than overriding fascination with the challenge of his Egyptian career that is blocking Joseph's re-engagement with his kindred. All that we can say with any certainty is that by the end of his life Joseph seems to have become completely disillusioned with Egypt, and very possibly with a project that has been his whole life.[6]

Perhaps this is the place to comment on the affinity between the natures of Jacob and Joseph. In many ways Joseph was a chip off the old block (and this may help to explain in part Joseph being his father's favorite). Of all his sons, Joseph was most like in character to his father. Both were, by nature, operators who became wise in the ways of the world, and whose "wisdom" propelled them to success, as the world sees success.[7] But then their paths diverge. Jacob eventually learns that there are things more important than material success. As a result he becomes Israel. His youthful dream of a ladder connecting earth and heaven, with angels ascending and descending, pointed in the direction of his eventual spiritual maturation. When we compare this with Joseph's youthful dreams of power and domination, the contrast could not be sharper. Joseph ends as he began: his brothers, now old men, groveling in terror before him. Joseph never learns, or if he does his new knowledge of what is important comes too late. A half-century of increasing racial rejection and isolation in his adopted homeland ultimately force upon him the realization that the way of Egypt is neither the way for him nor for the children of Israel. On his deathbed, he renounces Egypt and puts his hope in the God of Israel, the Redeemer. He, at his very end, finally accepts that all along his destiny lay with the Promise.

And so we have reached the ultimate irony of Joseph's remarkable life. Laid to rest in the gargantuan sarcophagus that he has prepared for himself,[8] on his deathbed he contracts to vacate it for a simple grave in the land of his fathers; a grave similar to that in which his father had insisted on being interred.

Joseph and Moses

Up to now we have been evaluating Joseph within the context of the Book of Genesis. But we must not lose sight of the fact that the story of Joseph is not contemporaneous with the events that it relates. While the data embedded in the tale go back to the seventeenth century BCE,[9] the narrative as we now have it was composed and written much later: probably in the tenth century BCE,[10] and certainly, by all accounts, after the Exodus from Egypt. This means that our narrative was written with the benefit of hindsight; that the rise of the Pharaoh "who did not know Joseph" (Exodus 1:8), the enslavement and persecution, the subsequent liberation and Exodus from Egypt could never have been far from the mind of the author. And therefore, if we wish to understand our tale as the author meant for us to understand it, we must widen our horizons to include the whole subsequent narrative of redemption, Sinai and the settlement of the Children of Israel in the Promised Land. This means seeing Joseph, the last great personage in Genesis, in contrast to his historical successor, Moses.

When we examine these two towering figures, we are struck by both startling similarity and equally dramatic difference. Both were outsiders; both were marginal men. A marginal man can be defined as a person whose fate it is to live in two societies which embody two not merely different but antagonistic cultures.[11] In this definition we can with no difficulty recognize Joseph, a boy brought up within the confines of a pastoral Hebrew family in Canaan, unwillingly transported to Egypt. But the same definition applies to Moses, brought up in an Egyptian palace, who ends up first representing, and then leading, a slave people in the midst of whom he has embedded himself. In both cases, a radical readjustment of mental processes, involving a calling into question of all the certainties and assumptions underlying one's upbringing, was forced upon them merely to allow them to function within their new social environments.

Karl Mannheim, the true father of the concept if not the phrase, insists that multiple displacement is the true mark of marginality.[12] Mere displacement in space (i.e., Joseph being transferred from Canaan to Egypt; Moses fleeing Egypt for Midian[13]) is usually not sufficient to break a person loose from the generally accepted preconceptions of the society in which he or she was brought up. Only when mobility in space[14] is accompanied by a rapid movement up or down the social scale (i.e., in a drop from the status of free pastoralist in line to be leader of his family to that of slave, then a rise to almost the top of the pyramid for Joseph; the overnight drop from the rank of Prince of Egypt to that of fugitive shepherd for Moses) is the faith in the eternal validity of one's own upbringing called into question. It is mobility which is usually the decisive factor in making persons skeptical of their traditional view of the world.

The practical implications of the transformation of an individual into a "marginal man" can be summed up as follows:

> The fate which condemns him to live, at the same time, in two worlds is the same which compels him to assume, in relation to the worlds in which he lives, the role of a cosmopolitan and a stranger. Inevitably he becomes ... the individual with the wider horizon, the keener intelligence, the more detached and rational viewpoint.[15]

In sum, the thesis of the marginal person is that the social environment in which people are brought up establishes their way of looking at things, a more or less closed ideological framework that excludes alternatives by its very nature. Only marginal persons, looking in from the outside, have the ability to question the system. Only a Joseph or a Moses could be sufficiently detached to question the certainties of the world in which they found themselves and to challenge the inevitability of the existing order. Marginality is the precondition for radical creativity and innovation, the mark of both Joseph and Moses.

When, however, we begin to examine the ways their creativity and innovation manifested themselves, it is the dissimilarity in the direction that they take that strikes the eye. While Joseph begins as a son of Israel he ends an Egyptian; Moses starts as an Egyptian yet his path leads to his becoming an Israelite. Joseph takes Israel out of Canaan and brings them into Egypt; Moses takes Israel out of Egypt and brings them to Canaan. These differences amount to night and day.

If we compare these two outstanding men, we discover that they are, to use Claude Levi-Strauss's evocative term, binary opposites. They are different in every conceivable dimension; their ... actions are mirror images.... The opposition between the two is so great and so consistent that it is difficult to believe it is unintended. The question arises then: What are we to make of this turn from Egypt toward Canaan, from Joseph-the-assimilator to Moses-the-lawgiver?[16]

I suggest that the narrative has been framed so as to specifically contrast the career of Joseph with that of the Great Liberator and Lawgiver; in the retrospect of history Joseph is being cast in the role of the anti-hero. The path Joseph so assiduously pursues is the way being rejected in favor of the path of the Promise championed by Moses. Not only does our narrative reject Joseph as leader of the people of the covenant, but the Bible as a whole rejects him, turning him into a kind of nonperson. As we have already noted, the dominating personage of almost a third of Genesis virtually vanishes from the subsequent biblical text.[17] This eclipse cannot be unintentional. It is Moses who

>...incarnates Judaism at its summit.... His genius for enraged vision, his direct dialogues with God, the mutinies he must endure from his own people, the momentary transgressions which forbid his entry into the promised land, crystallize the whole historical, psychological and moral condition of the Jew to this day.[18]

In the light of this incarnation, Joseph's achievement pales into insignificance; the way chosen eclipses the way rejected.

A Cautionary Tale

More than Joseph the man is being rejected. An entire way of life has been sampled and found wanting: the way of Egypt. This is not simply a question of idolatry but of the type of society the idolatry of Egypt created. Kass, analyzing the career of Joseph in modern terms, sees his failings "as emblematic of the administrative soul and the Egyptian way, in which the morally blind penchant for technical mastery over things and events logically implies the emergence of despotism and servitude."[19] However sound this analysis may be — and I think it has much to say not only about ancient Egypt but also about our twenty-first century world — I seriously doubt if the author of our narrative was thinking in these terms; these terms of reference were simply unavailable to him. But I think that our text does show that the author was very much aware that what we have termed "the way of Egypt" values the state above the lives and welfare of mere people, places expediency before moral concerns and by raising one human being to the status of godhood debases the rest of humanity to the role of expendable ciphers, subhuman tools of the Pharaoh and his entourage. It was this "way" that not only our author but all the authors of the biblical text reject decisively.

This rejection does not stop with ideology: it frames the story of Joseph as a cautionary tale, establishing how the spectacularly successful path to material prosperity in a society such as Egypt proves but a prelude to slavery and debasement. Nor is it content with drawing our attention to the moral mathematics involved in following the path of Egypt: as Joseph does to the Egyptian peasants, so will the Egyptians eventually do to the Israelites; the moral universe is an equation in which both sides must ultimately balance. The lessons of Egypt will finally lead to the construction of a new social order designed to repudiate all that Egypt stands for, with safeguards built in to prevent what happened in Egypt from happening in Israel.

Two examples will suffice to demonstrate this thesis. We have noted that there was one class of people whom Joseph had exempted from expropriation when he forced the Egyptian populace to sell their land: the priests. It was the vast land holdings of the Egyptian priesthood that made them part of the exploiting hierarchy that dominated Egypt. By the time Joseph was finished, all Egyptian peasants were either state slaves farming Pharaoh's lands or Temple serfs working priestly holdings. These vast holdings — possibly as much as one third of all Egypt at the time under discussion — together with their religious influence gave the priests a position of power that was unassailable, even by the Pharaoh. This power, and the corruption that secular power inevitably engenders, was seen up close by the Israelites. This is a situation that will not be allowed to develop in the Israelite Commonwealth that is to emerge. This phenomenon of an economically independent priesthood will be prevented by the simple expedient of depriving them, from the start, of any land holdings. At the time of the settlement in Canaan, the tribe of Levi, the priestly tribe, will not be given an allotment. Instead, the priests will be made dependent for their maintenance on the worshipers they are mandated to serve. A portion of every sacrifice will be designated as the perquisite of the priests, and from these portions they will obtain their sustenance. Never, during the Age of the First Commonwealth, will the priests of Israel ever attain to a ghost of the oppressive power taken for granted by the Egyptian priesthood.

The other side of the coin was the example of the impoverishment and despoilment of the Egyptian peasantry.

> The Egyptians sold all they owned and finally their persons.... Who was the author of this policy — Joseph. And who became its main victims — Joseph's descendants (a subtle critique of "Joseph the Wise; Joseph the Provider"). Our text's message is loud and clear: In Israel this must not happen! The preventive force is the institution of redemption.[20]

The institution of redemption (Hebrew *geulah*) was enshrined in a complex of custom and law. It mandated that should impoverishment force a landowner to sell a part or all of his land, the sale would not be final. The sale would, in truth, be merely a lease which would terminate in the Jubilee.[21] The purchaser would have the use of the land, but in the fiftieth year, whenever that would fall, the land would revert to its true owner, or his heirs should he no longer be living.[22] Furthermore, the seller would have the absolute right of repurchase at any time that he could scrape together the money needed. The purchaser would not have the right of refusal.[23] What is more, should the seller be unable to raise the necessary funds to repurchase his land, his closest relatives would find themselves under the obligation to buy the land from the purchaser to keep it in the family.[24] Here too the redeemer would merely be acquiring the use of the property; regardless of who held the land it would revert in the Jubilee to the original owner or his heirs.[25] As long as the institution of redemption functioned, no latter day Joseph would be able to perpetrate upon the independent farmers of the Israelite Commonwealth the enormity that the historical Joseph visited upon the hapless Egyptians.[26] In this manner the story of Joseph in Egypt, and the Israelite experience that lay behind it, were to prove a powerful force in the shaping of the Israelite Commonwealth of the Biblical Age. The way of Egypt was the way to be avoided at all costs.

The Rehabilitation of Joseph

The reading of the Joseph narrative we have developed presents a severely negative appraisal of the tale's central protagonist. We contend that this evaluation has not been superimposed upon the text, but rather that it elicits the way the narrative was originally written and structured. Beyond the underlying slant of the narrative itself stands the harsh fact of Jacob's choice of Judah as the designated leader of the family's future: a repudiation of a lifetime's favoritism shown to Joseph. We have the clear juxtaposition of Joseph with his successor, Moses, and it is the latter who emerges as the role model of the future: prophet, lawgiver and "man of God."[27] We have the fading of Joseph's name from the consciousness of the descendants of Jacob/Israel, an erasure reflected in the biblical text. The message would seem to be straightforward.

Yet this is not the way the story was always read. The ambiguous way in which the story has been framed permits more readings than one. During the period of the First Commonwealth, our sources indicate that there were differences of opinion as to how to read the Joseph Story. On the one hand there were those who viewed Joseph's rise as preordained by God.

> *Now He called forth a famine upon the land;*
>   *Every staff of bread He broke.*
> *He sent before them a man;*
>   *As a slave was Joseph sold.*
> *His feet were tortured with fetters;*
>   *His neck was put in iron;*
> *Until what he had said had come to pass*[28];
>   *The utterance of the Lord tested him.*
> *The king sent and released him;*
>   *The ruler of peoples set him free.*
> *He made him lord of his house;*
>   *And ruler of all his possessions.*
> *To bind*[29] *his princes at his pleasure,*
>   *And to teach his elders wisdom.*
> *So Israel came to Egypt;*
>   *And Jacob sojourned in the land of Ham*[30] [Ps. 105:16–23].

This portrayal could scarcely be called negative. On the other hand another historical Psalm chooses to recall Jacob's rejection of Joseph in favor of Judah. Presenting Jacob's choice as reflecting the will of God the psalmist proclaims:

> *And He rejected*[31] *the tent of Joseph,*
> *The tribe of Ephraim He did not choose;*
> *But He chose the tribe of Judah,*
> *Mount Zion which He loves* [Ps. 78:67–68].

These lines hardly amount to a positive assessment.[32]

It is only in the period of the Second Commonwealth and thereafter that more extreme attitudes begin to appear. Most outspoken is the so-called "Testament of Naphtali," which is to be found in the Pseudepigrapha.[33] In this work Joseph is painted as a villain who refuses to do as his father instructed and proves to be the cause of the eventual exile of the Israelites. Father Jacob is further pictured as commanding his sons and their progeny to have nothing to do with Joseph's descendants and to model themselves only on Levi (the progenitor of the priestly tribe) and on Judah.

> *He* [Jacob] *said to me, "My son ... my body is confounded by reason of Joseph my son, for I loved him above you all; and for the wickedness of my son Joseph you will be sent into captivity, and you will be scattered among the nations.... Therefore I command you not to unite with the sons of Joseph, but only with Levi and Judah"* [Naphtali 7:4–6].[34]

The negative portrayals, though having warrant in the text, were later to be submerged and superseded by an assessment just as extreme but positive. This interpretation, which was to become what might be termed "the standard model" of understanding the Joseph narrative, was promulgated by the rabbis of the second and third centuries of the Common Era, and later enlarged upon by their successors. It was they who promoted the picture of Joseph as the sole hero of the tale, and they who endowed him with the title that, in traditional circles, he bears to this day: Joseph the Saint.[35] The Wise — perhaps; the Provider — possibly; but the Saint? The title is unique; no other biblical personage has been awarded this title! Were the rabbis somehow blind to the plain meaning and implications of the text? What can explain such a radical reading — in effect a rewriting of the tale — turning the son whom his father rejected (and indeed whom the Bible as a whole dismissed) into a "Saint"?

Seeing one's past in the afterglow of a nostalgic hindsight is not an uncommon phenomenon. It is quite usual for peoples to transmute their ancestors, especially those seen as their distant progenitors, into heroic figures, conveniently overlooking their faults and supplying them with quite unwarranted virtues.[36] The Latin dictum *de mortuis nil nisi bonum*[37] would seem especially appropriate as an explanation for what amounts to a revisionist retelling of the Joseph Story. Yet the rabbis were a highly intelligent group of individuals who were acutely alive to the nuances of the biblical text. An individual might go astray, but as a collectivity they could hardly be expected to misunderstand so completely the principle thrust of the text. It makes far better sense to entertain the possibility that their reading of the narrative was deliberate.

I propose that what we are here witnessing is a conscious and considered program of rehabilitation, an agenda imposed by the vicissitudes of history. The year 70 CE marked a radical break in the history of ancient Israel. In that year the Second Commonwealth came to a tragic end: Jerusalem was sacked and burned, and the Temple destroyed. The triumph of the Roman legions created a new situation: the Jews were now a people stripped of their sovereignty, without a land and deprived of their spiritual center. They would henceforth, and for the foreseeable future, need to learn how to survive as a powerless minority within alien civilizations. From a religion focused on a central shrine, and built around an ethical system predicated upon the existence of national sovereignty and the ability to legislate and enforce rules of conduct, they would have to repackage their faith into a form that could be taken wherever they might be driven, while transforming their public ethics into a private morality dependent neither on sovereignty nor majority status. For this transformation of Judaism, people would need new role models.

Two biblical figures present themselves as candidates: Joseph and Mordechai. Both are examples of the success possible when an Israelite, insignificant and powerless, is embedded within an alien, indeed pagan, society. The counter to powerlessness is to serve the ruler and the state loyally wherever you find yourself, and thus rise to high station. Both Joseph and Mordechai demonstrate that successful careers and personal pride are possible in conditions of minority status in alien lands.[38]

Mordechai is the more straightforward case, one of the two heroes of the Book of Esther.[39] The case of Joseph, however, can only be made to serve the function of role model if his character can be rehabilitated, and his life given a positive spin. So I suggest that the life of Joseph was reconsidered, reevaluated and repackaged — his failings minimized and extenuated by means of legends which expanded and modified the biblical texts.[40] Thus his public life was played down, his private life highlighted, his failings trivialized or transmuted into virtues, and his virtues expanded to heroic proportions. The end result is a saintly human being who is also simultaneously a pious Jew and a worldly success; an example to be emulated by future generations of exiled Jews wandering the face of an inhospitable world.

The way this transformation was achieved is instructive. The biblical Joseph was a man who lived more than 90 percent of his life as a public figure in the public sphere, and the glimpses we are given of his private life, mainly in relation to his family, are not calculated to prompt emulation. Out of the vast compendium of legend woven by the rabbis, we single out two elements as examples of the rabbinic treatment.[41] The first involves Mrs. Potiphar. By dramatically painting her as the very queen of seductresses, elaborating on her numerous wiles and enticements, Joseph's steadfast refusal to fall into her trap and his success in maintaining his moral integrity becomes absolutely heroic in proportion. It is this episode more than anything else that earns Joseph, as the rabbis spin the tale, the designation of "Saint." He becomes, in this telling, the exemplar of the moral power to resist not only the sexual temptation of human seductresses, but the larger temptation of foreign religions and foreign customs as well.

Another prime goal of the rabbis was to promote the solidarity of the various Jewish communities. One of the central teachings of the rabbis was: the welfare and the fate of every Jew is bound up with the welfare and the fate of every other Jew. Lacking a police force and the coercive powers of the state, only the ethics of brotherly responsibility and the deep sense that every Jew was one's brother would suffice to maintain the cohesiveness of the various scattered communities, and the unity of the people as a whole. But the fratricidal relationship of Joseph and his brothers was hardly a model of brotherly love. Hence, I suggest, the myth of reconciliation had to be superimposed upon a text which quite explicitly disavows any such notion.

The purpose of these examples (and many more could be cited) should be sufficient to indicate what I think was the purpose behind the rabbinic rehabilitation of Joseph. And in his new career as saintly exemplar, Joseph was to prove an outstanding success. By the third century at the latest, virtually all Jews were reading Joseph through rabbinic-tinted glasses, the "rehabilitated Joseph" standing between the reader and the text. And not only Jews: the Church Fathers, influenced by the rabbinic commentators, adopted this portrayal of Joseph, as did the Koran. This picture of Joseph has reverberated down to the present day. The irony of the matter is: the one rejected by the Bible has become one of the foremost heroes of the heirs of the Bible—the Jews, the Christians and the Muslims.

While the needs for repackaging the Joseph Story by putting a positive spin on Joseph may have been compelling in late antiquity and the early Middle Ages, we are now in a period that appreciates a structured literary text more than legends, and clear-eyed realism more than interpretative spin. It would seem that the time has therefore come to return to the unadorned text. Our treatment of the Joseph Story is predicated on this assumption.

Telling It Like It Is

When we compare the revisionist reading of the rabbis with the original biblical narrative—multidimensional, complex and subtle—one can only be struck with how shallow and simplistic this reading is: As a precocious and pious youth, Joseph's divinely inspired dreams predict his future greatness, his father rightly preferring him over his loutish and evil brothers who are unable to tolerate his superior piety and learning. Any faults he manifests are brushed aside as mere youthful peccadilloes — boys, after all, will be boys.[42] One day, while far from home, and thus with no one to protect him, his evil brothers seize him, throw him into a pit, and finally rid themselves of him by selling him to passing merchants. But God protects him and eases his path, guaranteeing him success in Egypt and rapid promotion to the position of manager of his owner's estate.[43] His owner's wife, inflamed by Joseph's beauty and pious modesty, sets herself to seduce him. But despite her lascivious advances and practiced wiles, she can make no progress. Joseph never even looks at her, keeping his eyes modestly fixed on the ground. After each advance he retreats to his room, fasts and prays. When his chaste resistance once wavers, a sudden vision of his father (some say it was of his mother) stiffens his resolve and keeps him from falling into her grip. Failing utterly, she revenges herself by falsely accusing him of attempting to assault her, and has him thrown into prison. But God sends prophetic dreams to his fellow inmates which Joseph, through his great wisdom and learning, is able to interpret, which leads to interpreting Pharaoh's dreams. Pharaoh wants to appoint Joseph to be his Vizier, but there is an obstacle: the rabbis have invented a job description for the Vizier of Egypt that includes the ability to converse in all seventy languages of the world. So God sends an angel to teach Joseph, in one night, all seventy languages of the world so that he can qualify to be Vizier of Egypt. Appointed Vizier, he singlehandedly saves Egypt. When his brothers appear before him, he gets to work reforming their characters by a program of "tough love," and when he brings them to repent of their evil ways, he reveals himself to them and forgives them. The brothers reconciled, and united now in love, he brings his family to Egypt where they live happily forever after. This pious parody of the tale told in the Bible reminds one of the stories of young George Washington that appeared in children's books in the nineteenth century: of the youth who could throw a silver dollar over the Potomac and who cheerfully admitted to chopping down the cherry tree because he could not tell a lie.

When Oliver Cromwell, Lord Protector of England, sat for his portrait, Samuel Cooper, the miniaturist, asked him how he wished to be painted. The reported answer was, "With all the warts."[44] This reply was to become proverbial as a demand for total honesty. It is this sort of unflinching honesty that characterizes biblical narrative, resisting all temptation to prettify its heroes and to paint over their faults. The tale of Joseph and his brothers as told in the Bible, a tale told with all the warts, is an outstanding example of how biblical narrative approaches its subjects.

It is this honesty that has been one of the main factors in ensuring the widespread and long-lasting popularity of the Bible. Despite all attempts over the centuries to pretty up and "improve" the biblical narratives, the original text has remained available and people have kept returning to it. It is this honesty and refusal to pander to the special interests of varying reading groups that has kept these ancient tales perennially relevant. And, perhaps more than any other factor, this sense that the Bible "tells it like it is" has been instrumental in persuading generation after generation of readers that, through these biblical narratives, they are experiencing the Word of God.

A Being of a Higher Order

To wind up our concluding remarks to this work, we wish to correct a misplacement of emphasis. We have focused much of our analysis on the psychological aspects of the Joseph Story. This is largely a concession to modern tastes. The insistence on explaining all behavior psychologically is a relatively recent development, and when applied to some of the greatest classical literary creations it fails miserably. Take Sophocles' portrayal of Oedipus. Despite the protagonist having become a prototype and a byword of modern psychological understanding, the Greek dramatist offers no psychological explanation for his having killed his father and married his mother. Rather Sophocles insists on the inevitability of predestination. The events were preordained before the hero was born; and any effort to explain these acts in terms of single, or even multiple motives — conscious or unconscious — trivializes them.

It is similar with the story of Joseph. We have pointed out that the story of Joseph and his brothers was known, in outline, for centuries before the tale was committed to writing in the form we have before us today. Thus the suspense on which modern writers rely to such a great extent is lacking. As in virtually all tales of the Bible, the author has chosen a theme that insures that his audience would know the outcome in advance. But it did not occur to either him or to his public that this might in any way detract from the power of his work or the impact of its many meanings. That we know the overall outcome of the drama of Joseph and his brothers does not in the least lessen our sense of awe at Joseph's relentless striving, the anguish of his brothers, or of Jacob's terrible pain and disillusionment over the fate of his favorite son. And as the significance of Joseph's realization that he is but an instrument of God's overarching purposes sinks in, our understanding of this religious dimension transcends the social and psychological spheres and represents something of cosmic significance. The tale of human doings becomes transmuted before our eyes into a kind of revelation of man's place in the cosmos.

Joseph, by the end of the tale, stands revealed as one of those unique creations of God. He stands apart from all the others in the tale. No one really understands him: not his brothers, not Pharaoh, not even his father. He remains an enigma — the one set apart. He can only be likened to a tragic hero in one the dramas of Shakespeare or Aeschylus. Even in succeeding in what he comes to understand as his cosmic purpose in life — saving his family — he simultaneously condemns them to a future of four hundred years of slavery and oppression. There is an inevitability to his tragedy, and he alone is aware of it. Placed in a world not his own, suffocating in the provincialism of Canaan among people who do not understand him, he is propelled by forces he cannot comprehend into a new world: Egypt. In seizing the opportunity that has opened before him, in following what he deems to be his destiny, he turns his back on the heritage which is his true destiny as a great-grandson of Abraham. And in so doing he ends up in a world not his own that rejects him and enslaves his people.

The story of Joseph deals not only with the hero but with the society in which he finds himself. Unlike Abraham, Isaac and Jacob in a Canaan but sketchily delineated — heroic figures free-standing against a virtually non-existent background — Joseph's Egypt is brought to life. It is the Egyptian social background that is used by the author to model Joseph's character that much more clearly, and that enables us to empathize so intensely with this man, torn between his past and his vaunting ambition, between a world rejected and a vision of a future that increasingly becomes a mirage.

Joseph's fate is to appear on the cusp of a seismic transition between two epochs. He is a product of the Age of the Fathers, a world of towering personalities; a world in which the solitary individual was everything; a numinous world in which God walked with man. Ahead lies a world which Joseph cannot even dimly intuit: a world in which the central human protagonist will be not an individual but an entire people; where its heroes will not be solitary individuals walking with God but prophets, servants of God and tasked by Him with bringing His Word to this people. It is the transition between Genesis and Exodus.

These two epochs are separated by what amounts to an interregnum. Sandwiched between two ages resonant with the presence of God is to be found a secular hiatus in which God seems to have abandoned the affairs of the world to its inhabitants. It is in this lull between two eras of overt divine activity that Joseph, like his forbears a towering individual, finds himself deposited. Born into a secular world — a world not dominated by the presence of God — before the dawn of the Age of Peoples and Multitudes, and at the tail end of a Primal Age on the verge of disintegration, Joseph marks the epitome of the exaltation of the autonomous individual to a plane that is somehow higher than that reached by all subsequent individualisms.

And the author of this extraordinary work, no less than his hero into whom he breathed his spirit, may justly be called, in the words of Goethe, "a being of a higher order."[45]

NOTES

1. The only progression in Joseph's thinking that he reports remains in the physical realm: the extension of his concern for the preservation of life from the confines of his family to encompass the Egyptian people and the peoples of neighboring lands — commendable in and of itself yet still missing the spiritual dimension of a larger purpose.

2. See Chapter 13, note 41.

3. Genesis 17:1, God's central command to Abraham and his descendants.

4. We are not told of any such participation, and we have argued that the account we have been given indicates that Joseph kept his distance. See Chapter 11, and especially pages 159–160.

5. Samuel, 350. The kingdom here referred to is the United Kingdom created by David. Upon the death of his son, the kingdom broke apart, permanently dividing the children of Israel.

6. His deathbed instructions to his and his brothers' descendants to hold on to the hope that God would eventually redeem them from Egypt (what had Egypt become to them that their one hope was to escape it?) bespeaks a deep disappointment.

7. Jacob, by his manipulations in Paddan-aram, became extremely wealthy. As to Joseph, nothing needs to be said.

8. One of the prime tasks of upper-class Egyptians during the course of their adult lives was to prepare their burial arrangements. We have every reason to assume that as one of Egypt's elite, Joseph would do no less.

9. See Introduction, "When Did the Events Related in the Joseph Narrative Take Place?" (pages 11–13).

10. See Introduction, "When Was the Joseph Story Written?" (pages 13–16).

11. So Robert E. Park, the coiner of the phrase, "Introduction," in *The Marginal Man* by E. V. Stonequest (New York: Scribner, 1937), xv.

12. See Karl Mannheim, *Ideology and Utopia* (New York: Harcourt, Brace, 1936), especially page 7.

13. See Exodus 2:11–22.

14. Termed horizontal mobility by sociologists.

15. Park, xvii–xviii.

16. Wildavsky, 1.

17. See Chapter 11, note 48.

18. George Steiner, "A Preface to the Hebrew Bible," in *No Passion Spent: Essays 1978–1996* (London: Faber & Faber, 1996), 66.

19. Kass, 632, note 20.

20. Milgrom, *Leviticus 23–27*, 2,192.

21. The Jubilee (Hebrew *yovel*) was a cyclical sacred moment in time falling every fiftieth year; an interlude ordained by God and thus neither revocable nor circumventable. It commenced on the Day of Atonement (*Yom Kippur*) in that year and was proclaimed by a blast blown on the ram's horn (*shofar*). At that time all land returned to its legitimate owners or their heirs, and all slaves were set free. "Hebrew *yovel* means both 'ram' and 'ram's horn.' The fiftieth year is called 'Jubilee' because its advent is proclaimed by sounding the ram's horn" (Baruch Levine, *Leviticus* [Philadelphia: Jewish Publication Society, 1989], 172).

22. Leviticus 25:8–10.

23. Leviticus 25:23–24, 26–27.

24. Leviticus 25:25.

25. It is important to bear in mind that the land served more purposes than that of simply a source of agricultural production. One's ancestors were buried in one's landholding. This was one of the main motives for one's kin to repurchase the land from the purchaser. It was felt to be sacrilegious for the graves of one's family to pass out of the family.

26. The actual workings of the institution of redemption can be seen in Chapter 4 of the Book of Ruth (which chronicles the situation of the early eleventh century BCE) and in the thirty-second chapter of Jeremiah (the second decade of the sixth century BCE, the very end of the First Commonwealth).

27. Deuteronomy 33:1; Psalms 90:1.

28. Literally, "until the time of his word had come."

29. LXX, Syr., and Vulg. read "instruct."

30. The second son of Noah, and putative father of the Egyptian people (Gen. 10:6).

31. The Hebrew *ma'as* also has the sense of "despise, abhor."

32. In the only other mentions of Joseph in the Psalms, the descendants of Joseph are depicted as being redeemed at the Red Sea (77:15–17), while in Psalm 80 the term *Joseph* is used to depict the Northern Kingdom whose people God shepherds (v. 2); uses that are essentially neutral and from which we can learn little.

33. The "Testament of Naphtali," part of *The Testament of the Twelve Patriarchs*, composed, it would seem, during the last years of the reign of the Hasmonean king John Hyrcanus—109–106 BCE—purports to be the last will and testament of Naphtali, sixth son of Jacob. Its full Hebrew title is "The Testament of Naphtali, son of Jacob."

34. R. H. Charles, ed., *The Apocrypha and Pseudepigrapha of the Old Testament in English with Introductions and Critical Explanatory Notes to the Several Books* (Oxford: Clarendon, 1913), II: 363.

35. In Hebrew, *ha-Tzadik*, which, while usually rendered as "the Saint," is more properly an amalgam of the Just One, the Righteous One and the Saintly One.

36. The rabbis were not unaware of Joseph's multiple defects, but they usually found ways, some of them quite farfetched, to excuse them.

37. "One only speaks good of the dead."

38. Indeed, Yoram Hazony contends in his work, *The Dawn: Political Teachings of the Book of Esther* (Jerusalem: Genesis Jerusalem Press, 1995), that the Book of Esther, on one level, amounts to a "How-To" primer: instruction in the politics of communal and personal survival and success for minority ethnic groups.

39. The main hero, or rather heroine, of the tale is, of course, Esther. By the end of the book she has eclipsed Mordecai as the central figure of the little epic. This in no way detracts from Mordecai's suitability as a role model. See my *Four Biblical Heroines*, especially 178–187, for an analysis of the shifting centrality of the roles of Mordecai and Esther.

40. These legends, called *Midrashim*, would be used by preachers and teachers when expounding on the biblical text as a kind of commentary. In this way the text would be interpreted in the light of these stories. The classic compilation of these *Midrashic* expansions is Louis Ginsberg, *The Legends of the Jews* (Philadelphia: Jewish Publication Society of America, 1910–1946), vol. 2, to which the reader who desires concrete examples is referred. A summary of the rabbinic reading of the Joseph Story is given in the section, "Telling It Like It Is."

41. Ginsberg's terse retelling of the legendary material about Joseph invented by the rabbis covers more than one hundred pages.

42. Joseph's talebearing caused the rabbis real problems: in the rabbinic ethical system, talebearing and informing are major sins. Extreme ingenuity was required on their part to explain it away. Those who were unable to do so invented for Joseph a ten-year jail sentence where he could atone for his sin: one year for each brother he had slandered.

43. For example, it was God who had arranged for the merchants who bought Joseph to be carrying spices rather than some other cargo. This insured that Joseph was enveloped by sweet smells and did not have his delicate nostrils assaulted by the unpleasant odor of the camels. In Egypt small daily miracles insured that every task set Joseph by his master worked out exactly in accord with his master's expectations, etc.

44. The full quote, as reported by George Vertue, was, "I desire you would use all your skill to paint my picture truly like me and Flatter me not at all. But [pointing to his own face] remark all of these roughnesses, pimples, warts and everything as you see me. Otherwise I will never pay a farthing for it." All three warts were clearly delineated.

45. Goethe was referring to Shakespeare (Conversation with Eckerman, March 30, 1824).

Appendix 1

Who Sold Joseph into Egypt?

Why ever raise this question? The answer would seem obvious — Joseph's own brothers — but matters are not as simple as they may at first seem. Let us review the facts as they are presented in the text.

We begin with Joseph in the cistern and the brothers eating lunch. Seeing in the distance a caravan of Ishmaelites approaching on its way to Egypt (Dothan was a junction on an important caravan route leading to Egypt), Judah proposes to his brothers that they sell Joseph to the Ishmaelites rather than kill him. It appears that the brothers agree.[1] So far so good; it is at this point the problems begin.

> *Now some Midianite merchant men passed by, and* they *drew Joseph up and lifted him out of the cistern, and* they *sold Joseph to the Ishmaelites.... And* they *brought Joseph to Egypt* [Gen. 37:28, emphasis added].

Three times the pronoun *they* is repeated.[2] What is the subject of each of the respective verbs?

To begin with, who are the "they" who lifted Joseph out of the cistern? There are only three possibilities: the brothers, the Midianites and (a remote possibility to be sure) the Ishmaelites. Then who are the "they" who sell Joseph to the Ishmaelites? It would seem that whoever is the subject of the first pronoun is the subject of the second, so that the choice devolves upon either the brothers or the Midianites. Both choices present difficulties. If it is the brothers who draw Joseph out and sell him to the Ishmaelites, what part do the Midianites play? They seem superfluous.

We now face a further problem. After having been informed that the Ishmaelites, as purchasers of Joseph, bring him to Egypt, we are told a few verses later, "*Now the Midianites had sold him* [Joseph] *into Egypt, to Potiphar*" (37:36). So the Midianites do have a part to play, and on this reading they have somehow reacquired possession of Joseph and now sell him on the open market, one Potiphar being the purchaser. But wait, yet further problems surface: in 39:1 we are informed that it is the Ishmaelites, having taken Joseph down to Egypt, sell him to Potiphar.

There is one further problem to our making the brothers the subject of the action of lifting Joseph out of the cistern and selling him. Once the transaction has been completed and all the participants have dispersed, Reuben shows up and he is shocked to discover Joseph gone. He leaps to the conclusion that Joseph is dead, and tearing his clothes in mourning, he so informs his brothers. They do not disillusion him.

> *Now Reuben returned to the cistern and behold, Joseph was not in the cistern! And he rent his clothes and returned to his brothers and said, "The boy is gone! And as for me, where shall I go?"* [Gen. 37:29–30].

Where are the brothers when he rejoins them? And where was Reuben when his brothers were selling Joseph?[3] We are not told that he left them. What was he doing while the transaction was going on? The problems seem insuperable so let us explore the second option: that it was the Midianites who were the "they."

This reading assumes that the brothers, having thrown Joseph into the cistern, remove themselves from the vicinity to enjoy a quiet lunch elsewhere. We know that Joseph did not react to the violent treatment he was receiving with stoic silence.[4] A group of Midianite merchantmen passing on the same route, perhaps in the opposite direction to the approaching Ishmaelites, attracted by the screams and pleas emanating from the cistern, investigate, and drawing out Joseph sell him as a slave to the Ishmaelites. These proceed to carry him down to Egypt where they put him up for sale in the local slave market.

The advantages of this reading are that it explains Reuben's ignorance of the extraction and sale of Joseph, and also why the brothers seem to go along with the theory that a wild beast has killed and devoured Joseph.[5] The difficulties as to who sold Joseph to Potiphar remain.

Four solutions have been proposed to the conundrum of this ambiguous and confusing tale. The first is that of the ancients, followed by medieval commentators.[6] As they read the narrative, it is the brothers who pull Joseph out of the pit and sell him to the Midianites, who in turn sell him to the Ishmaelites. In this reading the Midianites served as middlemen in the transaction. This reading explains 37:36 to mean that the Midianites sold Joseph to Potiphar through the instrumentality of the Ishmaelites. This reading puts the full burden of guilt for selling their brother into slavery upon the brothers.

The second solution, favored by most modern commentators, is to reject the underlying assumption of both the ancients and of this study: that we are reading a unified narrative. These scholars claim that there originally existed two versions of the story, one in which the Midianites sell Joseph and it is Reuben who tries to save him, and the other in which it is the Ishmaelites who sell him, with Judah in the role of the putative savior. The redactor, unable to choose between them, used both and interwove them. It is this interweaving of two disparate tales that accounts for the ambiguities and the contradictions in the story we have today.[7] The main difficulty with this theory is that the redactor is posited to be either a literary incompetent or just plain stupid. It assumes that he was unable to see the contradictions he was building into the narrative, contradictions that have bothered readers from ancient times to the present. Considering the sophistication and brilliant construction of the narrative as a whole, this interpretation seems more than a bit naïve.

A third possibility is offered by Nahum Sarna. Basing himself upon Ibn Ezra, he postulates that "Ishmaelites" and "Midianites" are variant terms for one and the same group of people, "Midianite" being an ethnic designation while "Ishmaelite" has the connotation of "nomadic trader." The terms are, in the present context, roughly synonymous and are being used interchangeably.[8] In this reading it is the brothers who sell Joseph to the Ishmaelites-Midianites, and it is they that sell him to Potiphar.[9] Unanswered is the question of why Reuben is unaware of what happened, why the brothers don't correct his conclusion that Joseph is dead, and why Joseph later claims that he was kidnapped.

The fourth alternative is that proposed by Robert Sacks and seconded by Leon Kass.[10] In this reading the pronouns "they" in the phrase "Now some Midianite merchant-men passed by, and they drew Joseph up ... and they sold Joseph to the Ishmaelites" refers back to the Midianites. This actually makes much better grammatical sense than the other readings. Then the Ishmaelites put him up for sale in Egypt and Potiphar buys him. Interpreting the matter thus leads to understanding 37:36 to mean that the Ishmaelites serve as the middle men in the transaction, and that through them the Midianites sell Joseph to Potiphar. The advantages of this interpretation are that it explains Joseph's statement that he was kidnapped (40:15), an incongruous description of events if it was the brothers who were the sellers ("betrayed" or "sold by my family" would fit much better). It explains the shock of Reuben upon finding Joseph missing (37:29). It explains the continued belief on the part of the brothers that Joseph is dead (42:13). Finally, as Sacks puts it, "This explanation would also account for the fact that even after they repent the brothers never admit to selling Joseph."[11]

The basic obstacle to this view of the episode is that Joseph himself charges his brothers, not once but twice, with having sold him into Egypt (45:4–5). This requires us to understand Joseph's dramatic charge metaphorically: that it was the brothers who, by throwing Joseph into the cistern, began the process that led to his kidnapping and eventual sale in the Egyptian slave market.

This reading holds the brothers guilty of callous assault and vicious intention, but not of the actual implementation; the deed being effected by the Midianites and the Ishmaelites. While far from perfect, this reading seems to me the best of the alternatives, and I have based my understanding of the narrative on this reading.

But if this is the author's meaning, then why doesn't the author come right out and say it instead of writing in such an equivocal way? However, this very question can be asked at numerous points in the tale as a whole. Ambiguity seems to be built in to the way the story is written. It seems to be the intention of the author to constantly leave open the possibility of numerous interpretations of the events narrated. We can never be certain of the truth of the matter because we never know enough. But as in real life, because one has to act, one of necessity has to come to some conclusion, imperfect though it may be. So here, in writing this book, I have had to choose. And this choice, as well as many others I have been forced to make, will determine the direction this book will take and the conclusions that will be reached.

Notes

1. Literally the text states "and the brothers heard him," which could connote either acquiescence or simply that they pay attention to his remark. The word *heard* is ambivalent and does not necessarily indicate agreement.

2. In English translation the pronoun is a discrete word, in the original Hebrew we are referring to prefixes and suffixes that modify the verbs.

3. Kitchen proposes the following scenario: "[The text] suggests that Reuben had been absent from the first appearance of the caravan until it (and Joseph) had passed on.... Why should Reuben be absent? Of many possible reasons, the simplest is that when the foreign caravan was sighted, Reuben, the most conscientious of the brothers (and true to character), went off to mount guard among the sheep: passing foreigners could not be trusted not to filch a few choice animals. Reuben would have to wait till they had passed. By the time Reuben could safely return, Joseph was sold and gone" ("Joseph," 657). But all this is speculation; there is no hint of this in the text.

4. When they later reflect on their deed, the brothers state that Joseph had cried and pleaded with them from the depths of the cistern: "They said to one another, 'Surely we are guilty [or are being punished] on account of our brother, we saw the bitterness of his soul and we paid no heed when he pleaded with us; therefore this trouble has come upon us'" (Gen. 42:21).

5. The objection has been raised that had a wild beast killed and devoured Joseph, bones would have been left in the cistern. The absence of bones would decisively negate the theory of Joseph being killed. But this objection presumes that members of the cat family (the prime suspects) devour their prey at the point of kill. They usually don't; normally they carry the prey away and consume it elsewhere. People in those days knew this.

6. Genesis Rabbah 84:20; and, based on this, Rashi ad loc. See Glossary.
7. Westermann, 264–266; Speiser, 291–294; Alter, *Genesis*, 213–214; et al.
8. Ibn Ezra on Gen. 37:28. See Glossary. This theory is based on Judges 8:24 where Gideon, after having defeated the Midianites, asks as his share in the spoils of victory the golden earrings of the Midianites, "for they had golden earrings, because they were Ishmaelites." Here it is clear that Midianites is an ethnic designation while Ishmaelites is a term for nomads, a way of life. Kitchen is also of the opinion that the terms are synonymous and insists they are being alternated for stylistic variation, a usage common in the writing of the Ancient Near East. He brings an Egyptian example to demonstrate this usage ("Joseph," 657).
9. Sarna, *Genesis*, 260–263.
10. Sacks, 311–313; Kass, 523, note 19.
11. Sacks, 312.

Appendix 2

Can Judah and Tamar Be Fitted into the Joseph Narrative?

In many ways Genesis 38, the story of Judah and Tamar, seems an artificial intrusion into the Joseph saga. It breaks the flow of the narrative, as Genesis 39 (Joseph's travails beginning with his arrival in Egypt) follows directly upon Genesis 37 (the tale of Joseph's betrayal by his brothers and his sale to slave dealers who take him to Egypt). But while the various strands of the larger narrative may have been transmitted orally for centuries as separate stories, it has been demonstrated that the Saga of Joseph and his brothers as we know it today (Genesis 37–50) is the work of a single author, and that the story of Judah and Tamar fits in seamlessly as an integral part of the greater literary masterpiece.[1] This unity, however, poses a serious problem of chronology: too much seems to be packed into too few years.

Simply stated the problem is as follows: Joseph is declared to be 17 years of age at the time of his betrayal by his brothers (Genesis 37:2), and 30 years old when he becomes Viceroy of Egypt (41:46). As the descent of Jacob into Egypt and the reunification of the family there takes place after two years of famine (45:11), to the 13 years of Joseph's rise to power must be added the "seven years of plenty" and the first two years of the famine, making a total of, at the minimum, 22 years from the time Judah proposed Joseph's sale into slavery to the descent of the family, including Judah, into Egypt. Can all the events related in Genesis 38 — Judah's marriage, the birth of his three sons, their growth to maturity, the marriage of two of them to Tamar, their deaths, Tamar's return to her parent's home, her gradual discovery that she had been abandoned, her subsequent seduction of Judah, her pregnancy and the birth of her twin sons — can all this somehow be fitted into a mere 22 years? And if this were not difficult enough, we are informed that when the family migrated to Egypt, not only were Tamar's sons Perez and Zerah listed as part of the company, but her grandsons, Hezron and Hamul, are included in the list of the migrants as well (46:12)! This would seem to imply the passage of yet another generation before the descent into Egypt.

The real question here is: how could the author of the Joseph Saga not be cognizant of the impossibility of this simple calculation from the data that he himself has so carefully supplied? Or perhaps a better way of phrasing the question would be: how did he view the events so as to make it credible in his eyes to present the events he relates within the time frame he provides?[2]

Let us begin with the most serious problem: the inclusion of Tamar's grandsons, Hezron and Hamul, in the list of the migrants to Egypt. But wait a moment, *is* the list of names in Genesis 46:8–27 really a list of the persons who migrated with Jacob from Canaan to

Egypt? It includes the names of Er and Onan who died in Canaan (46:12 admits this fact). The list also includes Joseph's sons, Manasseh and Ephraim, who were born in Egypt and so were never part of the group that came to Egypt (46:20, 27). What we really have here is not a list of migrants but a list of the sons of Jacob who founded the tribes of Israel, and of their descendants who founded the clans that made up those tribes.[3] Umberto Cassuto has pointed out that the terminology used to introduce the names of Tamar's grandchildren is unlike that used to introduce everyone else except the sons of Joseph. His conclusion is that just as Joseph's sons were born in Egypt, so were Hezron and Hamul.[4]

Having disposed of Tamar's grandchildren in Genesis 46:12, we return to the events related in Genesis 38. Can all these events be credibly confined within the compass of twenty-two years? Both Cassuto and Sarna show that they can.[5] If Judah separated from his brothers, moved to Adullam and married in the same year that Joseph was sold into Egypt, and if his three sons were then born in rapid succession, then four years would more than suffice for this section of our chapter. Another fourteen years would be sufficient to bring Er to the marriageable age of sixteen. Assuming Er dies shortly after marriage, and Onan then married the widow, only to quickly follow his brother to the grave, we are talking of less than a year. If Tamar then waited two years until Shelah reached 16 years of age before realizing that she had been hung out to dry, we have covered a total of twenty years from the start of our tale. This leaves two years for Tamar to seduce Judah, give birth to twins, and they to be brought down to Egypt as infants.

The timing is tight but certainly possible. The author of the saga, as able to do the calculation as we, would know that the narrative as he penned it contained no inherent chronological impossibilities. Whether the events actually occurred as he described them is another matter, one that we have no way of knowing. Writing a minimum of six hundred years after the events he is depicting, he also would have had no way of knowing. All he could do was to rely on his sources[6] and so shape his narrative as to embody the messages he was trying to convey in the most elegant manner possible while avoiding internal contradictions and blatant impossibilities. In this he was brilliantly successful.

Notes

1. See Chapter 2, page 54, and especially notes 4 and 13 there. "Many readers have sensed this tale of Judah and Tamar as an 'interruption' of the Joseph story, or, at best, as a means of building suspense about Joseph's fate in Egypt. In fact, there is an intricate network of connections with what precedes and what follows" (Alter, *Genesis*, 217). "This digression heightens the reader's suspense at a critical moment in the Joseph narrative, but the skillful blending of the chapter into the larger story shows that the digression is deliberate and the result of careful literary design.... The present chapter, then, provides a foil to the Joseph-centered episodes" (Sarna, *Genesis*, 263–264).

2. We have to remember that the author was under no compulsion to set up a 22-year time frame. He could simply have kept quiet about how old Joseph was at each stage of the narrative, and so conceal the very existence of a problem. To go out of his way to give the relevant chronological information means that he saw no inherent difficulty in fitting the events he relates into the time frame he himself created.

3. Numbers 26:5–51 makes all this specific. The tribe of Judah is listed as made up of five clans. The first three are familiar to us: the clans founded by Shelah, Perez, and Zerah, the three surviving sons of Judah. But then, strangely, Er and Onan are also listed as sons of Judah. By rights they too should have founded clans, but "Er and Onan died in the land of Canaan" (v. 19). Who then takes their place? Judah's grandsons, the sons of Perez: Hezron and Hamul. They founded the clans of the Hezronites and the Hamulites (v. 21), thus insuring that Judah does not end up short two clans.

4. "The meaning of the passage in Genesis xlvi 12 ... now becomes self-evident in all its details: '*The sons of Judah: Er, Onan, Shelah, Perez and Zerah*,' that is to say, these five were born to Judah before he went down to Egypt; '*but Er and Onan died in the land of Canaan*,' that is, although these two sons were

not among those who emigrated to Egypt, nevertheless, '*there were the sons of Perez, Hezron and Hamul,*' who represented Er and Onan, and consequently retained their place among the sons of Judah. [Thus we] come to the conclusion that Hezron and Hamul did not emigrate to Egypt" (Cassuto, 38–39, italics indicating biblical quotation added. The lengthy analysis that leads to this conclusion begins on page 35).

5. Ibid., 39–40; Sarna, *Genesis*, 264–265.

6. "There is much in the narrative that testifies to great antiquity. Judah's wanderings take place in the border regions of the future tribe, not in its main area of settlement. He is not portrayed as a conqueror or even as a settler. He is still a pastoral nomad, not a city dweller. There is no hostility or tension between him and the Canaanites; later tradition would hardly have invented the uncomfortable account of a marriage to one. Thus the image of the tribe of Judah reflected here is, in general, not that of the post-conquest situation.... Finally, both the fact that no stigma is attached to what would, in later times, be the offspring of an incestuous marriage and the Narrator's need to offer an apologia for Judah's behavior ... combine to confirm an early date for the details of the action" (Sarna, *Genesis*, 264).

Appendix 3

What Is a Poem Doing in the Joseph Story?
The Testament of Jacob: Genesis 49

The "Testament of Jacob" is framed as a poem. As we remarked in chapter 12, the starting point for our discussion is the basic assumption that the poetry comprising Genesis 49, verses 2–27, is a unified composition.[1] The central problem that faces us is: why poetry? Why has a poem been intruded into a prose narrative? What function does its specific format fulfill?

There is widespread, indeed almost universal, agreement that the poem serves the purpose of foreshadowing, in a format reflecting prophetic oracle, the future condition of the tribes of Israel that will descend from their eponymous founders, the sons of Jacob/Israel. But at this point unanimity ends. Some commentators, notably those of the medieval and early modern period, accept Jacob as the poem's author. Considering him to have been graced with prophetic vision, they have no difficulty in ascribing to him the prediction of the future destiny of the tribes descended from his sons. The majority of modern commentators, on the other hand, see the situation reversed. They ascribe the origins of the poem to a time when the tribes had already taken on their definitive form. In this view the author of the poem has projected his contemporary situation into hoary antiquity, unhistorically attributing the authorship to the ancient patriarch, Jacob. The choice between these, as well as any other theory, will be dependent on our ability to date the poem's composition.

As we have said, there is general agreement that our poem belongs to one of the oldest strata of the Bible. Wenham goes so far as to state that "there is universal agreement that we are here dealing with one of the oldest parts of the Bible."[2] But then how old is "oldest"? Wenham then quotes Seebass' opinion that it "probably originated in the twelfth century,"[3] that is, the early part of the Age of the Judges. Others have pushed back the origins of the poem still further.[4] But attempts to definitively date it by means of orthographic analysis (essentially the spelling of the words) and that of syntax founder on issues inherent to the transmission of ancient texts: the tendency of scribes to constantly "modernize" ancient spellings and grammatical constructions.[5] So we are thrown back on an analysis of the contents.

When one turns to the content of the Testament, one cannot avoid being struck, first and foremost, by the incongruity of the depiction of Levi. He is painted as a vicious warrior with not the slightest hint of the sacerdotal functions which later typify the tribe. This would suggest a date of composition prior to the tribe of Levi assuming these functions. A comparison between the treatment of Levi in our poem and that of Levi in Deuteronomy

33:8–11, "The Blessing of Moses," which stresses these very sacerdotal functions and their historic origins, further emphasizes the antiquity of our composition.[6] All biblical traditions concur that the change in the status and the functions of the tribe of Levi took place under the leadership of Moses, whose tribe it was. This would imply that our poem antedates the Mosaic Period.

To my mind the most decisive evidence for dating the composition lies in the blatant ignorance displayed by the poet who authored these verses of the actual destinies of many, perhaps even the majority of the tribes. Most scholars, both those who see the poem in terms of prophecy and those who see it as a disguised description of current reality, have focused on finding ways, no matter how tortured and convoluted, to harmonize the content of our poem within an often recalcitrant reality. But these attempts fall far short of being uniformly convincing. The hard fact remains that the gap between the "future" depicted by father Jacob for his sons, and what actually happened to their descendants, is too wide to bridge.

We have already alluded to the incongruity of the depiction of the Levi in our poem with the future role of the tribe. The contradiction runs deeper: Levi is paired with the Simeon in our text, and cursed with division and extinction ("scattering"), yet their historic destinies bear little relation to this curse. Levi became the spiritually preeminent tribe, responsible for divine worship and serving as the repository of the Word of God in Israel.[7] Simeon, on the other hand, far from being scattered, merged with Judah to become part of a compact kingdom—one not riven by the intertribal dissension that so plagued the rival kingdom of Israel that emerged to its north.

Zebulun's future is depicted as maritime oriented, a coastal power incorporating a large part of Phoenicia. Yet the reality that emerged historically was that of a land-locked tribe with no access to the sea. Nor did the Phoenicians ever lose control of their coastline or their maritime dominance. Issachar is depicted as bovine in character, lethargic and materialistic, whose destiny is that of serfdom. Yet this depiction bears no relationship to the historical data at our disposal. Far from behaving like stolid serfs, Issachar was in the forefront of Deborah's national liberation movement which broke the armies of the Canaanite kingdom dominating all northern Israel.[8]

One could continue, but I believe that the point has been made. The vague phrasing and the poetic imagery of Genesis 49 cannot disguise, to one unencumbered by preconceived notions, that the poet had no actual knowledge of the real situation of early post-settlement Israel—the "Age of the Judges"—much less that of the Age of the Monarchy. This rules out any possibility of dating the composition of the poem to those periods; a contemporary could hardly have gotten things so blatantly wrong. It also puts paid to any notion of "prophetic powers" on the part of Jacob.[9] But beyond the implications for dating, this analysis calls into question the generally accepted reason for the composition of the poem.

I would therefore wish to propose an alternative theory to account for both the composition of the poem and the reasons for its inclusion in our narrative. My main premise, based primarily on the poet's ignorance of historical outcomes, is that the origin of the poem must be dated to pre–Mosaic times.[10] As noted in chapter 12, the poem must have antedated the composition of our narrative, perhaps by centuries, being transmitted orally until being reduced to writing probably no later than the Age of the Judges, and had become part of the cultural legacy of ancient Israel. Its attribution to the patriarch Jacob was accepted as self-evident. I propose that the author of our narrative had it before him when he composed the gripping tale of Joseph and his family that we have been examining.

I further propose that, from the start, he intended to use the poem as the climax to his dramatic narrative, and he designed the narrative to build up to the poem, consciously incorporating some of its terminology into his composition and providing background, so as to make some of the more obscure references in the poem understandable,[11] thus making the poem and the narrative dovetail.[12]

To summarize: I hold that the "Testament" or "Legacy of Jacob" which occupies most of chapter 49 of Genesis is an ancient poem, deriving from pre–Mosaic times. The poem is in the first person, the speaker being the patriarch Israel. Jacob's authorship is assumed and was unquestioningly accepted by ancient Israelites. This poem was very much a part of Israel's cultural heritage, and it may have served as a prime, possibly the prime inspiration for the composition of the Joseph saga. It certainly was deployed by the author to serve as the centerpiece of the narrative. And thus it would appear that it was the poem that in large part set the agenda for the story line of the Joseph narrative.

Notes

1. This view runs counter to the current majority of opinion which holds that these verses are nothing more then "a collection of tribal sayings ... it originated in an independent collection" (Westermann, 326). Von Rad is of the opinion that "it cannot be maintained at all ... that these aphorisms regarding Jacob's sons are a single and compact poem" (von Rad, *Genesis*, 416). But contra von Rad, this is exactly what I shall maintain. (I am not alone. Dillman, Gunkel, Seebass, Skinner, and Wenham also argue for the essential unity of the poem.) My reasons will become evident in the following discussion.
2. Wenham, 471.
3. Ibid., 470–471; Van Horst Seebass, "Die Stammespruche Gen 49:3–27," *ZAW* 96 (1984): 333–350.
4. For example Cross and Freedman: "It may be remarked that certain blessings, e.g. Reuben, Simeon and Levi, etc., may go back to patriarchal traditions" (Frank Moor Cross Jr. and David Noel Freedman, *Studies in Ancient Yahwistic Poetry*, SBL Dissertation Ser. 21 [Missoula, MT: Scholars, 1975], 70).
5. Cross and Freedman, Chapter 1. The most the authors can say is that the poem probably antedates the eleventh century and is possibly much older (6).
6. The poem in Deuteronomy reads as follows:

> "And of Levi he said:
> Let your Thummim and Urim
> Be with your faithful one,
> Whom you tested at Massah,
> Challenged at the waters of Meribah;
>
> Who said of his father and mother,
> 'I consider them not.'
> His brothers he disregarded,
> Ignored his own children.
>
> Your precepts alone they observed,
> And kept Your covenant.
>
> They shall teach Your laws to Jacob,
> And Your instructions to Israel.
> They shall offer You incense to savor
> And whole-offerings on Your altar.
>
> Bless, O Lord, his substance,
> And favor his undertakings.
> Smite the loins of his foes;
> Let his enemies rise no more" [Deut. 33:8–11].

7. The price of becoming the priestly tribe was the surrender of any territorial integrity. Persons ministering to the religious needs of a people must dwell with the people they serve and cannot be separated from them geographically. To depict this trade-off as a fulfillment of the "scattering" curse, as so many

commentators conclude, is shortsighted to say the least. Historically, the tribe of Levi was promoted to preeminence; in the trade-off that was involved they traded up.

8. See Judges 4–5.

9. Whatever the meaning of the term *prophet* in Genesis (as in 20:7), nowhere does the text apply this term to Jacob.

10. The revolutionary changes in the role of the tribe of Levi that took place in this period could hardly have been overlooked had a contemporary been the poem's author.

11. Specifically the background of Reuben's transgression (Gen. 35:22) and the rape of Dinah that gives context to Jacob's denunciation of Simeon and Levi (Gen. 34).

12. "It has rarely been noted how well the song dovetails into the larger story of Jacob, with *Leitworter* and motifs that link the song to earlier episodes in his life" (Ackerman, 109). In this observation Ackerman is undoubtedly correct but, in my estimation, he is wrong in attributing cause and effect. He assigns precedence to the narrative and assumes that it was the narrative that shaped the poem. I come to the opposite conclusion on the basis of simple chronological priority: as the poem predates the narrative, it is the poem that shaped the narrative.

Glossary of Terms and Place Names

*Words appearing in **bold** are themselves in the Glossary. Names appearing in italics are in the Who's Who in the Joseph Story section (following).*

Abel Mizraim The name given to **Goren ha-Atad** by the locals following *Joseph*'s prolonged lamentation there.
Adulam A **Canaanite** city about 13 miles southwest of Bethlehem.
Akhenaten The name that the **Pharaoh Amenophis** IV assumed to signal his exclusive devotion to the Aten, the sun-disc, to the exclusion of all other Egyptian gods, and his resolve to impose his radical theology on all Egypt.
Amenemhat I **Pharaoh**, founder of the Twelfth Dynasty, who established a royal residence in **Ro-wati** in the Eastern **Delta** somewhat prior to 1944 BCE, making it a part-time capital of Egypt. It was in **Ro-wati** that *Joseph* served one of his successors.
Amen-hotep A variant form of the royal name **Amenophis**.
Amenophis III The ninth **Pharaoh** of the Eighteenth Dynasty.
Amenophis IV See **Akhenaten**.
Apocrypha Literally, hidden or dubious [books]; 14 books never admitted into the canon of the Hebrew Bible, but included in the Vulgate or Catholic Bible.
Aramaic A Western-**Semitic language** spoken in the Ancient Near East from Syria to southern **Mesopotamia**; it is a sister language to **Hebrew**. Some parts of the Bible are written in Aramaic.
Athena Greek civic goddess, wise in industries of peace and the arts of war.
AV Authorized Version; the 1611 translation of the Bible, often called the King James Bible.
Avaris The name by which the **Hyksos** capital of **Hat-waret** was known to **Manetho**.
Baal Literally, "Lord," "Master." The title of Hadad, chief God of the **Canaanites**; he was a storm and fertility deity who was thought to die each summer and to be resurrected with the winter rains.
Babylonian Exile Sometimes known as the Babylonian Captivity. The historical period following the destruction of the Kingdom of Judah (586 BCE) during which the remainder of its population was removed from the land by the victorious Babylonians and resettled in **Mesopotamia**. This period is deemed to end with a proclamation by **Cyrus the Great** (538 BCE) allowing the Jews to return to their homeland.
BCE Abbreviation for Before the Common Era.
Beer-sheba A town approximately 45 miles southwest of Jerusalem and traditionally marking the southern extremity of the Land of Israel.

Bronze Age An archaeological term relating to the period in the Ancient Near East between approximately 3100 to 1200 BCE, the era when the main material used for tools and armaments was bronze. It was preceded by the Stone Age and followed by the Iron Age. It is usually divided into:

Early Bronze	3100 to 2100 BCE
Middle Bronze	2100 to 1550 BCE
Late Bronze	1550 to 1200 BCE

Canaan The name given by the Egyptians to the geographical region of their empire that eventually became known as the Land of Israel. Prior to the Israelite conquest it had been inhabited by various peoples and ethnic groups, and organized into independent city-states.

Canaanites One of the largest of the ethnic groups inhabiting the Promised Land prior to the Israelite conquest. Sometimes this term is used collectively for all the pre-conquest peoples.

Canon The collection or list of books which are received as genuine and inspired Holy Scripture.

Canonization The process by which the various books that now make up the Bible were accepted and certified as genuine and inspired Holy Scripture.

CE Abbreviation for Common Era.

Chezib Probably identical with the town of Achzib, a lowland town southwest of **Adulam**.

Commonwealth, First The six century historical period from the settlement of the Land of Israel until the destruction of Judah and the exile of its surviving inhabitants in 586 BCE This period is the heart of the Biblical Age.

Commonwealth, Second The historical period, comprising almost six centuries, beginning with the return from the **Babylonian Exile** in 538 BCE until the destruction of Jerusalem by the Romans in 70 CE. The first centuries of this period bring the Biblical Age to a close.

Concubine A marriage partner, but one of lower status than a wife.

Covenant, The Literally, "agreement," "treaty." Hebrew, *brit*. Originally, the agreement or contract between God and Abraham, pledging that Abraham's descendants will become a great people and will inherit the Promised Land in return for accepting the Lord exclusively and walking in His ways.

Cyrus the Great Cyrus II, the founder of the Persian or Achaemenian Empire, ruled from 559–530 BCE One of the greatest conquerors and rulers in recorded history; he is famous for having freed the Jews from the **Babylonian Exile**.

Davidic Empire The empire carved out by David stretching from the border of Egypt to the Euphrates River.

Delta The northernmost portion of the Nile River where it empties into the Mediterranean Sea; the alluvial tract of land at the mouth of the Nile.

Dothan Ancient fortress town less than 15 miles north of **Shechem**. It was here that *Joseph* was sold into Egypt.

Egypt A country located in the northeast corner of Africa; the oldest nation-state in the world.

Ephrath Another name for Bethlehem.

Etruscan Of or pertaining to ancient Etruria in Italy, its inhabitants, art, language or civilization.

Exodus 1. The second Book of the Bible.
2. The name given to the historic event of the liberation of the ancient Israelites from slavery, and their departure from Egypt.

Fathers, The The name given to the progenitors of the People of Israel: *Abraham, Isaac and Jacob/Israel.*

Genesis The first Book of the Bible, which includes the *Joseph* Story.

Gerar Principality in southwest Canaan peopled by Aegean Greeks (probably from Caphtor, i.e., Crete).

Geulah Redemption: the institution in ancient Israel that guaranteed that land would never be permanently alienated from its owner.

Goren ha-Atad The site on the way to Hebron where *Joseph* and his brothers halted for a seven day period of mourning before proceeding to bury their father.

Goshen The lush pasture land situated between the Egyptian border and the region of the capital, **Ro-wati**.

Haran Ancient city and the major commercial center located in northern **Mesopotamia** on the Balih River (a tributary of the Euphrates). It was in Haran that *Abraham* received his call.

Hat-waret The **Hyksos** capital during the period they ruled Egypt. It was called **Avaris** by **Manetho**. Hat-waret was situated on the site of the former Egyptian capital of **Ro-wati**.

Hazor Large city in the Upper Galilee, less than nine miles north of the Sea of Galilee and dominating the main north-south trade routes.

Hebrew A Western-**Semitic language** spoken in its various dialects by **Canaanites**, Moabites, Amonites, Edomites and **Phoenicians** among others. When the **Fathers** of the Israelites settled in **Canaan** they made the language their own. The Bible is largely written in Hebrew.

Hebron Ancient city about 20 miles south of Jerusalem. The burial place of **The Fathers** is located at Hebron.

Hieroglyphics The writing system of the ancient Egyptians consisting of pictures or symbols representing whole words, pictures or symbols representing syllables, and unpronounced signs (determinatives) indicating to what class of objects or actions the word belongs.

Hm Literally, "Majesty," a title referring to the human nature of the person holding it, thus, in practical terms, the **Pharaoh**'s body as distinct from his divine nature. See ***niswit***.

Hyksos The name by which the Semitic conquerors of Egypt were known. They ruled Egypt from the end of the Fourteenth Dynasty until the Eighteenth Dynasty.

Ibn Ezra, Abraham (1089–1164 CE). Medieval Spanish philosopher, poet, grammarian and Bible Commentator.

Intermediate Period, The First (2181–2133 BCE). The half-century of social collapse, chaos and foreign incursion brought on by the collapse of the **Old Kingdom**.

Intermediate Period, The Second (1786–1567 BCE). The term used to designate a time of social collapse and foreign domination following the disintegration of the **Middle Kingdom**.

Ishmaelites 1. Descendants of *Abraham* and his **concubine** *Hagar*.
2. Itinerant merchants.

Israelites The descendants of *Jacob/Israel*, otherwise known as the Children of Israel.

JPS The Jewish Publication Society of America 1917 translation of the Bible.

Jubilee The institution in ancient Israel that, every half-century, mandated the return of all landed property to its original owner and the freeing of all slaves.

Ka Egyptian term for the spirit, the personality and vitality of the individual (human or divine).

Kavod Honor; more properly, the God-endowed quality that distinguishes humans from other forms of life.

Kimchi, Rabbi David (c. 1160–1235 CE). Medieval French philologist, philosopher and biblical commentator; also known by his acronym Radak.

Lachish Ancient city about 30 miles southwest of Jerusalem.

Luz The original name of Beth-el.

Luzzato, Samuel David (1800–1865 CE). Italian scholar, Bible commentator philosopher and translator.

LXX Abbreviation for Septuagint, the ancient Greek translation of the Bible.

Maat Literally, "right order, justice, morality." The determination of what was *maat* and what wasn't was the prerogative of the **Pharaoh** who embodied *maat* and dispensed it.

Machpelah The term refers to both a field in the vicinity of **Hebron**, and to a cave within the perimeter of the field which *Abraham* purchased from one Ephron the Hittite to serve as a family sepulcher.

Manetho Third century BCE Egyptian priest who wrote the first systematic history of Egypt.

Masorites The term for the persons who, over the generations, were concerned with the precise preservation and transmission of the text of the Bible. The end product of the millennium-long endeavor is the current definitive text of the Hebrew Bible, known as the **Masoretic Text (MT)**.

Memphis (Noph) The capital of Egypt during the **Old Kingdom**, situated at the junction of Upper and Lower Egypt near present day Cairo.

Mesopotamia The name given to the region in the Near East watered by the Euphrates and Tigris rivers. The region today goes by the name of Iraq.

Middle Kingdom (2133–1786 BCE) The name given to the feudal reconsolidation of Egypt following the **First Intermediate Period**. During most of this time Egypt was ruled from **Thebes** (No-ammon).

MT Abbreviation for **Masoretic** Text, the standard **Hebrew** text of the Bible.

Nahmanidies See **Ramban**.

Narmer Egyptian king of Upper Egypt who conquered Lower Egypt at approximately 3100 BCE and unified the two kingdoms into one nation-state, known thereafter as "**The Two Lands**." As the first **Pharaoh** of unified Egypt, he was the founder of the First Dynasty.

Nefesh Often translated as "soul," this biblical term more accurately expresses the essence of one's life and animation.

New Empire, The (1567–1085 BCE) The name given to the age following the **Second Intermediate Period**, when Egyptian society reconstituted itself after the expulsion of the **Hyksos** and expanded out of the Nile basin, carving out an empire in Canaan and Syria.

NJPS The New Jewish Publication Society of America 1985 translation of the Bible.

Niswit Literally, "bearer of the office," a title referring to the divine nature of the Pharaohs. As *niswit* the Pharaoh was all the gods.

Nomarch The governor of a **Nome**.

Glossary of Terms and Place Names

Nome A term denoting an administrative district in ancient Egypt.

Novella A work of prose fiction, longer than a short story but shorter than a novel. The literary form was invented in Italy in the fourteenth century CE.

NT Abbreviation for New Testament.

Old Kingdom (2686–2181 BCE). The name which Egyptologists give to the period of the Third to Sixth Dynasties, the first great crystallization of Egyptian civilization. It is sometimes known as the Pyramid Age.

On The ancient center of the worship of **Re**, the Egyptian sun god, located approximately 7 miles northeast of present-day Cairo.

Osiris Egyptian god of the underworld and of the dead.

OT Abbreviation for Old Testament.

Paddan-aram The region in **Mesopotamia** in which the city of **Haran** was situated.

Peniel Site on the Jabbok River in the Trans-Jordan, a few miles from where it flows into the Jordan River. Here, in a night encounter, *Jacob*'s name was changed to *Israel* (Gen. 32:23–32).

Pentateuch The first five Books of the Bible; "The Five Books of Moses."

People of Israel Synonym for "Children of Israel" and "Israelites."

Pepi II Last **Pharaoh** of the Sixth Dynasty. With his death in approximately 2181 BCE, the **Old Kingdom** came to an end.

Pharaoh Literally, "Great House"; the official title of the king of Egypt.

Philistines An Aegean people, part of a coalition that invaded Egypt during the reign of Ramses III and, unable to conquer her, carved out a principality in southwest Canaan for themselves. They established themselves in Gaza, Ashdod, Ashkelon, Gath and Ekron.

Phoenicia The land area from present-day Acre northward fronting on the Mediterranean, including Western Lebanon. The Phoenicians were a mercantile people who developed a large commercial empire in the Mediterranean basin.

Pi-Ramesses Capital of Egypt from approximately 1295–1130 BCE, located in the Eastern Delta near the site of **Avaris**, the **Hyksos** capital.

Pseudepigrapha Dubious works purporting to have been authored by biblical characters.

Ramban Acronym for Rabbi Moses ben Nahman (1194–1270 CE), otherwise known as Nahmanides. Spanish philosopher, poet and biblical scholar, author of an extensive commentary on the **Pentateuch** and other books of the Bible.

Ramses II (1279–1213 BCE). Greatest **Pharaoh** of the Nineteenth Dynasty, considered by many as the "Pharaoh of the oppression."

Rashi Acronym for Rabbi Shlomo ben Isaac (1040–1105 BCE); probably the greatest of the medieval Jewish biblical commentators.

Re Egyptian god of the sun; the Pharaoh was believed to be the incarnation of Re or the son of Re.

Ro-wati Egyptian capital between 1970–1540 BCE, situated in the Eastern Delta.

RSV Revised Standard Version (1952) translation of the Bible.

Saite Referring to the rulers of the Twenty-Sixth Dynasty who ruled from Sais in the Western Delta.

Sam. Abbreviation for Samaritan Bible, the Samaritan text of the **Pentateuch** and Joshua.

Semitic Languages The language group that includes **Hebrew**, **Aramaic**, Akkadian and Arabic.

Sesostris III Fifth Pharaoh of the Twelfth Dynasty. Around 1860 BCE he expanded **Ro-wati** from an occasional Royal residence into the capital of Egypt.

Seth   Egyptian god of the desert and of evil. In Egyptian mythology he was the murderer of his brother **Osiris**.

Shechem   Ancient city about 50 miles north of Jerusalem.

Sheol   The Underworld; the realm of the dead.

Sidon   A major **Phoenician** port city about 25 miles north of **Tyre**.

Solomonic Enlightenment   The literary renaissance proposed by G. von Rad; beginning during the last years of the reign of *David* and continuing during the reign of his successor, *Solomon*. Several of the books of the Bible are likely to have been written during this period.

Sumerians   The founders of the earliest known civilization. It flourished in **Mesopotamia** and present-day Western Iran from before 3500 until 1750 BCE, when its remains were incorporated into the Babylonian empire by Hammurabi. The greatest accomplishment of the Sumerians was the invention of writing.

Syr.   Abbreviation for the Syriac translation of the Bible, called the Peshita.

Talmud   The 24 volume corpus of Jewish law, tradition and theology that provided the authoritative formulation of Rabbinic Judaism.

Targ.   Abbreviation of Targum, the Aramaic translations of the Bible.

Thebes   (No-ammon) The capital of Upper Egypt, and the capital of all Egypt during most of the **Middle Kingdom** and during the Eighteenth Dynasty.

Timnah   A Canaanite town southeast of **Hebron**.

Two Lands, The   The name by which Egypt was known to its own people.

Tyre   Major **Phoenician** port city in present-day south Lebanon, approximately 30 miles north of Haifa Bay.

United Monarchy   The name by which the political union created by *David* between the Kingdom of Judah and the Kingdom of Israel is known. It endured during the reign of *David* and his son *Solomon*.

Ur of the Chaldees   One of the greatest commercial centers of the ancient world; the birthplace of *Abraham*.

Vulg. or **Vul.**   Abbreviation for **Vulgate**. The translation of the Bible from Hebrew into Latin made by St. Jerome in Bethlehem, completed approximately 405 CE

Walls of the Ruler, The   The moat and line of forts securing Egypt's northeast frontier.

Ziggurat   Temple-topped pyramid typical of ancient **Sumerian** cities.

Who's Who in the Joseph Story

*(Including Some Who Have No Part in the
Tale But Are Nonetheless Mentioned in This Book)*

Words appearing in ***bold italics*** are entries in the Glossary (preceding). Names in *italics* are themselves in the Who's Who.

Above and beyond the human actors there is One who covertly dominates the entire Joseph Story and indeed, overtly, the entire Bible: known alternatively as God, the Lord, the Redeemer of Israel and Judge of Mankind, etc. His role in the Joseph Story is that of the Director of the entire drama as well as the Critic of how all the actors play their parts.

Aaron Older brother of *Moses*, first High Priest in Israel and founder of the priesthood.
Abel Son of the first human beings on earth; murdered by his older brother, *Cain*.
Abimelech King of the principality of **Gerar**; host to *Isaac*.
Abiram One of the chiefs of the tribe of *Reuben*. He and his brother *Dathan* were leaders of a rebellion against *Moses*.
Abraham The first of "The Fathers" of the people that will be known as the Israelites, later as the Jews, and devoted to founding and embodying a new way of life designed to bring blessing to humanity.
Abram The original name of *Abraham*. See *Abraham*.
Ahazuerus (Xerxes I) Persian king who occupies a central role in the Book of Esther.
Ahuzzath Holder of the office "Friend of the King" (i.e., royal advisor) to King *Abimelech* of **Gerar**.
Aper-el Semitic Grand Vizier of Egypt under ***Amenophis III*** and his son, ***Amenophis IV (Akhenaten)***.
Artaxerxes I Persian king (reigned 465–424 BCE).
Asenath Daughter of *Poti-phera*, priest of **On**; wife of Joseph and mother of *Manasseh* and *Ephriam*.
Asher Eighth son of Jacob; son of *Zilpah*, maid of *Leah* and concubine of *Jacob*.
Benjamin Youngest son of *Jacob*; son of *Rachel* who died giving birth to him.
Bethuel Son of Nahor, brother of *Abraham*, and father of *Rebecca*.
Bilhah Slave presented to *Rachel* as a wedding gift by her father *Laban* to serve as her personal servant. Presented by her mistress to *Jacob* as a concubine, to whom she bore *Dan* and *Naphtali*.
Cain First offspring of the first human beings and accounted as the initiator of violence

on earth: murderer of his brother *Abel*. He is also credited as the builder of the first city and thus the father of civilization.

Dan Fifth son of *Jacob*, born to *Bilhah*, maid of *Rachel*.

Dathan One of the chiefs of the tribe of *Reuben*. He and his brother *Abiram* were leaders of a rebellion against *Moses*.

David (c. 1032–962 BCE). Youngest son of *Jesse* of Bethlehem; warrior, liberator of his people from Philistine domination, statesman, empire-builder, king of Judah, king of Israel and conqueror of Jerusalem.

Deborah Judge, poet and prophetess; liberator of the Israelites from the domination of Yabin, king of **Hazor**.

Dinah Daughter of *Jacob* and *Leah*.

Ephraim Younger son of *Joseph* and *Asenath*.

Ephron the Hittite Resident of **Hebron** or the vicinity thereof, from whom *Abraham* purchased the field of **Machpelah** for use as a family burial site.

Er First-born son of *Judah*; husband of *Tamar*.

Esau Older twin brother of *Jacob*.

Gad Seventh son of Jacob, born of *Zilpah*, maid of *Leah*.

Hagar Slave of *Sarah*, presented to *Abraham* as a concubine. The mother of *Ishmael*.

Ham Second son of Noah; father of the Egyptians.

Haman Grand Vizier of the Persian Empire; initiator of a program to exterminate the Jews. The "villain" of the Book of Esther.

Hamul Son of *Perez*.

Hezron Son of *Perez*.

Hirah A friend of *Judah* resident in **Adulam**.

Isaac The second of "The Fathers." Son of *Abraham* and father of *Jacob*.

Ishmael Son of *Abraham* by his concubine *Hagar*.

Israel Alternative name of *Jacob*, bestowed on him upon his return to the Promised Land after an absence of almost two decades.

Issachar Ninth son of *Jacob*, born to *Leah*.

Jacob Son of *Isaac*, grandson of *Abraham*; father to twelve sons and one daughter. Due to his alternative name of *Israel*, his offspring and their descendants will become known as "The Children of Israel." The third and last of "The Fathers."

Jonathan Crown prince and heir apparent to the throne of his father King Saul; brilliant and charismatic military commander and devoted lifelong friend of *David*. Killed at the battle of Gilboa (c. 1003 BCE).

Joseph Eleventh son of *Jacob* and his father's favorite; born to *Rachel*; later Grand Vizier of Egypt.

Judah Fourth son of Jacob, born to *Leah*; ultimately accepted by his brothers as their spokesman and leader.

Keturah Concubine of *Abraham* and mother of Midian.

Korah Prominent Levite who spearheaded a rebellion against *Moses*.

Laban: Brother of *Rebecca* and father of *Leah* and *Rachel*, wives of *Jacob*.

Leah Wife of *Jacob* who bore him six sons—Reuben, Simeon, Levi, Judah, Issachar and Zebulun—and a daughter, *Dinah*. One of "The Mothers" of the Jewish People.

Levi Third son of *Jacob*, born to *Leah*.

Manasseh First born son of *Joseph* and *Asenath*.

Miriam Older sister of *Moses*.

Moses Prophet, lawgiver and liberator of the Israelites from Egyptian bondage; the most important single personage in all Israelite history.
Mut-em-enet Thomas Mann's invented name for "Mrs. *Potiphar*" in his novel *Joseph and His Brothers*.
Naphtali Sixth son of *Jacob*, born to *Bilhah*, maid of *Rachel*.
Nehemiah High official during the reign of *Artaxerxes I*. Appointed governor of the province of Yehud (Judea), he was responsible for fortifying Jerusalem and stabilizing the security of the province.
Onan Second son of *Judah*; husband of *Tamar*, *Er's* widow.
Perez Son of *Judah* and *Tamar*; ancestor of *King David*.
Potiphar High official in charge of Egyptian prisons and (probably) state security. Purchaser of *Joseph*.
Poti-phera High Priest of **Re** at his shrine of **On**; father of *Asenath* and father-in-law of *Joseph*.
Rachel Favorite wife of *Jacob*; mother of *Joseph* and *Benjamin*. One of "The Mothers" of the Jewish People, and the only one not buried in the Cave of **Machpelah**, the family sepulcher.
Ramses II Egyptian king (reigned c. 1290–1224 BCE). Probably the Pharaoh of the oppression.
Rebecca Wife of *Isaac*, mother of *Jacob* and *Esau*.
Reuben First-born son of *Jacob*, whose mother was *Leah*. The presumptive leader of his generation due to his place in the birth order, he forfeits his position due to his lack of leadership ability and his general ineptness.
Sarah First of "The Mothers" of the Jewish People. Wife of *Abraham* and mother of *Isaac*.
Shelah Third son of *Judah*.
Shua Canaanite father of *Judah's* wife.
Simeon Second son of *Jacob* and *Leah*.
Solomon Son of *David*; king of Israel and Judah (reigned c.961–922 BCE).
Tamar *Judah's* daughter-in-law and mother to his two sons, *Perez* and *Zerah*. Ancestress to *King David*.
Terah Father of *Abraham*.
Zaphenath-paneah *Joseph's* Egyptian name.
Zebulun Tenth son of *Jacob*, born to *Leah*.
Zerah Son of *Judah* and *Tamar*.
Zilpah Slave woman presented to *Leah* as a wedding gift by her father *Laban* to serve as her personal maid servant. Presented by her mistress to *Jacob* as a concubine. She bore him *Gad* and *Asher*.
Zuleika Name invented by an ancient rabbi for "Mrs. *Potiphar*."

Bibliography

Ackerman, James S. "Joseph, Judah and Jacob." In *Literary Interpretations of Biblical Narratives*, edited by K. R. R. Gros Louis and J. S. Ackerman, II, 85–113. 2 vols. Nashville: Abingdon, 1982.
Alter, Robert. "A Literary Approach to the Bible." *Commentary* 60, no. 6 (1975): 70–77.
———. *The Art of Biblical Narrative*. New York: Basic, 1981.
———. *Genesis: Translation and Commentary*. New York: W. W. Norton, 1996.
Brueggermann, Walter. "Genesis L 15–21: A Theological Exploration." In *Congress Volume: Salamanca, 1983*, edited by J. A. Emerton, *VTS* 36. Leiden: E. J. Brill, 1985.
Bury, J. B. *The Ancient Greek Historians*. New York: Dover, 1958.
Caine, Ivan. "Numbers in the Joseph Narrative." In *Jewish Civilization: Essays and Studies, Volume I*, edited by Ronald A. Brauner, 3–17. Philadelphia: Reconstructionist Rabbinical College, 1979.
Cassuto, Umberto. "The Story of Tamar and Judah." In *Biblical and Oriental Studies*, vol. 1. Translated by Israel Abrahams. Jerusalem: Magnus, 1975.
Charles, R. H., ed. *The Apocrypha and Pseudepigrapha of the Old Testament in English with Introductions and Critical Explanatory Notes to the Several Books*. 2 vols. Oxford: Clarendon, 1913.
Cross, Frank Moor Jr., and David Noel Freedman. *Studies in Ancient Yahwistic Poetry*. SBL Dissertation Ser. 21. Missoula, MT: Scholars, 1975.
Dahood, M. J. "MKRTYHM in Genesis 49,5." *CBQ* 23 (1961): 54–56.
———. "Northwest Semitic Notes on Genesis." *Biblica* 55 (1974): 76–82.
Davidson, A. B. *The Book of the Prophet Ezekiel*. Cambridge Bible for Schools and Colleges, 22. UK: Cambridge University Press, 1906.
de Hoop, Raymond. *Genesis 49 in Its Literary and Historical Context*. Leiden: Brill, 1999.
Diamond, Jared. *Guns, Germs and Steel: The Fates of Human Societies*. New York: W. W. Norton, 1999.
Diodorus of Sicily. *Bibliotheca Historica*. Various editions.
Dor-Shav, Ethan. "Soul of Fire: A Theory of Biblical Man." *Azure* 22 (Autumn 2005): 78–113.
Dostoyevsky, Fyodor. *The Brothers Karamazov*. Numerous editions.
Driver, S. R. *The Book of Genesis*. 3rd ed. London: Methuen, 1904.
Eliot, T. S. "Hamlet and His Problems." In *The Sacred Wood: Essays on Poetry and Criticism*, 4th ed., 95–103. London: Methuen, 1934.
Fagan, Brian. *The Great Warming: Climate Change and the Rise and Fall of Civilizations*. New York: Bloomsbury, 2008.
Feder, Avraham H. *Torah Through a Zionist Vision*. 2 vols. Jerusalem: Gefen, 2008.
Frankfort, H., H. A. Frankfort, J. A. Wilson, T. Jacobson. *Before Philosophy: The Intellectual Adventure of Ancient Man*. Harmondsworth, UK: Penguin, 1949.
Ginsberg, Louis. *The Legends of the Jews*. 7 vols. Philadelphia: Jewish Publication Society of America, 1910–1946.
Good, Edwin M. "The 'Blessing' on Judah, Gen. 49:8–12." *JBL* 82 (1963): 427–432.
Gooding, David W. "An Approach to the Literary and Textual Problems in the David-Goliath Story." In *The Story of David and Goliath: Textual and Literary Criticism*, edited by D. Barthelemy, D. W. Gooding, J. Lust, and E. Tov. Gottingen: Vandenhoeck und Ruprecht, 1986.
Gordis, Robert. *The Book of God and Man: A Study of Job*. Chicago: University of Chicago Press, 1965.
Greenberg, Moshe. *Ezekiel 21–37*. The Anchor Bible, 22A. New York: Doubleday, 1997.
Gunkel, Hermann. *Genesis*. Translated from German by Mark E. Biddle. Macon, GA: Mercer University Press, 1997.
Hamilton, Victor P. *The Book of Genesis: Chapters 18–50*. Grand Rapids: Eerdmans, 1995.
Haran, Menachem. "Book-Scrolls in Israel in Pre-Exilic Times." *Journal of Jewish Studies* 33 (1982): 161–73.

———. "Scribal Workmanship in Biblical Times." *Tarbiz* 50 (1980–1981): 65–87.
Hazony, David. "Plowshares into Swords: The Lost Biblical Ideal of Peace." *Azure* 3 (Winter 1988): 90–119.
Hazony, Yoram. *The Dawn: Political Teachings of the Book of Esther*. Jerusalem: Genesis Jerusalem Press, 1995.
Herodotus. *Histories*. Various editions.
Hoffmeier, James K. *Israel in Egypt: The Evidence for the Authenticity of the Exodus Tradition*. New York: Oxford University Press, 1996.
Humphreys, W. Lee. "Novella." In *Saga, Legend, Tale, Novella, Fable: Narrative Forms in Old Testament Literature*, edited by G. W. Coats, 82–96. London: Sheffield Academic Press, 1985.
Johnson, Paul. *The Civilization of Ancient Egypt*. London: Seven Dials, 2000.
Kass, Leon. *The Beginning of Wisdom: Reading Genesis*. New York: Free Press, 2003.
Kikawada, Isaac M., and Arthur Quinn. *Before Abraham Was: The Unity of Genesis 1–11*. Nashville: Abingdon Press, 1985.
King, P. J., and L. E. Stager. *Life in Biblical Israel*. Louisville: Westminster John Knox Press, 2001.
Kitchen, K. A. *The Bible in Its World: The Bible and Archaeology Today*. Eugene, OR: Wipf & Stock, 1977.
———. "Joseph." In *The New Bible Dictionary*, edited by J. D. Douglas, 656–660. Grand Rapids: Eerdmans, 1962.
———. *On the Reliability of the Old Testament*. Grand Rapids: Eerdmans, 2003.
———. "Review of Redford, *A Study of the Biblical Story of Joseph* (1970)." *Oriens Antiquus* 12 (1973): 233–243.
Levine, Baruch. *Leviticus*. JPS Torah Commentary. Philadelphia: Jewish Publication Society, 1989.
Mann, Thomas. *Joseph and His Brothers*. 4 vols. Translated from German by H. T. Lowe-Porter. New York: Alfred A. Knopf, 1935, 1938, 1943.
Mannheim, Karl. *Ideology and Utopia: An Introduction to the Sociology of Knowledge*. Translated from German by Louis Wirth and Edward Shils. New York: Harcourt, Brace & World, 1936.
Mathews, Kenneth A. *Genesis 1–11:26*. The New American Commentary, vol. 1A. Nashville: Broadman & Holman, 1996.
———. *Genesis 11:27–50:26*. The New American Commentary, vol. 1B. Nashville: Broadman & Holman, 2005.
Menn, Esther M. *Judah and Tamar (Genesis 38) in Ancient Jewish Exegesis: Studies in Literary Form and Hermeneutics*. New York: Brill, 1997.
Milgrom, Jacob. *Leviticus 1–16*. The Anchor Bible, C3. New York: Doubleday, 1991.
———. *Leviticus 17–22*. The Anchor Bible, C3A. New York: Doubleday, 2000.
———. *Leviticus 23–27*. The Anchor Bible, C3B. New York: Doubleday, 2000.
———. *Numbers*. JPS Torah Commentary. Philadelphia: Jewish Publication Society, 1990.
Millgram, Hillel I. *Four Biblical Heroines and the Case for Female Authorship: An Analysis of the Women of Ruth, Esther and Genesis 38*. Jefferson, NC: McFarland, 2008.
———. *The Invention of Monotheist Ethics*. 2 vols. Lanham, MD: University Press of America, 2010.
Moran, W. L. "Gen. 49,10 and Its Use in Ez. 21,32." *Biblica* 39 (1958): 405–425.
O'Brien, Mark A. "The Contribution of Judah's Speech, Genesis 44:18–34, to the Characterization of Joseph." *CBQ* 59 (1997): 429–447.
Park, Robert E. "Introduction." In E. V. Stonequist, *The Marginal Man*, xii–xviii. New York: Scribner's Sons, 1937.
Pirson, Ron. *The Lord of Dreams: A Semantic and Literary Analysis of Genesis 37–50*. London: Sheffield Academic Press, 2002.
Podhoretz, Norman. *The Prophets: Who They Were, What They Are*. New York: Free Press, 2002.
Redford, D. B. *A Study of the Biblical Story of Joseph (Genesis 37–50)*, (VTS 20). Leiden, E. J. Brill, 1970.
Rendsberg, G. A. *The Redaction of Genesis*. Winona Lake, IN: Eisenbrauns, 1986.
Robinson, Ira. "*Bepetah Enayim* in Genesis 38:14." *Journal of Biblical Literature* 96 (1977): 569.
Rosenberg, Joel. "Meanings, Morals, and Mysteries: Literary Approaches to the Torah." *Response* 9:2 (Summer 1975): 67–94.
Ryle, Herbert E. *The Book of Genesis*. The Cambridge Bible. UK: Cambridge University Press, 1914.
Sacks, Robert D. *A Commentary on the Book of Genesis*. Lewiston, NY: Edwin Mellen, 1990.
Samuel, Maurice. "The Brilliant Failure." In *Certain People of the Book*, 299–363. New York: Alfred A. Knopf, 1959.
Sarna, Nahum M. *Exodus*. JPS Torah Commentary. Philadelphia: Jewish Publication Society, 1991.
———. *Genesis*. JPS Torah Commentary. Philadelphia: Jewish Publication Society, 1989.

Seebass, Van Horst. "Die Stammespruche Gen 49:3–27." *ZAW* 96 (1984): 333–350.
Skinner, John. *The Book of Ezekiel.* The Expositor's Bible. London: Hodder and Stoughton, 1895.
———. *A Critical and Exegetical Commentary on the Book of Genesis.* 2nd ed. Edinburgh: T. & T. Clark, 1930.
Soggin, J. A. "Notes on the Joseph Story." In *Understanding Poets and Prophets: Essays in Honour of George Wishart Anderson,* edited by A. Graeme Auld, 336–349. London: Sheffield Academic Press, 1993.
Speiser, E. A. *Genesis.* The Anchor Bible. Garden City, NY: Doubleday, 1985.
Steiner, George. "A Preface to the Hebrew Bible." In *No Passion Spent: Essays 1978–1996,* 40–87. London: Faber & Faber, 1996.
Sternberg, Meir. *The Poetics of Biblical Narrative.* Bloomington: Indiana University Press, 1987.
Tigay, Jeffrey H. *Deuteronomy.* JPS Torah Commentary. Philadelphia: Jewish Publication Society, 1996.
Turner, Laurence A. *Announcements of Plot in Genesis.* London: Sheffield Academic Press, 1990.
von Rad, Gerhard. *Genesis.* Translated by D. M. G. Stalker. Philadelphia: Westminster, 1972.
———. "The Joseph Narrative and Ancient Wisdom." Translated from "Josephsgeschichte und Altere Chokma." In *Studies in Ancient Israelite Wisdom,* edited by J. Crenshaw. New York: Ktav, 1976.
———. *Old Testament Theology.* 2 vols. Translated by D. M. G. Stalker. New York: Harper, 1962, 1965.
Wellhausen, Julius. *Prolegomena to the History of Ancient Israel.* Translated from German by Black and Menzies. New York: Meridian, 1957.
Wenham, Gordon J. *Genesis 16–50.* World Biblical Commentary, vol. 2. Dallas, TX: World, 1994.
Westermann, Claus. *Genesis: A Practical Commentary.* Translated by David E. Green. Grand Rapids: Eerdmans, 1987.
Wildavsky, Aaron. *Assimilation versus Separation: Joseph the Administrator and the Politics of Religion in Biblical Israel.* New Brunswick, NJ: Transaction, 1993.
Woolley, Sir Leonard. *Ur of the Chaldees: A Record of Seven Years of Excavation.* Revised ed. Harmondsworth, UK: Penguin, 1952.

Scriptural Index

This book contains the entire text of Genesis 37–50. Specific verses can be located in their sequential order. All other references to biblical verses, including those additional citations from Genesis 37–50 that are not in sequential order, are listed below. The order of the books follows that of the Hebrew Bible.

Genesis
1:2 $51n23$
1:22 $38n4$
1:28 $38n4$
1:29 $51n23$
2:19f $94n4$
4:17–26 32
6:11 32
8:22 204
10:6 $219n30$
11:8 $38n9$
12:1–3 34
12:2–3 $195n41$
12:3f 199
12:5 $39n20$
12:7 34, 199
12:10–20 37, 137
12:7 34
15:5f $39n23$
15:6 34
15:7 $39n16$
15:7–14 136
15:11 $86n28$
15:13 137, $156n4$
15:13f 192
15:17f 136
17:1 36, $218n3$
17:4f $147n10$
17:5 $39n12$
17:9–14 $40n29$
18:1 $148n43$
18:19 36, 43
18:22f 125
18:25 125
18:31f 125
19:11 $156n8$
20:1–18 $147n12$
20:7 231
22 $64n6$
22:2 46
22:7 46
22:11–13 135
22:15–18 36
22:18 $195n41$
24:3f $65n14$
25:7f $149n60$
26:1–22 $147n12$
26:2f $147n16$
26:3–5 199

26:6–11 $40n31$
26:8 $75n36$
26:25 $147n15$
26:26 $67n57$
26:31 $193n2$
27:28f $168n35$
28:1f $65n15$
28:3f $168n35$
28:12–15 $51n25$, $196n65$
28:13f $167n11$, $195n41$, 199
28:13–21 $74n12$
29:17, 30 162
30:1f $168n25$
30:2 $194n38$
30:14 $67n55$
31:10f $51n25$
31:10–13 44, $196n65$
31:19 162
31:30–35 162
32:22–33 $23n5$
32:23–33 $51n19$, $179n18$
34 $168n47$, $231n11$
34:1–31 $67n54$
34:7 $168n39$
34:25–29 $179n26$
34:25–31 $119n2$
34:27–29 108
35:2 $50n11$, $168n25$
35:6f $167n12$
35:9–12 43, $167n12$
35:9–15 $51n19$
35:10–12 $168n36$
35:10–15 $179n18$
35:16–20 162
35:22 $52n32$, $67n54$, 172, $179n18$, $231n11$
35:27f $50n2$
35:28f $149n60$
37:2 $148n35$, 202, 225
37:3 98
37:4 43, 130
37:5–11 203
37:7 $196n61$
37:7–10 190
37:8 147
37:9f $166n3$, $196n61$
37:11 $64n6$
37:12 98
37:12–16 203

37:13 46
37:14 46
37:21f $65n22$, $132n2$
37:21–24 203
37:26f 203
37:28 $107n37$, 221
37:29 223
37:29f 221
37:32 $67n43$
37:35 $n13$
37:36 221
38: $147n2$
38:17f 111
38:26 $67n46$
39:1 $65n13$, $147n2$, 221
39:2 129, $205n4$
39:6 $167n24$
39:21 129, $206n4$
39:23 $206n4$
40:3 $53n59$
40:5 $51n24$
40:14f $95n12$
41:15 $51n24$
41:41–44 184
41:46 225
41:47–49 $156n10$
42:13 $53n58$, 223
42:21 114, $223n4$
42:22 123
42:30, 33 $119n3$
43:26 190
43:27f $132n23$
43:28 190
43:32 $149n50$
44:14 124
44:19, 23 110
44:33 135
45:3 187
45:4f 187, 223
45:5 198, 200
45:7 187, 198
45:8 200
45:11 225
45:14f $193n7$
45:20 142
45:28 138, $149n46$
46:1–4 $205n2$
46:2–4 $196n65$
146:4 $148n36$, 186

247

46:5 147n13
46:8–27 225
46:12 67n59, 225, 226
46:20 226
46:20 226
46:27 226
46:29 183
46:30 149n46, 183
47:6 156n21
47:27 147
48:5 180n34
48:21 38n11, 171, 192
49:8 190
49:18 206n4
49:23 194n30
49:26 209
49:28 193n2
50:17 188
50:18 196n61
50:20 199, 201, 206n9

Exodus
1:1 148n26
1:8 209
1:16–21 75n36
2:11–22 218n13
3:4 147 n 22
4:25 178n26
7:14 156n8
10:9 193n22
13:5 38n11
22:25 51n23
24:13 74n6
30:12 86 n 26

Leviticus
1:3 39n25
19:18 194n37
20:10 66n42
25:8–10 218n22
25:23f 219n23
25:25 218n24
25:26f 219n23

Numbers
1:2, 49 86n26
2:3–10 179n25
4:2, 22 86n26
12:2 179n23
12:6 127
13:22 50n1
13:32 50n8
14:36f 50n8
16:1–3 179n25
26:5–51 226n3
26:12 148n27
26:15 148n32
26:16 148n33
26:24 148n31
26:38–41 148n36
31:26, 49 86n26
34:11 168n43
34:25f 180n42

Deuteronomy
1:8 38n11
6:18 38n11
7:9 25n30
9:5 38n11
10:15 38n11
12:2f 25n30
13:2 189
16:22 25n30
18:10, 12 189
18;13 39n25
22:21 66n42
25:5f 56
25:7, 10 65n18
26:5 145
29:12 38n11
32:35 194n37
33 178n1
33:1 219n27
33:8–10 229, 230
33:18 180n42

Joshua
15:8, 10f 168n43
15:44 64n9
15:557 66n30
18:12f 168n43
19:10–17 180n42
24:3 38n11
24:14 39n25

Judges
4–5 231n8
5:15f 179n25
7:13 51n24
8:24 53n50, 224n8
19–21 181n53

1 Samuel
1:17 51n23
1:24 51n23
1:27 51n23
2:13 51n23
2:28 51n23
4:7 194n29
7:2 66n28
7:7 194n29
16:22 95n23
20:25 85n3

2 Samuel
13:18 51n15
14:20 75n24
16:16 149n58
23:3 120n18

1 Kings
1:2 95n23
1:31 149n58
3:26 121n37
6:15 74n6
25:8 53n59

Isaiah
11:14 168n43
59:21 31

Jeremiah
17:10 101

Ezekiel
19 180n37
21:32 180n37
34:25 53n56

Hosea
4:13 25n30

Jonah
2:7 148n21

Micah
1:14 64n9

Nahum
1:2 194n37

Zephaniah
3:9 168n44

Psalms
18:3, 32, 47 120n18
45:18 180n35
49:19 180n35
77:15–17 219n32
78:67f 213
80:2 219n32
90:1 219n27
92:16 120n18
94:1 194n37
105:16–23 213
123:1f 74n19

Proverbs
16:9 197

Job
36:28 195n42
40:14 180n35

Ruth
2:13 195n43
4:12 62
4:18–22 62

Esther
2:7 167n24

Daniel
2:3, 5 51n24

Nehemiah
2:1 85n3
9:7 39n16

1 Chronicles
4:24 148n28
7:1 148n30, n31
7:6 148 n 36
8:1f 148n36

Pseudepigrapha
Naftali
7:4–6 213

General Index

Aaron 133
Abel 32, 95
Abomination 114, 121, 142, 149, 172
Abraham 6, 12, 15, 25, 26, 33, 34, 36–40, 43, 46, 49, 52, 55, 69, 74, 86, 91, 95, 100, 101, 125, 129, 135–139, 145, 147–149, 154, 158, 160, 161, 163, 164, 165, 167, 169, 178, 181, 182, 185, 188, 191, 192, 196, 198, 199, 201, 205, 208, 217, 218
Achzib 64, 97, 135
Ackerman, James 106, 147, 231
Adam 32, 95
Adullam 55, 63, 64, 226
Ahasuerus 52
Akedah 46, 64
Akhenaten 91, 93, 94, 156
Akh-en-aten *see* Akhenaten
Akkadian language 51, 53, 120, 179
Albright, W.F. 24
Almighty 120, 163, 167, 169, 181; *see also* Shaddai
alphabet 17, 18, 26, 28
Alter, Robert 8, 24, 28, 53, 54, 59, 66, 147, 168, 180, 224, 226
ambiguity 41, 67, 71, 95, 133, 166, 194, 202–204, 213, 222, 223
ambition 44, 71, 76, 88, 195, 217
ambivalence 71, 126, 132
Amen-hotep IV 89, 93; *see also* Amenophis IV
Amenophis IV 91, 156
Amos, Book of 31
The Ancient Greek Historians 24
Ancient Near East 8, 12, 16, 17, 23, 24, 40, 42, 52, 66, 71, 77, 83, 120, 147, 189, 224
Aramaic 23, 27
Asenath 89, 92, 139
Asher 51, 139, 176
assimilation 16, 87, 101, 142, 162, 163, 211
Avaris 12, 29, 146

Baal 12
Babylonian Exile 27
Baker, Chief 77, 79, 80, 85
Beer-sheba 50, 137, 138, 147, 180, 186, 196, 205
The Beginning of Wisdom 2, 38
Benjamin 6, 51, 63, 97, 100, 103–126, 129–132, 135, 139, 142, 146, 148, 176, 178, 181, 186, 190, 193–195, 205
Beth-el 160, 167, 196
Bethlehem 64, 161, 162
The Bible in Its World 25, 27
The Biblical Age 7, 10, 11, 16, 40, 145, 179, 197
Bilhah 42, 50, 51, 139, 148, 170, 172, 176, 178, 179, 202
biological determinism 164
birthday 79, 81, 82, 86
blessing 32–34, 37, 38, 40, 43, 47, 62, 68, 69, 104, 120, 136, 144, 145, 147, 149, 159, 160, 163, 164, 168, 174, 177, 178, 181, 188, 193, 194, 199, 206, 208
Boaz 62, 195
Boccaccio, Giovanni 24
The Brothers Karamazov 54
Brueggermann, Walter 195
Bury, J.B. 11, 24

Cain 32, 95
Caine, Ivan 155, 157
Canaan 17, 25, 26, 29, 34, 41, 42, 44, 49, 52, 64, 71, 78, 88, 92, 93, 99, 101, 104–106, 109, 117, 120, 126, 130, 131, 133–138, 142, 143, 147, 151, 156, 160, 167, 181, 182, 184–186, 194, 196, 200, 210, 212, 217, 225, 226
Canaanites 12, 17, 27, 29, 51, 55, 56, 59, 61, 62, 64–66, 108, 135, 139, 185, 188, 198, 227, 229
canonization 23
Cassuto, Umberto 65, 226, 227
cat-and-mouse 72, 100, 102, 115, 117, 132, 190, 178
Chezib 55; *see also* Achzib
Children of Israel 7, 139, 148, 171, 177, 208, 209, 218
Chosen People 138, 166
civilization 7, 19, 28, 32, 34, 38
The Civilization of Egypt 29
close reading 1, 8
coat of many colors *see* robe of many colors
command economy 93
consent of the governed 174, 175, 190
The Covenant 7, 31, 36, 40, 41, 43, 86, 95, 136, 147, 155, 211

Cupbearer, Chief 77–82, 85, 200
Cyrus the Great 23

Dahood, M.J. 66, 86, 179, 180, 181
Dan 51, 139, 148, 168, 176, 180
David 6, 13, 25, 62, 168, 174, 206, 210
Davidic Empire 13
death 6, 13, 20, 28, 38, 42, 47, 49–53, 56, 58, 59, 62, 64, 70, 77, 97, 104, 110, 117, 121, 126, 132, 137, 142, 144, 148, 149, 159, 161, 162, 183, 185, 186, 188, 189, 191, 193, 196
the Delta 12, 19, 24, 86, 133, 142, 146, 148
determinatives 17
Deuteronomy, Book of 38, 55, 65, 66, 168, 178–180, 189, 194, 228, 230
Diamond, Jared 27
Dinah 51, 62, 119, 139, 147, 148, 172, 173, 231
Diodorus 184, 193
Dor-shav, Ethan 180
Dothan 45, 47, 52, 102, 123, 181, 189, 195, 221
dream 21, 29, 43–46, 51, 52, 69, 76–83, 85, 86, 88, 96, 97, 99, 101, 106, 113, 116, 121, 127, 131, 136, 166, 173, 182, 189–191, 195, 196, 203, 205, 215, 216
Driver, S.R. 75, 157

Ebla 16
Eliot, T.S. 14, 26
embalming 183, 192, 193
Empire *see* New Empire
Empson, William 24
Enayim 58–60, 66, 111
Enlightenment, Solomonic 13, 25
Ephraim 92, 139, 148, 160–165, 167, 170, 171, 180, 191, 193, 208, 226
Er 55–58, 63, 65, 67, 111, 139, 148, 226, 227
Esau 50, 111, 120, 168
Esther, Book of 24, 205, 206, 214, 219
eternity 20, 144, 149
Eve 32, 95

249

Exodus, Book of 24, 31, 74, 86, 147, 149, 168, 179, 193, 206, 209, 217, 218

Fagan, Brian 156
famine 83, 84, 93, 97, 98, 103, 105–108, 127, 129, 138, 143, 149, 151, 154, 156, 184, 187, 195, 199, 200, 209, 213, 225
the Fathers 23, 25, 32–37, 39, 40, 120, 139, 140, 144, 145, 147, 162, 165, 169, 170, 217
Feder, A.H. 39, 47, 52, 181
fiction 10–12, 25, 26
The First Historians 10, 21
First Intermediate Period 19
firstborn 92, 105, 108, 115, 161, 163, 164, 167, 180
forgiveness 100, 186–189, 195, 209
Four Biblical Heroines 1, 3, 25, 26, 29, 52, 54, 67, 95, 195, 205, 206, 219
François de Bellforest 14
Frankfort, Henri 39, 40
freedom 56, 80, 89, 107, 126, 152, 154, 155, 158, 194, 200, 205
friendship 63, 67

Gad 51, 139, 176
Ginsberg, Louis 219
goblet 115, 117, 118, 121, 124, 125, 186
God: hidden 199, 200, 218; no mention of 46, 197, 198; plan of 133, 199, 200; sent me 128, 187, 198, 200; Way of 208
Goethe 218
Gooding, D.W. 23
Gordis, Robert 194
Goren ha-Atad 185, 194
Goshen 129, 131, 133, 137, 140, 142, 143, 146, 149, 151, 157–159, 167, 185, 195, 205
granaries 92–95, 98, 152
Grand Vizier 85, 87, 95, 96, 98, 104, 116, 118, 133, 144, 200; *see also* Viceroy; vizier
Great Sin 70, 71, 74
Greece 17, 26
Greek language 23
Greek translation of the Bible 94
Greenberg, Moshe 53
Gressmann, H. 23, 24
guilt 47, 49, 64, 77, 80, 88, 96, 102–104, 112, 117, 119, 128, 133, 173, 186, 189, 195, 222
Gunkel, H. 23, 24, 230
Guns, Germs and Steel 27

Hagar 49
Halpern, Baruch 10, 24
Haman 52
Hamilton, V.P. 3, 64, 66, 67, 179, 181, 184, 193–195
Hamlet 14, 15, 26
Hammurabi, laws of 52
Hamul 139, 225–227
Haran 33, 39, 50, 155
Haran, M. 25

Hazony, D. 86, 219
Hazor 25
Hebrew: Bible 7, 23, 38, 166, 198; ethnic designation 33, 37, 72–74, 78, 82, 85, 86, 88, 89, 92, 108, 114, 135, 143, 149, 152, 167, 184, 185, 210; language 6, 7, 18, 22, 23, 26–29, 47, 50, 51, 60, 64, 67, 71, 75, 81, 82, 92, 94, 95, 102, 103, 106, 119–121, 128, 129, 132, 147, 149, 160, 165, 168, 179–181, 194, 196, 198, 202, 206, 219
Hebron 41, 45, 50, 52, 55, 64, 66, 137, 162, 184, 185, 194
Herodotus 86, 94, 193
hesed (kindness) 75, 78, 85
Hezron 55, 139, 225–227
Hirah 55, 58, 59, 63, 66, 67
historical narrative 10–14, 16, 24
history 8, 10–14, 17–19, 26, 39, 91, 119, 152, 158, 161, 191, 207, 210, 214
Hoffmeier, James 24, 92, 95, 148
Hoop, Raymond de 167, 180
Humphreys, W.L. 9, 16, 24–26
Hyksos 12, 25, 29, 146

Ibn Ezra 50, 133, 222, 224
immortality 21, 79
indifference 48, 103, 140, 167, 189
intransigence, human 32
The Invention of Monotheist Ethics 24, 26, 194
Isaac 6, 12, 37, 40, 46, 50, 55, 64, 69, 74, 91, 95, 101, 135–137, 146, 147, 149, 155, 160, 161, 163, 164, 167–169, 181, 182, 191, 196, 199, 205, 217
Ishmael 168
Ishmaelites 48, 68, 112, 203, 222–224
Israel: House of 168, 170, 192; nation of 142; People of 11, 166, 197; Tribes of 180, 182, 193, 228; *see also* Children of Israel
Israel in Egypt 24
Issachar 51, 139, 168, 175, 178, 180, 229
Izbet Sarta 18, 27

Jacob, story of 205
Jericho 194
Jerome 194
Jerusalem 23, 27, 50, 214
Jesse 62
Job, Book of 31, 180, 194
Johnson, Paul 20, 29, 74, 94, 95
the Jordan 179, 185, 194
Joseph and His Brothers 74, 91
Joseph and the Amazing Technicolor Dreamcoat 5
Joseph narrative *see* Joseph Story
Joseph Story 1–6, 9–16, 18, 21, 23–26, 31, 38, 91, 170, 197–202, 204, 205, 213–216, 218, 225, 230
Jubilee 212, 219
Judah 13, 16, 26, 48, 50–68, 95, 97, 105–110, 118–124, 132–135, 139, 140, 147, 148, 168, 170, 171, 173–175, 178–180, 194, 203, 208, 213, 221, 222, 225, 226, 228, 229

Kass, Leon 2, 38, 51, 52, 61, 63–67, 75, 77, 79, 85, 86, 114, 120, 121, 133, 136, 140, 147, 149, 150, 162, 166, 168, 193, 211, 218, 222, 224
Keturah 49
Kikawada, I. 32, 38
Kimchi 104
King, P.J. 52
King James translation 18, 28, 51, 168
Kitchen, K.A. 12, 13, 17, 25–27, 39, 52, 53, 65, 86, 94, 146, 149, 223, 224
Kuntillet Ajrud 18
Kyd, Thomas 14, 15

Laban 50, 51, 65, 120, 139, 146
Lachish 17, 27
Leah 42, 50, 51, 62, 139, 148, 160, 170, 175, 176, 178, 182
Levi 51, 62, 119, 139, 168, 170, 172, 173, 178, 228–231
Levine, Baruch 218
levirate marriage 56, 57, 65
literacy 16, 24, 26, 69, 200
literary conventions 8
livestock 142, 149, 152, 156
Lloyd Webber, Andrew 5
logograms 17
Lord 34, 43, 56, 65, 68–71, 73, 74, 94, 125, 127, 129, 133, 136, 145, 147, 148, 180, 197, 199, 213
Lord of Dreams 47, 190, 191
Lower Egypt 19, 28, 95
Luzzato, S.D. 86

maat 20
Machpelah 162, 165, 182, 185, 194
Manasseh 92, 96, 139, 148, 160–165, 167, 170, 171, 180, 191, 193, 208, 226
Manetho 12, 29
Mann, Thomas 74, 91, 131
Mannheim, Karl 210, 218
marginal man 210, 218
Mari 16, 52
Mathews, Kenneth 10, 23, 25
Mazer, A. 25
Memphis 19, 28, 86
Menn, Esther 67
Mesopotamia 24, 28, 33, 50, 53, 95, 147
Middle Kingdom 13, 19
Midianites 48, 50, 210, 221–224
Milgrom, Jacob 39, 51, 75, 121, 193, 194, 218
Miriam 133
monotheistic revolution 10, 24
Mordecai 214, 219
Moses 6, 12, 25, 74, 133, 147, 178, 179, 185, 193, 210, 213, 229, 230

motives 11, 42, 48, 62, 65, 98, 101–103, 108, 132, 142, 187, 198–200, 303, 217
mummies 86, 94, 138, 144, 145, 183–185, 192–194
Mut-em-enet 74

Nahmanides 206
Naphtali 51, 139, 176, 213, 219
narrator 12, 31, 43, 47–51, 61, 67–71, 73, 74, 81, 86, 87, 99, 101, 104, 109, 110, 114, 116, 119, 126, 127, 131, 132, 146, 148, 154, 155, 183, 185, 195, 201, 205, 227
natural law 204
New Empire 29, 105, 149
New Testament 23
New Way 15, 33, 23, 36, 38, 41, 137, 151, 155, 162
the Nile 20, 21, 28, 75, 81, 83, 86, 88, 93, 94, 133, 144, 149, 153–156, 181
Noah 32, 95, 219
novella 9, 24, 25

Obed 62
O'Brien, Mark 100, 106
Old Kingdom 19, 20, 29, 89, 151, 152, 155, 196
Old Testament 17, 23–25, 133
old way *see* way of the world
On 89, 91, 92, 94, 139
On the Reliability of the Old Testament 24, 25, 27, 39, 52, 65, 86, 94, 149
Onan 55–58, 63, 65, 139, 148, 225, 227
one set apart 129, 177, 178, 181, 188, 191, 209, 217

Paddan-aram 41, 50, 65, 95, 139, 146, 160–162, 167, 196, 218
peasants 89, 152–154, 192, 196, 211, 212
Peniel 43, 47
Perez 13, 25, 62, 67, 139, 206, 225–227
Pharaoh 12, 19, 20, 29, 50, 68, 74, 77, 79–83, 85–89, 91, 92, 94, 125, 127, 128, 130–133, 142–160, 162, 167, 184, 185, 193, 195, 200, 208, 209, 211, 212, 216, 217
Pharonic divinity, doctrine of 20, 29, 85, 86, 144, 145, 149
Phoenicians 17, 27, 180, 229
Pi-Ramesses 12, 146
Pirson, Ron 133, 166, 168, 181, 189, 195
Podhoretz, Norman 28
The Poetics of Boblical Narrative 38
poetry 7, 15, 17, 164, 169, 177, 178, 181, 182, 228–230
Potiphar 50, 53, 68, 69, 73, 76, 77, 86, 88, 96, 129, 200, 205, 221, 222
Poti-phera 89, 92, 139
priests 19, 29, 86, 89, 152, 153, 156, 183, 184, 193, 212
The Primeval History 31, 32

primogeniture 108, 164, 170, 172
the Promise 34, 36, 40, 43, 46, 56, 62, 137, 160, 199, 207–209, 211
Promised Land 34, 50, 136–138, 143, 146, 147, 159, 166, 179, 180, 192, 199, 210
Providence 1, 47, 129, 196, 199, 201, 206
provisions 97, 98, 103–108, 115, 131, 151
Pyramid Age 20, 89, 155; *see also* Old Kingdom
pyramids 29

Rachel 42, 50, 51, 63, 74, 97, 121, 126, 139, 148, 161–163, 167, 169, 170, 172, 176, 178, 190, 194
Rad, Gerhard von 13, 25, 64, 156, 164, 168, 195, 199, 206, 230
Ramban 50
Ramses 12, 24, 146, 157, 158
Re 19, 29, 91, 94, 149
Rebecca 95, 182
reconciliation 63, 100, 102, 131, 186, 188, 189, 195, 205, 209, 215
redemption 6, 109, 192, 196, 199, 207, 210, 212, 218
Redford, D.B. 24, 25
religiously neutral 183, 198
Rendsberg, G. 25
Reuben 47, 51, 52, 62, 103–105, 108, 109, 111, 119, 120, 123, 139, 160–162, 164, 170, 172, 178–180, 203, 221–223, 230, 231
revenge 15, 49, 100–102, 116, 120, 187, 188, 191
Rice, Tim 5
Richards, I.A. 24
robe of many colors 42, 44, 47, 49, 51, 66, 67, 88, 108, 116, 200
Robinson, Ira 66
Rosenberg, Joel 24
Ro-wati 12, 19, 106
Rowley, H.H. 94
Ruth, Book of 13, 25, 56, 58, 62, 64, 67, 195, 201, 205, 206
Ryle, H.E. 133

Sacks, Robert 51, 53, 64, 105, 116, 121, 168, 171, 179, 222–224
The Sacred Wood 26
sacrifice 20, 40, 51, 64, 94, 111, 120, 135, 137, 147, 154, 205, 212
Saint 214, 215, 219
Samson 24, 66
Samuel, Book of 13, 25, 66, 168
Samuel, Maurice 71, 73–75, 131, 132, 134, 176, 181, 186, 194, 218
sanctity of life 32
Sarah 12, 37, 39–41, 95, 139, 183
Sarna, Nahum M. 50, 51, 53, 70, 74, 75, 94, 95, 119, 120, 147, 148, 167, 168, 178–180, 206, 222, 224, 226, 227
Scripture 1, 10, 23–26
Second Intermediate Period 13, 19
secularism 128, 198, 206, 207, 212, 218

Shaddai (Almighty) 111, 120, 167, 169, 177, 181; *see also* Almighty
Shakespeare, William 14, 15, 26, 76, 88, 217, 219
shaving 82, 83, 86, 88, 106, 148
Shechem 41, 45, 97, 108, 119, 165–168, 172, 203
Shelah 55, 57, 60, 61, 63, 65, 66, 111, 139, 226
Sheol 49, 64, 105, 126, 132, 138, 146
shepherds 44, 48, 58, 143, 149, 166, 186, 219
Shua 55, 58
silver 48, 52, 59, 104, 107, 111–113, 115–118, 120, 131, 156
Simeon 51, 62, 103–105, 112, 113, 116, 119–121, 132, 139, 142, 160, 161, 168, 170, 172, 173, 178, 180, 186, 229–231
slavery 48, 49, 52, 61, 62, 64, 66, 68–70, 72, 73, 76, 78, 79, 82, 92, 96, 112, 116–119, 121, 124, 126, 135, 136, 138, 151–156, 186, 192, 194, 196, 200, 203, 210, 212, 213, 217, 218, 222, 225
Soggin, J.A. 23, 189, 195
Solomon 13, 26, 121
source criticism 1, 7
Speiser, E.A. 64, 133, 165, 168, 179, 180, 193, 224
Stager, L.E. 52
standard model 214
Sternberg, Meir 31, 38, 119, 195, 204, 206
A Study of the Biblical Story of Joseph 25
Sumer 17, 39
syllabaries 17

Talmud 8, 206
Tamar 13, 54–60, 95, 97, 109–111, 120, 180, 206, 225, 226
Tell Deir Alla 17
test 100–102, 115, 196
The Testament of Israel 14, 169–171, 173, 178, 182, 188, 189, 194, 228–230
Tetragrammaton 28, 74, 180
Thebes 19, 91, 184
theocracy 19, 20
theology 1, 2, 6, 8, 10, 15, 31, 89, 91, 128, 145, 149, 188, 194, 195, 197, 198, 201, 203, 206, 208
Third Dynasty 19
Thoreau, Henry 33
Thucydides 11
Tigay, Jeffrey 66
Timnah 58–60, 66
tomb 20, 27, 29, 48, 89, 94, 145, 184
totalitarian 19, 20, 36, 38, 89, 151, 152, 184, 196
The Travails of the Fathers 31–36, 201, 205
tribe of Joseph 161, 166
Turner, Laurence A. 100, 106, 121, 149, 168, 195

Ugarit (Ugaritic) 16, 66, 86, 181
United Kingdom 13
Upper Egypt 19, 24, 28, 29, 95, 184
Ur-Hamlet 14, 15, 25
Ur-Joseph 14, 15, 26
Ur of the Chaldees 32–34, 38, 39, 155

vengeance 170, 186, 187, 194
Viceroy 64, 85, 162, 178, 188, 190, 198, 225
vizier 93, 104–106, 216

The Walls of the Ruler 140, 148
way of Egypt 136, 151, 155, 162, 178, 208, 209, 211, 212; *see also* the way of the world
the way of the world 15, 34, 36, 38, 39
weeping 49, 103, 113, 121, 127, 129, 140, 159, 182, 183, 186, 193
Wellhausen, Julius 16, 23, 25, 26
Wenham, G. 25, 180, 228, 230
Westermann, C. 25, 64, 106, 181, 195, 196, 224, 230

wife of Potiphar 70–74, 76, 86, 215, 216
Wildavsky, A. 156, 157, 218
Woolley, Sir Leonard 39

Zaphenath-paneah 89, 92
Zebulun 51, 139, 175, 180, 229
Zerah 62, 139, 225, 226
Ziggurat 33, 38, 39
Zilpah 42, 50, 51, 139, 148, 170, 178, 179, 202
Zuleika 74

www.ingramcontent.com/pod-product-compliance
Lightning Source LLC
Chambersburg PA
CBHW081549300426
44116CB00015B/2807